# REBOUND

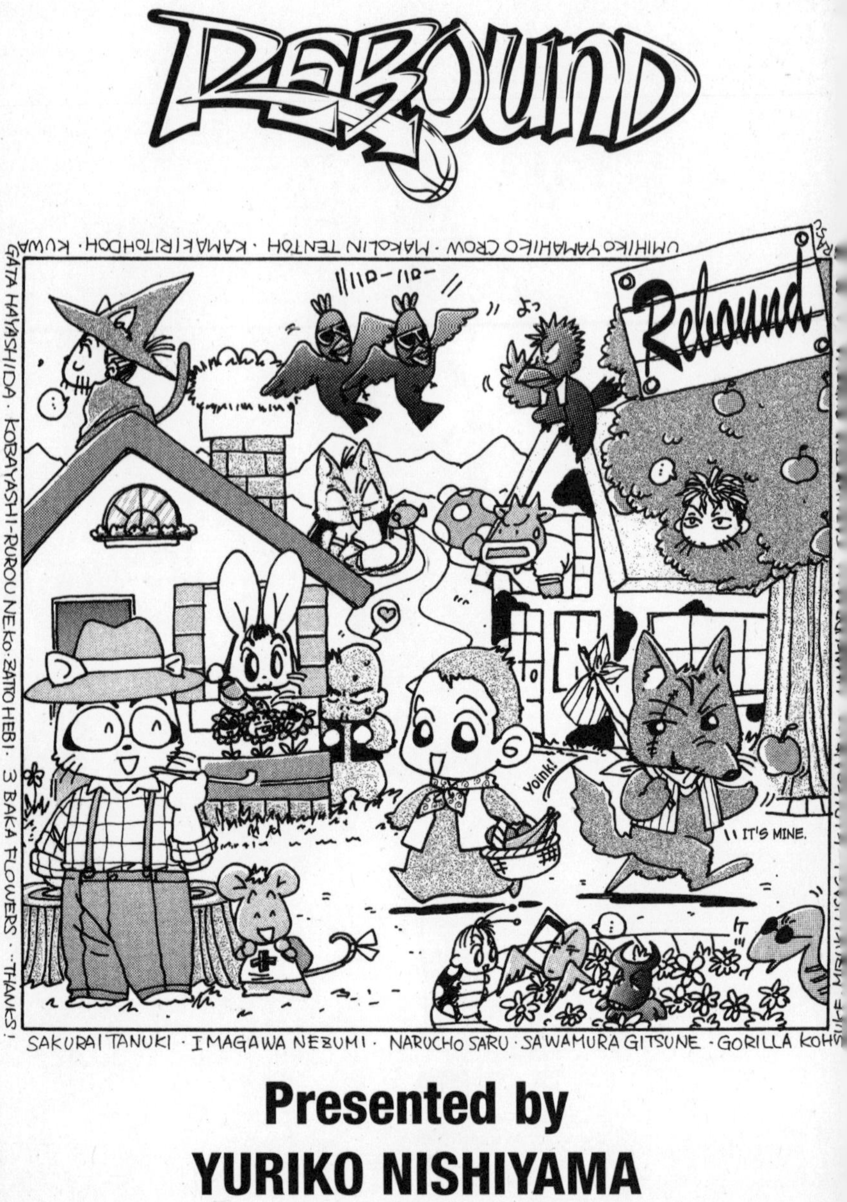
UMIHIKO YAMAHIKO CROW · MAKOLIN TENTOH · KAMAKIRITOHDOH · KUWA
GATA HAYASHIDA · KOBAYASHI-RUROU NEKO · ZATTO HEBI · 3 BAKA FLOWERS · ...THANKS!
Rebound
Yoink!
IT'S MINE.
SAKURAI TANUKI · IMAGAWA NEZUMI · NARUCHO SARU · SAWAMURA GITSUNE · GORILLA KOHSUKE

**Presented by**
**YURIKO NISHIYAMA**

By Yuriko Nishiyama

Volume 8

Los Angeles • Tokyo • London • Hamburg

Translator - Shirley Kubo
English Adaption - Jordan Capell
Associate Editor - Troy Lewter
Retouch and Lettering - Steven Redd
Cover Layout - Patrick Hook
Graphic Designer - John Lo

Editor - Luis Reyes
Associate Editor - Troy Lewter
Digital Imaging Manager - Chris Buford
Pre-Press Manager - Antonio DePietro
Production Managers - Jennifer Miller, Mutsumi Miyazaki
Art Director - Matt Alford
Managing Editor - Jill Freshney
VP of Production - Ron Klamert
President & C.O.O. - John Parker
Publisher & C.E.O. - Stuart Levy

E-mail: info@TOKYOPOP.com
Come visit us online at www.TOKYOPOP.com

A  Manga

TOKYOPOP Inc.
5900 Wilshire Blvd. Suite 2000
Los Angeles, CA 90036

*Rebound Vol. 8*

## ISBN: 1-59182-532-6

First TOKYOPOP printing: June 2004

10  9  8  7  6  5  4  3  2  1

Printed in the USA

## -Play by Play-
## The Season So Far...

The Season So Far...

The Johnan High basketball team has beaten the odds and made it to the national championships in Sapporo. However, it's definitely a high-wire act without a net, because just one loss and they're on the short bus for the long ride back to Tokyo.

After a slow start, Team Johnan have managed to emerge as victors in their game against Yokohama International. This places them in final eight, and next in line to face the nearly flawless machine that is Team Kanakita. Kanakita's offense and their "Unlimited Triangle" strategy will definitely prove to be tough obstacles to surmount; Johnan will really have to focus and do their homework for this one. Meanwhile, Tomomi's team advances as well, and will play their next game at the same venue as Nate and Johnan. Nate and Tomomi finally find time to go on a date to the zoo, and later run into Team Kanakita's Sasuke while shopping. They all end up having lunch together, where Nate learns he must not fear Sasuke, since Sasuke doesn't fear losing. Besides—no one on Johnan has time to second-guess. With Kanakita firmly blocking the road to victory, can the Johnan boys up their game along with the ante? Or will their championship dreams make like a match and go up in smoke?

You're Reading...

# REBOUND

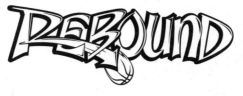

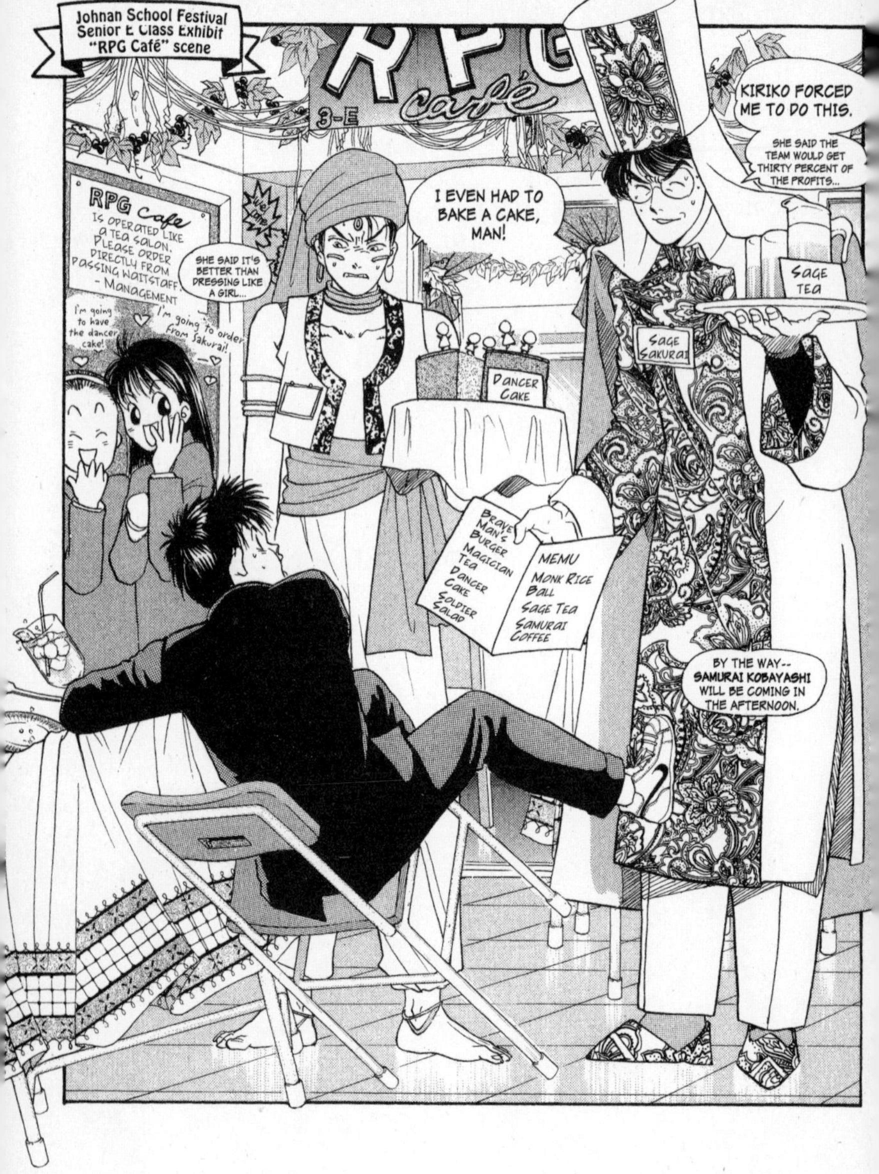
Johnan School Festival
Senior E Class Exhibit
"RPG Café" scene
RPG Café
3-E
KIRIKO FORCED ME TO DO THIS.
SHE SAID THE TEAM WOULD GET THIRTY PERCENT OF THE PROFITS...
I EVEN HAD TO BAKE A CAKE, MAN!
Sage Tea
Sage Sakurai
SHE SAID IT'S BETTER THAN DRESSING LIKE A GIRL...
RPG Cafe IS OPERATED LIKE A TEA SALON. PLEASE ORDER DIRECTLY FROM PASSING WAITSTAFF. - Management
I'm going to order from Sakurai!
I'm going to have the dancer cake!
Dancer Cake
Brave Man's Burger
Magician Tea
Dancer Cake
Soldier Salad
MEMU
Monk Rice Ball
Sage Tea
Samurai Coffee
BY THE WAY-- SAMURAI KOBAYASHI WILL BE COMING IN THE AFTERNOON.

# Today on REBOUND

EIGHT

# REBOUND

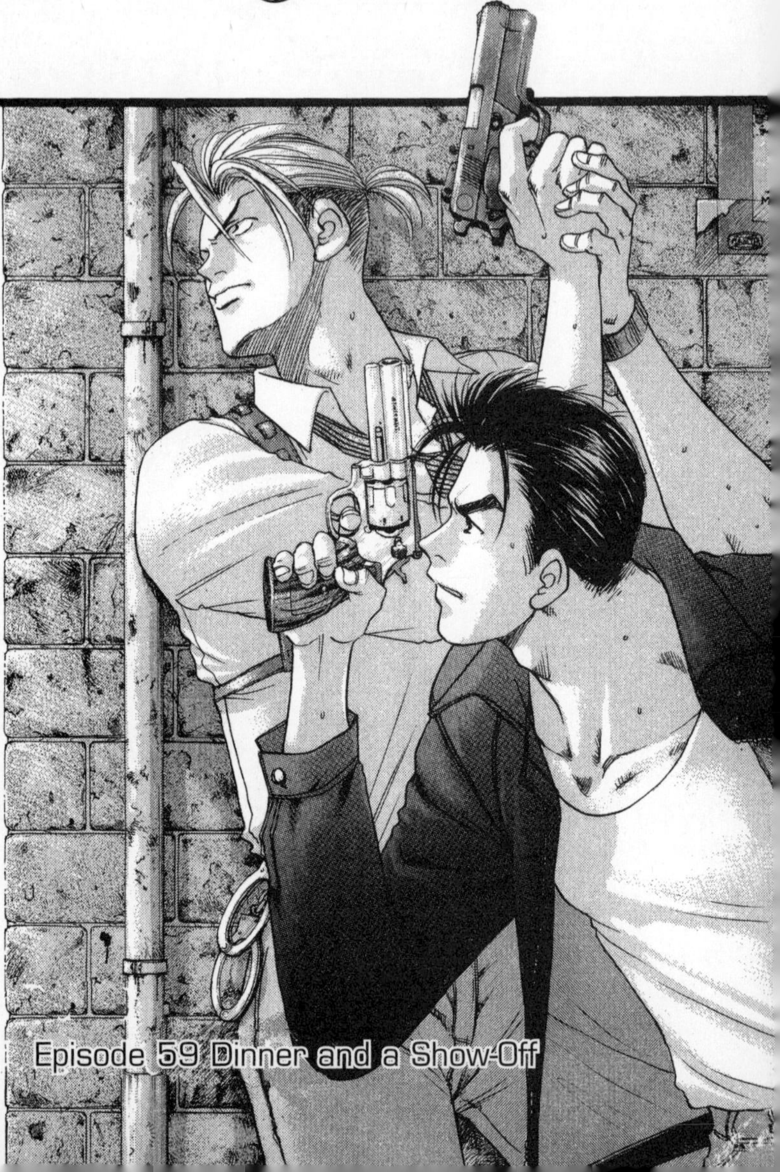
Episode 59 Dinner and a Show-Off

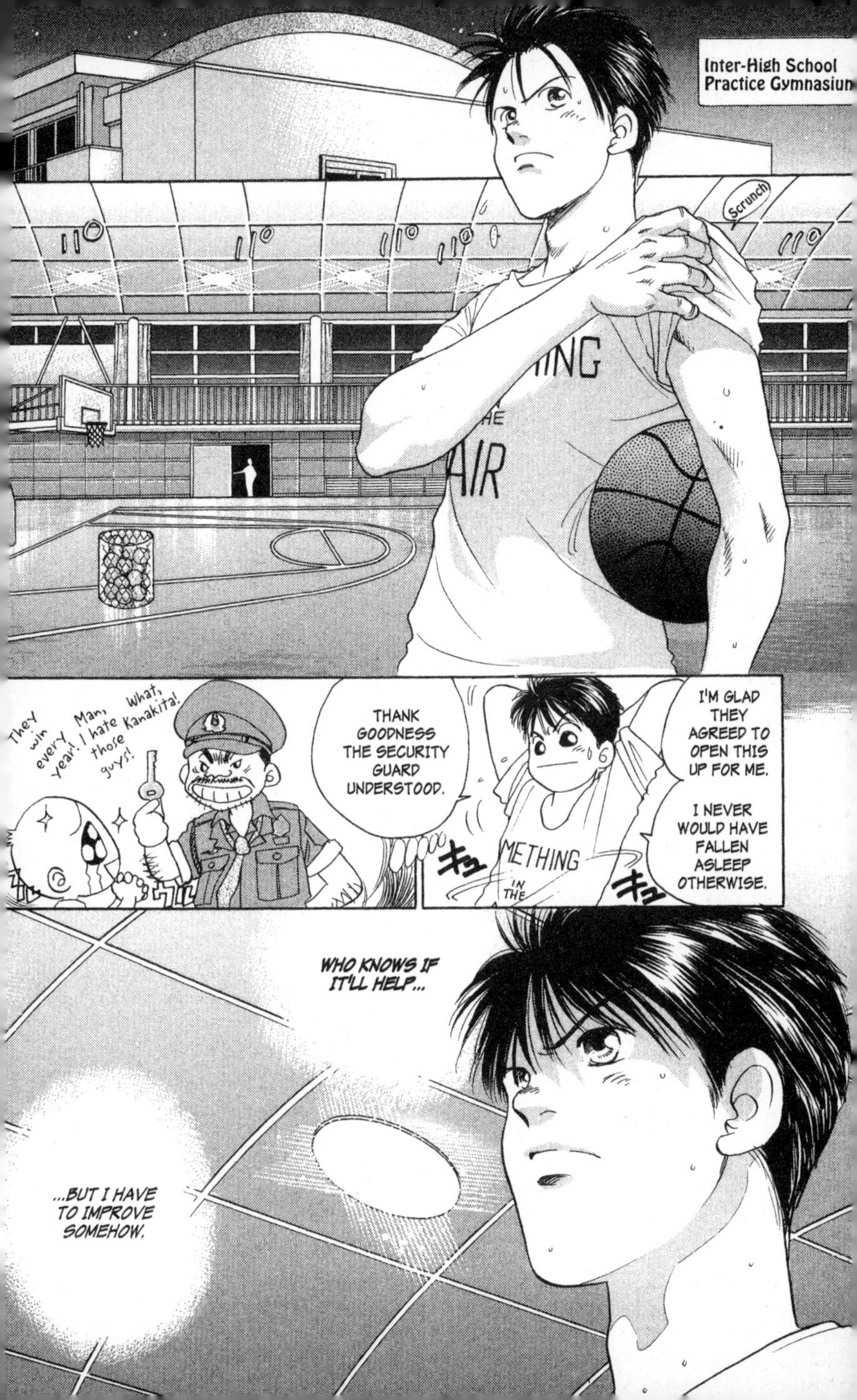
Inter-High School Practice Gymnasiun
Scrunch
I'M GLAD THEY AGREED TO OPEN THIS UP FOR ME.
I NEVER WOULD HAVE FALLEN ASLEEP OTHERWISE.
THANK GOODNESS THE SECURITY GUARD UNDERSTOOD.
What, Kanakita!
Man, I hate those guys!
They win every year!
WHO KNOWS IF IT'LL HELP...
...BUT I HAVE TO IMPROVE SOMEHOW.

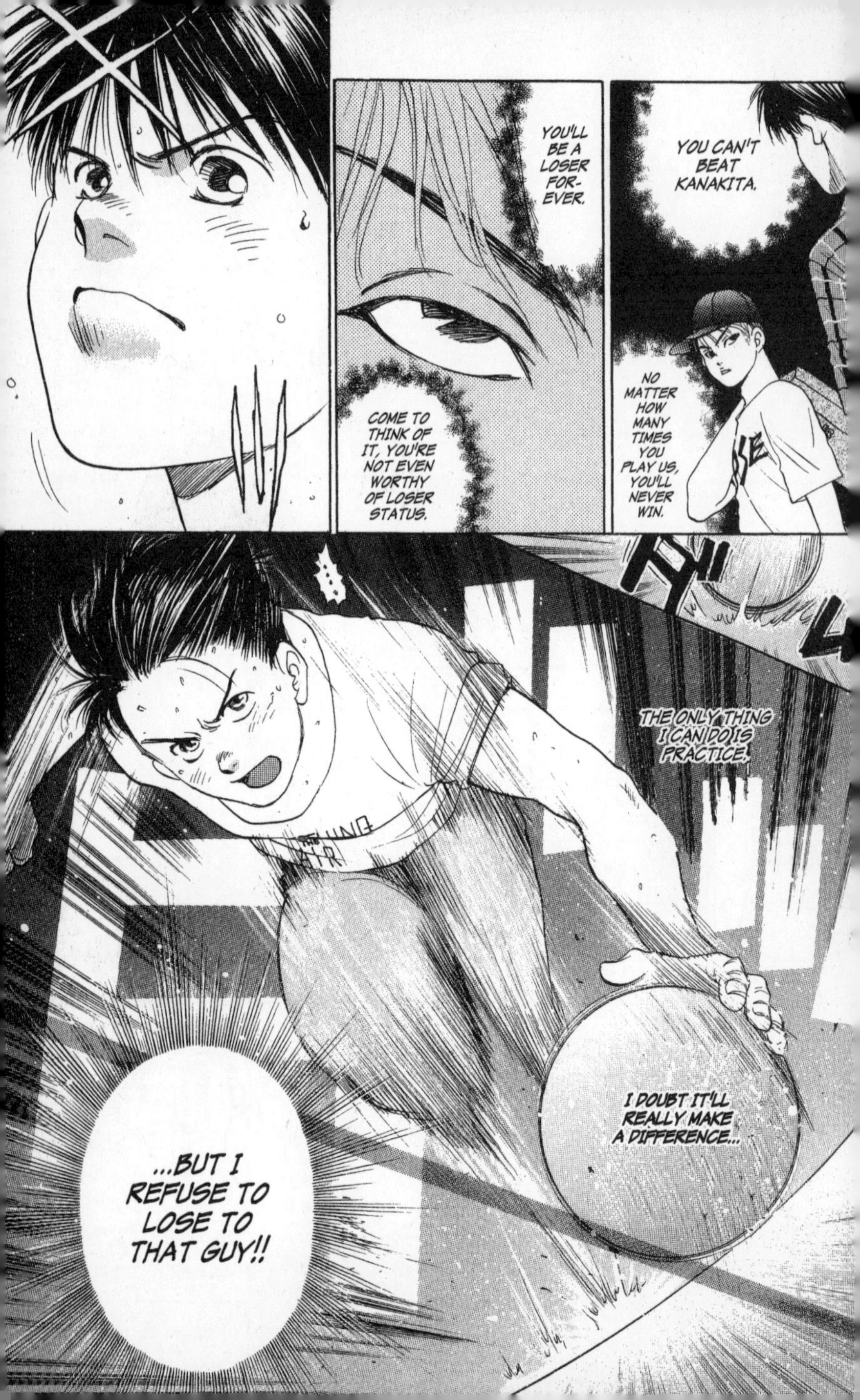
YOU CAN'T BEAT KANAKITA.
NO MATTER HOW MANY TIMES YOU PLAY US, YOU'LL NEVER WIN.
YOU'LL BE A LOSER FOR-EVER.
COME TO THINK OF IT, YOU'RE NOT EVEN WORTHY OF LOSER STATUS.
THE ONLY THING I CAN DO IS PRACTICE.
I DOUBT IT'LL REALLY MAKE A DIFFERENCE...
...BUT I REFUSE TO LOSE TO THAT GUY!!

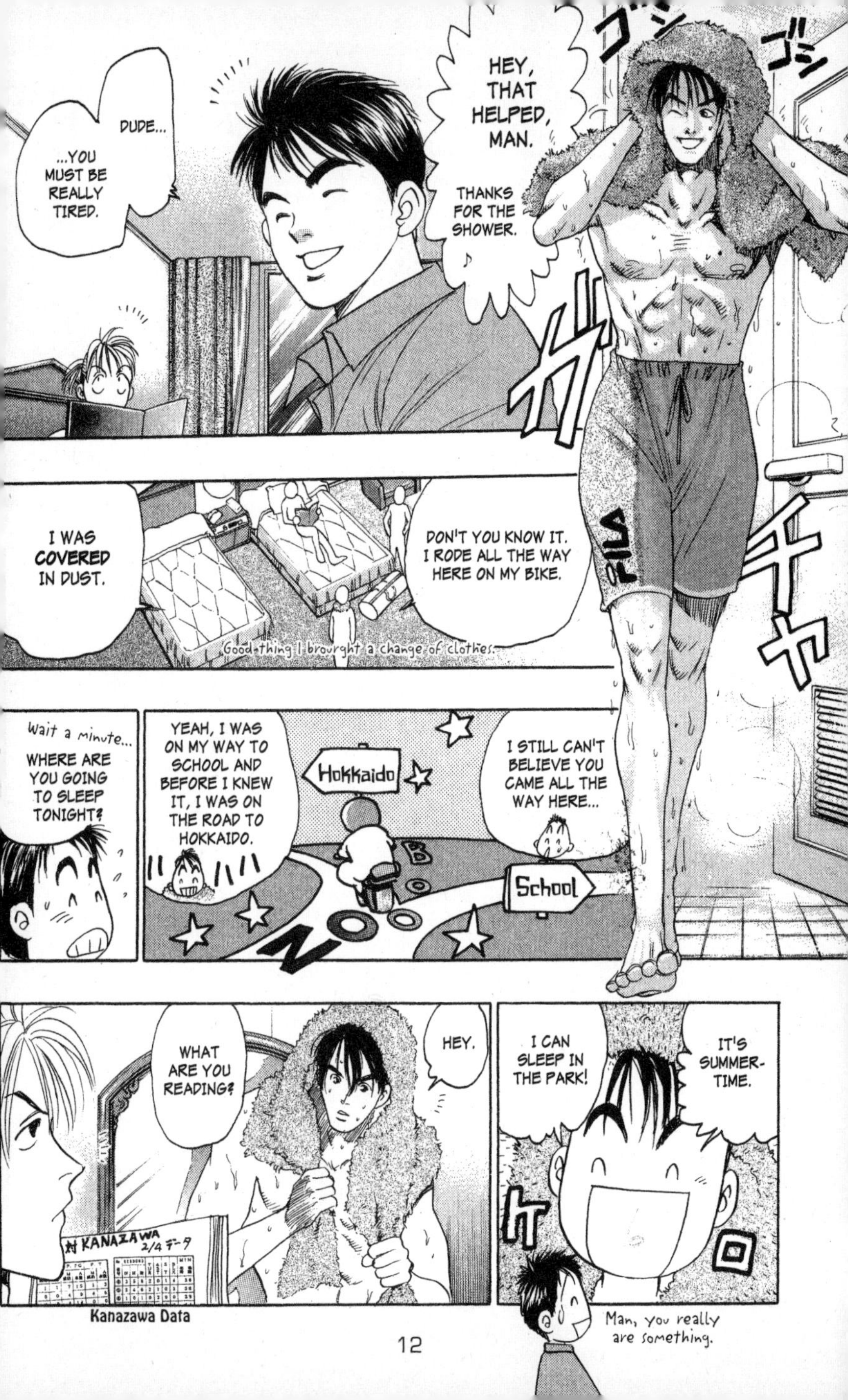
ゴシ
ゴシ
HEY, THAT HELPED, MAN.
THANKS FOR THE SHOWER. ♪
ガ
チャ
DUDE...
...YOU MUST BE REALLY TIRED.
DON'T YOU KNOW IT. I RODE ALL THE WAY HERE ON MY BIKE.
I WAS COVERED IN DUST.
Good thing I brourght a change of clothes.
I STILL CAN'T BELIEVE YOU CAME ALL THE WAY HERE...
School
Hokkaido
YEAH, I WAS ON MY WAY TO SCHOOL AND BEFORE I KNEW IT, I WAS ON THE ROAD TO HOKKAIDO.
NOOO
Wait a minute...
WHERE ARE YOU GOING TO SLEEP TONIGHT?
IT'S SUMMER-TIME.
I CAN SLEEP IN THE PARK!
ケロ
Man, you really are something.
HEY.
WHAT ARE YOU READING?
対 KANAZAWA 2/4 データ
Kanazawa Data

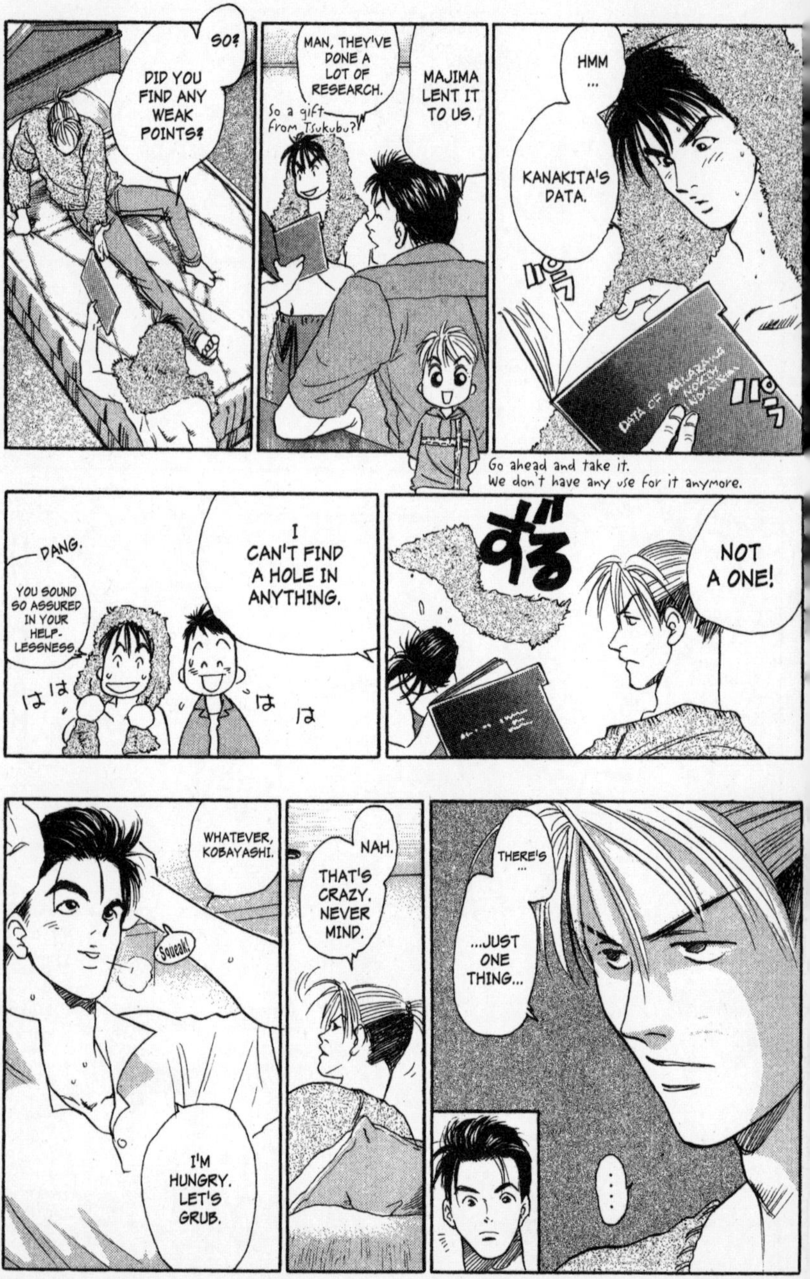
HMM ...
KANAKITA'S DATA.
パラ
パラ
MAJIMA LENT IT TO US.
MAN, THEY'VE DONE A LOT OF RESEARCH.
So a gift from Tsukubu?
Go ahead and take it. We don't have any use for it anymore.
SO? DID YOU FIND ANY WEAK POINTS?
ずる
NOT A ONE!
I CAN'T FIND A HOLE IN ANYTHING.
DANG.
YOU SOUND SO ASSURED IN YOUR HELP-LESSNESS.
はは
はは
THERE'S ...
...JUST ONE THING...
.....
NAH.
THAT'S CRAZY. NEVER MIND.
WHATEVER, KOBAYASHI.
Squeak!
I'M HUNGRY. LET'S GRUB.

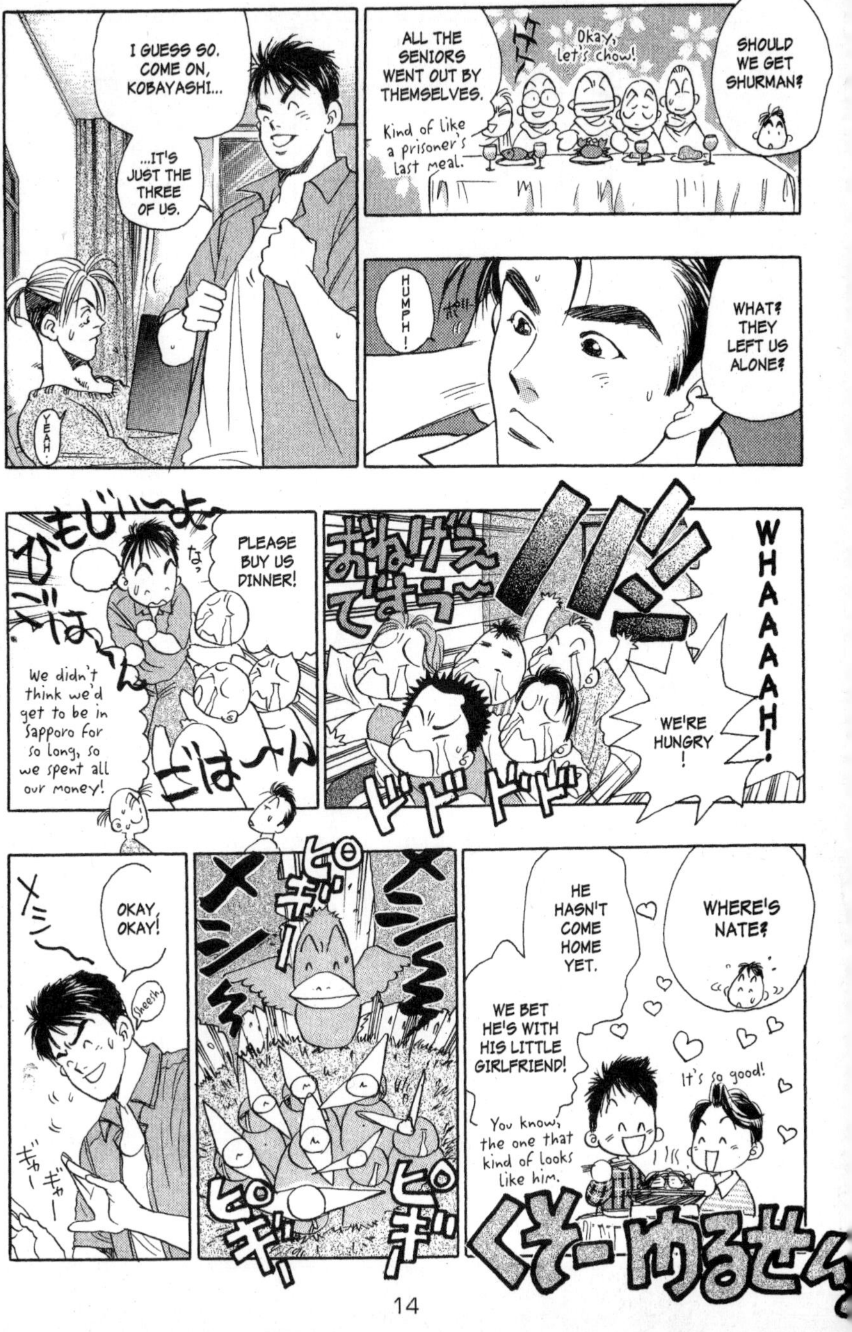
SHOULD WE GET SHURMAN?
Okay, let's chow!
ALL THE SENIORS WENT OUT BY THEMSELVES.
Kind of like a prisoner's last meal.
WHAT? THEY LEFT US ALONE?
HUMPH!
I GUESS SO. COME ON, KOBAYASHI...
...IT'S JUST THE THREE OF US.
YEAH.
WHAAAAAH!
おねげえですう~
WE'RE HUNGRY!
ドドドド
PLEASE BUY US DINNER!
ひもじい~よ~
な
ごは~ん
We didn't think we'd get to be in Sapporo for so long, so we spent all our money!
ごは~ん
WHERE'S NATE?
HE HASN'T COME HOME YET.
WE BET HE'S WITH HIS LITTLE GIRLFRIEND!
It's so good!
You know, the one that kind of looks like him.
くそーゆるせん
メシ~
ピギー
ピギ
ピギ
OKAY, OKAY!
Sheesh.
メシ~
ギャーギャー

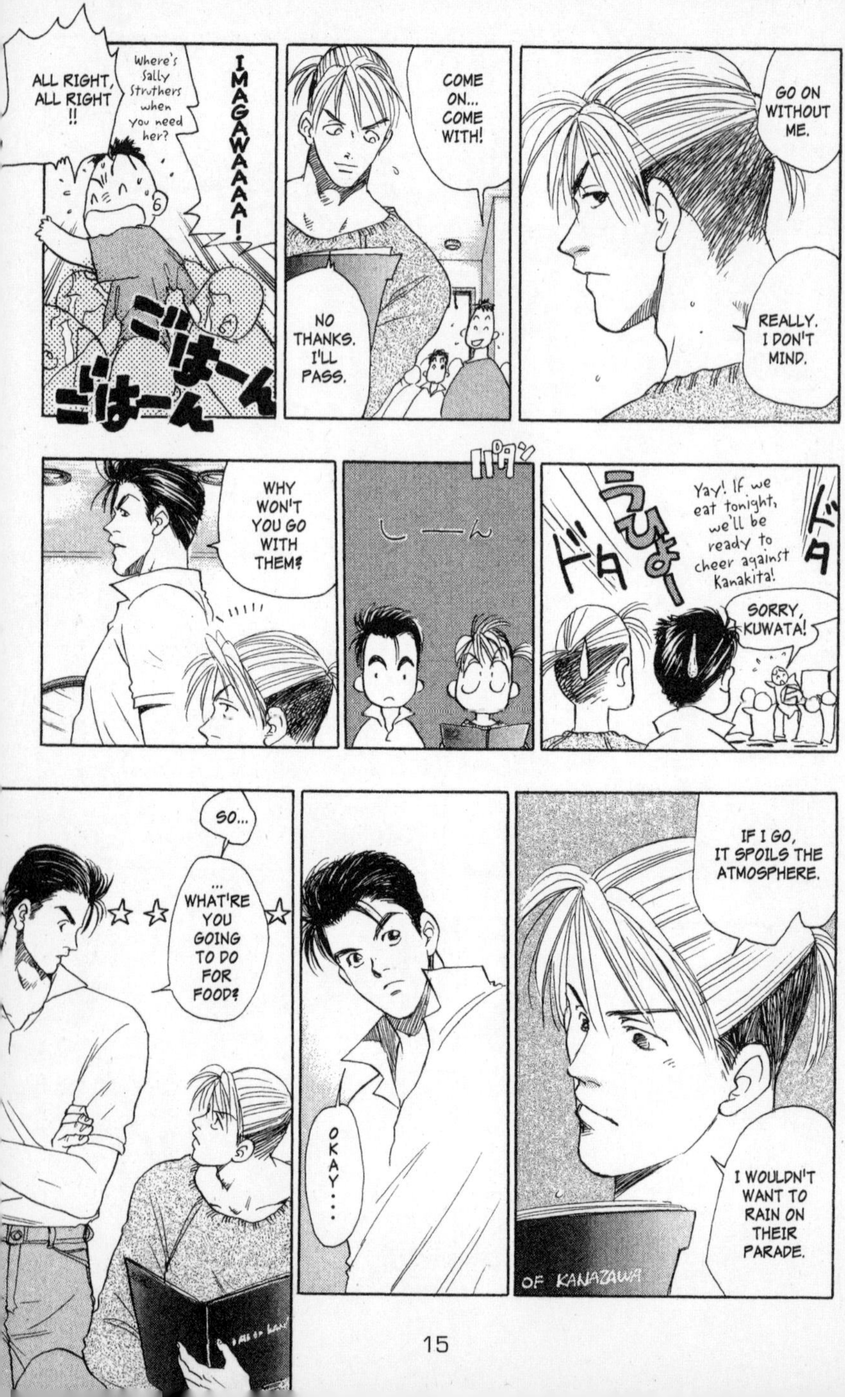
GO ON WITHOUT ME.
REALLY. I DON'T MIND.
COME ON... COME WITH!
NO THANKS. I'LL PASS.
IMAGAWAAAAA!
Where's Sally Struthers when you need her?
ALL RIGHT, ALL RIGHT !!
ごはーん
ごはーん
ドタ
うひょー
Yay! If we eat tonight, we'll be ready to cheer against Kanakita!
ドタ
SORRY, KUWATA!
パタン
しーん
WHY WON'T YOU GO WITH THEM?
IF I GO, IT SPOILS THE ATMOSPHERE.
I WOULDN'T WANT TO RAIN ON THEIR PARADE.
OF KANAZAWA
OKAY...
SO...
...WHAT'RE YOU GOING TO DO FOR FOOD?

*Sign: Liquor *Banner: Brothers of the North

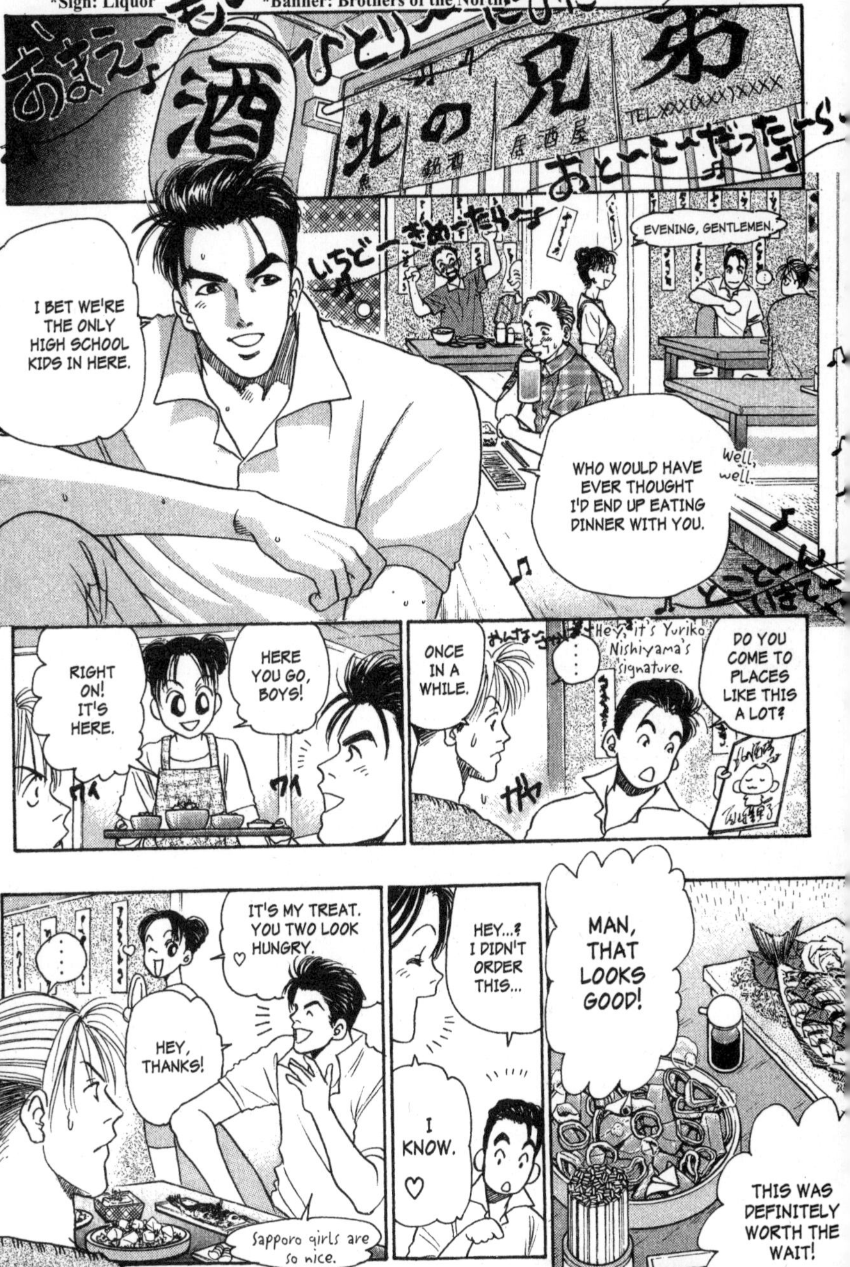
酒
北の兄弟
居酒屋
TEL XXX(XXX)XXXX
EVENING, GENTLEMEN.
WHO WOULD HAVE EVER THOUGHT I'D END UP EATING DINNER WITH YOU.
Well, well.
I BET WE'RE THE ONLY HIGH SCHOOL KIDS IN HERE.
DO YOU COME TO PLACES LIKE THIS A LOT?
Hey, it's Yuriko Nishiyama's signature.
ONCE IN A WHILE.
HERE YOU GO, BOYS!
RIGHT ON! IT'S HERE.
MAN, THAT LOOKS GOOD!
THIS WAS DEFINITELY WORTH THE WAIT!
HEY...? I DIDN'T ORDER THIS...
I KNOW.
IT'S MY TREAT. YOU TWO LOOK HUNGRY.
HEY, THANKS!
Sapporo girls are so nice.

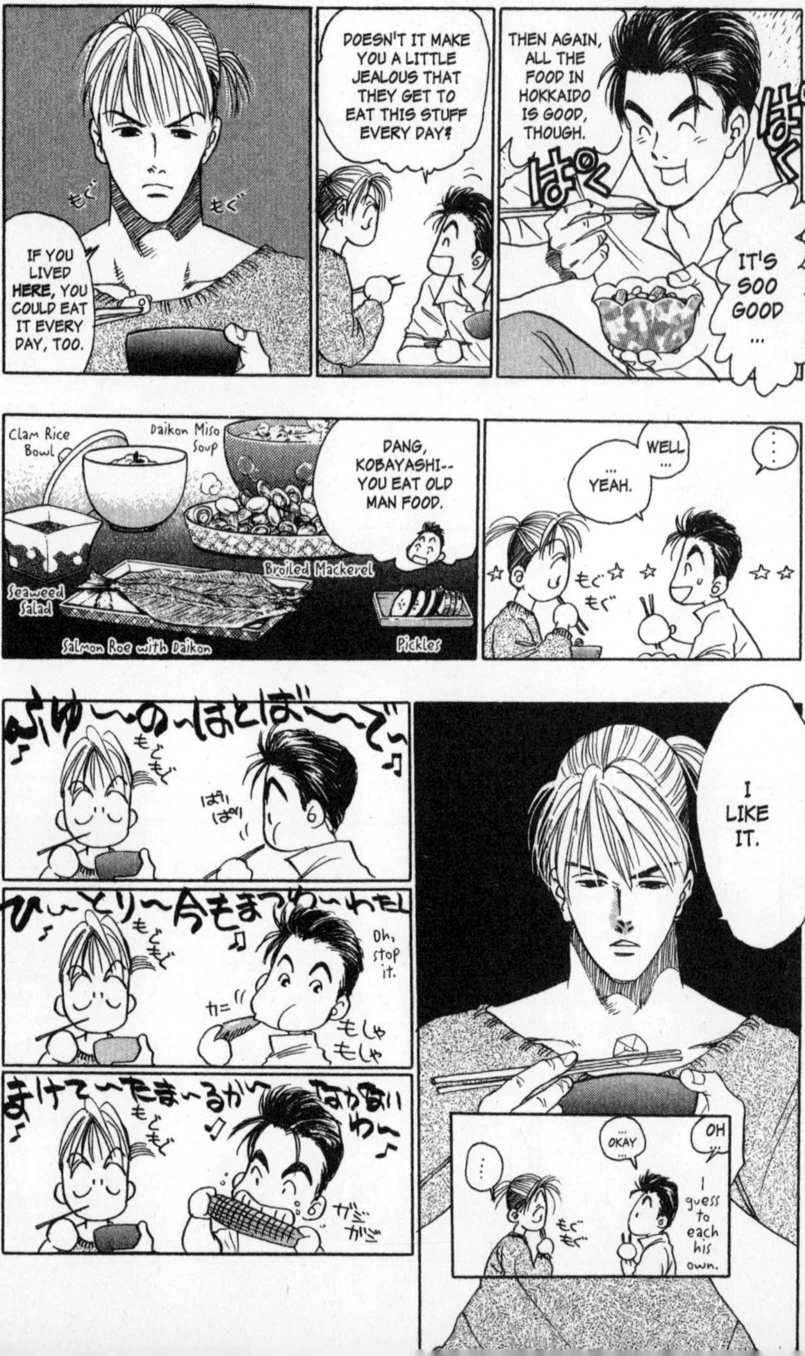
THEN AGAIN, ALL THE FOOD IN HOKKAIDO IS GOOD, THOUGH.
ぱく
ぱく
IT'S SOO GOOD ...
DOESN'T IT MAKE YOU A LITTLE JEALOUS THAT THEY GET TO EAT THIS STUFF EVERY DAY?
もぐ
もぐ
IF YOU LIVED HERE, YOU COULD EAT IT EVERY DAY, TOO.
WELL ...
... YEAH.
....
もぐ もぐ
DANG, KOBAYASHI-- YOU EAT OLD MAN FOOD.
Daikon Miso Soup
Clam Rice Bowl
Broiled Mackerel
Seaweed Salad
Pickles
Salmon Roe with Daikon
I LIKE IT.
OH ...
I guess to each his own.
... OKAY ...
...
もぐ もぐ
ふゆ〜の〜はとば〜で〜
もぐもぐ
ぱり ぱり
ひ〜とり〜今もまつわ〜わたし
もぐもぐ
Oh, stop it.
カニ
もしゃ もしゃ
まけて〜たま〜るか〜 なかない わ〜
もぐもぐ
ガジ ガジ

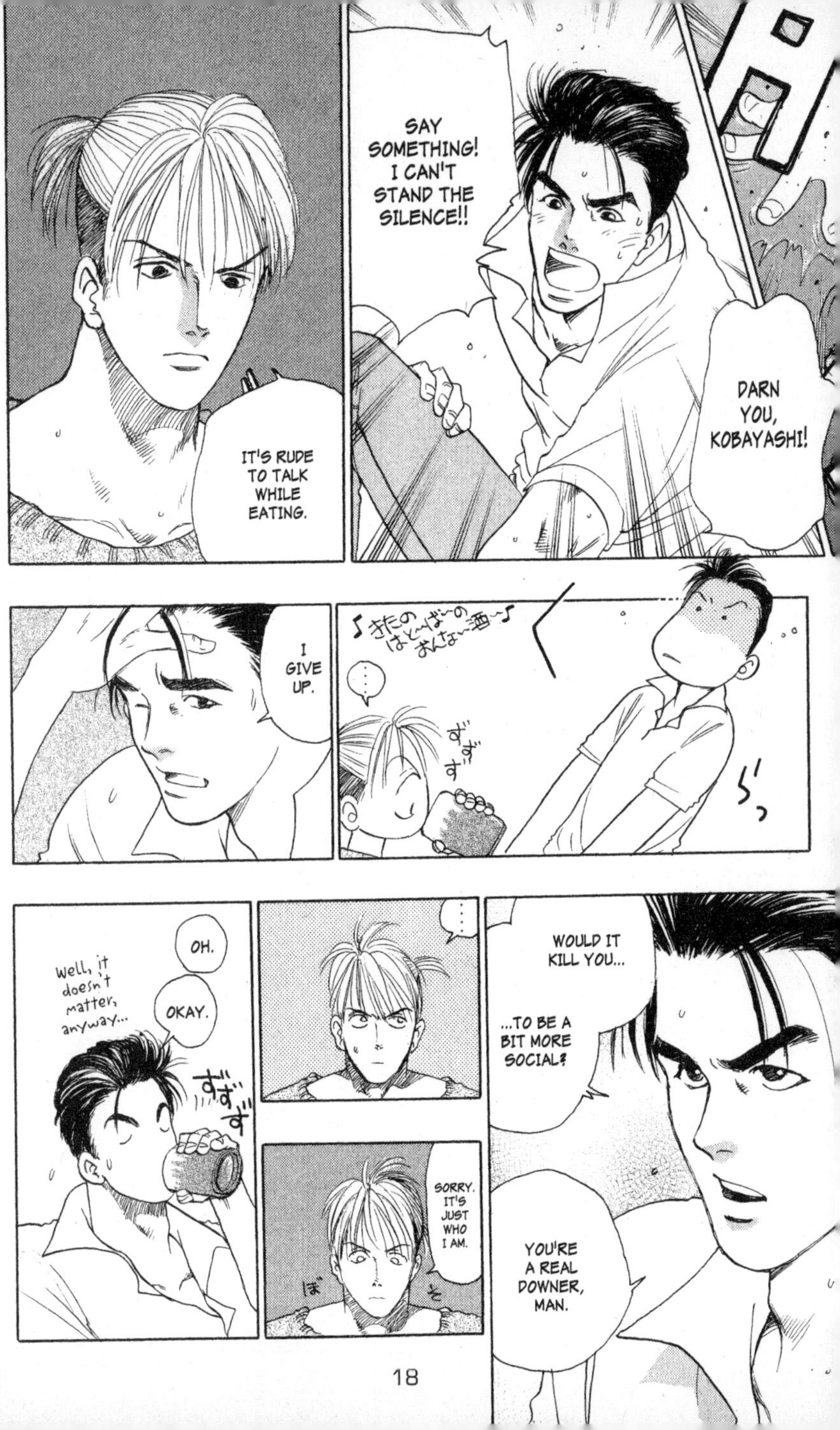
SAY SOMETHING! I CAN'T STAND THE SILENCE!!
DARN YOU, KOBAYASHI!
IT'S RUDE TO TALK WHILE EATING.
♪きたの はと~ば~の おんな~酒~♪
……
ずずず
らっ
I GIVE UP.
WOULD IT KILL YOU...
...TO BE A BIT MORE SOCIAL?
YOU'RE A REAL DOWNER, MAN.
……
SORRY. IT'S JUST WHO I AM.
ぼそ
OH.
OKAY.
Well, it doesn't matter, anyway...
ずずず

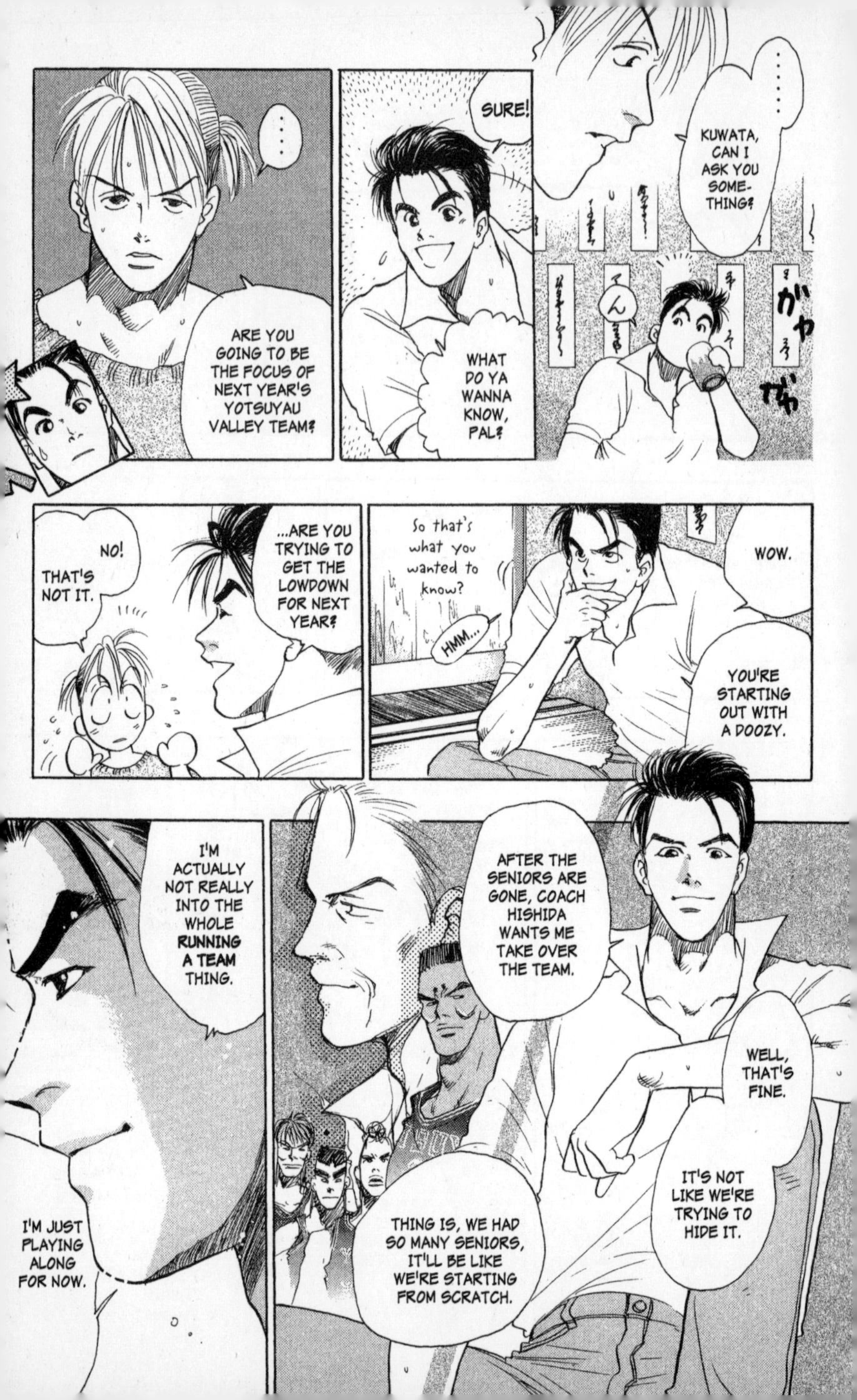
......
KUWATA, CAN I ASK YOU SOME-THING?
ん
がや
SURE!
WHAT DO YA WANNA KNOW, PAL?
......
ARE YOU GOING TO BE THE FOCUS OF NEXT YEAR'S YOTSUYAU VALLEY TEAM?
WOW.
So that's what you wanted to know?
YOU'RE STARTING OUT WITH A DOOZY.
HMM...
...ARE YOU TRYING TO GET THE LOWDOWN FOR NEXT YEAR?
NO! THAT'S NOT IT.
AFTER THE SENIORS ARE GONE, COACH HISHIDA WANTS ME TAKE OVER THE TEAM.
WELL, THAT'S FINE.
IT'S NOT LIKE WE'RE TRYING TO HIDE IT.
THING IS, WE HAD SO MANY SENIORS, IT'LL BE LIKE WE'RE STARTING FROM SCRATCH.
I'M ACTUALLY NOT REALLY INTO THE WHOLE RUNNING A TEAM THING.
I'M JUST PLAYING ALONG FOR NOW.

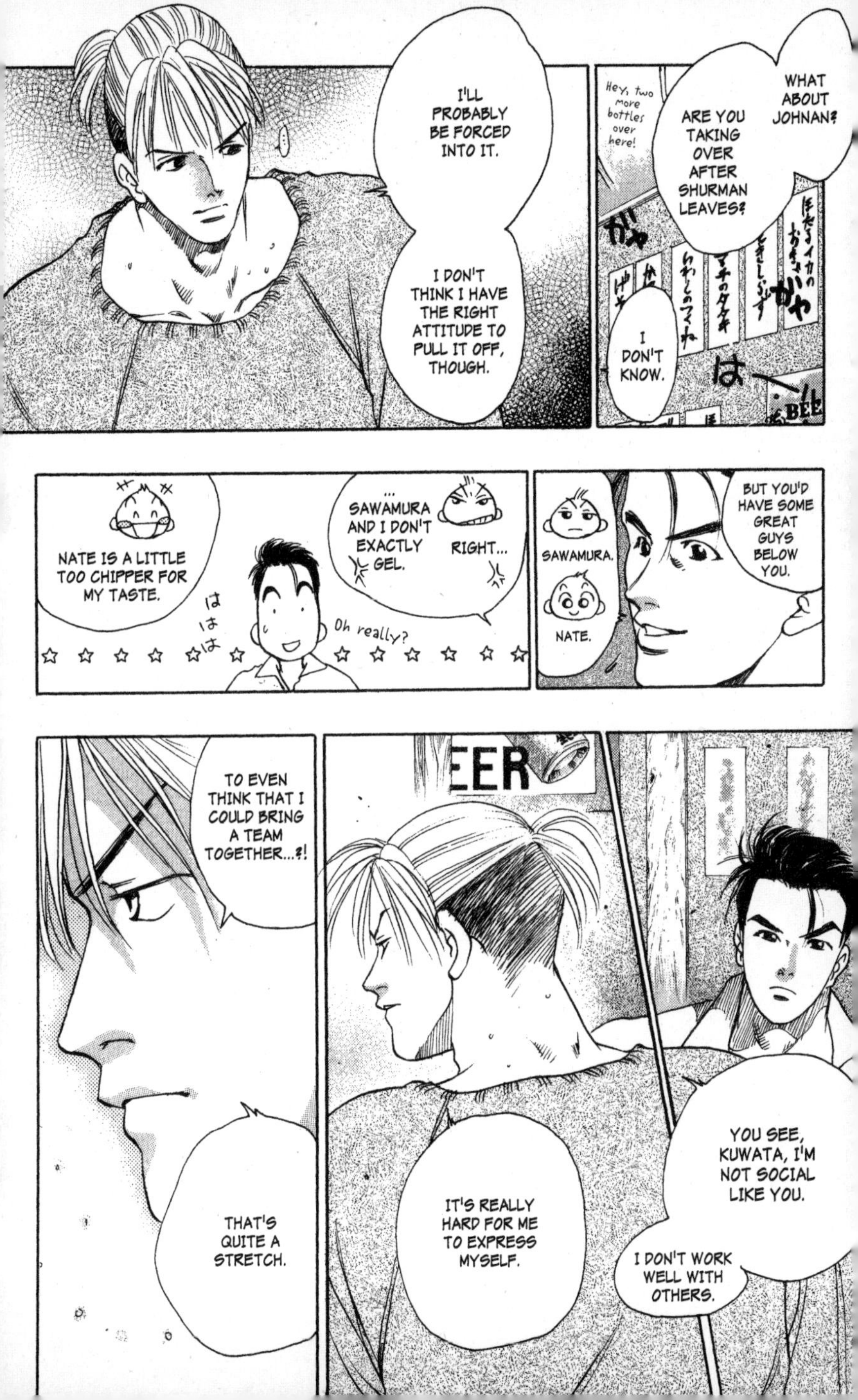
WHAT ABOUT JOHNAN?
Hey, two more bottles over here!
ARE YOU TAKING OVER AFTER SHURMAN LEAVES?
I DON'T KNOW.
I'LL PROBABLY BE FORCED INTO IT.
I DON'T THINK I HAVE THE RIGHT ATTITUDE TO PULL IT OFF, THOUGH.
BUT YOU'D HAVE SOME GREAT GUYS BELOW YOU.
SAWAMURA.
NATE.
... SAWAMURA AND I DON'T EXACTLY GEL.
RIGHT...
Oh really?
NATE IS A LITTLE TOO CHIPPER FOR MY TASTE.
ははは
YOU SEE, KUWATA, I'M NOT SOCIAL LIKE YOU.
I DON'T WORK WELL WITH OTHERS.
IT'S REALLY HARD FOR ME TO EXPRESS MYSELF.
TO EVEN THINK THAT I COULD BRING A TEAM TOGETHER...?!
THAT'S QUITE A STRETCH.

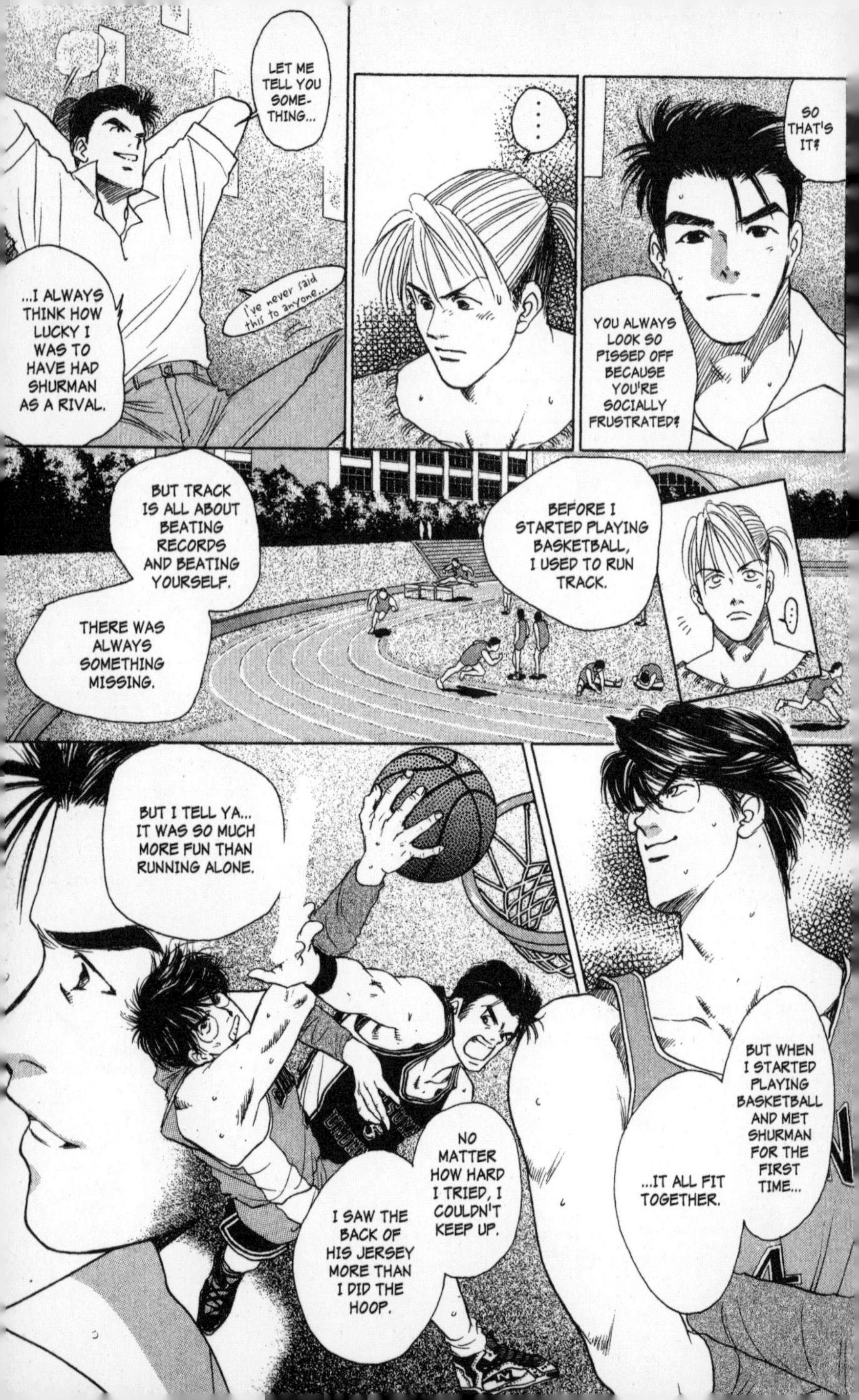
SO THAT'S IT?
YOU ALWAYS LOOK SO PISSED OFF BECAUSE YOU'RE SOCIALLY FRUSTRATED?
.....
LET ME TELL YOU SOME-THING...
I've never said this to anyone...
...I ALWAYS THINK HOW LUCKY I WAS TO HAVE HAD SHURMAN AS A RIVAL.
...
BEFORE I STARTED PLAYING BASKETBALL, I USED TO RUN TRACK.
BUT TRACK IS ALL ABOUT BEATING RECORDS AND BEATING YOURSELF.
THERE WAS ALWAYS SOMETHING MISSING.
BUT WHEN I STARTED PLAYING BASKETBALL AND MET SHURMAN FOR THE FIRST TIME...
...IT ALL FIT TOGETHER.
NO MATTER HOW HARD I TRIED, I COULDN'T KEEP UP.
I SAW THE BACK OF HIS JERSEY MORE THAN I DID THE HOOP.
BUT I TELL YA... IT WAS SO MUCH MORE FUN THAN RUNNING ALONE.

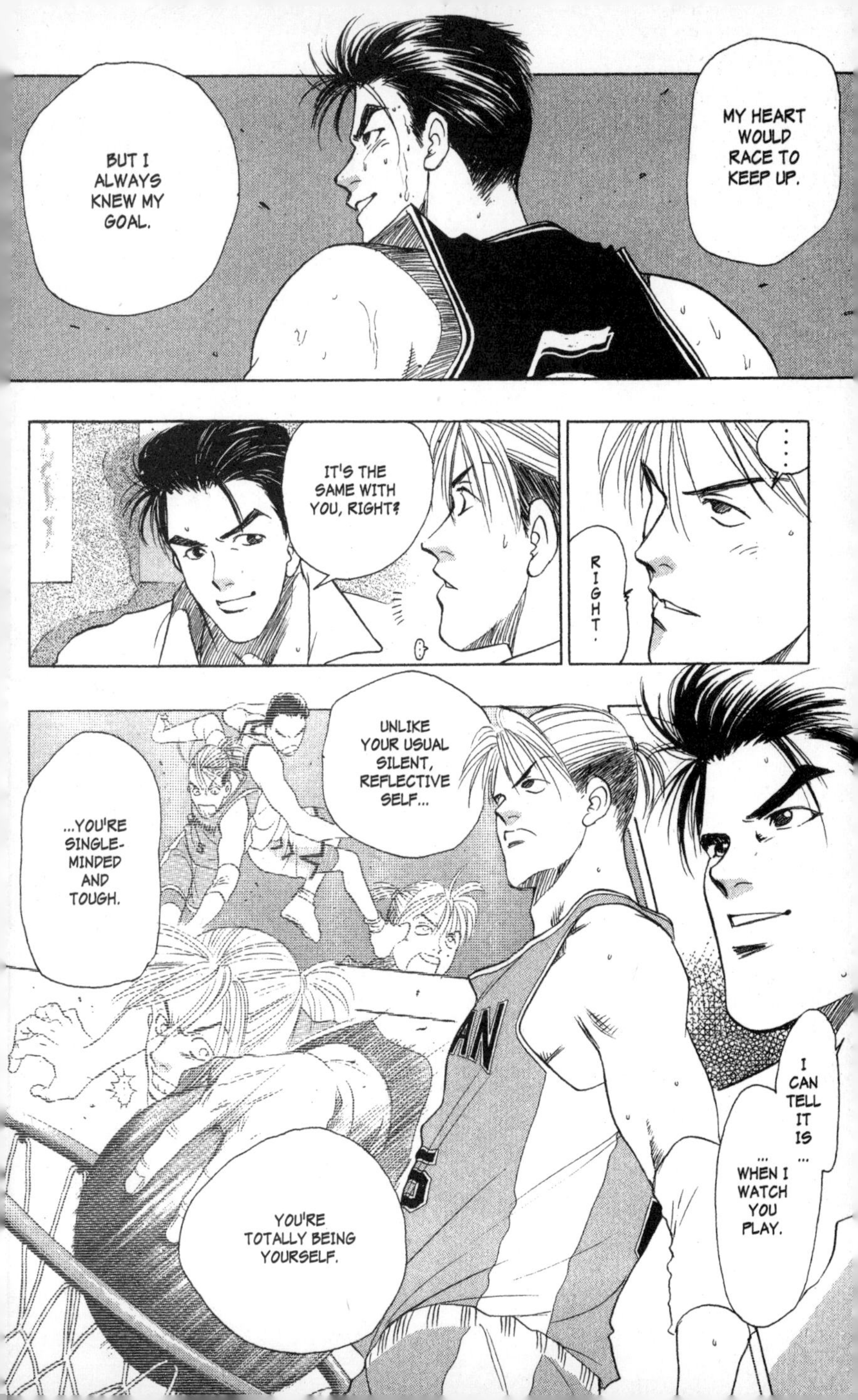
MY HEART WOULD RACE TO KEEP UP.
BUT I ALWAYS KNEW MY GOAL.
....
RIGHT.
IT'S THE SAME WITH YOU, RIGHT?
I CAN TELL IT IS ... WHEN I WATCH YOU PLAY.
UNLIKE YOUR USUAL SILENT, REFLECTIVE SELF...
...YOU'RE SINGLE-MINDED AND TOUGH.
YOU'RE TOTALLY BEING YOURSELF.

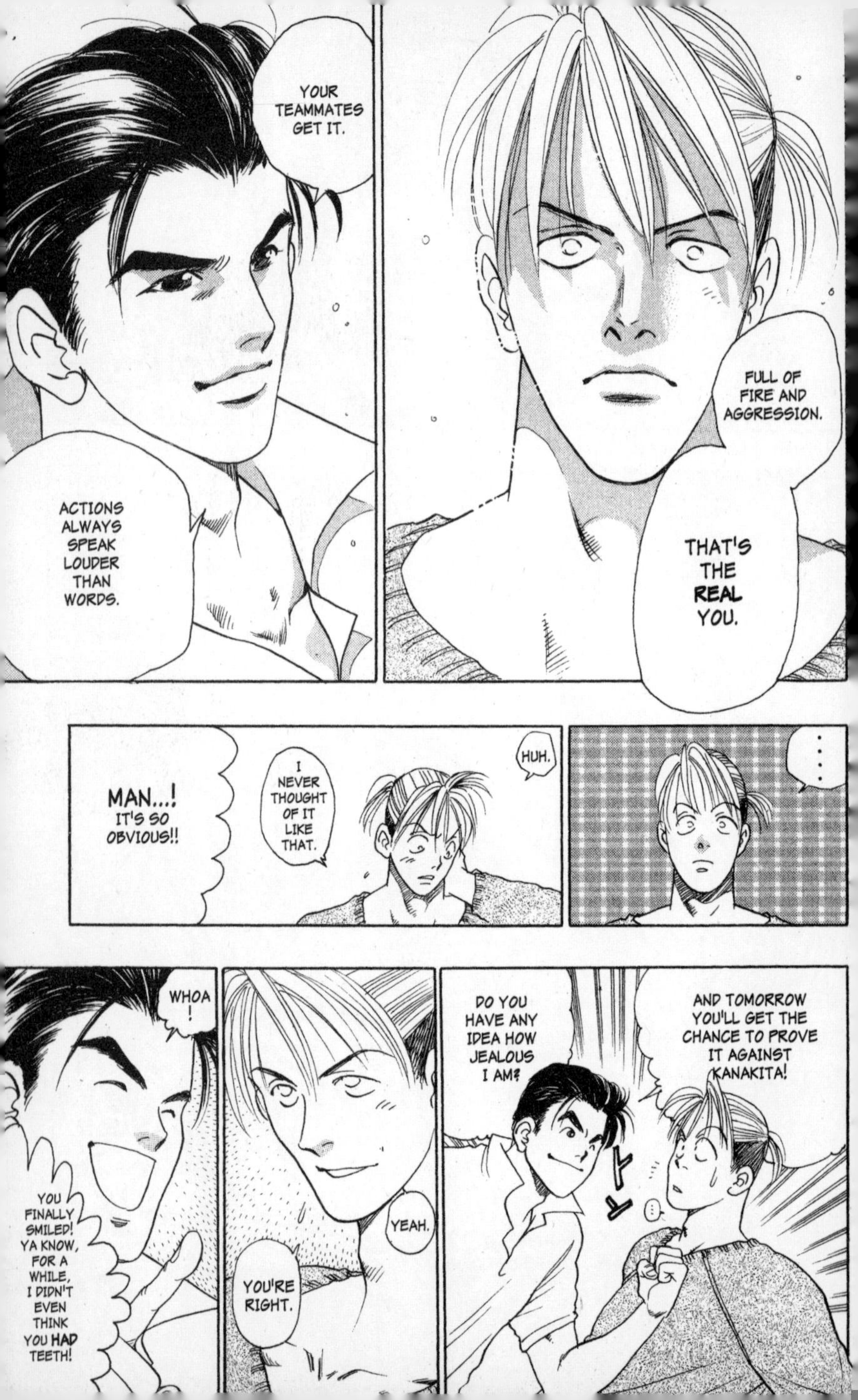

FULL OF FIRE AND AGGRESSION.
THAT'S THE **REAL** YOU.
YOUR TEAMMATES GET IT.
ACTIONS ALWAYS SPEAK LOUDER THAN WORDS.
....
HUH.
I NEVER THOUGHT OF IT LIKE THAT.
MAN...! IT'S SO OBVIOUS!!
AND TOMORROW YOU'LL GET THE CHANCE TO PROVE IT AGAINST KANAKITA!
DO YOU HAVE ANY IDEA HOW JEALOUS I AM?
...
YEAH.
YOU'RE RIGHT.
WHOA!
YOU FINALLY SMILED! YA KNOW, FOR A WHILE, I DIDN'T EVEN THINK YOU **HAD** TEETH!

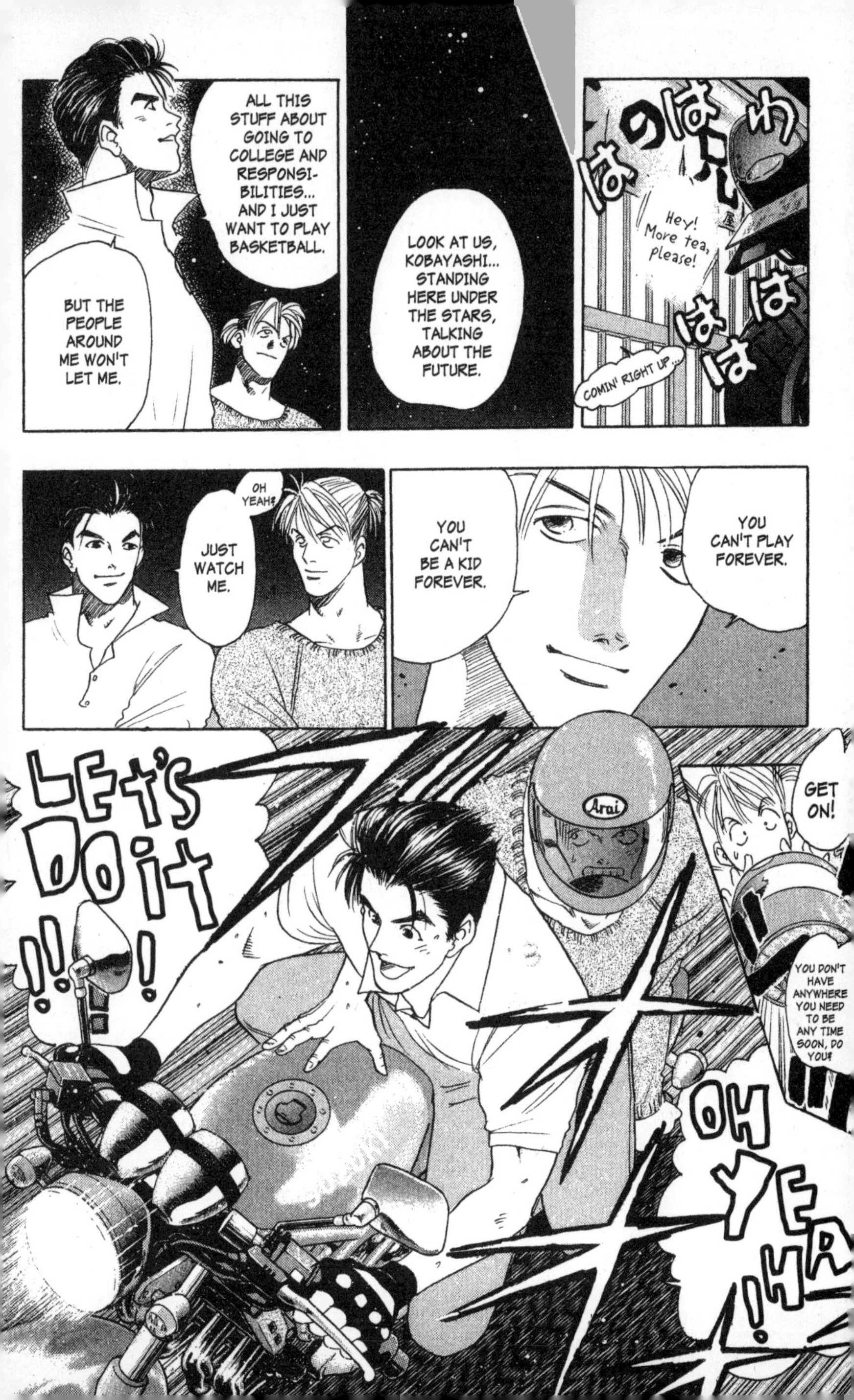
Hey! More tea, please!
COMIN' RIGHT UP...
LOOK AT US, KOBAYASHI... STANDING HERE UNDER THE STARS, TALKING ABOUT THE FUTURE.
ALL THIS STUFF ABOUT GOING TO COLLEGE AND RESPONSI-BILITIES... AND I JUST WANT TO PLAY BASKETBALL.
BUT THE PEOPLE AROUND ME WON'T LET ME.
YOU CAN'T PLAY FOREVER.
YOU CAN'T BE A KID FOREVER.
OH YEAH?
JUST WATCH ME.
GET ON!
YOU DON'T HAVE ANYWHERE YOU NEED TO BE ANY TIME SOON, DO YOU?
OH YEAHA!
Arai
LET'S DO IT !!!

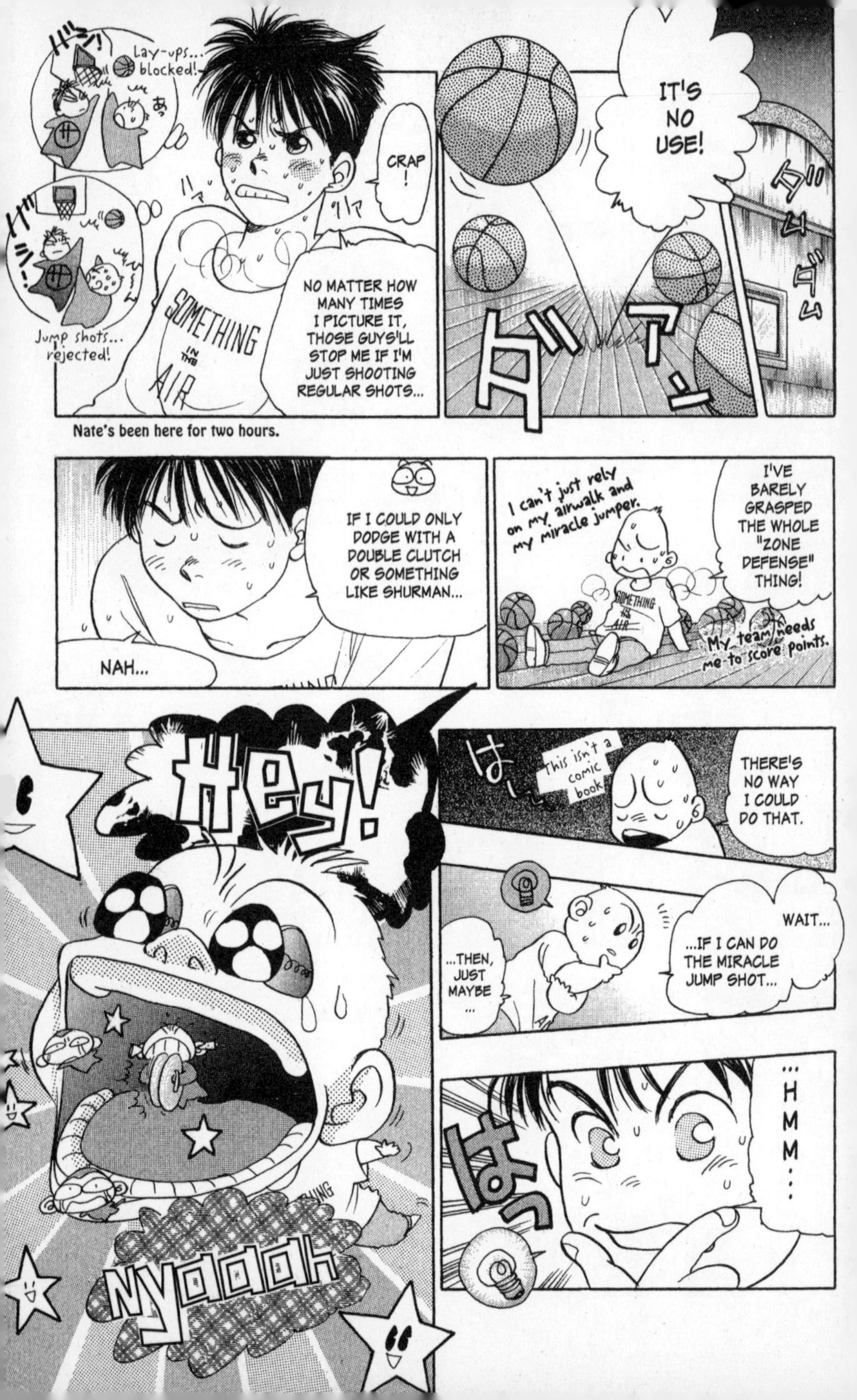
IT'S NO USE!
CRAP!
NO MATTER HOW MANY TIMES I PICTURE IT, THOSE GUYS'LL STOP ME IF I'M JUST SHOOTING REGULAR SHOTS...
Lay-ups... blocked!
Jump shots... rejected!
SOMETHING IN THE AIR
I'VE BARELY GRASPED THE WHOLE "ZONE DEFENSE" THING!
I can't just rely on my airwalk and my miracle jumper.
My team needs me to score points.
IF I COULD ONLY DODGE WITH A DOUBLE CLUTCH OR SOMETHING LIKE SHURMAN...
NAH...
THERE'S NO WAY I COULD DO THAT.
This isn't a comic book
WAIT...
...IF I CAN DO THE MIRACLE JUMP SHOT...
...THEN, JUST MAYBE ...
...HMM...
Hey!
Nyaaah
Nate's been here for two hours.

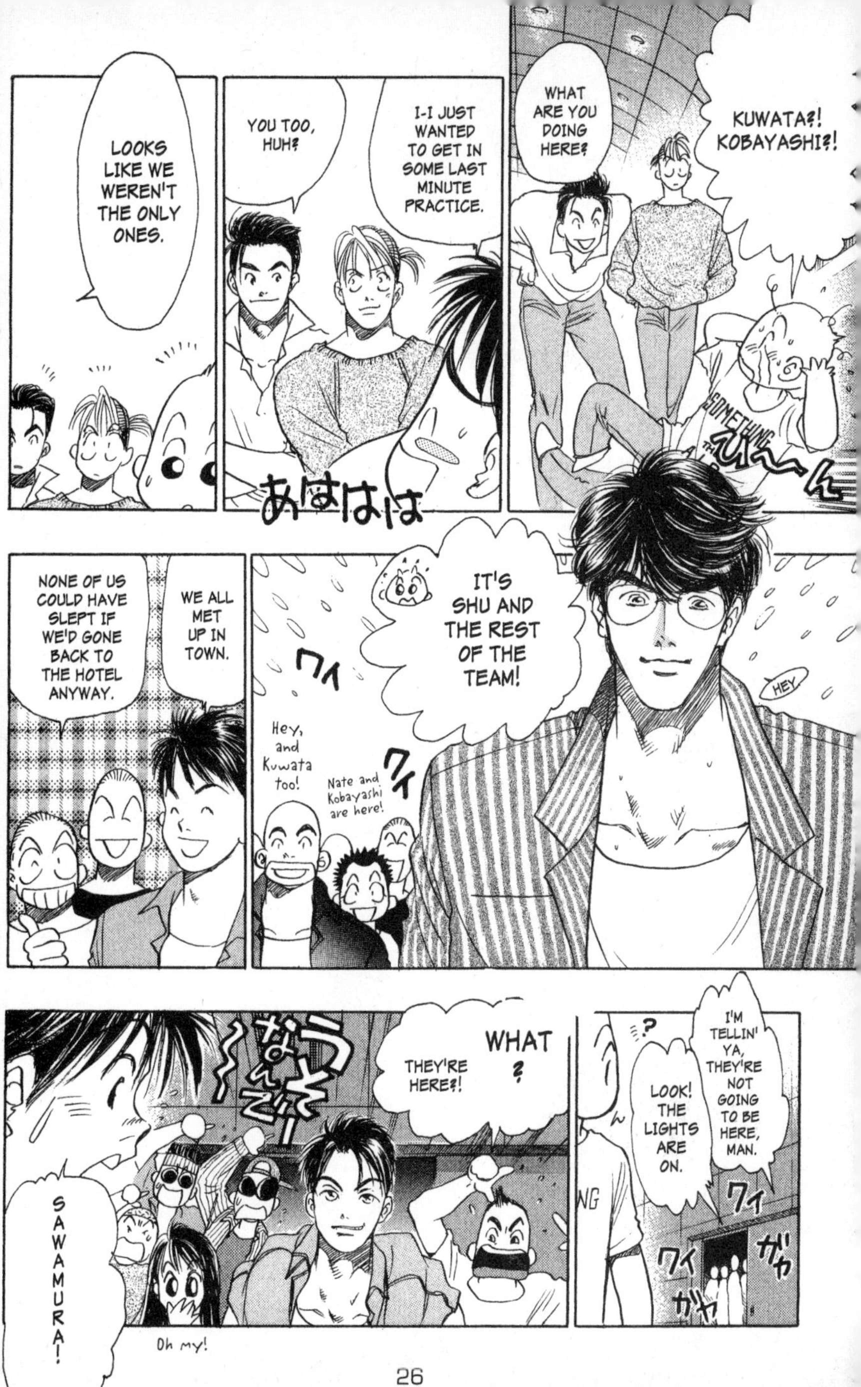
KUWATA?! KOBAYASHI?!
WHAT ARE YOU DOING HERE?
うぃ〜ん
I-I JUST WANTED TO GET IN SOME LAST MINUTE PRACTICE.
YOU TOO, HUH?
あははは
LOOKS LIKE WE WEREN'T THE ONLY ONES.
HEY
IT'S SHU AND THE REST OF THE TEAM!
ワイ
Nate and Kobayashi are here!
Hey, and Kuwata too!
ワイ
WE ALL MET UP IN TOWN.
NONE OF US COULD HAVE SLEPT IF WE'D GONE BACK TO THE HOTEL ANYWAY.
I'M TELLIN' YA, THEY'RE NOT GOING TO BE HERE, MAN.
LOOK! THE LIGHTS ARE ON.
?
ワイ
ガヤ
ワイ
ガヤ
WHAT?
THEY'RE HERE?!
うそ〜
なんで〜!
SAWAMURA!
Oh my!

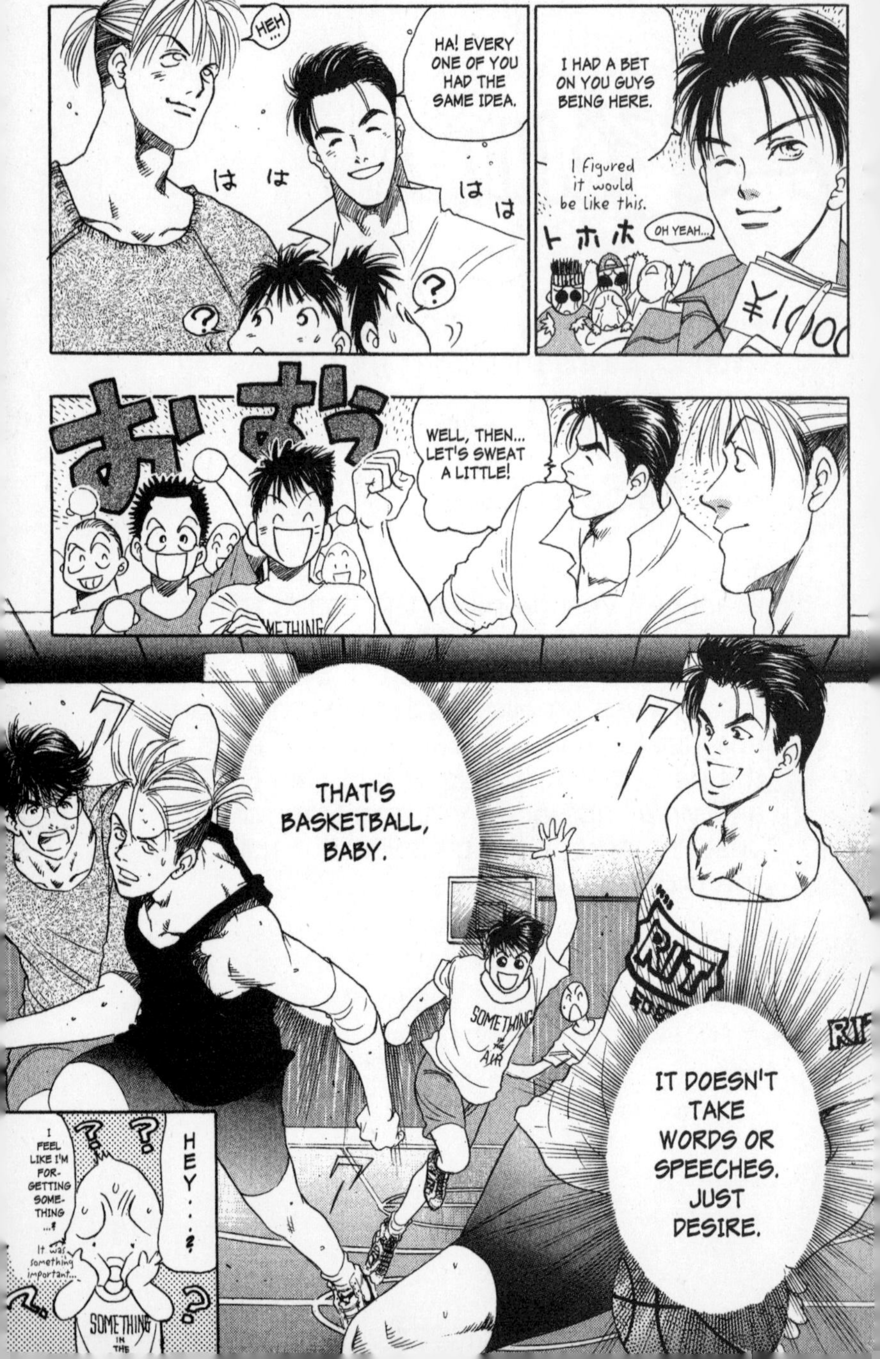
I HAD A BET ON YOU GUYS BEING HERE.
I figured it would be like this.
OH YEAH...
トホホ
HEH...
HA! EVERY ONE OF YOU HAD THE SAME IDEA.
はは
はは
?
?
WELL, THEN... LET'S SWEAT A LITTLE!
おおう
IT DOESN'T TAKE WORDS OR SPEECHES. JUST DESIRE.
THAT'S BASKETBALL, BABY.
HEY...?
I FEEL LIKE I'M FOR-GETTING SOME-THING...!
It was something important...

You're Reading...

From the vaults of TOKYOPOP–
Product tie-ins that didn't make it

Rejected Product #46

Rebound Can O' Sweat

Tired of busting your hump at basketball
practice? Wanna make the coach think
you're working hard while hardly working?
Then try our Rebound Can O' Sweat! Looks,
tastes–even smells like the real thing! And it's
not just for sports! Wanna go all Ferris on
the parents? A few squirts of Can O' Sweat,
and *viola!* Instant Amazonian fever of 110!
Just remember–it's no sweat for usto help
you with your problems!

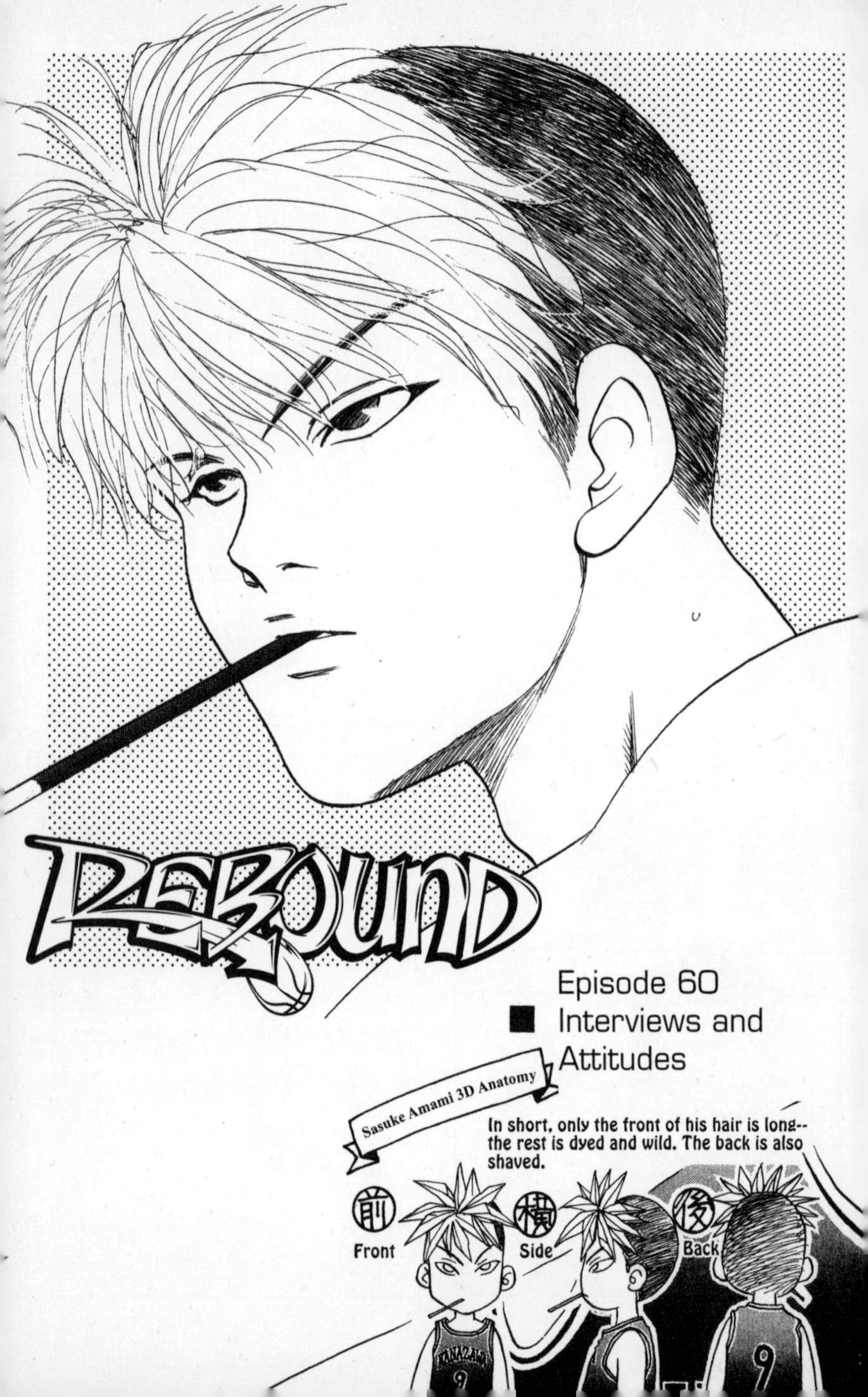
REBOUND
Episode 60 ■ Interviews and Attitudes
Sasuke Amami 3D Anatomy
In short, only the front of his hair is long--the rest is dyed and wild. The back is also shaved.
前 Front
横 Side
後 Back

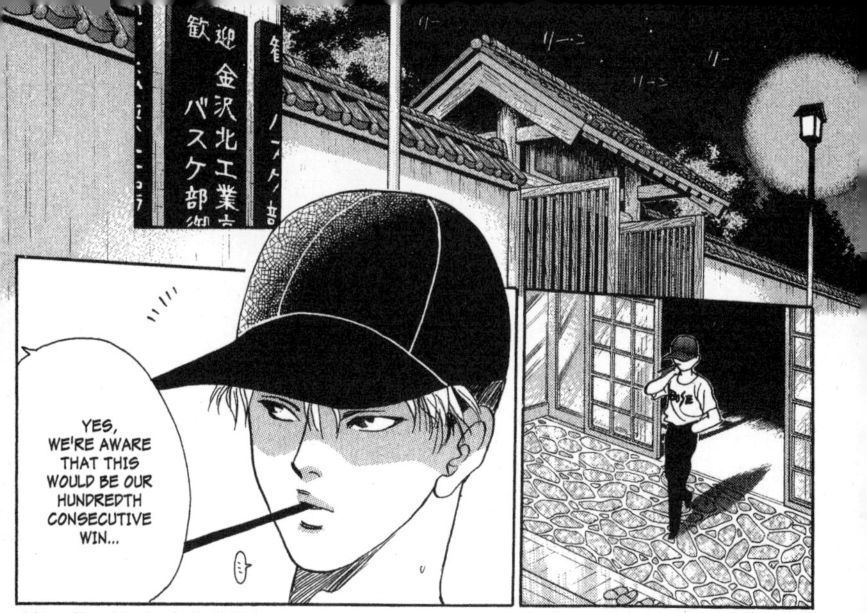
YES, WE'RE AWARE THAT THIS WOULD BE OUR HUNDREDTH CONSECUTIVE WIN...

*Sign: Kanakita Basketball Club.

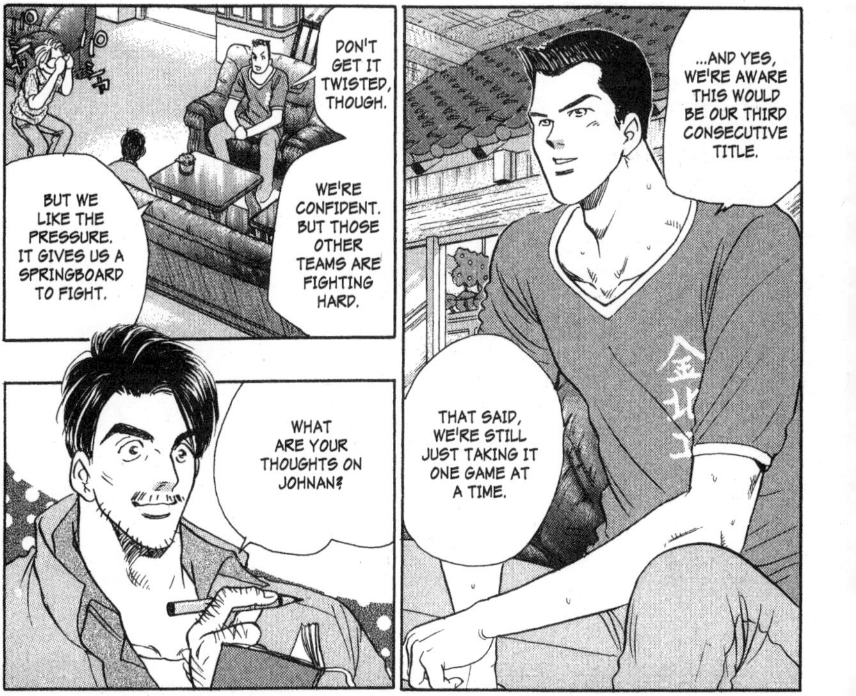
...AND YES, WE'RE AWARE THIS WOULD BE OUR THIRD CONSECUTIVE TITLE.
THAT SAID, WE'RE STILL JUST TAKING IT ONE GAME AT A TIME.
DON'T GET IT TWISTED, THOUGH.
WE'RE CONFIDENT. BUT THOSE OTHER TEAMS ARE FIGHTING HARD.
BUT WE LIKE THE PRESSURE. IT GIVES US A SPRINGBOARD TO FIGHT.
WHAT ARE YOUR THOUGHTS ON JOHNAN?

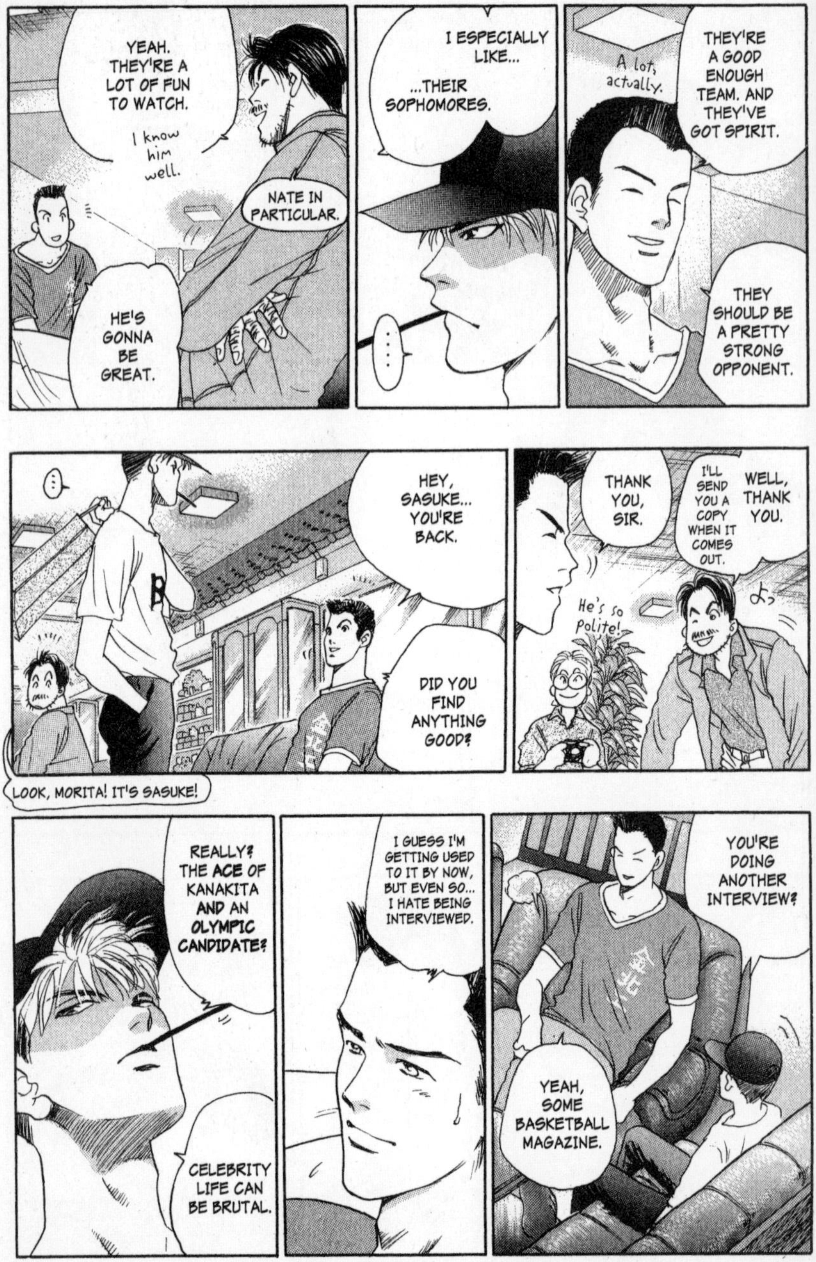
A lot, actually.
THEY'RE A GOOD ENOUGH TEAM. AND THEY'VE GOT SPIRIT.
THEY SHOULD BE A PRETTY STRONG OPPONENT.
I ESPECIALLY LIKE... ...THEIR SOPHOMORES.
....
YEAH. THEY'RE A LOT OF FUN TO WATCH.
I know him well.
NATE IN PARTICULAR.
HE'S GONNA BE GREAT.
WELL, THANK YOU.
I'LL SEND YOU A COPY WHEN IT COMES OUT.
THANK YOU, SIR.
He's so polite!
よっ
HEY, SASUKE... YOU'RE BACK.
...
DID YOU FIND ANYTHING GOOD?
LOOK, MORITA! IT'S SASUKE!
YOU'RE DOING ANOTHER INTERVIEW?
YEAH, SOME BASKETBALL MAGAZINE.
I GUESS I'M GETTING USED TO IT BY NOW, BUT EVEN SO... I HATE BEING INTERVIEWED.
REALLY? THE ACE OF KANAKITA AND AN OLYMPIC CANDIDATE?
CELEBRITY LIFE CAN BE BRUTAL.

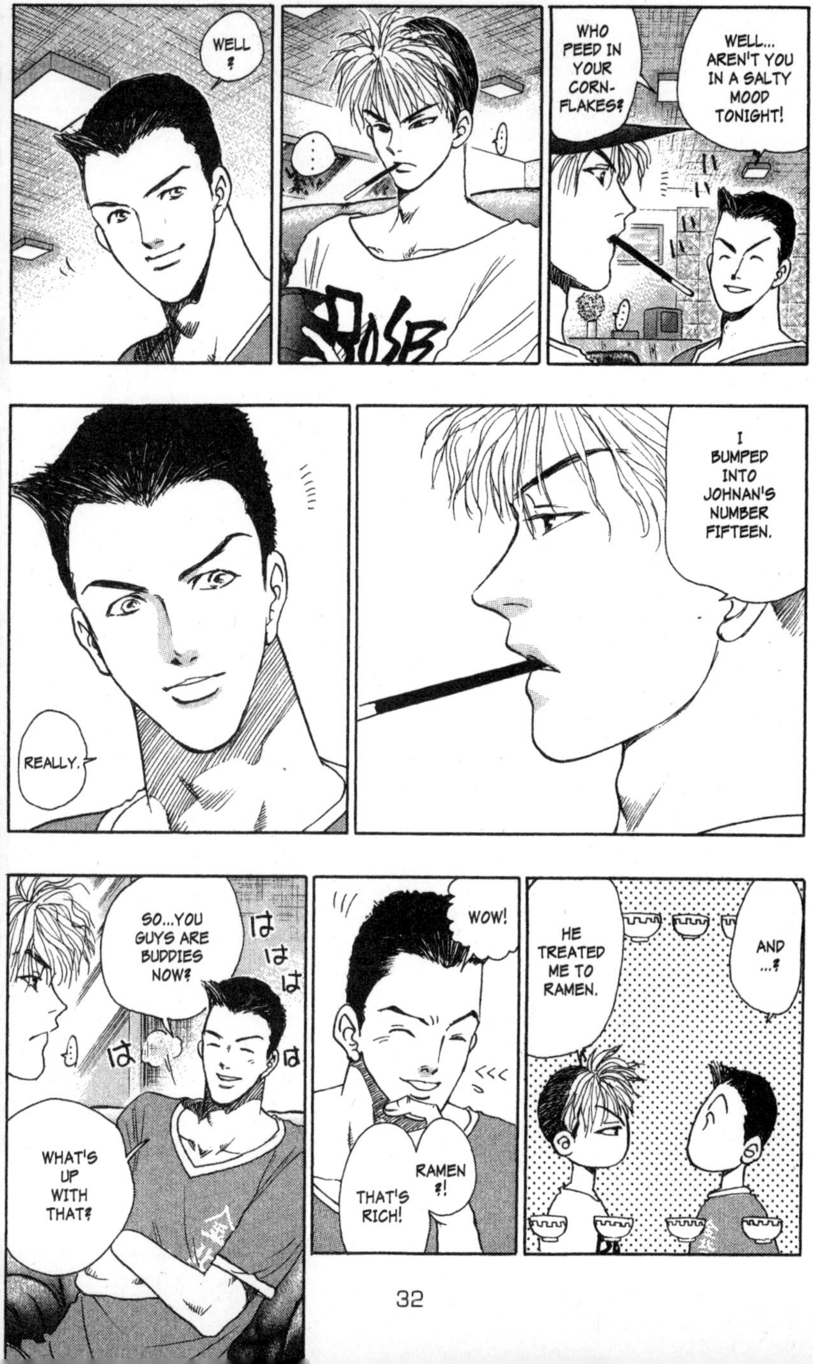
WELL... AREN'T YOU IN A SALTY MOOD TONIGHT!
WHO PEED IN YOUR CORN-FLAKES?
...
...
WELL?
I BUMPED INTO JOHNAN'S NUMBER FIFTEEN.
REALLY.
AND ...?
HE TREATED ME TO RAMEN.
WOW!
RAMEN?!
THAT'S RICH!
はは
はは
SO...YOU GUYS ARE BUDDIES NOW?
...
WHAT'S UP WITH THAT?

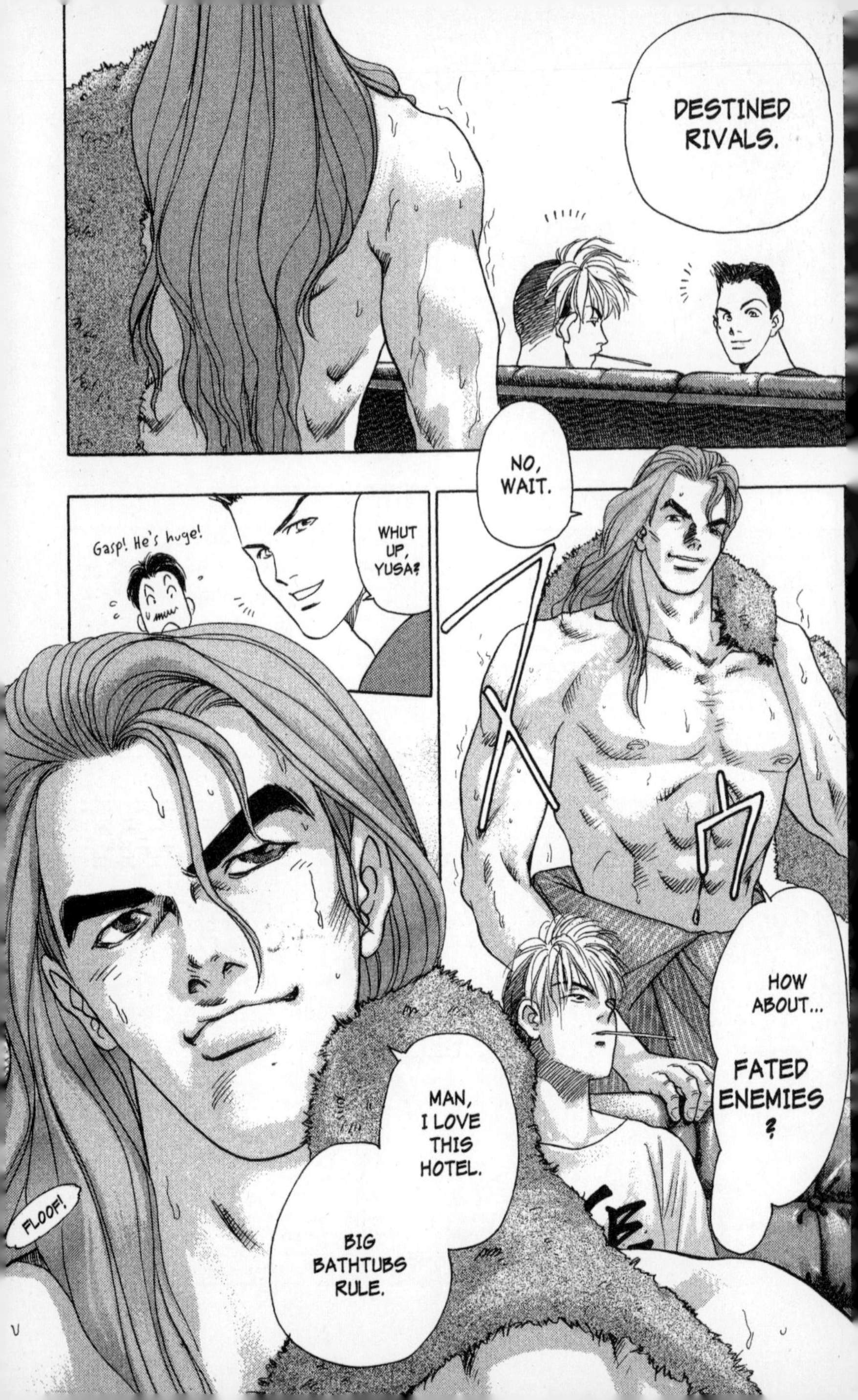
DESTINED RIVALS.
NO, WAIT.
HOW ABOUT...
FATED ENEMIES?
WHUT UP, YUSA?
Gasp! He's huge!
MAN, I LOVE THIS HOTEL.
BIG BATHTUBS RULE.
FLOOF!

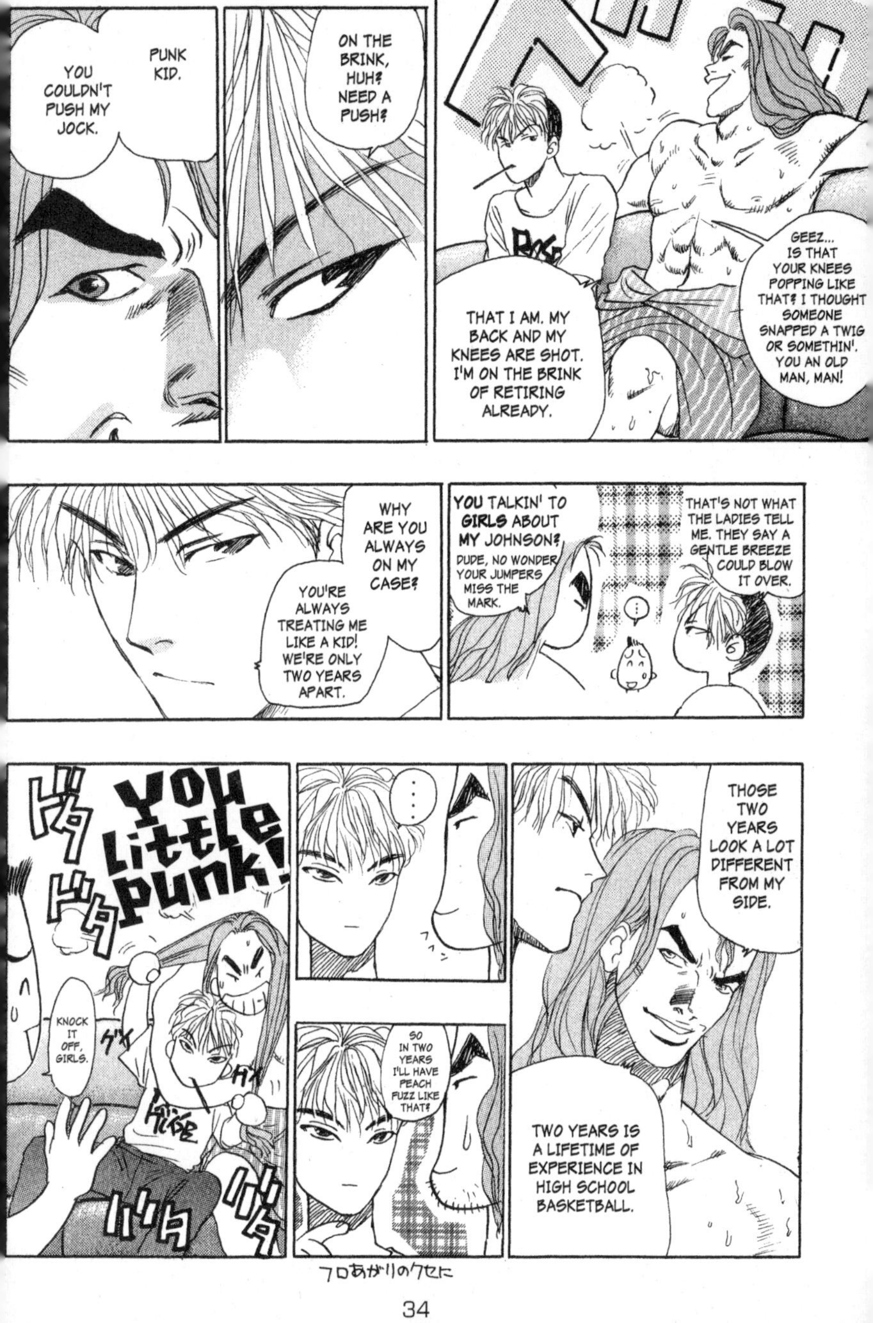
GEEZ... IS THAT YOUR KNEES POPPING LIKE THAT? I THOUGHT SOMEONE SNAPPED A TWIG OR SOMETHIN'. YOU AN OLD MAN, MAN!
THAT I AM. MY BACK AND MY KNEES ARE SHOT. I'M ON THE BRINK OF RETIRING ALREADY.
ON THE BRINK, HUH? NEED A PUSH?
PUNK KID.
YOU COULDN'T PUSH MY JOCK.
THAT'S NOT WHAT THE LADIES TELL ME. THEY SAY A GENTLE BREEZE COULD BLOW IT OVER.
YOU TALKIN' TO GIRLS ABOUT MY JOHNSON?
DUDE, NO WONDER YOUR JUMPERS MISS THE MARK.
...
WHY ARE YOU ALWAYS ON MY CASE?
YOU'RE ALWAYS TREATING ME LIKE A KID! WE'RE ONLY TWO YEARS APART.
THOSE TWO YEARS LOOK A LOT DIFFERENT FROM MY SIDE.
TWO YEARS IS A LIFETIME OF EXPERIENCE IN HIGH SCHOOL BASKETBALL.
....
SO IN TWO YEARS I'LL HAVE PEACH FUZZ LIKE THAT?
YOU LITTLE PUNK!
ドタ
ドタ
KNOCK IT OFF, GIRLS.
バタ
バタ

フロあがりのクセに

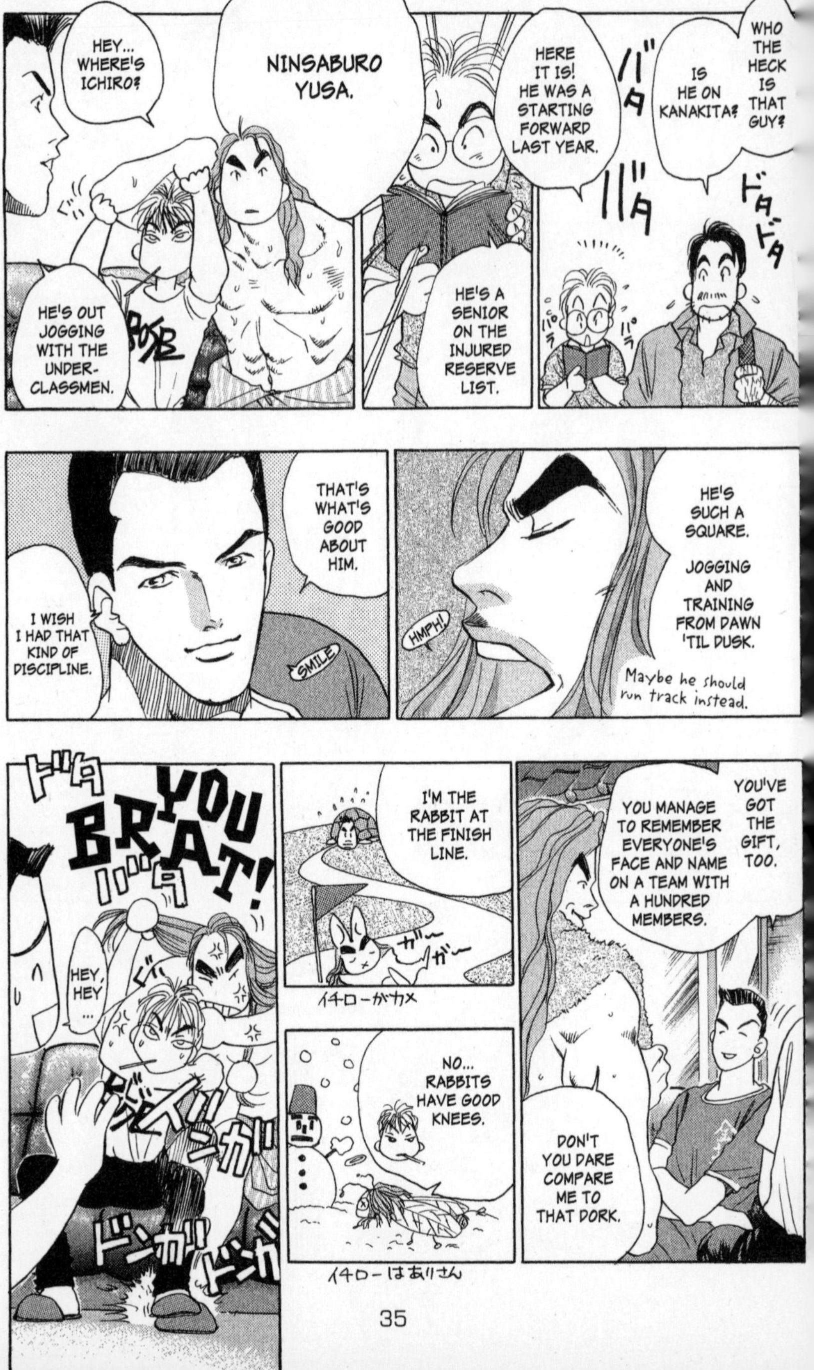
WHO THE HECK IS THAT GUY?
IS HE ON KANAKITA?
バタ
バタ
ドタドタ
HERE IT IS! HE WAS A STARTING FORWARD LAST YEAR.
HE'S A SENIOR ON THE INJURED RESERVE LIST.
NINSABURO YUSA.
HEY... WHERE'S ICHIRO?
HE'S OUT JOGGING WITH THE UNDER-CLASSMEN.
HE'S SUCH A SQUARE.
JOGGING AND TRAINING FROM DAWN 'TIL DUSK.
HMPH!
Maybe he should run track instead.
THAT'S WHAT'S GOOD ABOUT HIM.
I WISH I HAD THAT KIND OF DISCIPLINE.
SMILE
YOU'VE GOT THE GIFT, TOO.
YOU MANAGE TO REMEMBER EVERYONE'S FACE AND NAME ON A TEAM WITH A HUNDRED MEMBERS.
DON'T YOU DARE COMPARE ME TO THAT DORK.
I'M THE RABBIT AT THE FINISH LINE.
ガ～ ガ～
イチローがカメ
NO... RABBITS HAVE GOOD KNEES.
イチローはありさん
ドタ
YOU BRAT!
バタ
HEY, HEY...
ドンガ
ドンガ

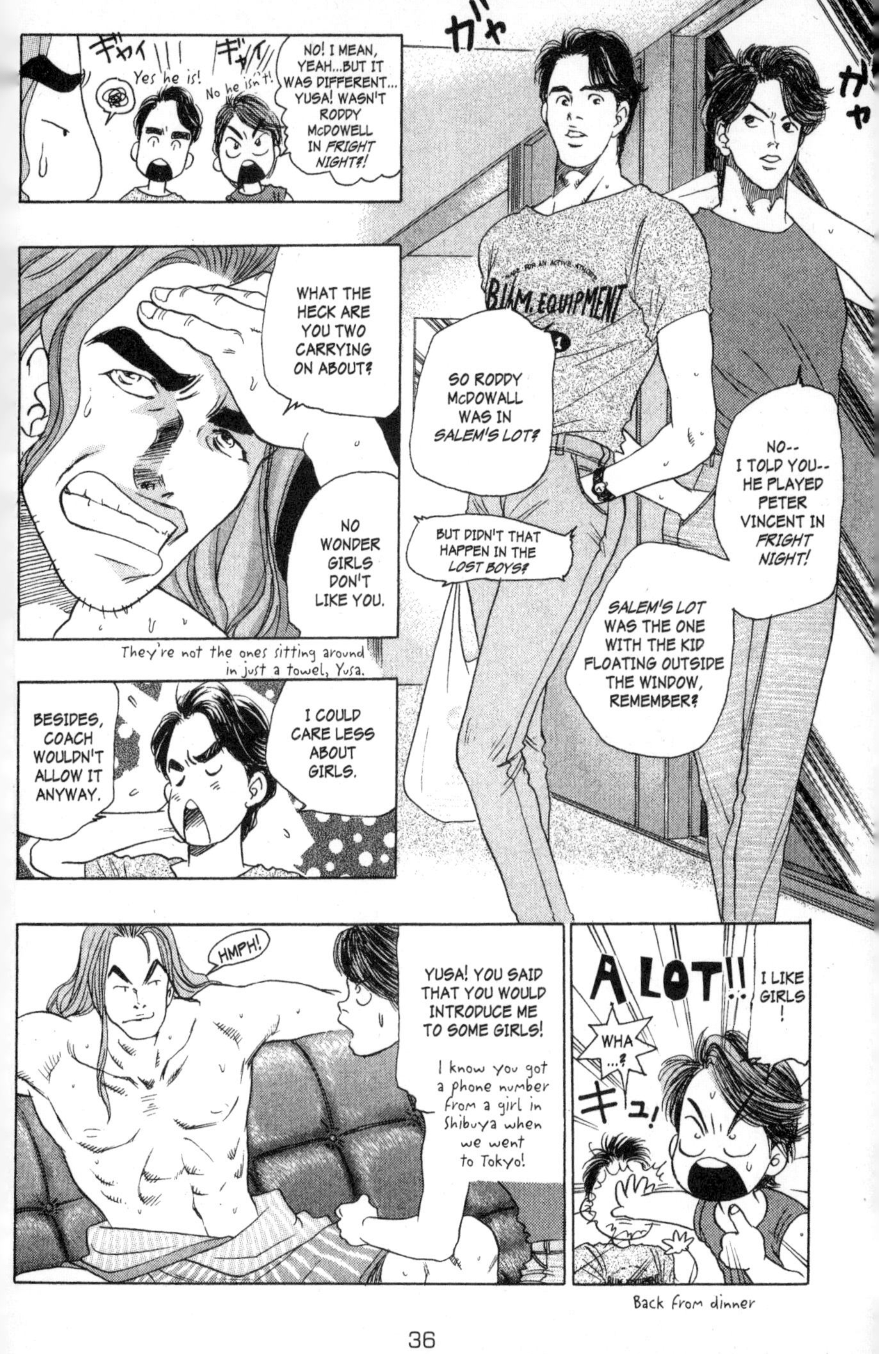

ガャ
ガャ
SO RODDY McDOWALL WAS IN SALEM'S LOT?
NO-- I TOLD YOU-- HE PLAYED PETER VINCENT IN FRIGHT NIGHT!
BUT DIDN'T THAT HAPPEN IN THE LOST BOYS?
SALEM'S LOT WAS THE ONE WITH THE KID FLOATING OUTSIDE THE WINDOW, REMEMBER?
NO! I MEAN, YEAH...BUT IT WAS DIFFERENT... YUSA! WASN'T RODDY McDOWELL IN FRIGHT NIGHT?!
ギャイ
ギャイ
No he isn't!
Yes he is!
WHAT THE HECK ARE YOU TWO CARRYING ON ABOUT?
NO WONDER GIRLS DON'T LIKE YOU.
They're not the ones sitting around in just a towel, Yusa.
I COULD CARE LESS ABOUT GIRLS.
BESIDES, COACH WOULDN'T ALLOW IT ANYWAY.
I LIKE GIRLS!
A LOT!!
WHA...?
キュ!
HMPH!
YUSA! YOU SAID THAT YOU WOULD INTRODUCE ME TO SOME GIRLS!
I know you got a phone number from a girl in Shibuya when we went to Tokyo!

Back from dinner

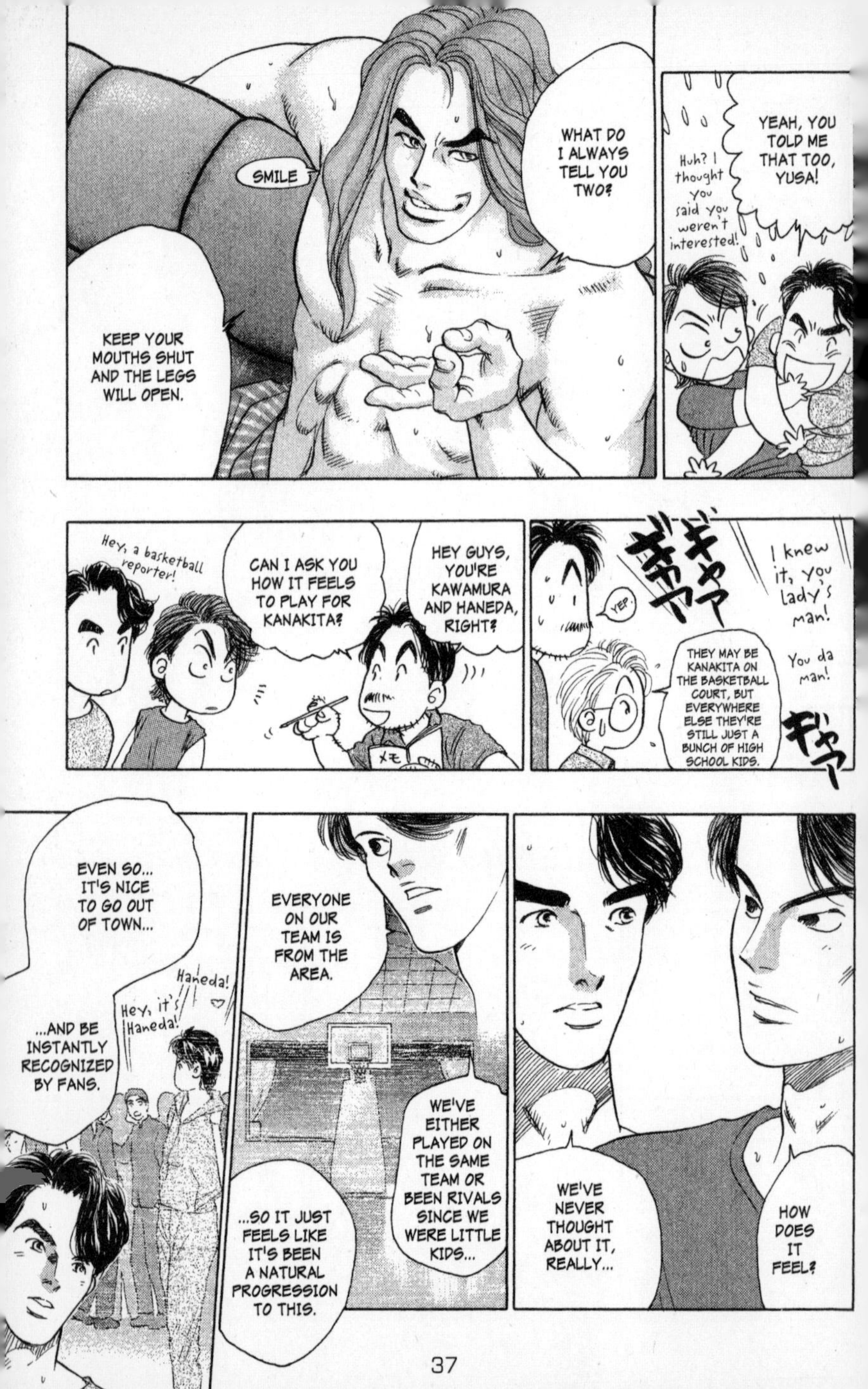
YEAH, YOU TOLD ME THAT TOO, YUSA!
Huh? I thought you said you weren't interested!
WHAT DO I ALWAYS TELL YOU TWO?
SMILE
KEEP YOUR MOUTHS SHUT AND THE LEGS WILL OPEN.
ギャア
ギャア
I knew it, you lady's man!
YEP.
You da man!
THEY MAY BE KANAKITA ON THE BASKETBALL COURT, BUT EVERYWHERE ELSE THEY'RE STILL JUST A BUNCH OF HIGH SCHOOL KIDS.
ギャー
HEY GUYS, YOU'RE KAWAMURA AND HANEDA, RIGHT?
CAN I ASK YOU HOW IT FEELS TO PLAY FOR KANAKITA?
Hey, a basketball reporter!
メモ
HOW DOES IT FEEL?
WE'VE NEVER THOUGHT ABOUT IT, REALLY...
EVERYONE ON OUR TEAM IS FROM THE AREA.
WE'VE EITHER PLAYED ON THE SAME TEAM OR BEEN RIVALS SINCE WE WERE LITTLE KIDS...
...SO IT JUST FEELS LIKE IT'S BEEN A NATURAL PROGRESSION TO THIS.
EVEN SO... IT'S NICE TO GO OUT OF TOWN...
Haneda!
Hey, it's Haneda!
...AND BE INSTANTLY RECOGNIZED BY FANS.

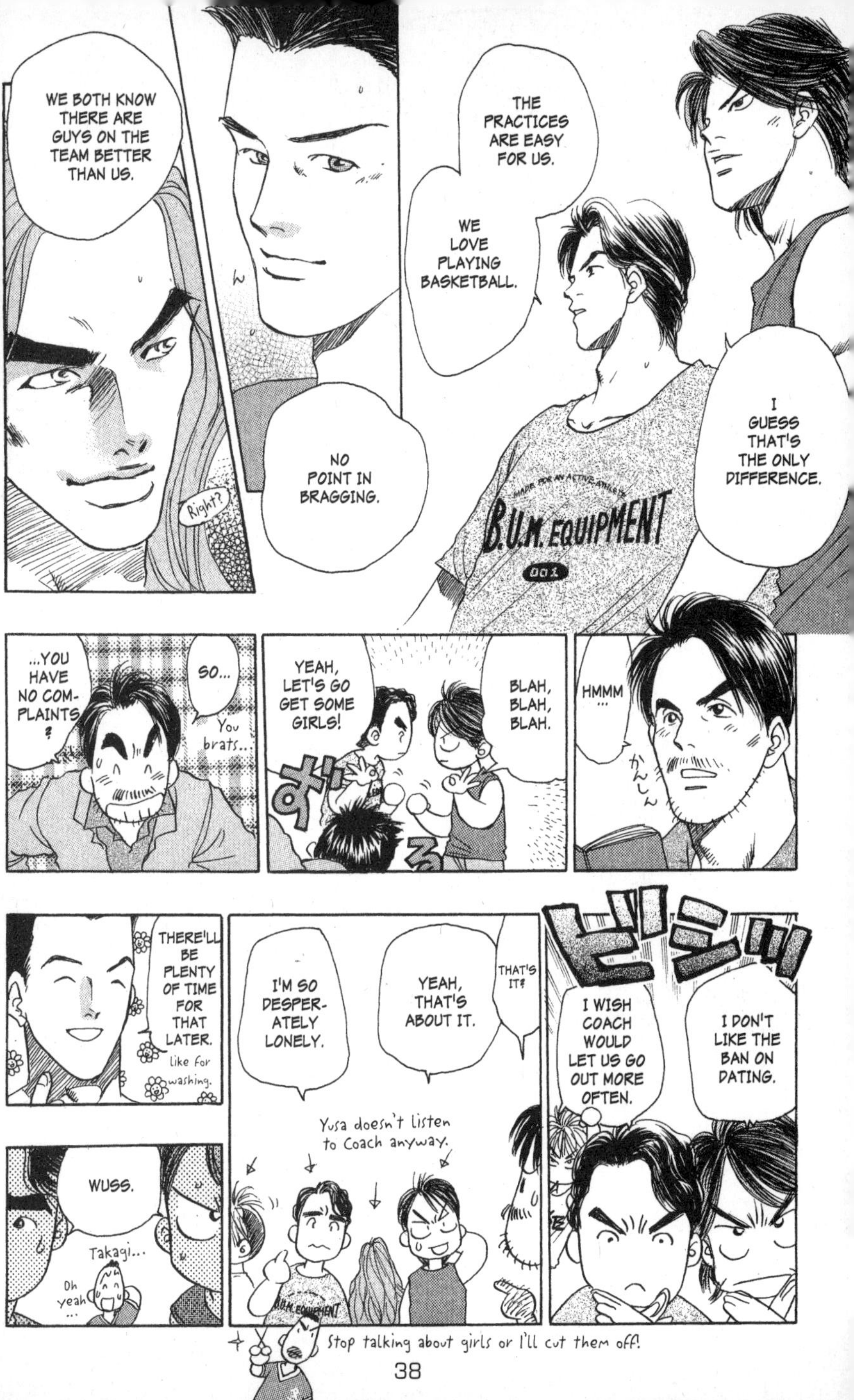
THE PRACTICES ARE EASY FOR US.
WE LOVE PLAYING BASKETBALL.
I GUESS THAT'S THE ONLY DIFFERENCE.
WE BOTH KNOW THERE ARE GUYS ON THE TEAM BETTER THAN US.
Right?
NO POINT IN BRAGGING.
B.U.M. EQUIPMENT
HMMM...
かんしん
BLAH, BLAH, BLAH.
YEAH, LET'S GO GET SOME GIRLS!
SO...
You brats...
...YOU HAVE NO COMPLAINTS?
ビシッ
I DON'T LIKE THE BAN ON DATING.
I WISH COACH WOULD LET US GO OUT MORE OFTEN.
THAT'S IT?
YEAH, THAT'S ABOUT IT.
I'M SO DESPERATELY LONELY.
Yusa doesn't listen to Coach anyway.
THERE'LL BE PLENTY OF TIME FOR THAT LATER.
like for washing.
WUSS.
Takagi...
Oh yeah...
Stop talking about girls or I'll cut them off!

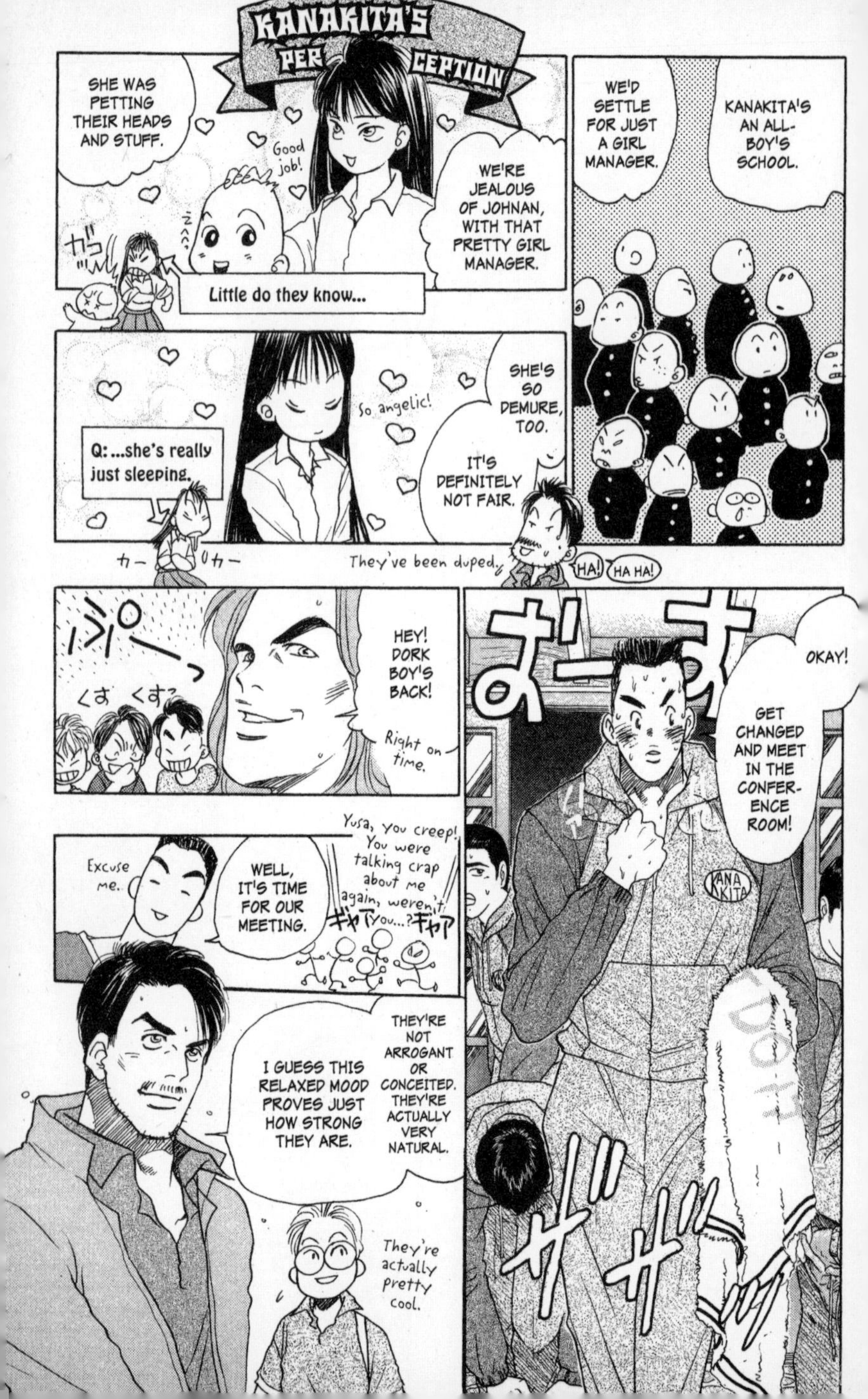
KANAKITA'S PERCEPTION
KANAKITA'S AN ALL-BOY'S SCHOOL.
WE'D SETTLE FOR JUST A GIRL MANAGER.
WE'RE JEALOUS OF JOHNAN, WITH THAT PRETTY GIRL MANAGER.
Good job!
SHE WAS PETTING THEIR HEADS AND STUFF.
Little do they know...
SHE'S SO DEMURE, TOO.
IT'S DEFINITELY NOT FAIR.
So angelic!
Q: ...she's really just sleeping.
They've been duped.
HA!
HA HA!
OKAY!
GET CHANGED AND MEET IN THE CONFERENCE ROOM!
KANAKITA
HEY! DORK BOY'S BACK!
Right on time.
くすくす
Yusa, you creep! You were talking crap about me again, weren't you...?
ギャア ギャア
WELL, IT'S TIME FOR OUR MEETING.
Excuse me.
THEY'RE NOT ARROGANT OR CONCEITED. THEY'RE ACTUALLY VERY NATURAL.
I GUESS THIS RELAXED MOOD PROVES JUST HOW STRONG THEY ARE.
They're actually pretty cool.

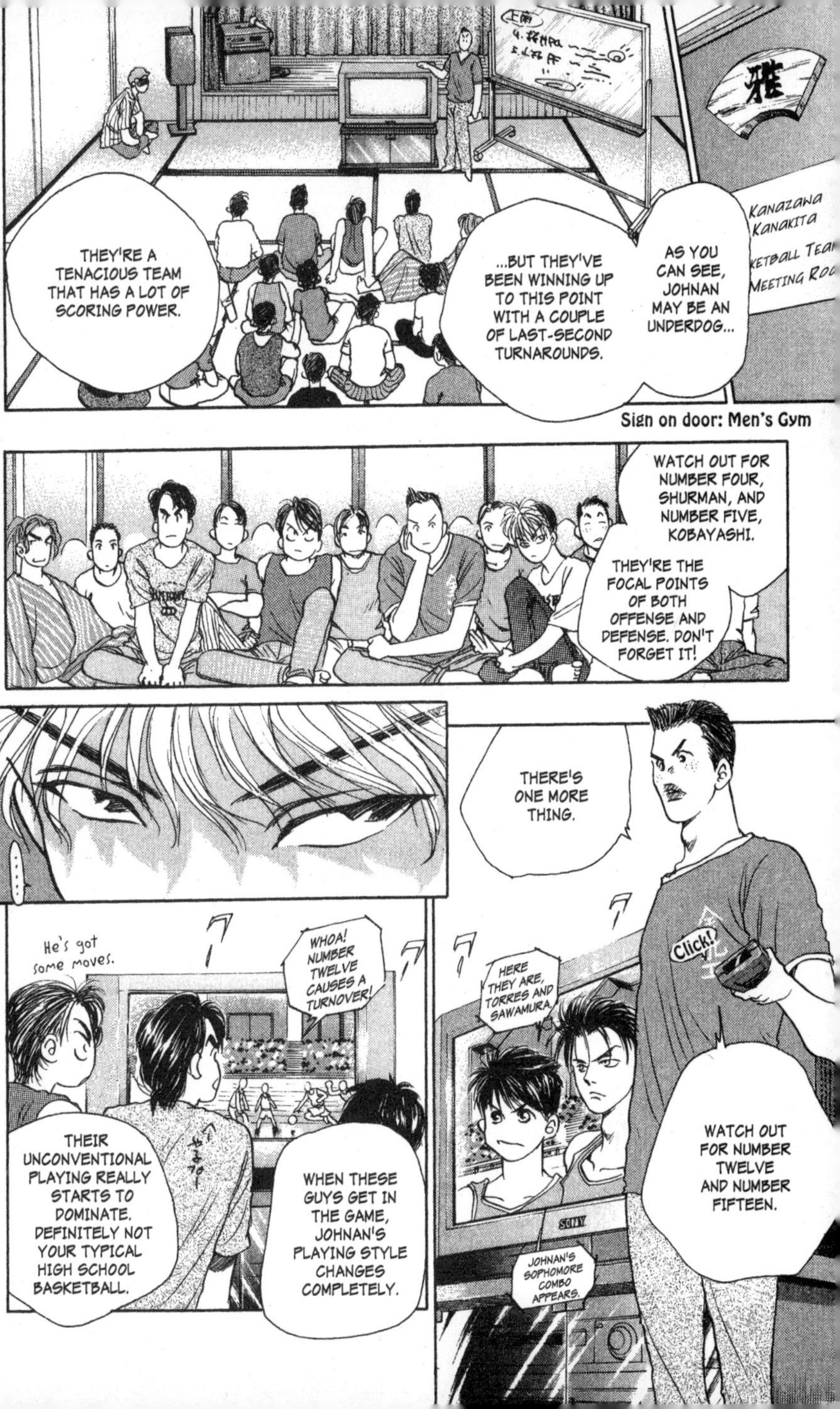
Kanazawa Kanakita
ketball Team Meeting Roo
AS YOU CAN SEE, JOHNAN MAY BE AN UNDERDOG...
...BUT THEY'VE BEEN WINNING UP TO THIS POINT WITH A COUPLE OF LAST-SECOND TURNAROUNDS.
THEY'RE A TENACIOUS TEAM THAT HAS A LOT OF SCORING POWER.
Sign on door: Men's Gym
WATCH OUT FOR NUMBER FOUR, SHURMAN, AND NUMBER FIVE, KOBAYASHI.
THEY'RE THE FOCAL POINTS OF BOTH OFFENSE AND DEFENSE. DON'T FORGET IT!
THERE'S ONE MORE THING.
Click!
HERE THEY ARE, TORRES AND SAWAMURA.
WATCH OUT FOR NUMBER TWELVE AND NUMBER FIFTEEN.
SONY
JOHNAN'S SOPHOMORE COMBO APPEARS.
...
WHOA! NUMBER TWELVE CAUSES A TURNOVER!
He's got some moves.
WHEN THESE GUYS GET IN THE GAME, JOHNAN'S PLAYING STYLE CHANGES COMPLETELY.
THEIR UNCONVENTIONAL PLAYING REALLY STARTS TO DOMINATE. DEFINITELY NOT YOUR TYPICAL HIGH SCHOOL BASKETBALL.

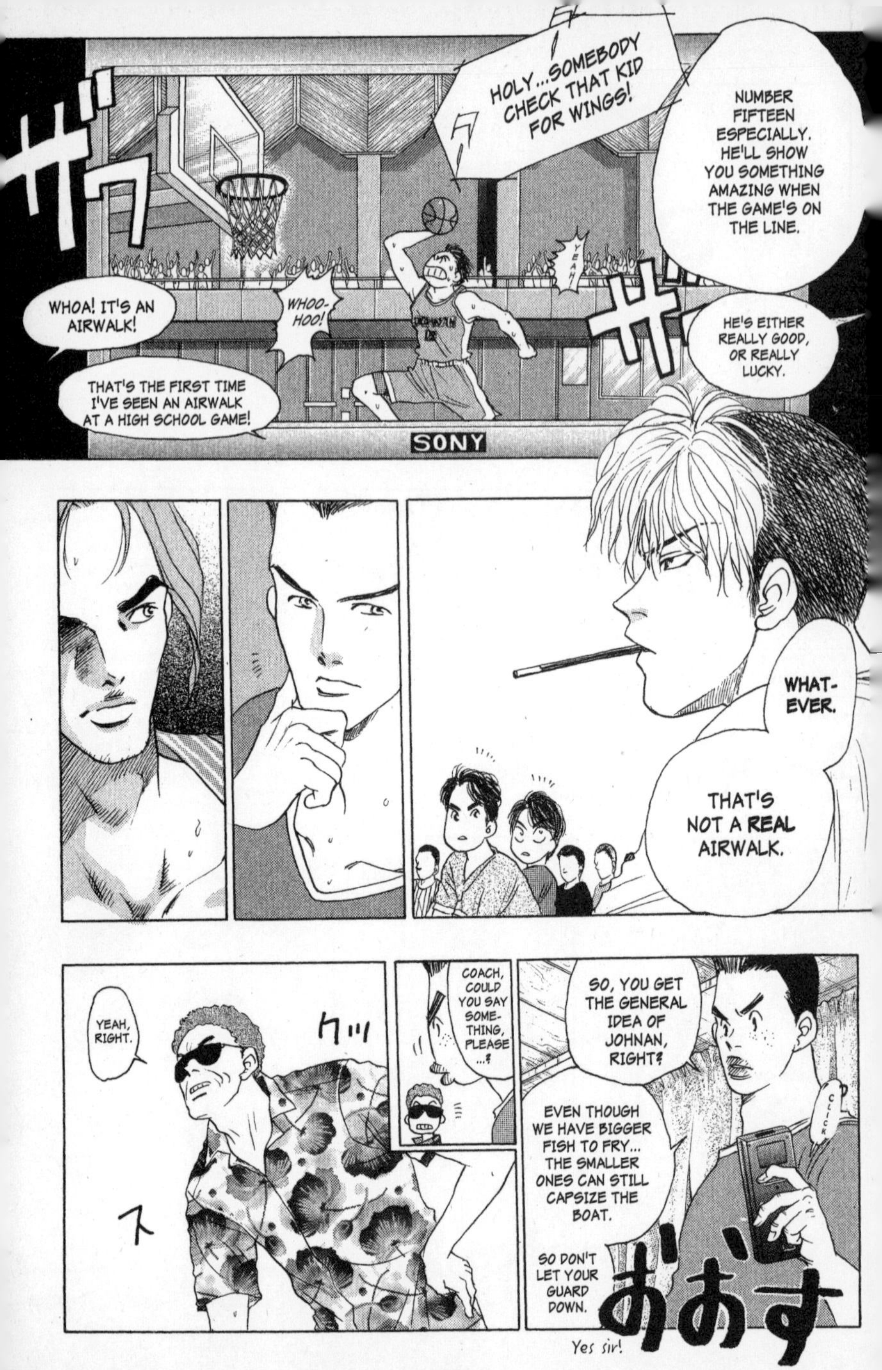

NUMBER FIFTEEN ESPECIALLY. HE'LL SHOW YOU SOMETHING AMAZING WHEN THE GAME'S ON THE LINE.
HOLY...SOMEBODY CHECK THAT KID FOR WINGS!
ザワ
YEAH!
WHOO-HOO!
HE'S EITHER REALLY GOOD, OR REALLY LUCKY.
WHOA! IT'S AN AIRWALK!
THAT'S THE FIRST TIME I'VE SEEN AN AIRWALK AT A HIGH SCHOOL GAME!
SONY
WHAT-EVER.
THAT'S NOT A REAL AIRWALK.
SO, YOU GET THE GENERAL IDEA OF JOHNAN, RIGHT?
CLICK
EVEN THOUGH WE HAVE BIGGER FISH TO FRY... THE SMALLER ONES CAN STILL CAPSIZE THE BOAT.
SO DON'T LET YOUR GUARD DOWN.
おおす
Yes sir!
COACH, COULD YOU SAY SOMETHING, PLEASE...?
クッ
YEAH, RIGHT.
ス

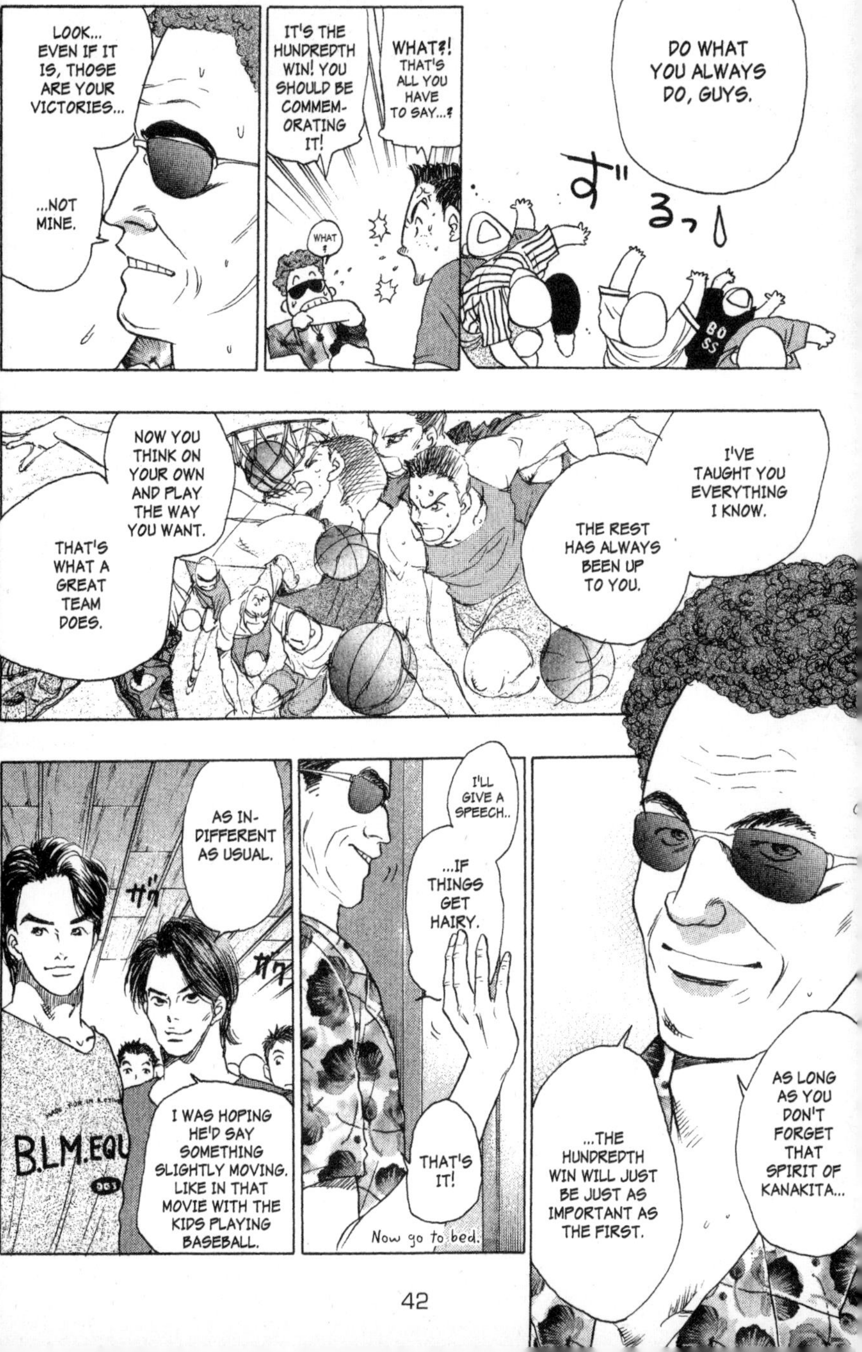
DO WHAT YOU ALWAYS DO, GUYS.
ずるっ
WHAT?! THAT'S ALL YOU HAVE TO SAY...?
IT'S THE HUNDREDTH WIN! YOU SHOULD BE COMMEM-ORATING IT!
WHAT?
LOOK... EVEN IF IT IS, THOSE ARE YOUR VICTORIES...
...NOT MINE.
I'VE TAUGHT YOU EVERYTHING I KNOW.
THE REST HAS ALWAYS BEEN UP TO YOU.
NOW YOU THINK ON YOUR OWN AND PLAY THE WAY YOU WANT.
THAT'S WHAT A GREAT TEAM DOES.
AS LONG AS YOU DON'T FORGET THAT SPIRIT OF KANAKITA...
...THE HUNDREDTH WIN WILL JUST BE JUST AS IMPORTANT AS THE FIRST.
I'LL GIVE A SPEECH..
...IF THINGS GET HAIRY.
THAT'S IT!
Now go to bed.
AS IN-DIFFERENT AS USUAL.
ガク
ガク
I WAS HOPING HE'D SAY SOMETHING SLIGHTLY MOVING. LIKE IN THAT MOVIE WITH THE KIDS PLAYING BASEBALL.
B.L.M.EQU

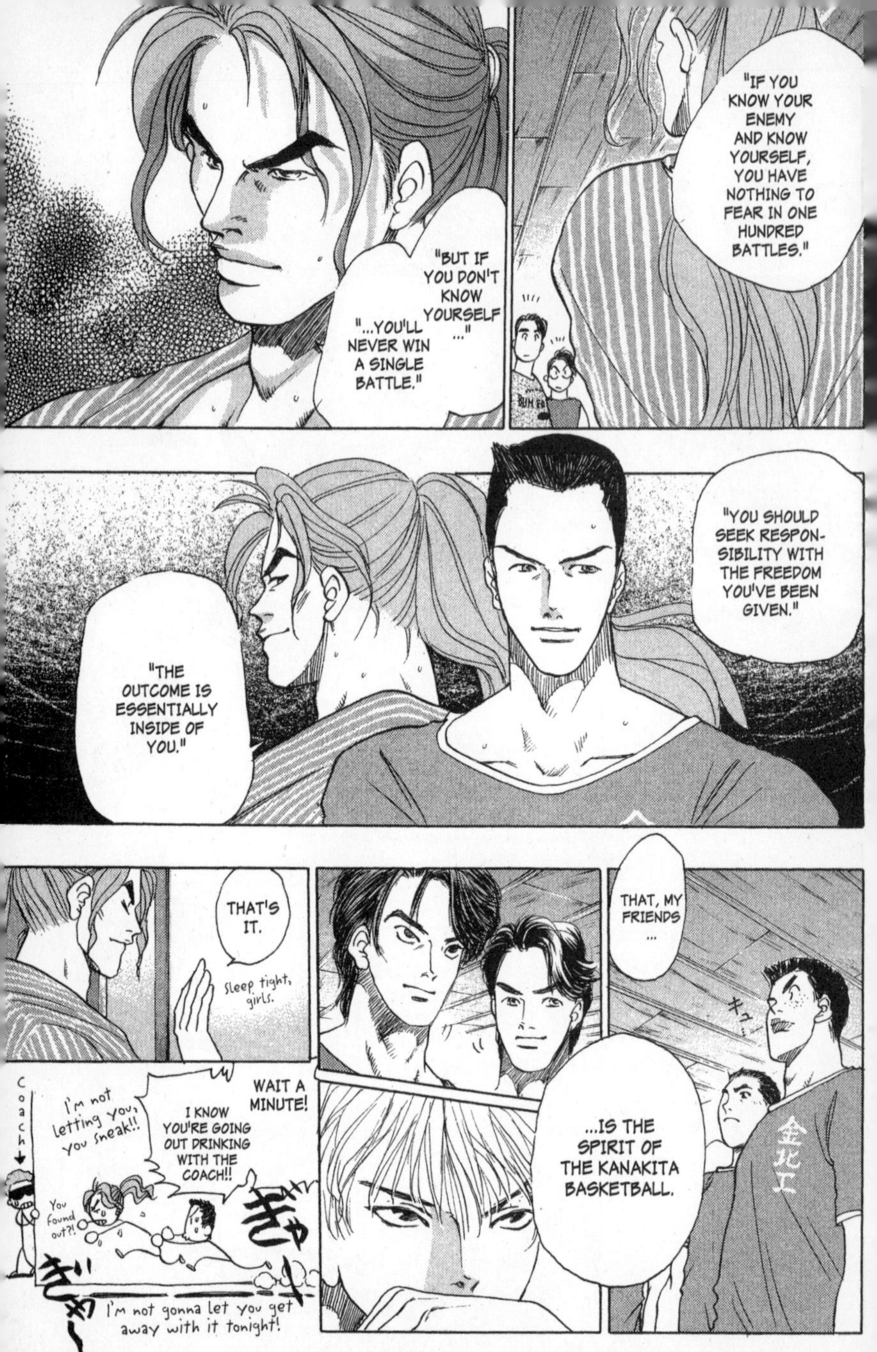
"IF YOU KNOW YOUR ENEMY AND KNOW YOURSELF, YOU HAVE NOTHING TO FEAR IN ONE HUNDRED BATTLES."
"BUT IF YOU DON'T KNOW YOURSELF ..."
"...YOU'LL NEVER WIN A SINGLE BATTLE."
"YOU SHOULD SEEK RESPON-SIBILITY WITH THE FREEDOM YOU'VE BEEN GIVEN."
"THE OUTCOME IS ESSENTIALLY INSIDE OF YOU."
THAT, MY FRIENDS ...
キュ...
...IS THE SPIRIT OF THE KANAKITA BASKETBALL.
金北工
THAT'S IT.
Sleep tight, girls.
WAIT A MINUTE!
I KNOW YOU'RE GOING OUT DRINKING WITH THE COACH!!
I'm not letting you, you sneak!!
Coach
You found out?!
ぎゃー
ぎゃ〜
I'm not gonna let you get away with it tonight!

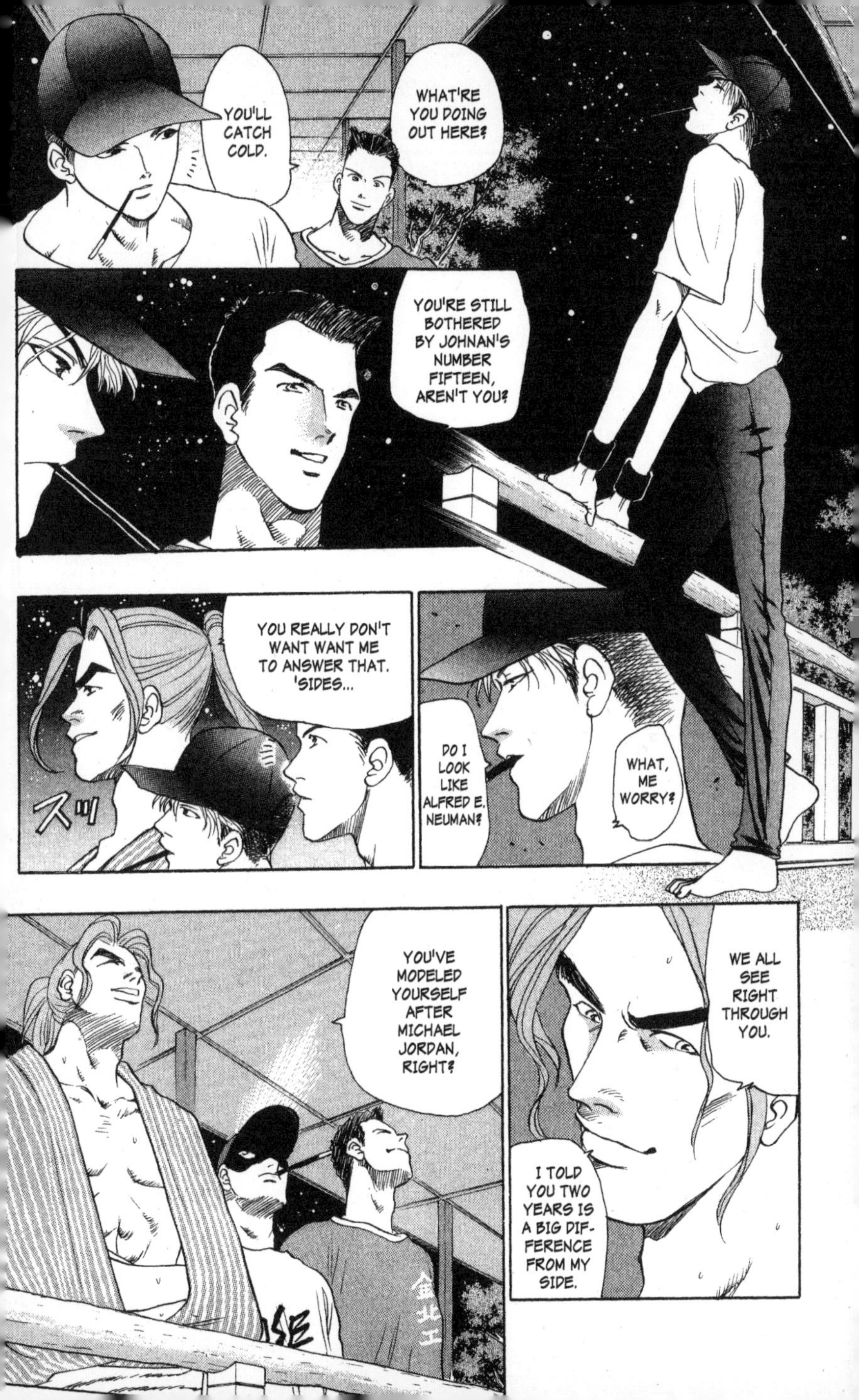
WHAT'RE YOU DOING OUT HERE?
YOU'LL CATCH COLD.
YOU'RE STILL BOTHERED BY JOHNAN'S NUMBER FIFTEEN, AREN'T YOU?
WHAT, ME WORRY?
DO I LOOK LIKE ALFRED E. NEUMAN?
YOU REALLY DON'T WANT WANT ME TO ANSWER THAT. 'SIDES...
スッ
WE ALL SEE RIGHT THROUGH YOU.
I TOLD YOU TWO YEARS IS A BIG DIFFERENCE FROM MY SIDE.
YOU'VE MODELED YOURSELF AFTER MICHAEL JORDAN, RIGHT?

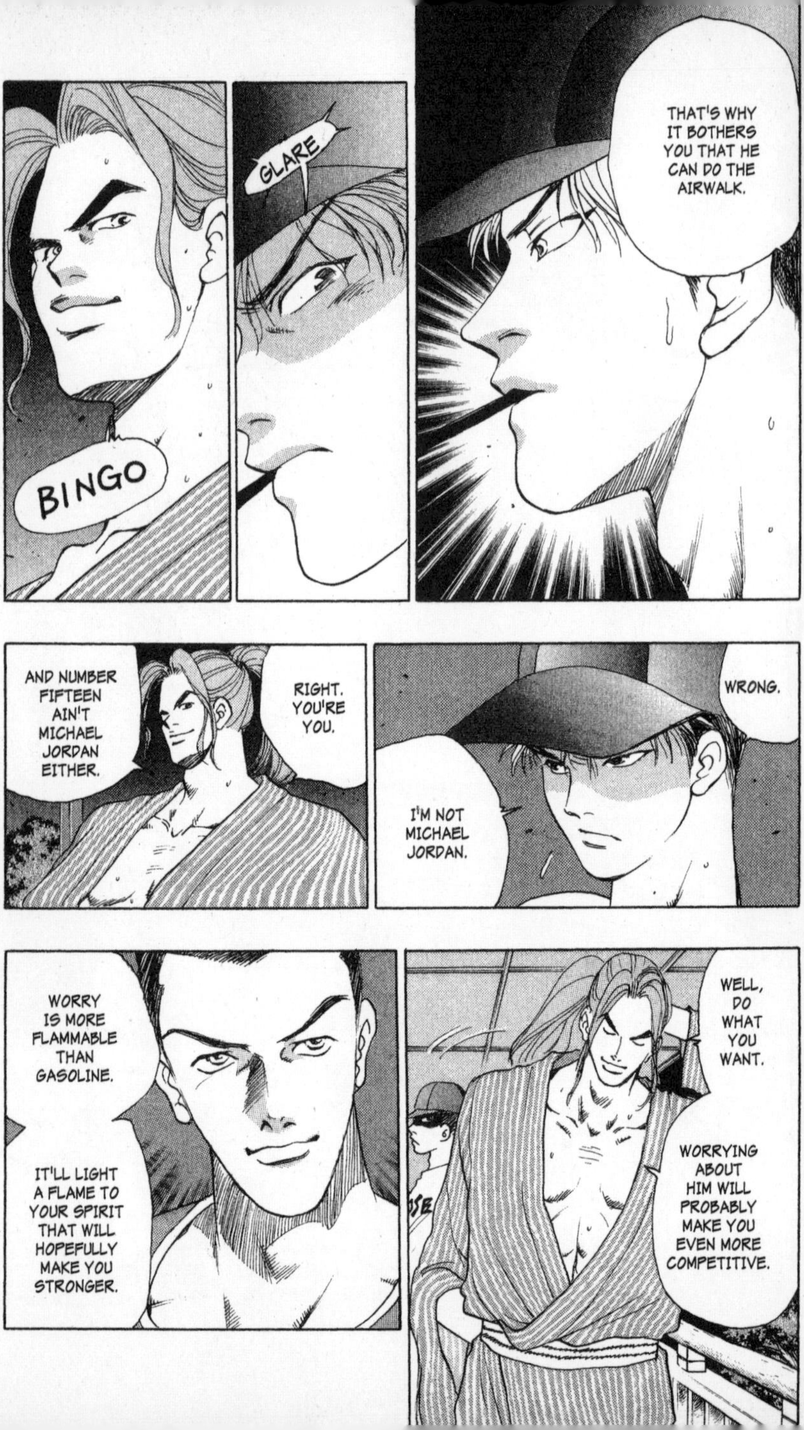
THAT'S WHY IT BOTHERS YOU THAT HE CAN DO THE AIRWALK.
GLARE
BINGO
WRONG.
I'M NOT MICHAEL JORDAN.
RIGHT. YOU'RE YOU.
AND NUMBER FIFTEEN AIN'T MICHAEL JORDAN EITHER.
WELL, DO WHAT YOU WANT.
WORRYING ABOUT HIM WILL PROBABLY MAKE YOU EVEN MORE COMPETITIVE.
WORRY IS MORE FLAMMABLE THAN GASOLINE.
IT'LL LIGHT A FLAME TO YOUR SPIRIT THAT WILL HOPEFULLY MAKE YOU STRONGER.

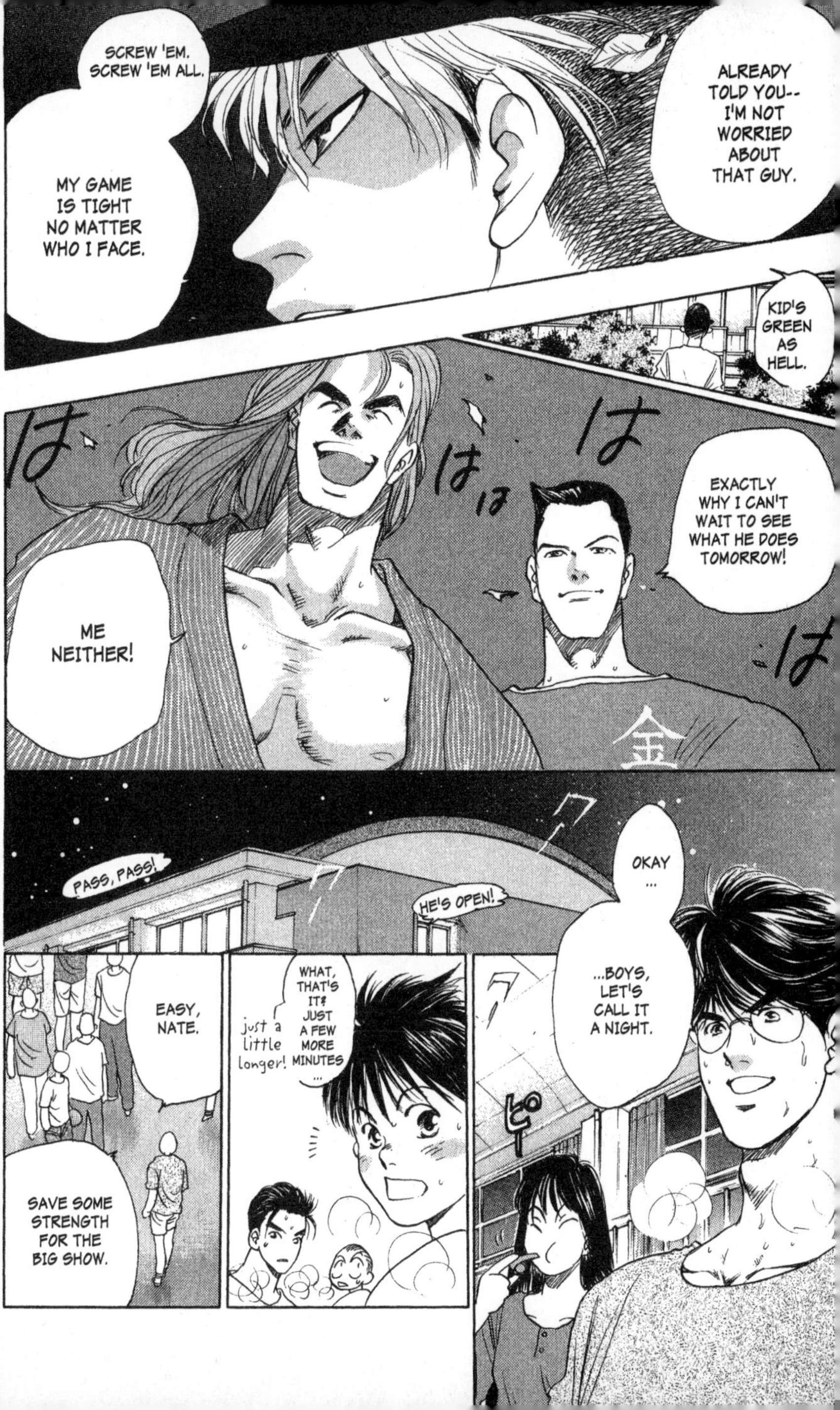
ALREADY TOLD YOU-- I'M NOT WORRIED ABOUT THAT GUY.
SCREW 'EM. SCREW 'EM ALL.
MY GAME IS TIGHT NO MATTER WHO I FACE.
KID'S GREEN AS HELL.
は
EXACTLY WHY I CAN'T WAIT TO SEE WHAT HE DOES TOMORROW!
はは
は
ME NEITHER!
は
OKAY ...
...BOYS, LET'S CALL IT A NIGHT.
ピー
HE'S OPEN!
PASS, PASS!
WHAT, THAT'S IT? JUST A FEW MORE MINUTES ...
just a little longer!
EASY, NATE.
SAVE SOME STRENGTH FOR THE BIG SHOW.

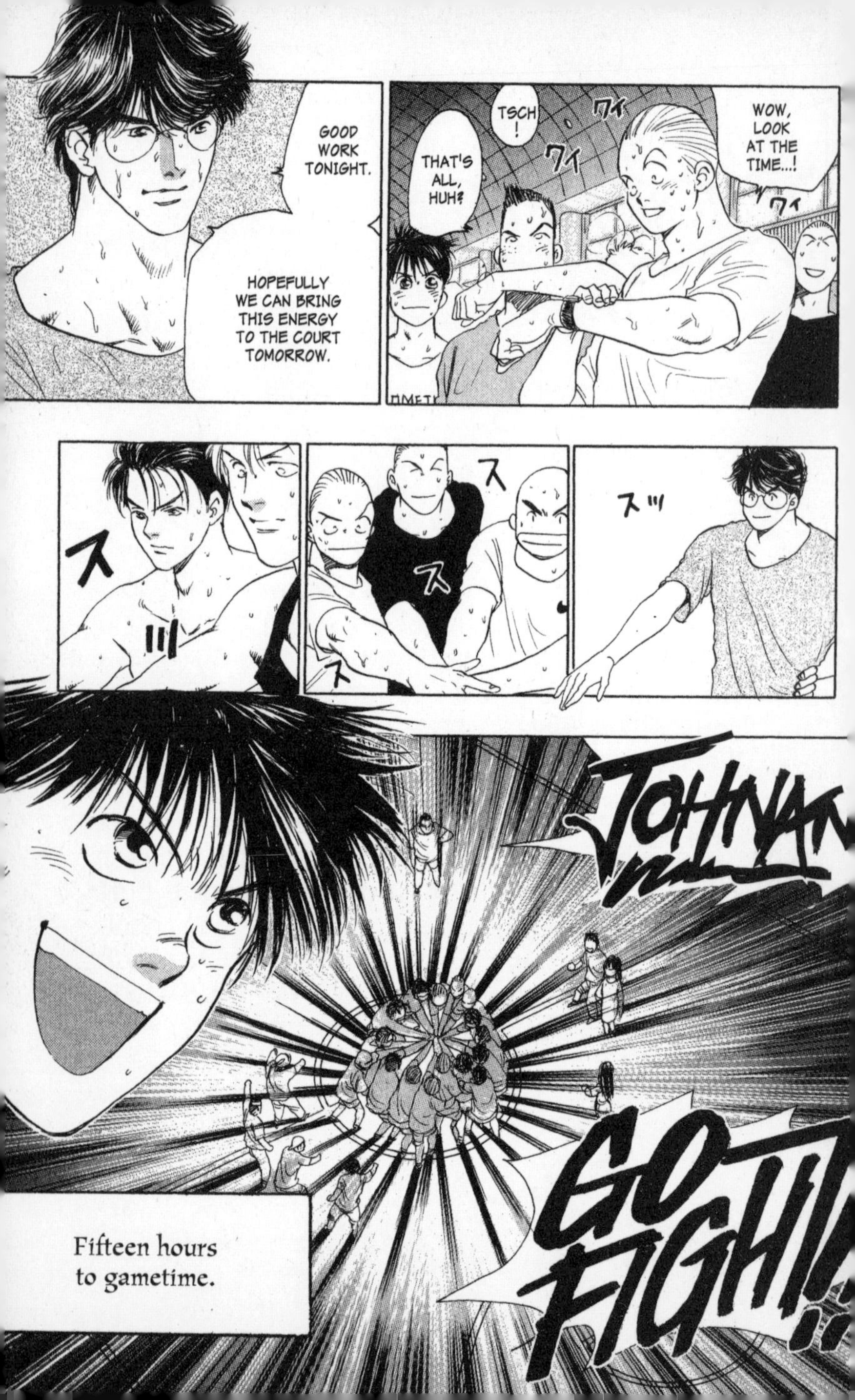
WOW, LOOK AT THE TIME...!
ワイ ワイ ワイ ワイ
TSCH!
THAT'S ALL, HUH?
GOOD WORK TONIGHT.
HOPEFULLY WE CAN BRING THIS ENERGY TO THE COURT TOMORROW.
ズッ
ス
ス
ス
ス
TOHNAN
GO FIGHT!!
Fifteen hours to gametime.

You're Reading...

And now, an anonymous message to Yusa...

Dear Dude,

'Sup. I feel kinda funny writin' a letter to another dude, 'cause, you know...ew. But I had to do somethin', and I was afraid if I told you in person, you might go all skipper on me and "little buddy" and "noogie" me to death (which is what you do to anyone smaller than you, which just so happens to be everyone). It's like this—you can't sit around in just a towel anymore. I know it's comfortable and all, but it just ain't cool. Last thing I need is to look up from my hot pocket to see your trouser snake winkin' at me. Not to mention the butt sweat you leave behind on the chair...not cool. So call me a towel Nazi, whatever—just put on some frickin' shorts for now on (And John Ritter thigh highs aren't acceptable. Only knee length shorts need apply.).

Thanx

Blinded With Science

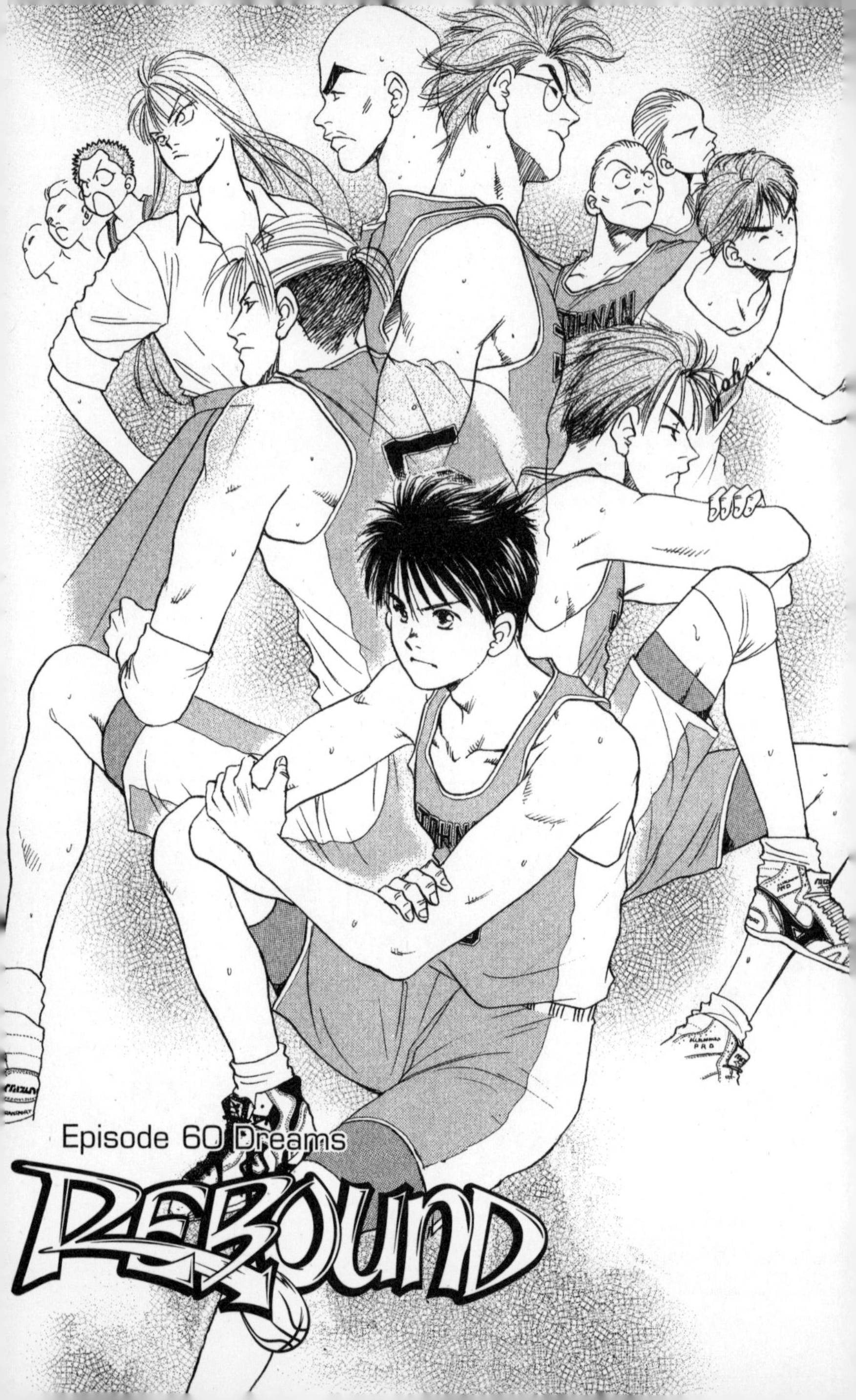
Episode 60 Dreams
REBOUND

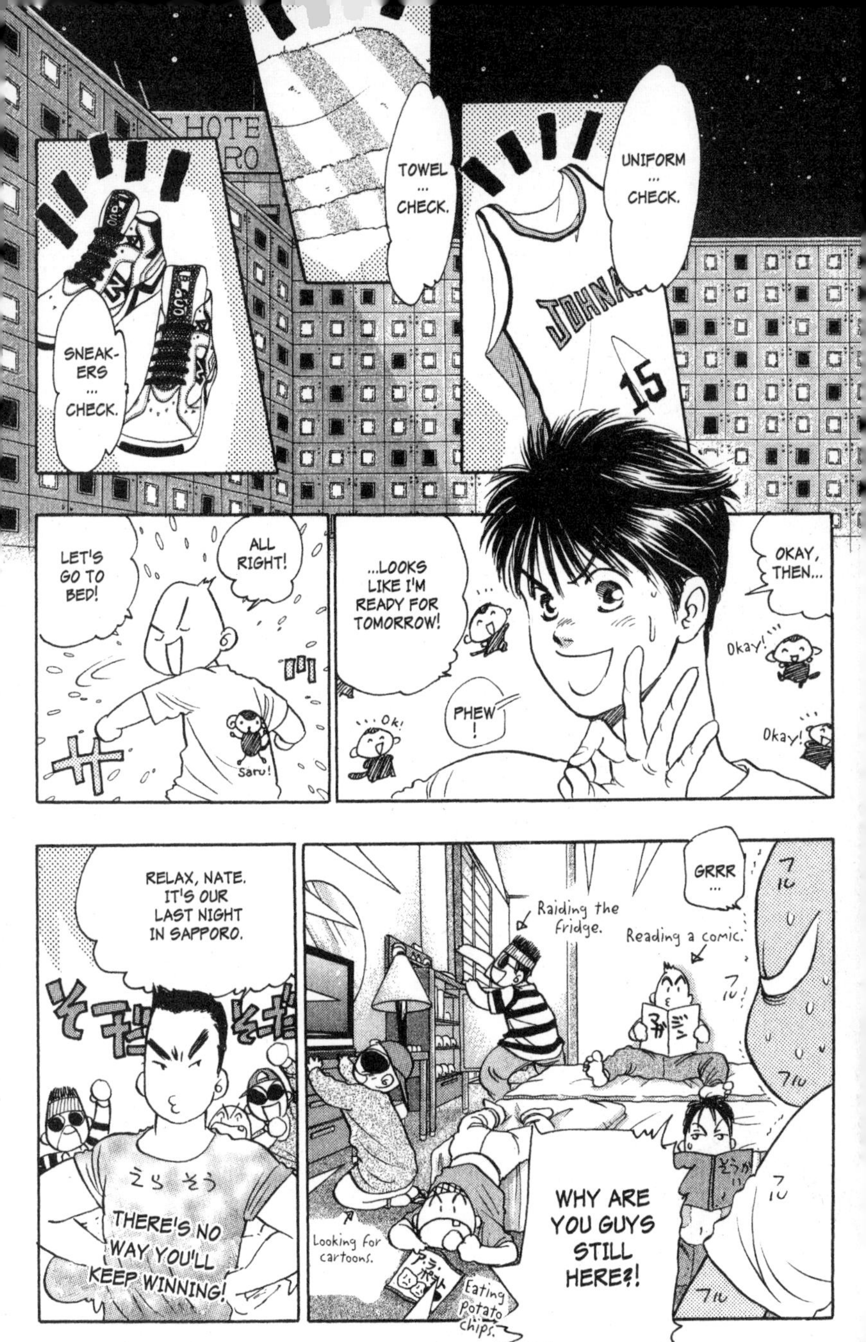
UNIFORM ... CHECK.
TOWEL ... CHECK.
SNEAK-ERS ... CHECK.
OKAY, THEN...
Okay!
...LOOKS LIKE I'M READY FOR TOMORROW!
PHEW!
Okay!
Ok!
ALL RIGHT!
LET'S GO TO BED!
Saru!
GRRR ...
Raiding the fridge.
Reading a comic.
WHY ARE YOU GUYS STILL HERE?!
Looking for cartoons.
Eating potato chips.
RELAX, NATE. IT'S OUR LAST NIGHT IN SAPPORO.
THERE'S NO WAY YOU'LL KEEP WINNING!

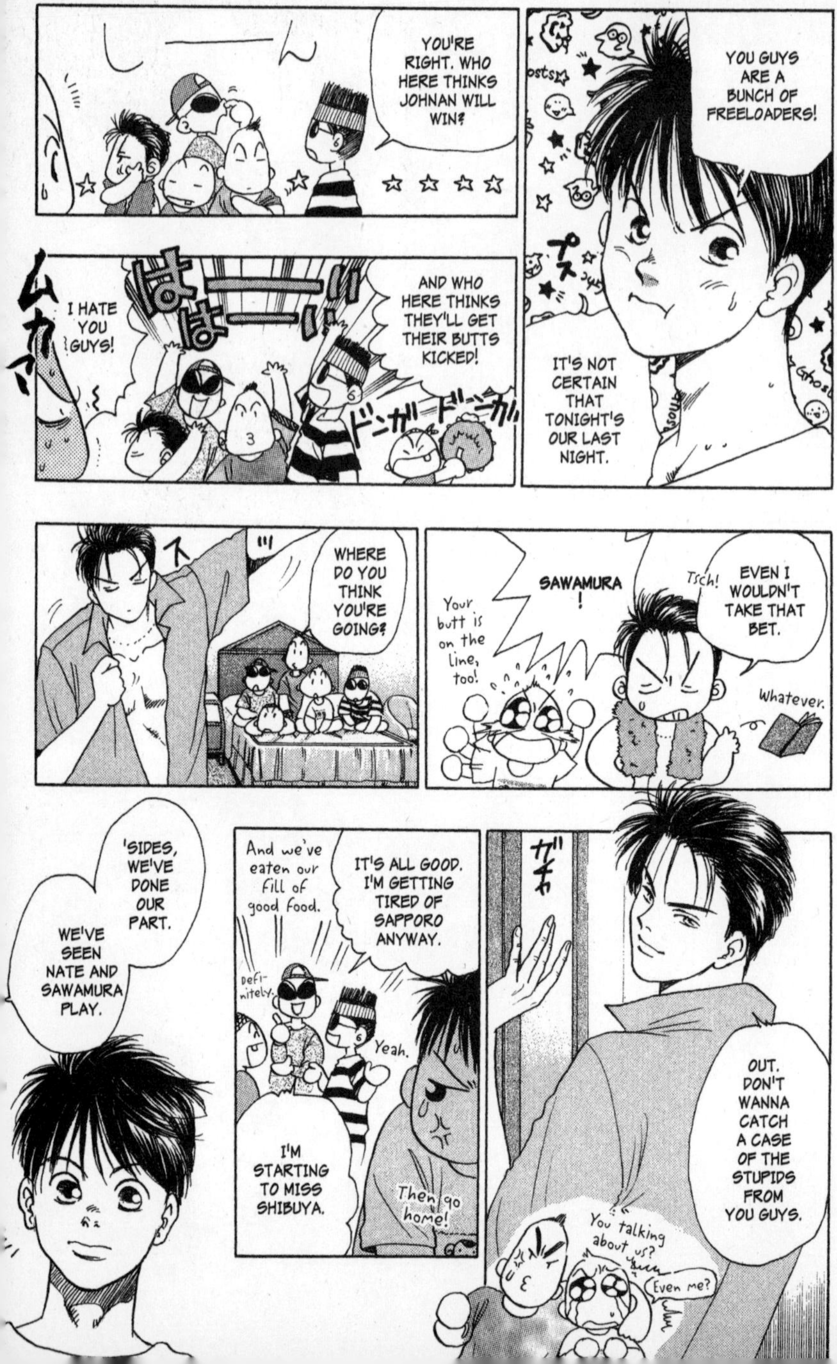

YOU GUYS ARE A BUNCH OF FREELOADERS!
IT'S NOT CERTAIN THAT TONIGHT'S OUR LAST NIGHT.
しーん
YOU'RE RIGHT. WHO HERE THINKS JOHNAN WILL WIN?
AND WHO HERE THINKS THEY'LL GET THEIR BUTTS KICKED!
はーい はーい
I HATE YOU GUYS!
SAWAMURA!
Tsch!
EVEN I WOULDN'T TAKE THAT BET.
Your butt is on the line, too!
Whatever.
WHERE DO YOU THINK YOU'RE GOING?
ガチャ
OUT. DON'T WANNA CATCH A CASE OF THE STUPIDS FROM YOU GUYS.
You talking about us?
Even me?
IT'S ALL GOOD. I'M GETTING TIRED OF SAPPORO ANYWAY.
And we've eaten our fill of good food.
Defi-nitely.
Yeah.
I'M STARTING TO MISS SHIBUYA.
Then go home!
'SIDES, WE'VE DONE OUR PART.
WE'VE SEEN NATE AND SAWAMURA PLAY.

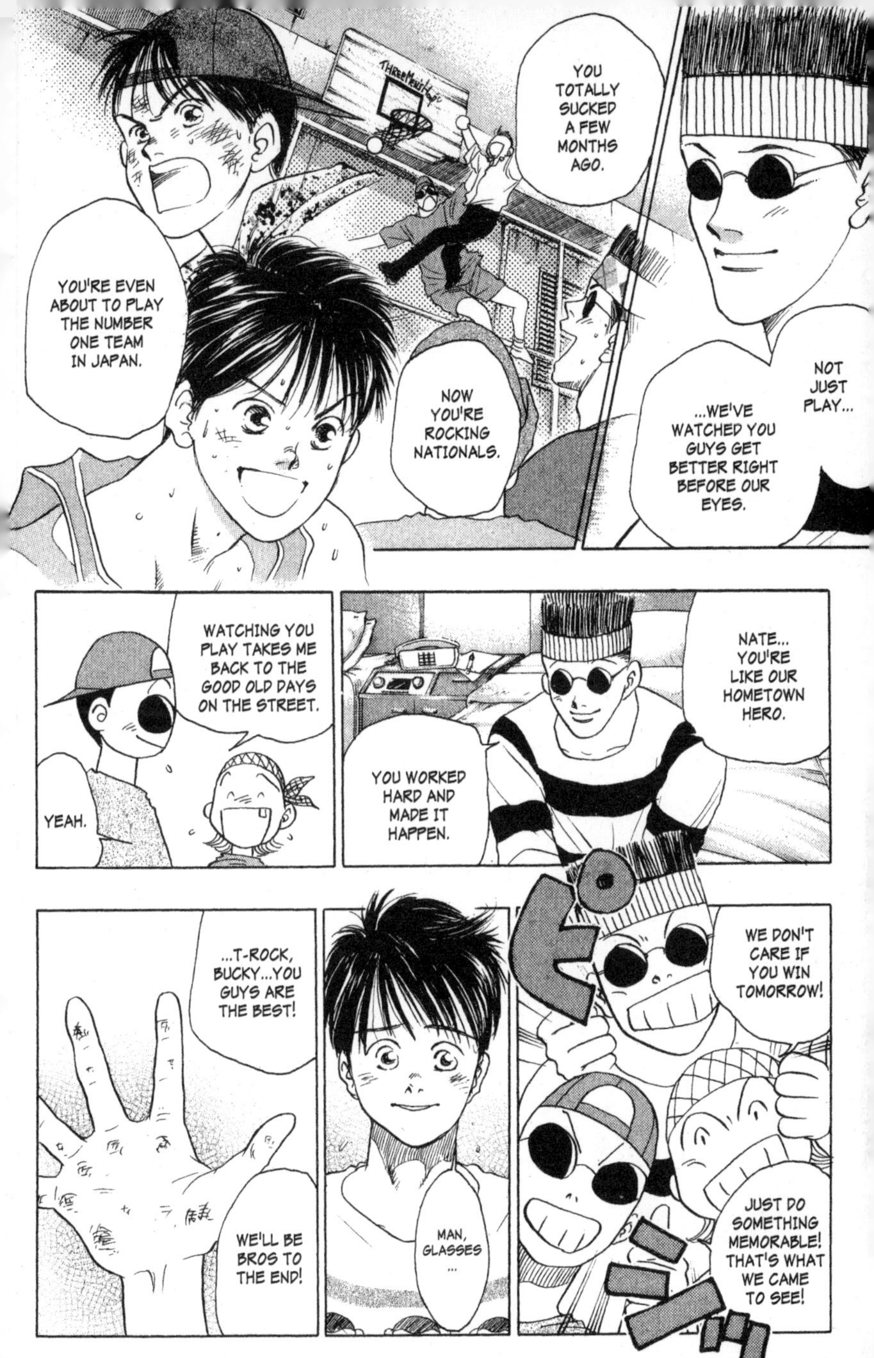
NOT JUST PLAY...
...WE'VE WATCHED YOU GUYS GET BETTER RIGHT BEFORE OUR EYES.
YOU TOTALLY SUCKED A FEW MONTHS AGO.
NOW YOU'RE ROCKING NATIONALS.
YOU'RE EVEN ABOUT TO PLAY THE NUMBER ONE TEAM IN JAPAN.
NATE... YOU'RE LIKE OUR HOMETOWN HERO.
YOU WORKED HARD AND MADE IT HAPPEN.
WATCHING YOU PLAY TAKES ME BACK TO THE GOOD OLD DAYS ON THE STREET.
YEAH.
WE DON'T CARE IF YOU WIN TOMORROW!
JUST DO SOMETHING MEMORABLE! THAT'S WHAT WE CAME TO SEE!
MAN, GLASSES ...
...T-ROCK, BUCKY...YOU GUYS ARE THE BEST!
WE'LL BE BROS TO THE END!

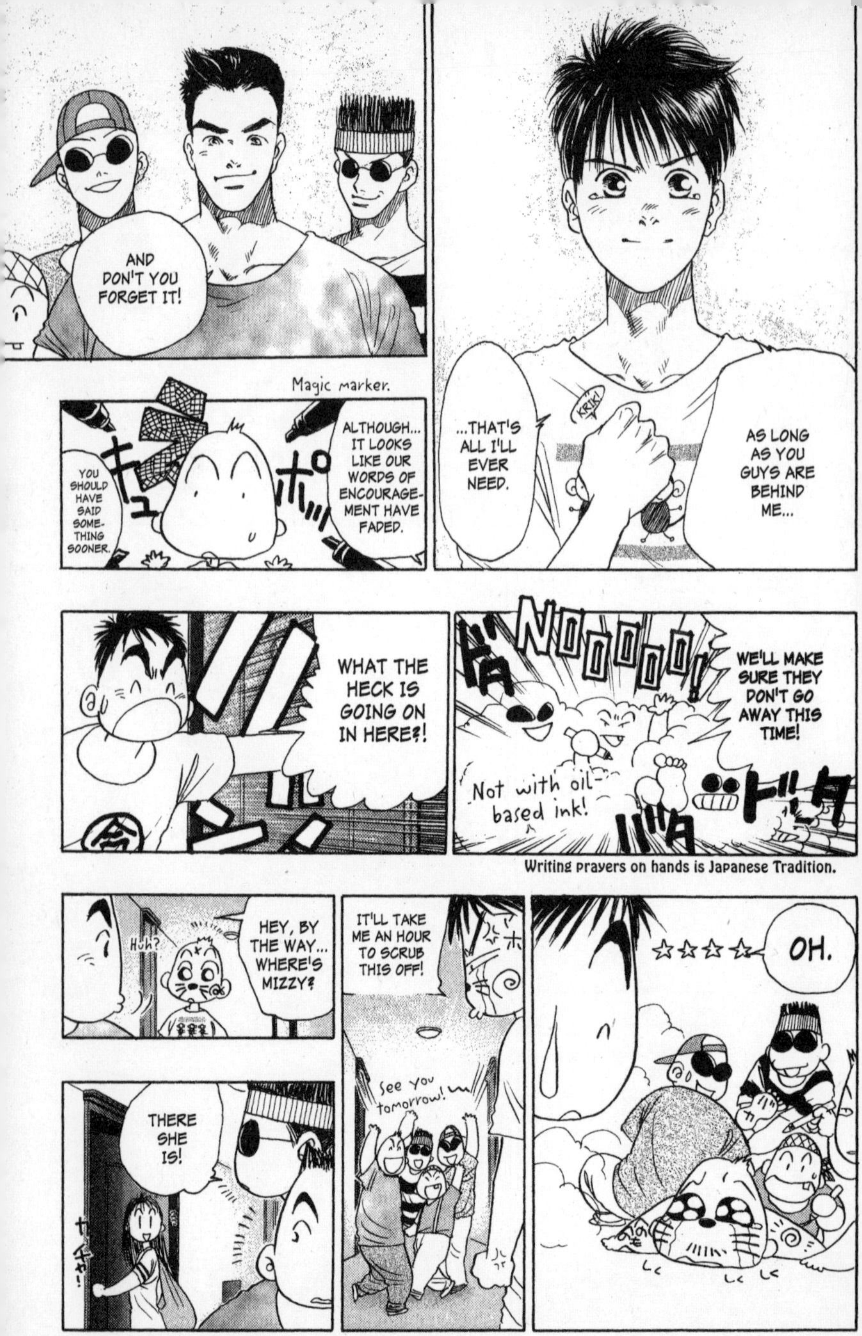
AS LONG AS YOU GUYS ARE BEHIND ME...
KRIK!
...THAT'S ALL I'LL EVER NEED.
AND DON'T YOU FORGET IT!
Magic marker.
ALTHOUGH... IT LOOKS LIKE OUR WORDS OF ENCOURAGEMENT HAVE FADED.
YOU SHOULD HAVE SAID SOMETHING SOONER.
NOOOOOO!
WE'LL MAKE SURE THEY DON'T GO AWAY THIS TIME!
Not with oil-based ink!
WHAT THE HECK IS GOING ON IN HERE?!
Writing prayers on hands is Japanese Tradition.
OH.
IT'LL TAKE ME AN HOUR TO SCRUB THIS OFF!
See you tomorrow!
HEY, BY THE WAY... WHERE'S MIZZY?
Huh?
THERE SHE IS!

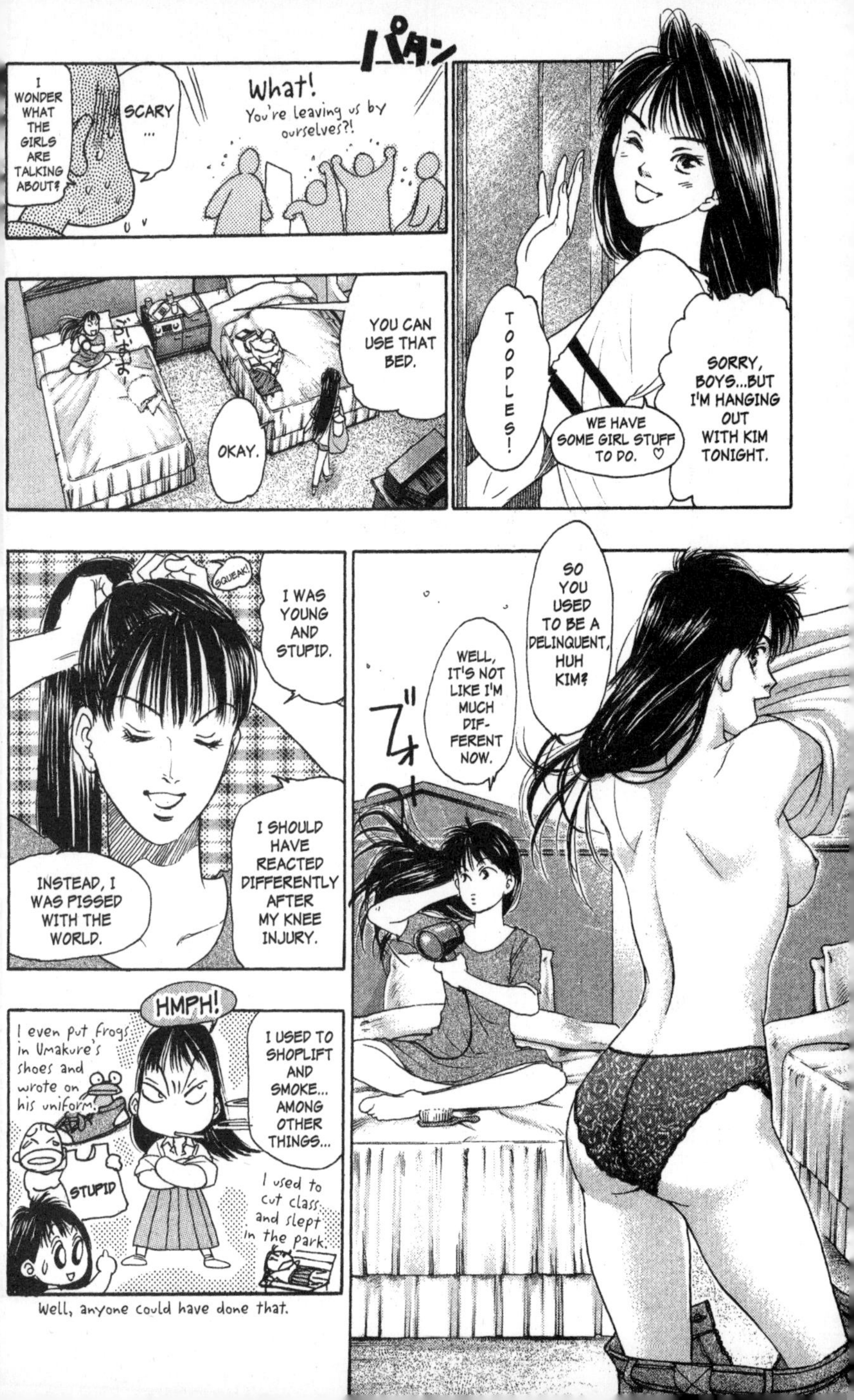
パタン
SORRY, BOYS...BUT I'M HANGING OUT WITH KIM TONIGHT.
WE HAVE SOME GIRL STUFF TO DO. ♡
TOODLES!
What! You're leaving us by ourselves?!
SCARY...
I WONDER WHAT THE GIRLS ARE TALKING ABOUT?
YOU CAN USE THAT BED.
OKAY.
SO YOU USED TO BE A DELINQUENT, HUH KIM?
WELL, IT'S NOT LIKE I'M MUCH DIF-FERENT NOW.
ブォー
SQUEAK!
I WAS YOUNG AND STUPID.
I SHOULD HAVE REACTED DIFFERENTLY AFTER MY KNEE INJURY.
INSTEAD, I WAS PISSED WITH THE WORLD.
HMPH!
I USED TO SHOPLIFT AND SMOKE... AMONG OTHER THINGS...
I even put frogs in Umakure's shoes and wrote on his uniform.
STUPID
I used to cut class and slept in the park.
Well, anyone could have done that.

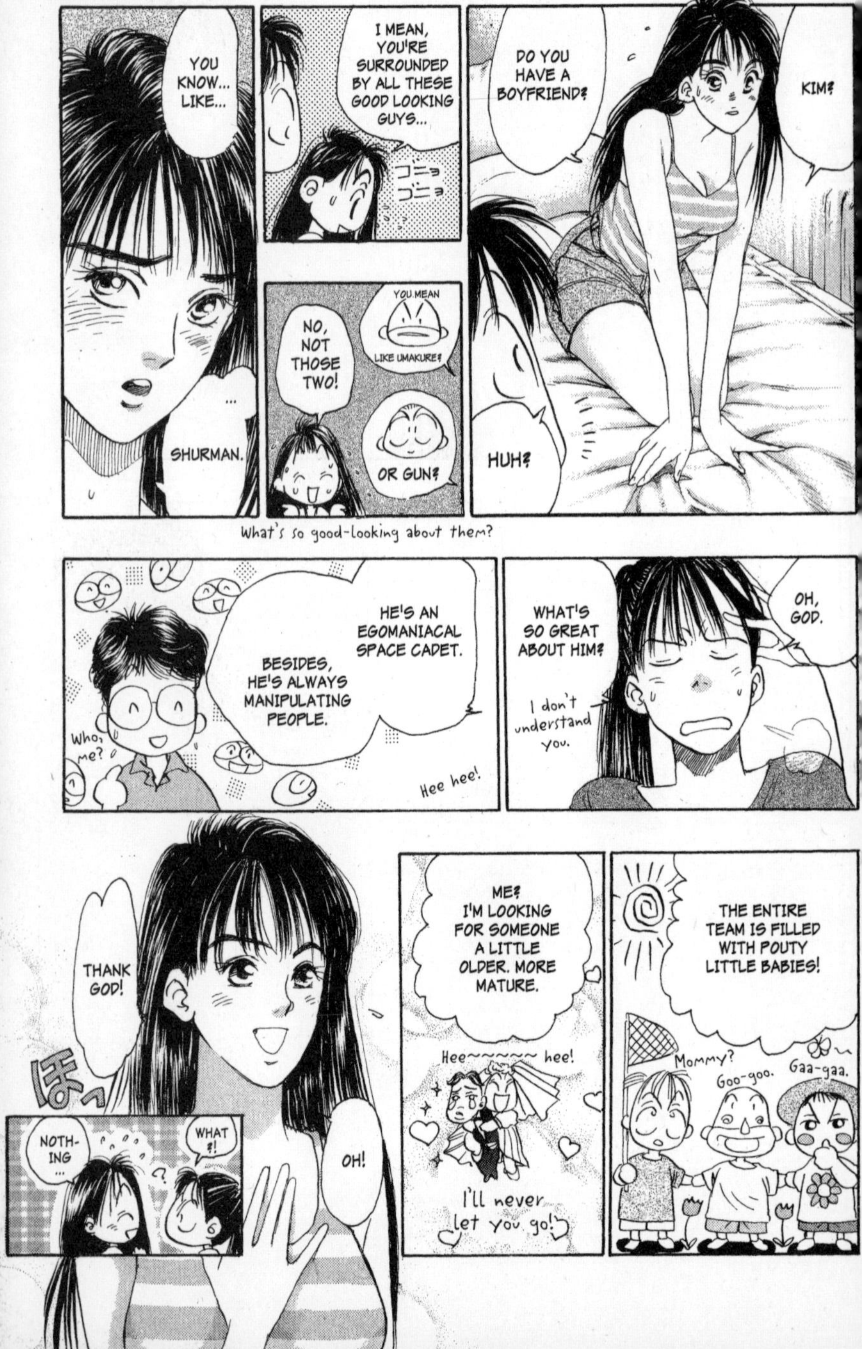
KIM?
DO YOU HAVE A BOYFRIEND?
HUH?
I MEAN, YOU'RE SURROUNDED BY ALL THESE GOOD LOOKING GUYS...
ゴニョゴニョ
YOU MEAN LIKE UMAKURE?
OR GUN?
NO, NOT THOSE TWO!
YOU KNOW... LIKE...
...
SHURMAN.
What's so good-looking about them?
OH, GOD.
WHAT'S SO GREAT ABOUT HIM?
I don't understand you.
HE'S AN EGOMANIACAL SPACE CADET.
BESIDES, HE'S ALWAYS MANIPULATING PEOPLE.
Who, me?
Hee hee!
THE ENTIRE TEAM IS FILLED WITH POUTY LITTLE BABIES!
Mommy?
Goo-goo.
Gaa-gaa.
ME? I'M LOOKING FOR SOMEONE A LITTLE OLDER. MORE MATURE.
Hee~~~~~ hee!
I'll never let you go!
OH!
THANK GOD!
ほっ
WHAT?!
NOTHING...

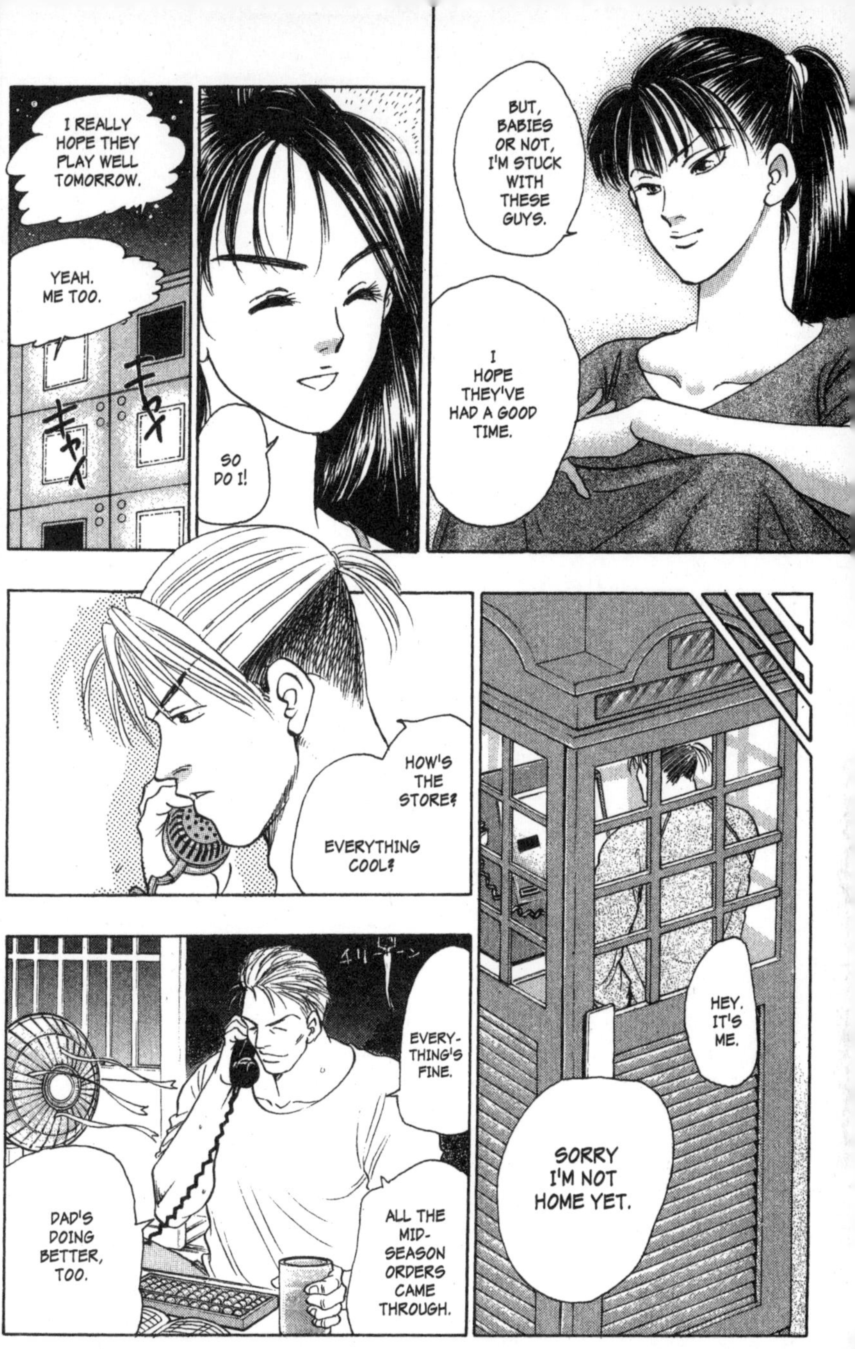
BUT, BABIES OR NOT, I'M STUCK WITH THESE GUYS.
I HOPE THEY'VE HAD A GOOD TIME.
SO DO I!
I REALLY HOPE THEY PLAY WELL TOMORROW.
YEAH. ME TOO.
キャイ
キャイ
HEY. IT'S ME.
SORRY I'M NOT HOME YET.
HOW'S THE STORE?
EVERYTHING COOL?
EVERY-THING'S FINE.
ALL THE MID-SEASON ORDERS CAME THROUGH.
DAD'S DOING BETTER, TOO.

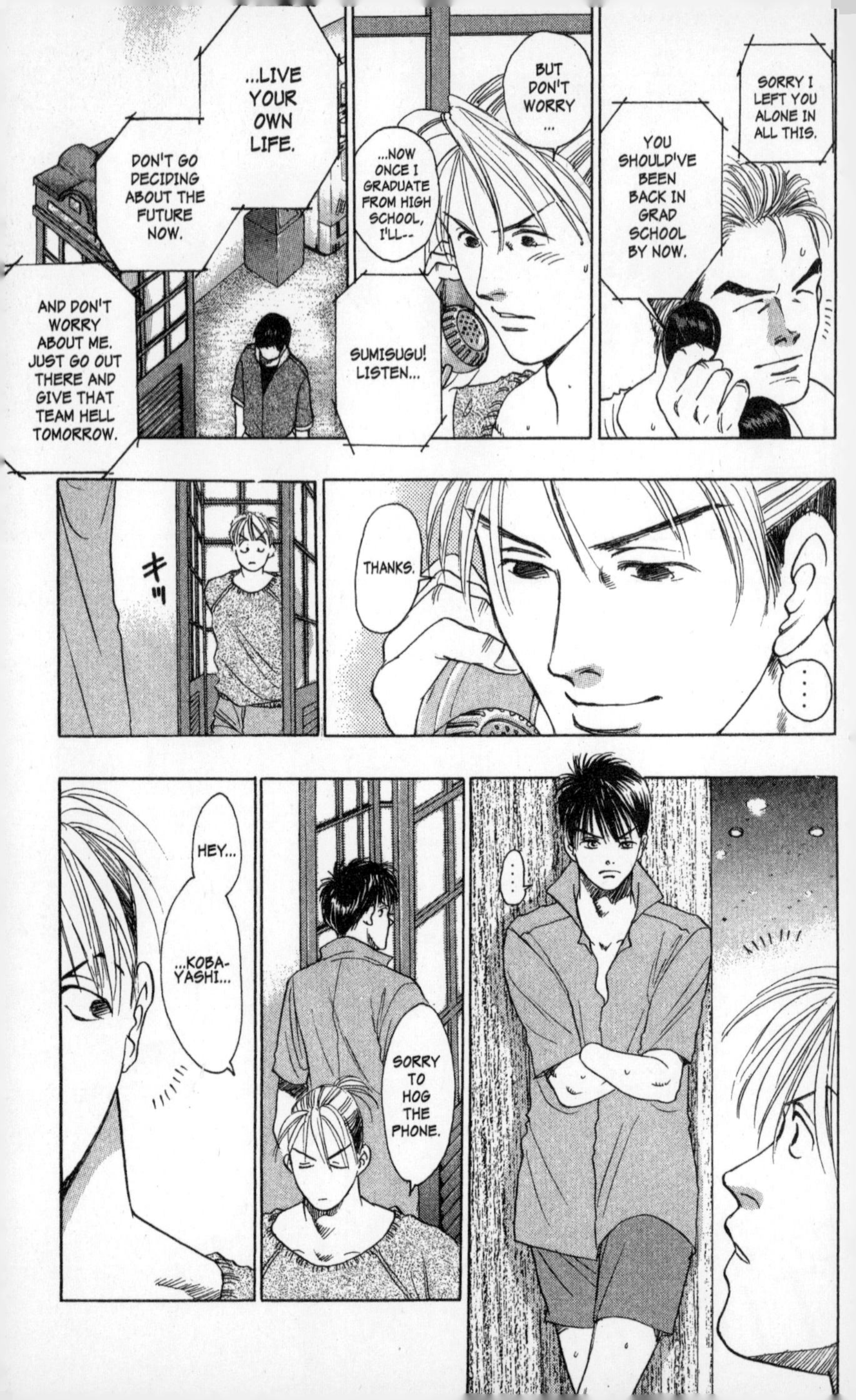
SORRY I LEFT YOU ALONE IN ALL THIS.
YOU SHOULD'VE BEEN BACK IN GRAD SCHOOL BY NOW.
BUT DON'T WORRY ...
...NOW ONCE I GRADUATE FROM HIGH SCHOOL, I'LL--
SUMISUGU! LISTEN...
...LIVE YOUR OWN LIFE.
DON'T GO DECIDING ABOUT THE FUTURE NOW.
AND DON'T WORRY ABOUT ME. JUST GO OUT THERE AND GIVE THAT TEAM HELL TOMORROW.
......
THANKS.
キッ
...
SORRY TO HOG THE PHONE.
HEY...
...KOBA-YASHI...

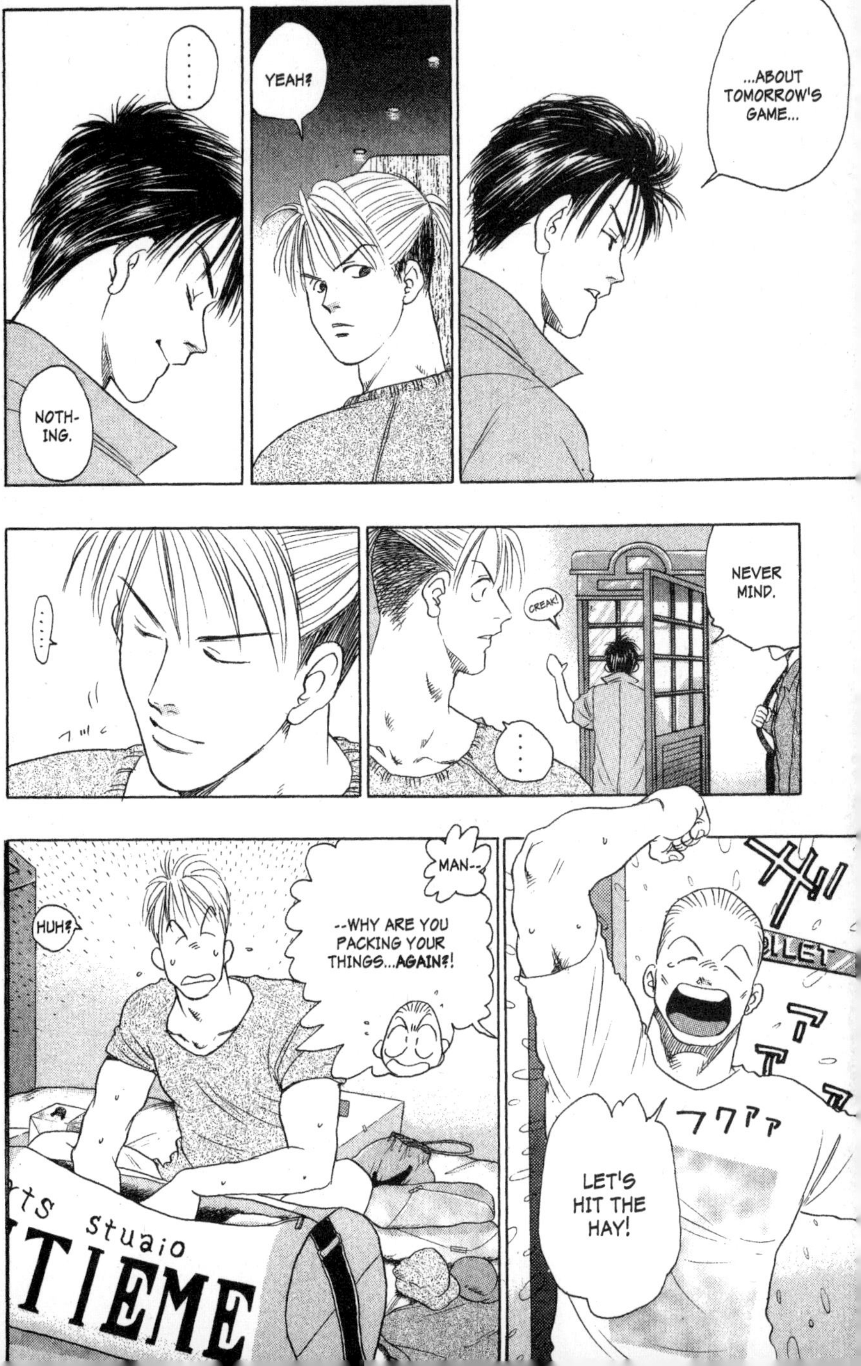
...ABOUT TOMORROW'S GAME...
YEAH?
......
NOTH-ING.
NEVER MIND.
CREAK!
......
......
LET'S HIT THE HAY!
MAN--
--WHY ARE YOU PACKING YOUR THINGS...AGAIN?!
HUH?

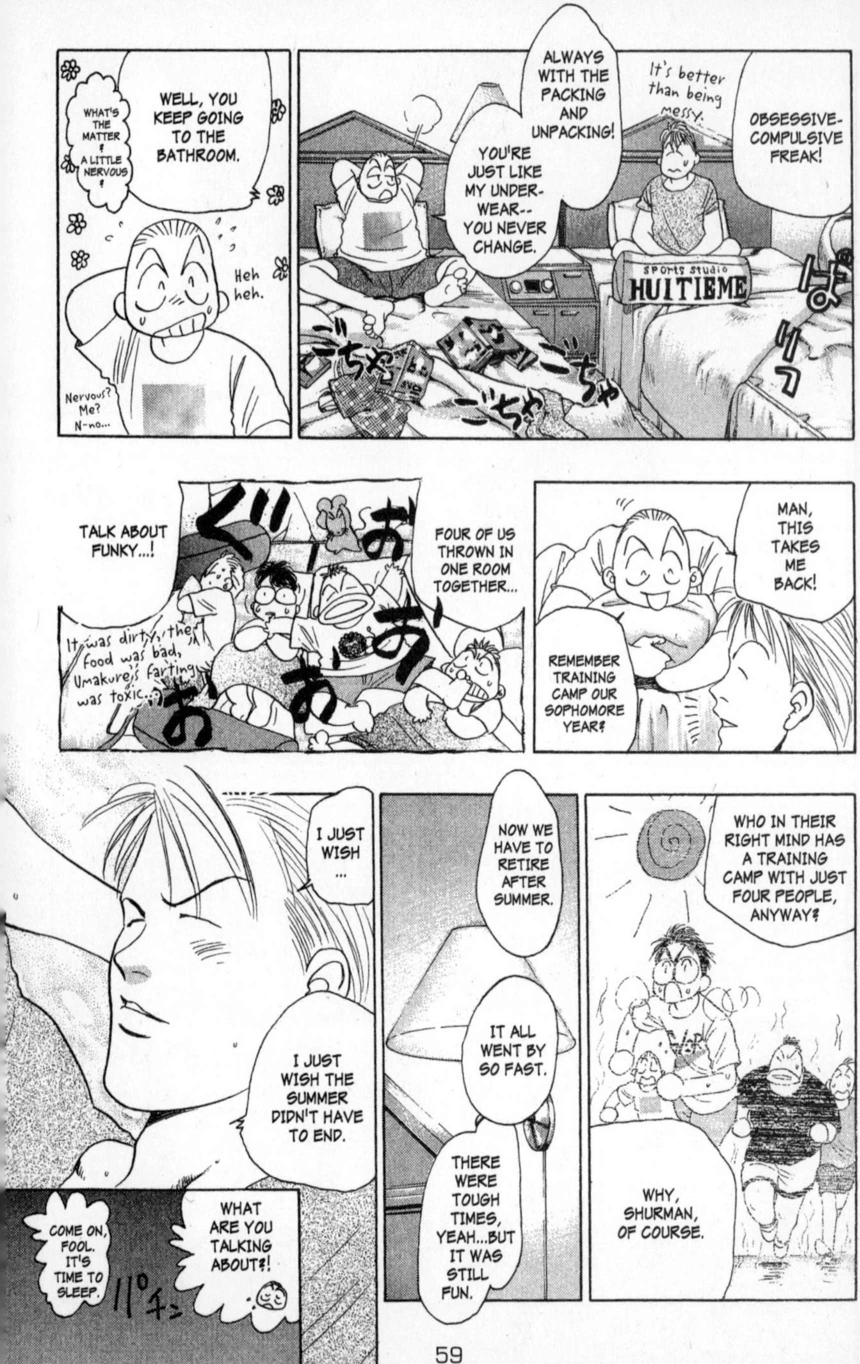

OBSESSIVE-COMPULSIVE FREAK!
It's better than being messy.
ALWAYS WITH THE PACKING AND UNPACKING!
YOU'RE JUST LIKE MY UNDER-WEAR-- YOU NEVER CHANGE.
SPORTS STUDIO HUITIEME
ごちゃ ごちゃ ごちゃ ごちゃ
WELL, YOU KEEP GOING TO THE BATHROOM.
WHAT'S THE MATTER? A LITTLE NERVOUS?
Heh heh.
Nervous? Me? N-no...
MAN, THIS TAKES ME BACK!
REMEMBER TRAINING CAMP OUR SOPHOMORE YEAR?
FOUR OF US THROWN IN ONE ROOM TOGETHER...
TALK ABOUT FUNKY...!
ぐおおお
It was dirty, the food was bad, Umakure's farting was toxic...
WHO IN THEIR RIGHT MIND HAS A TRAINING CAMP WITH JUST FOUR PEOPLE, ANYWAY?
WHY, SHURMAN, OF COURSE.
NOW WE HAVE TO RETIRE AFTER SUMMER.
IT ALL WENT BY SO FAST.
THERE WERE TOUGH TIMES, YEAH...BUT IT WAS STILL FUN.
I JUST WISH...
I JUST WISH THE SUMMER DIDN'T HAVE TO END.
WHAT ARE YOU TALKING ABOUT?!
COME ON, FOOL. IT'S TIME TO SLEEP.
パチン

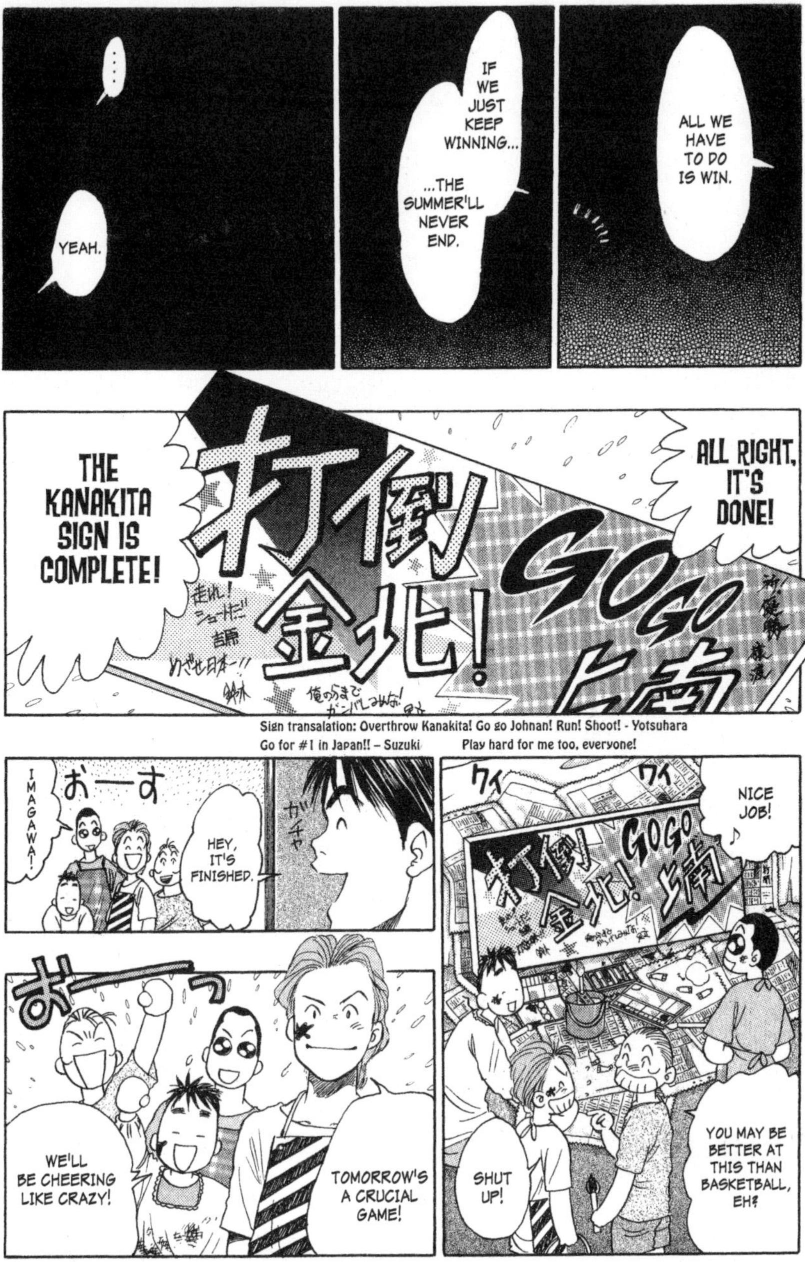
ALL WE HAVE TO DO IS WIN.
IF WE JUST KEEP WINNING...
...THE SUMMER'LL NEVER END.
...
YEAH.
ALL RIGHT, IT'S DONE!
THE KANAKITA SIGN IS COMPLETE!
打倒金北!
GOGO
Sign transalation: Overthrow Kanakita! Go go Johnan! Run! Shoot! - Yotsuhara
Go for #1 in Japan!! – Suzuki Play hard for me too, everyone!
ワイ ワイ
NICE JOB!
YOU MAY BE BETTER AT THIS THAN BASKETBALL, EH?
SHUT UP!
ガチャ
HEY, IT'S FINISHED.
おーす
IMAGAWA!
おーっ
TOMORROW'S A CRUCIAL GAME!
WE'LL BE CHEERING LIKE CRAZY!

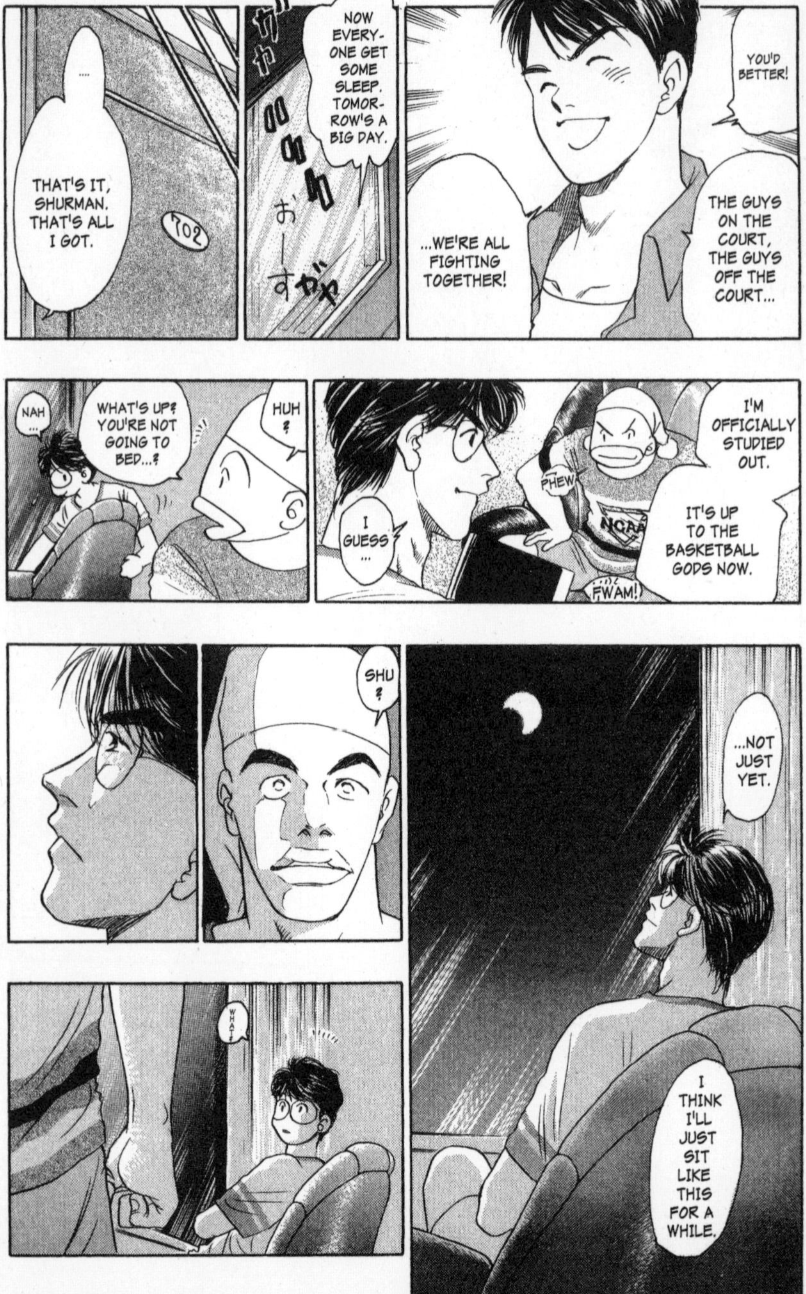
YOU'D BETTER!
THE GUYS ON THE COURT, THE GUYS OFF THE COURT...
...WE'RE ALL FIGHTING TOGETHER!
NOW EVERYONE GET SOME SLEEP. TOMORROW'S A BIG DAY.
....
THAT'S IT, SHURMAN. THAT'S ALL I GOT.
702
I'M OFFICIALLY STUDIED OUT.
IT'S UP TO THE BASKETBALL GODS NOW.
PHEW
FWAM!
I GUESS...
HUH?
WHAT'S UP? YOU'RE NOT GOING TO BED...?
NAH...
...NOT JUST YET.
I THINK I'LL JUST SIT LIKE THIS FOR A WHILE.
SHU?
WHAT?

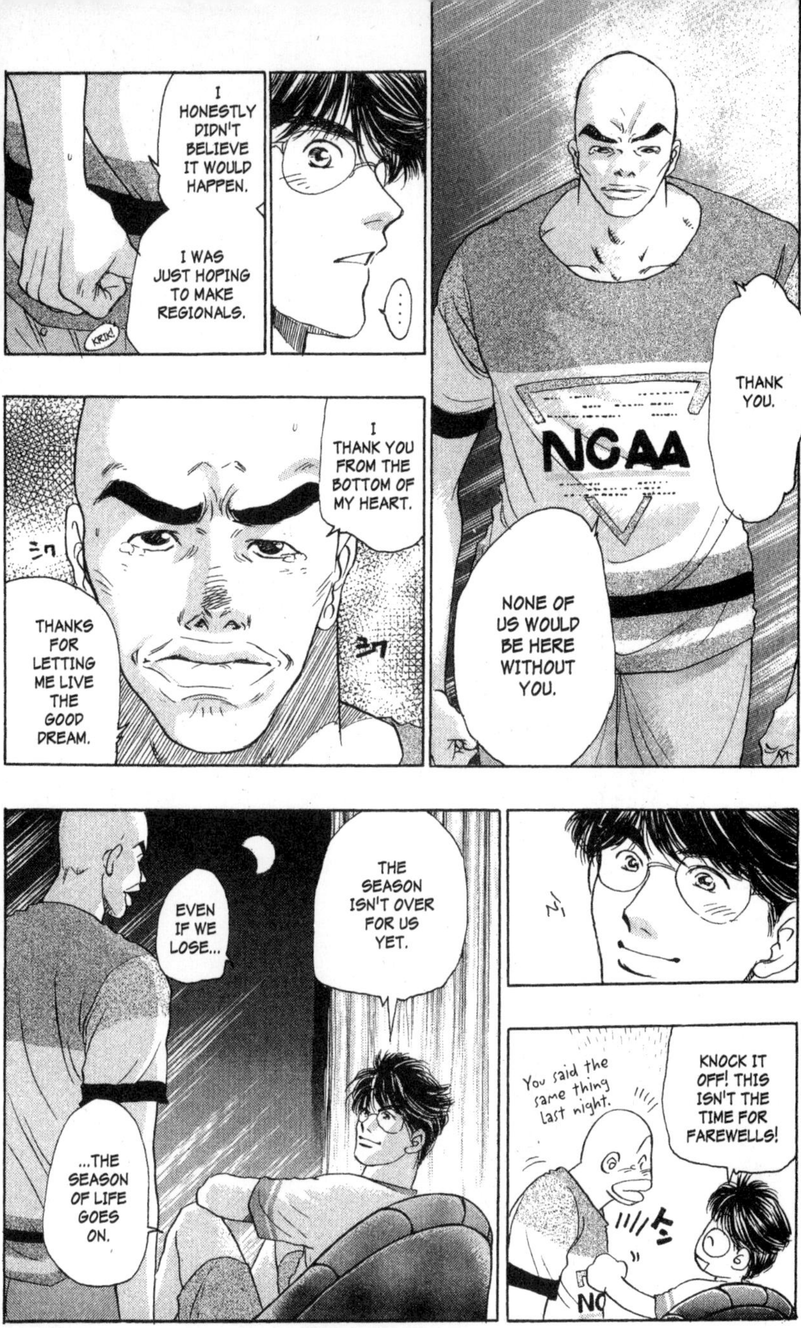
THANK YOU.
NONE OF US WOULD BE HERE WITHOUT YOU.
...
I HONESTLY DIDN'T BELIEVE IT WOULD HAPPEN.
I WAS JUST HOPING TO MAKE REGIONALS.
KRIK!
I THANK YOU FROM THE BOTTOM OF MY HEART.
THANKS FOR LETTING ME LIVE THE GOOD DREAM.
You said the same thing last night.
KNOCK IT OFF! THIS ISN'T THE TIME FOR FAREWELLS!
THE SEASON ISN'T OVER FOR US YET.
EVEN IF WE LOSE...
...THE SEASON OF LIFE GOES ON.

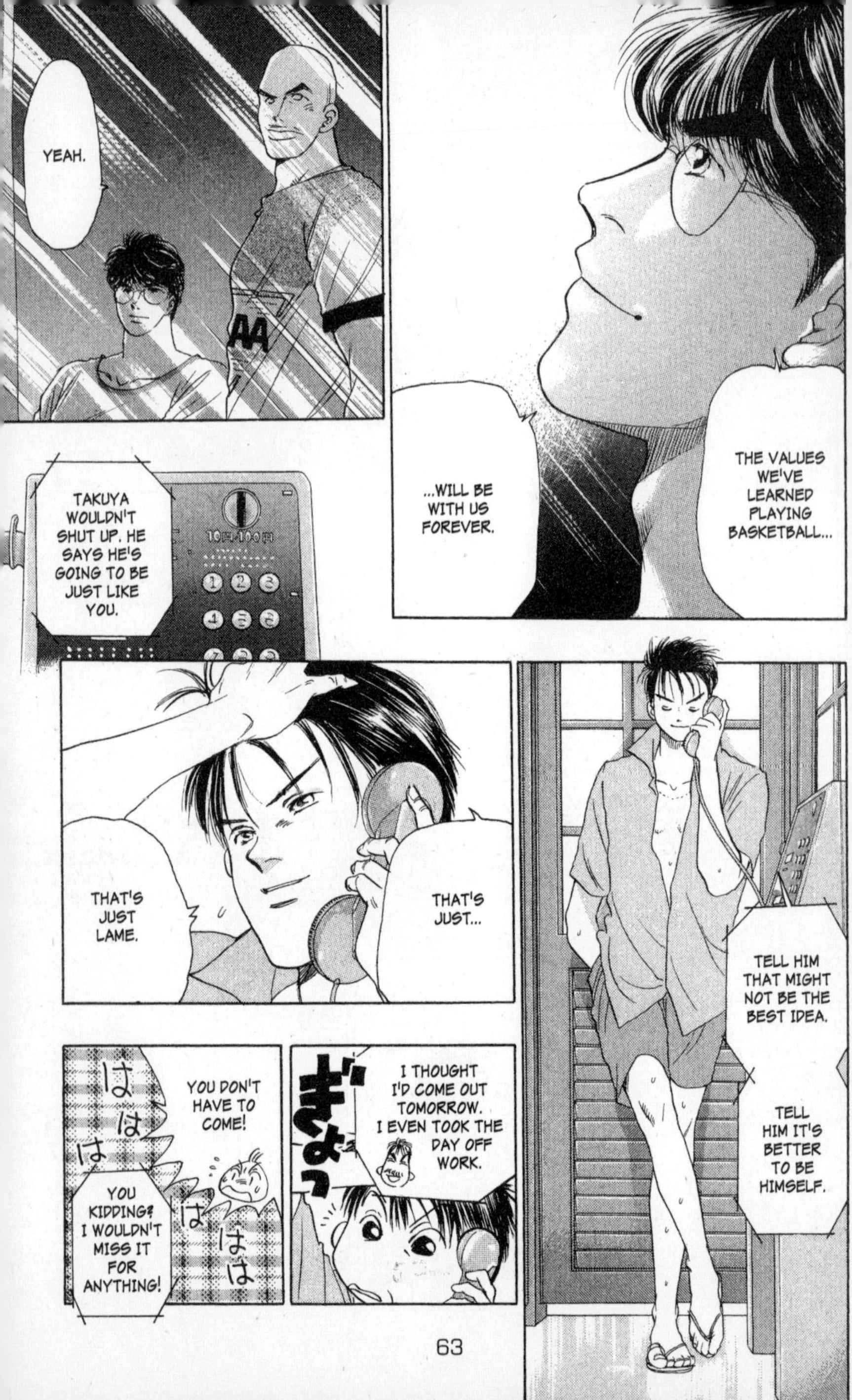
THE VALUES WE'VE LEARNED PLAYING BASKETBALL...
...WILL BE WITH US FOREVER.
YEAH.
TAKUYA WOULDN'T SHUT UP. HE SAYS HE'S GOING TO BE JUST LIKE YOU.
10円·100円
TELL HIM THAT MIGHT NOT BE THE BEST IDEA.
TELL HIM IT'S BETTER TO BE HIMSELF.
THAT'S JUST...
THAT'S JUST LAME.
I THOUGHT I'D COME OUT TOMORROW. I EVEN TOOK THE DAY OFF WORK.
ぎょっ
YOU DON'T HAVE TO COME!
ははは
YOU KIDDING? I WOULDN'T MISS IT FOR ANYTHING!
はは

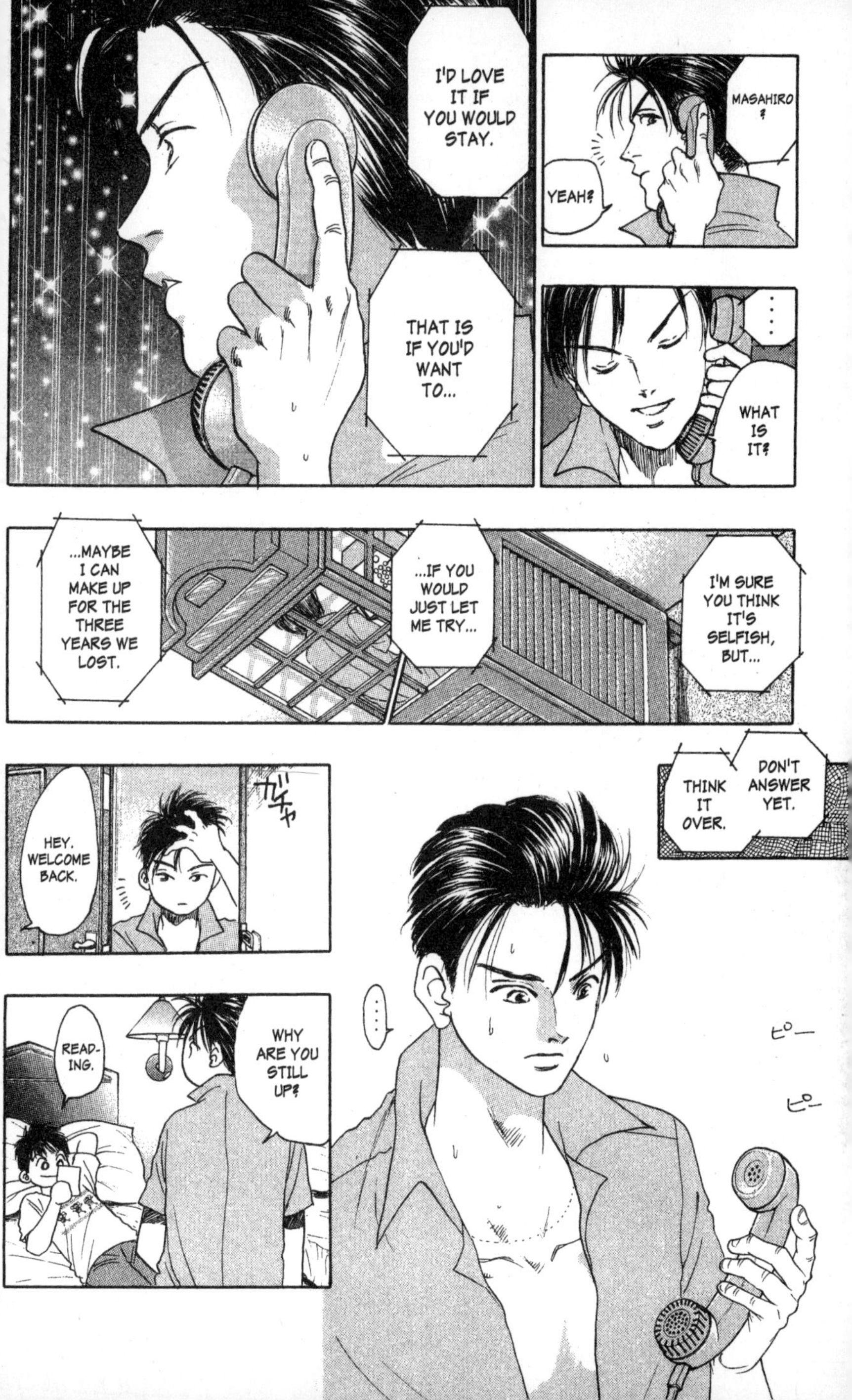
MASAHIRO?
YEAH?
...
WHAT IS IT?
I'D LOVE IT IF YOU WOULD STAY.
THAT IS IF YOU'D WANT TO...
I'M SURE YOU THINK IT'S SELFISH, BUT...
...IF YOU WOULD JUST LET ME TRY...
...MAYBE I CAN MAKE UP FOR THE THREE YEARS WE LOST.
DON'T ANSWER YET.
THINK IT OVER.
...
ピー
ピー
ガチャ
HEY. WELCOME BACK.
WHY ARE YOU STILL UP?
READ-ING.

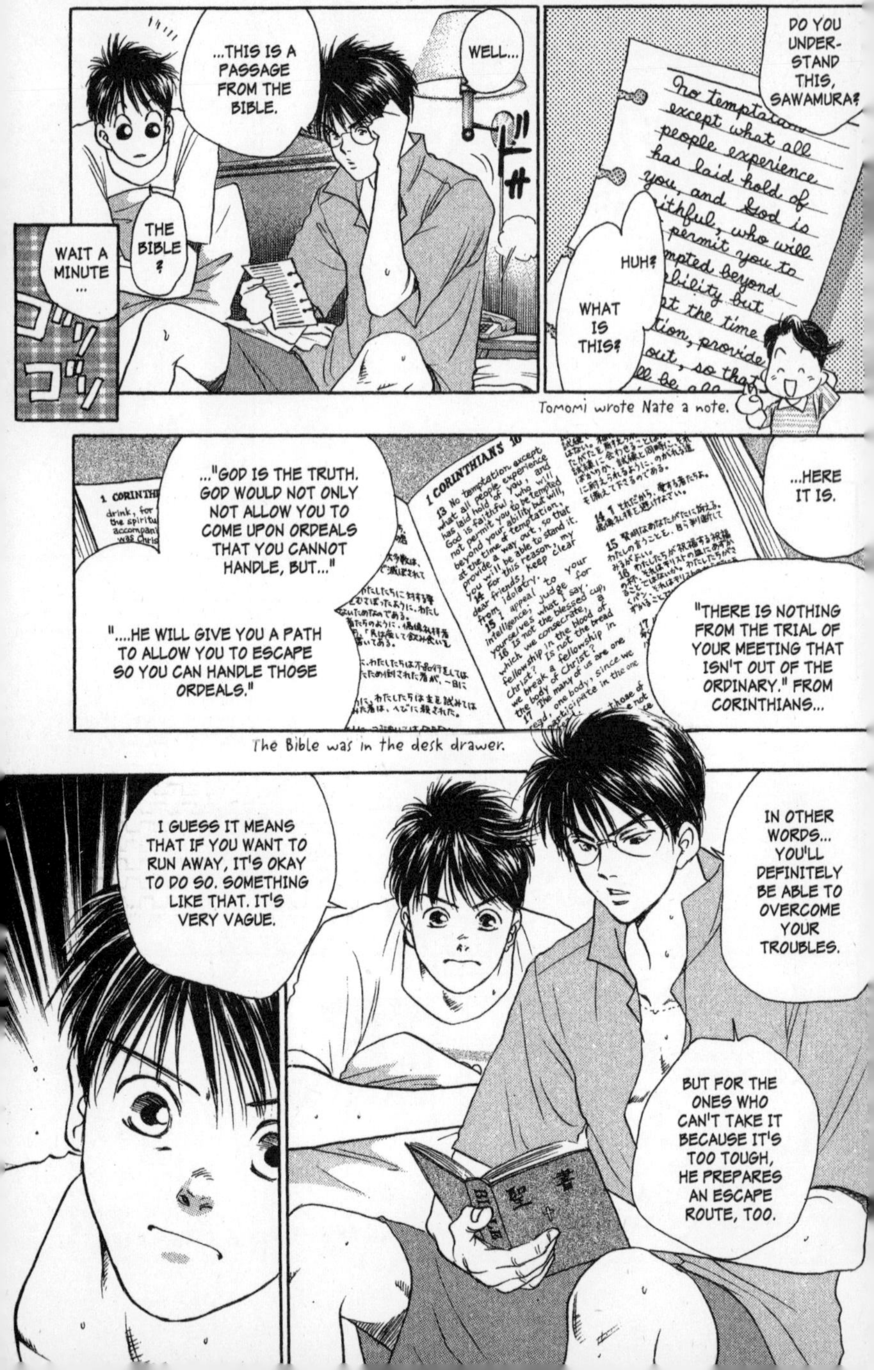
DO YOU UNDERSTAND THIS, SAWAMURA?
HUH? WHAT IS THIS?
Tomomi wrote Nate a note.
WELL...
...THIS IS A PASSAGE FROM THE BIBLE.
THE BIBLE?
WAIT A MINUTE...
...HERE IT IS.
"THERE IS NOTHING FROM THE TRIAL OF YOUR MEETING THAT ISN'T OUT OF THE ORDINARY." FROM CORINTHIANS...
..."GOD IS THE TRUTH. GOD WOULD NOT ONLY NOT ALLOW YOU TO COME UPON ORDEALS THAT YOU CANNOT HANDLE, BUT..."
"....HE WILL GIVE YOU A PATH TO ALLOW YOU TO ESCAPE SO YOU CAN HANDLE THOSE ORDEALS."
The Bible was in the desk drawer.
IN OTHER WORDS... YOU'LL DEFINITELY BE ABLE TO OVERCOME YOUR TROUBLES.
BUT FOR THE ONES WHO CAN'T TAKE IT BECAUSE IT'S TOO TOUGH, HE PREPARES AN ESCAPE ROUTE, TOO.
I GUESS IT MEANS THAT IF YOU WANT TO RUN AWAY, IT'S OKAY TO DO SO. SOMETHING LIKE THAT. IT'S VERY VAGUE.

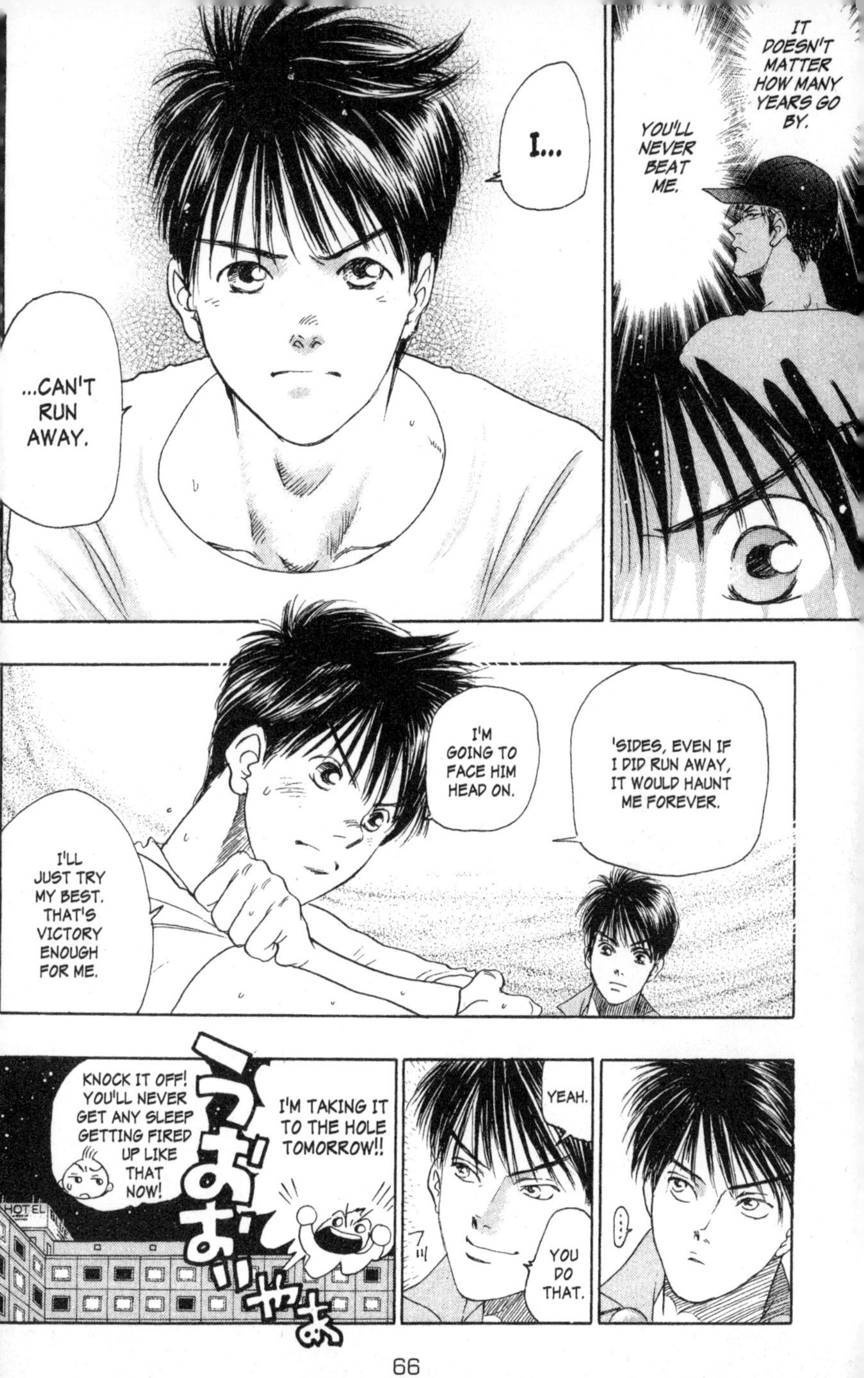

IT DOESN'T MATTER HOW MANY YEARS GO BY.
YOU'LL NEVER BEAT ME.
I...
...CAN'T RUN AWAY.
'SIDES, EVEN IF I DID RUN AWAY, IT WOULD HAUNT ME FOREVER.
I'M GOING TO FACE HIM HEAD ON.
I'LL JUST TRY MY BEST. THAT'S VICTORY ENOUGH FOR ME.
…
YEAH.
YOU DO THAT.
I'M TAKING IT TO THE HOLE TOMORROW!!
KNOCK IT OFF! YOU'LL NEVER GET ANY SLEEP GETTING FIRED UP LIKE THAT NOW!
HOTEL

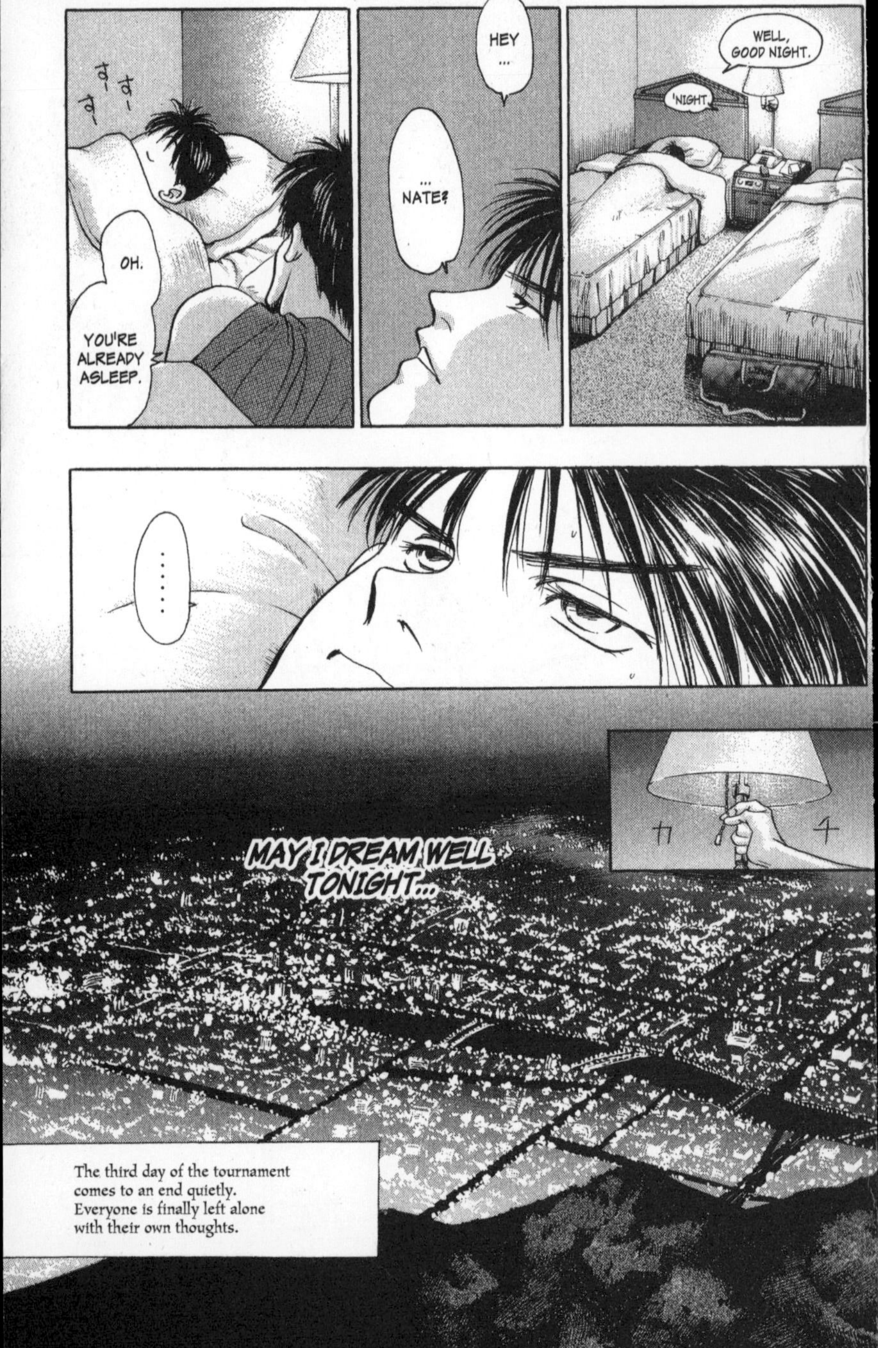
WELL, GOOD NIGHT.
'NIGHT.
HEY ...
... NATE?
OH.
YOU'RE ALREADY ASLEEP.
......
カチ
MAY I DREAM WELL TONIGHT...
The third day of the tournament comes to an end quietly. Everyone is finally left alone with their own thoughts.

You're Reading...

REBOUND

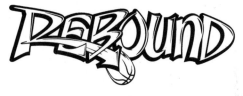

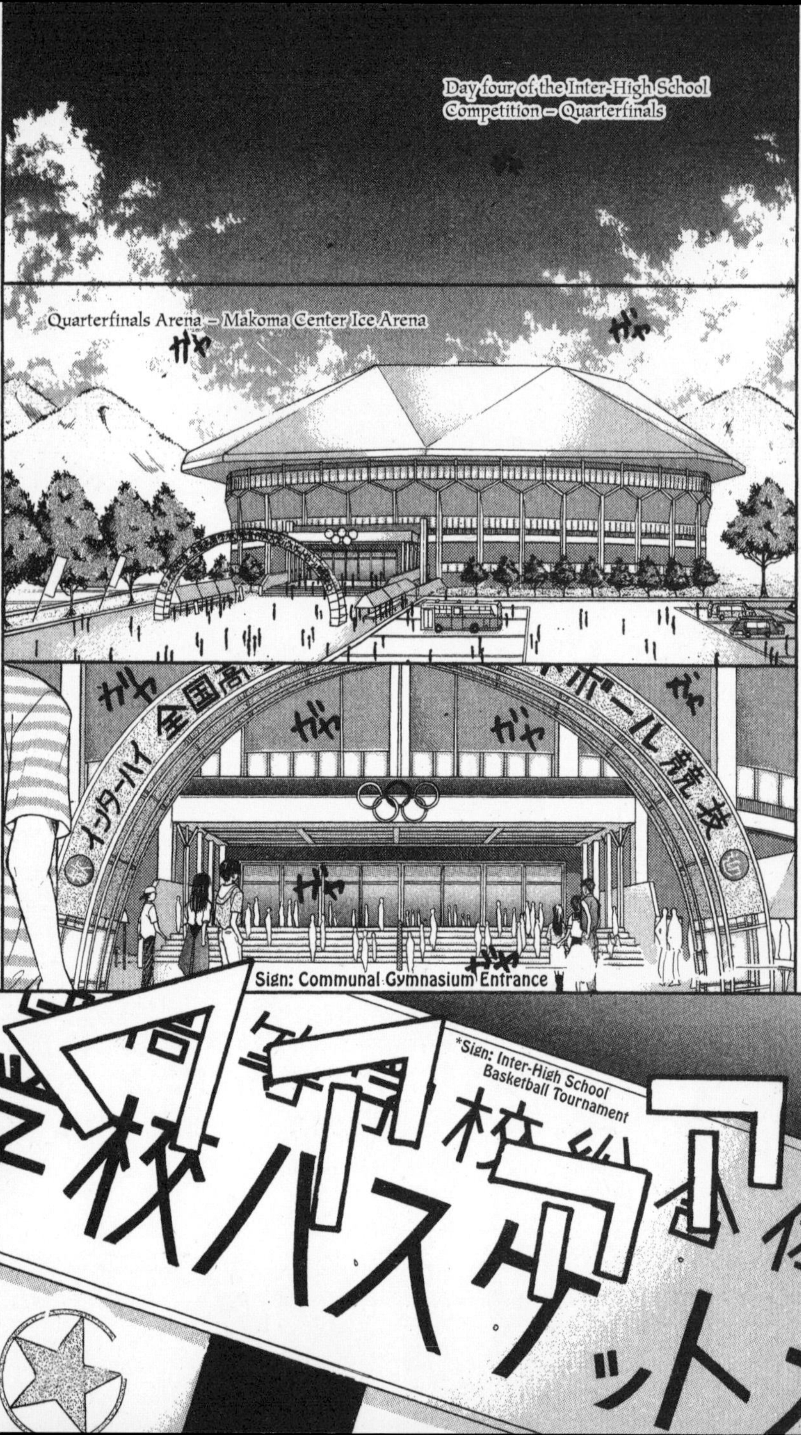
Day four of the Inter-High School Competition – Quarterfinals
Quarterfinals Arena – Makoma Center Ice Arena
ガヤ
ガヤ
ガヤ
ガヤ
ガヤ
ガヤ
Sign: Communal Gymnasium Entrance
*Sign: Inter-High School Basketball Tournament

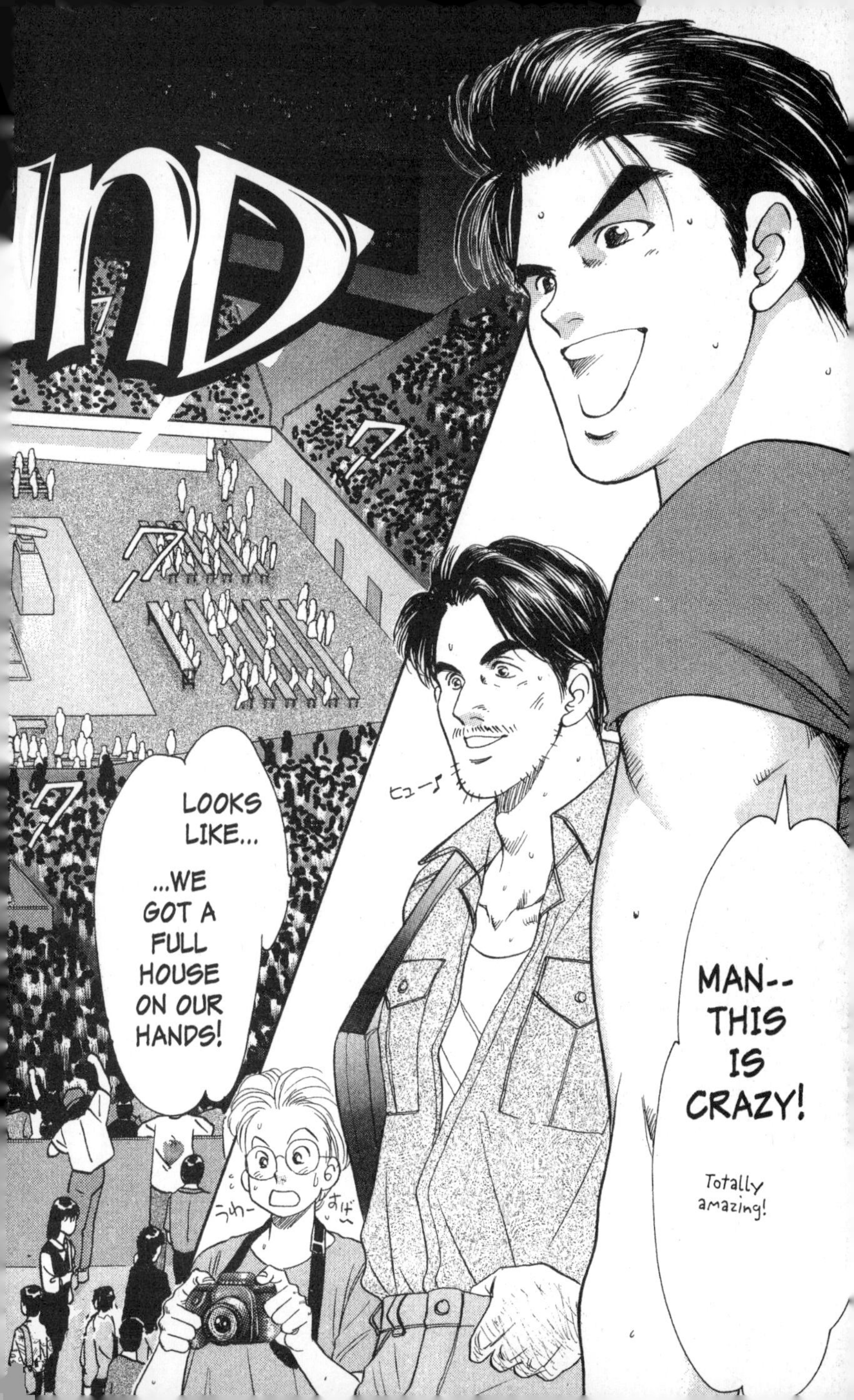
MAN-- THIS IS CRAZY!
Totally amazing!
ヒュー♪
LOOKS LIKE...
...WE GOT A FULL HOUSE ON OUR HANDS!
うわー

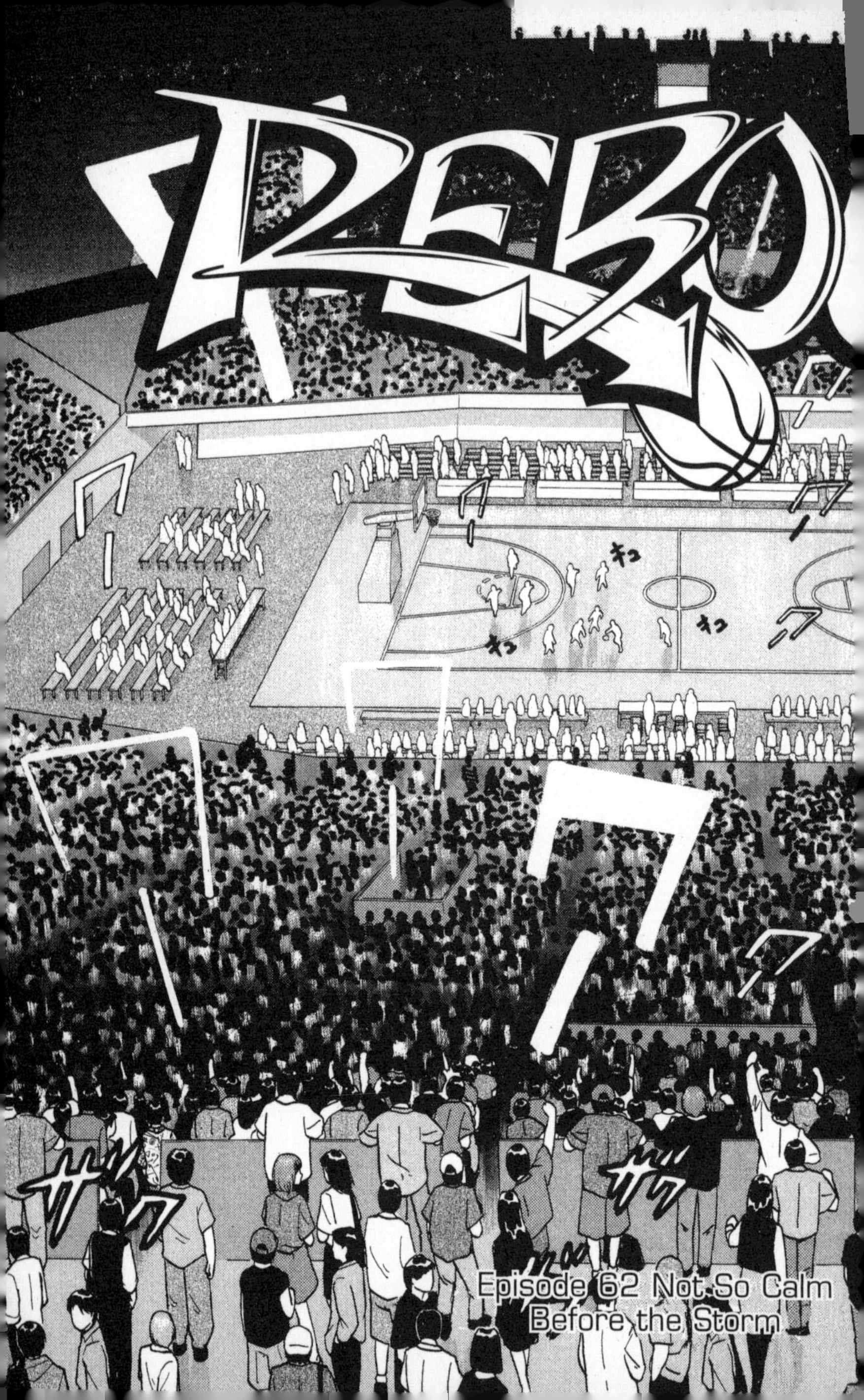
REBOUND
Episode 62 Not So Calm Before the Storm

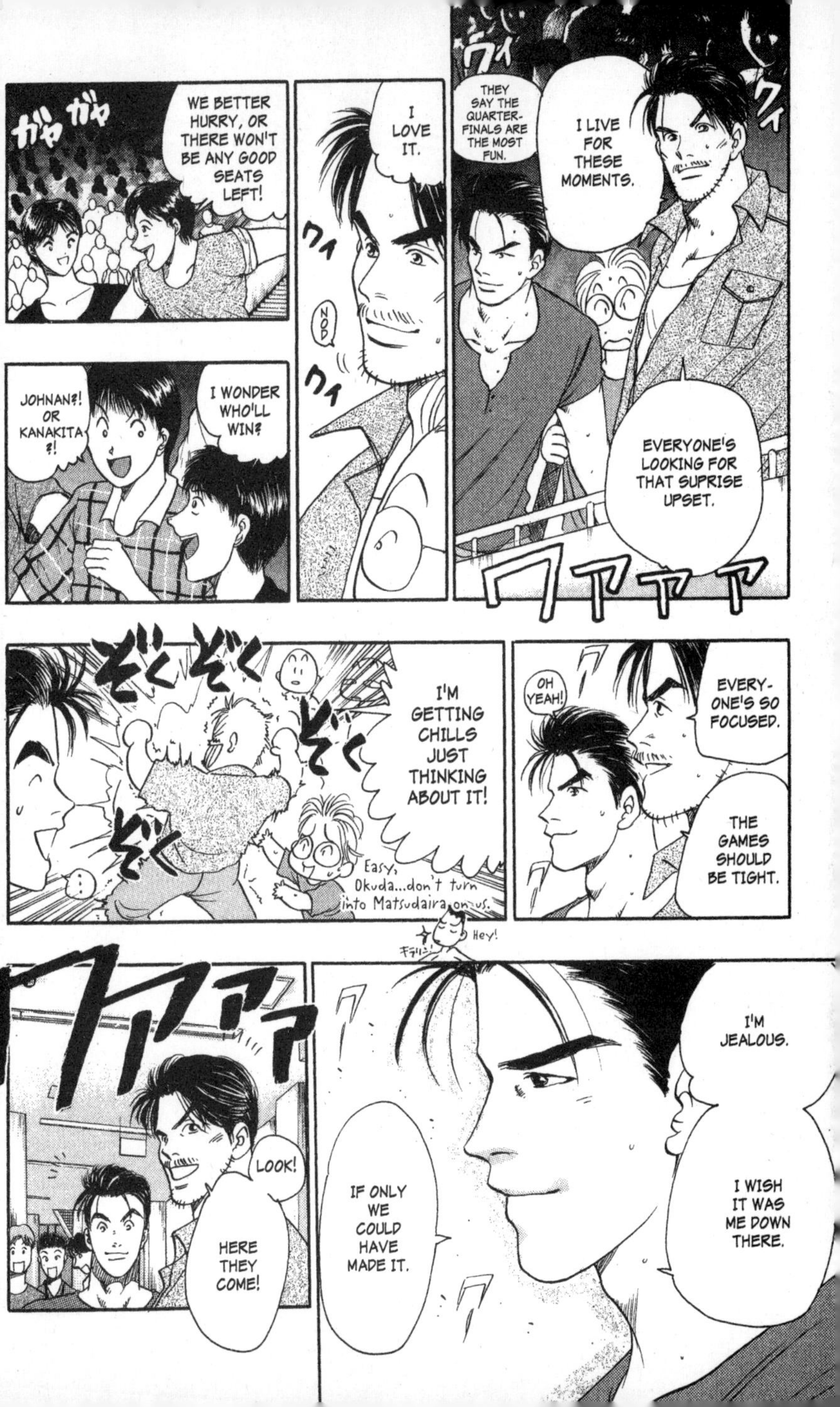
THEY SAY THE QUARTER-FINALS ARE THE MOST FUN.
I LIVE FOR THESE MOMENTS.
EVERYONE'S LOOKING FOR THAT SUPRISE UPSET.
I LOVE IT.
NOD
WE BETTER HURRY, OR THERE WON'T BE ANY GOOD SEATS LEFT!
I WONDER WHO'LL WIN?
JOHNAN?! OR KANAKITA?!
EVERY-ONE'S SO FOCUSED.
OH YEAH!
THE GAMES SHOULD BE TIGHT.
I'M GETTING CHILLS JUST THINKING ABOUT IT!
Easy, Okuda...don't turn into Matsudaira on us.
Hey!
I'M JEALOUS.
I WISH IT WAS ME DOWN THERE.
IF ONLY WE COULD HAVE MADE IT.
LOOK!
HERE THEY COME!

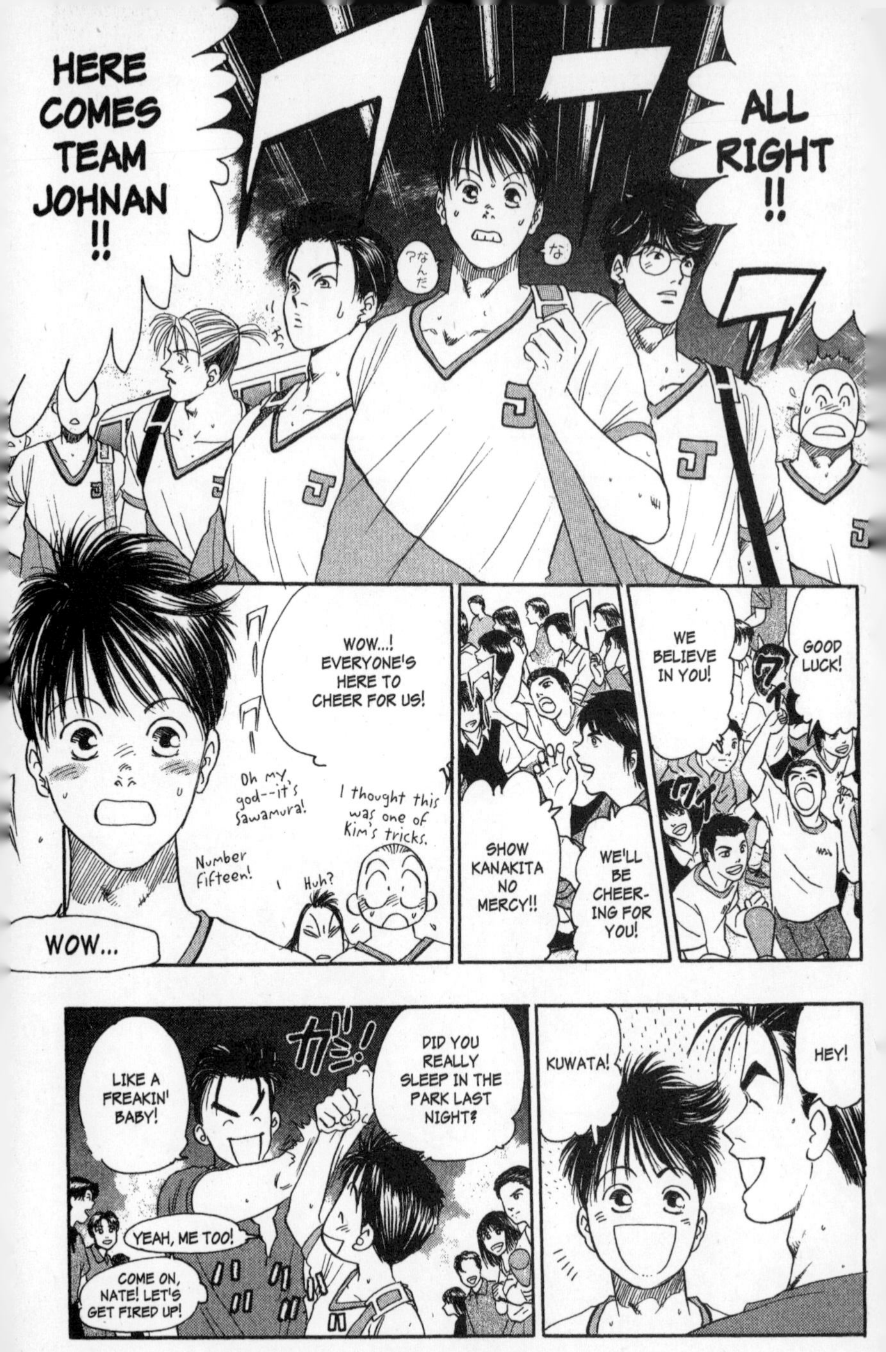
ALL RIGHT!!
な
?なんだ
おっ
HERE COMES TEAM JOHNAN!!
GOOD LUCK!
WE BELIEVE IN YOU!
WE'LL BE CHEER-ING FOR YOU!
SHOW KANAKITA NO MERCY!!
WOW...! EVERYONE'S HERE TO CHEER FOR US!
I thought this was one of Kim's tricks.
Oh my god--it's Sawamura!
Huh?
Number fifteen!
WOW...
HEY!
KUWATA!
DID YOU REALLY SLEEP IN THE PARK LAST NIGHT?
LIKE A FREAKIN' BABY!
YEAH, ME TOO!
COME ON, NATE! LET'S GET FIRED UP!

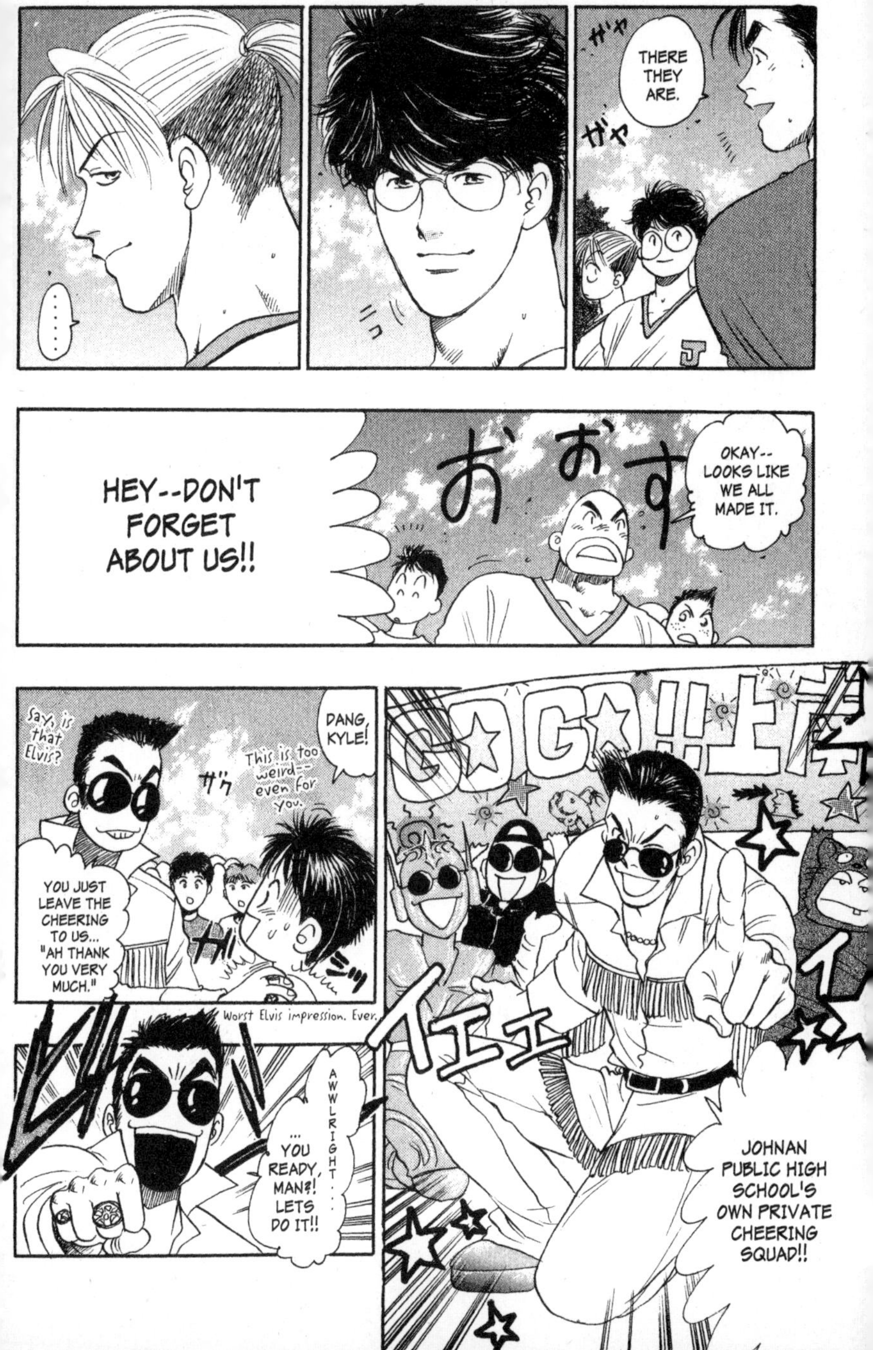
ザヤ
ガヤ
THERE THEY ARE.
ニコ
......
OKAY-- LOOKS LIKE WE ALL MADE IT.
おおす
HEY--DON'T FORGET ABOUT US!!
GO☆GO!!上南
イェェ
JOHNAN PUBLIC HIGH SCHOOL'S OWN PRIVATE CHEERING SQUAD!!
DANG, KYLE!
This is too weird-- even for you.
Say, is that Elvis?
ザク
YOU JUST LEAVE THE CHEERING TO US... "AH THANK YOU VERY MUCH."
Worst Elvis impression. Ever.
AWWLRIGHT...
... YOU READY, MAN?! LETS DO IT!!

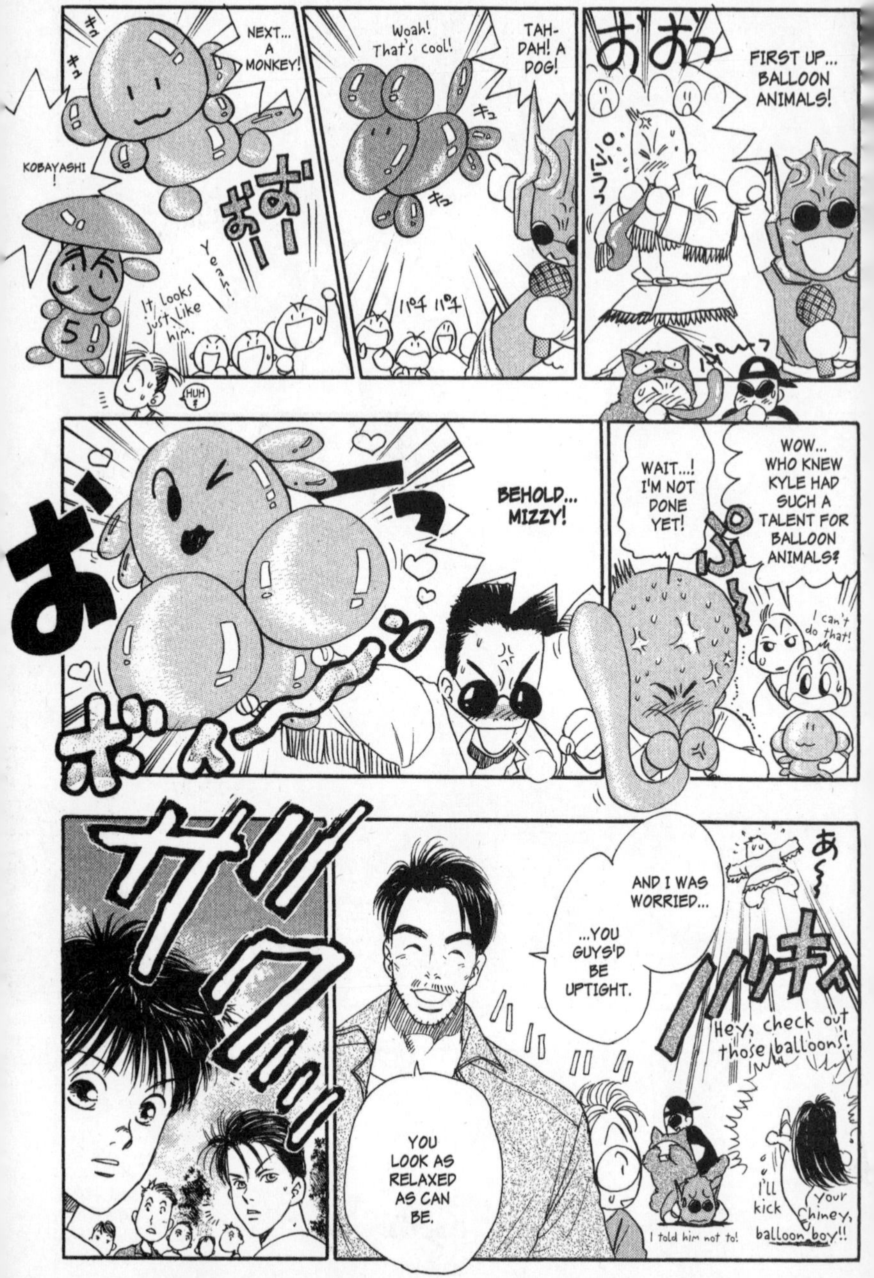
おおっ
FIRST UP... BALLOON ANIMALS!
TAH-DAH! A DOG!
Woah! That's cool!
NEXT... A MONKEY!
KOBAYASHI!
Yeah!
It looks just like him.
HUH?
WOW... WHO KNEW KYLE HAD SUCH A TALENT FOR BALLOON ANIMALS?
WAIT...! I'M NOT DONE YET!
I can't do that!
BEHOLD... MIZZY!
Hey, check out those balloons!
AND I WAS WORRIED...
...YOU GUYS'D BE UPTIGHT.
YOU LOOK AS RELAXED AS CAN BE.
I'll kick your chiney, balloon boy!!
I told him not to!

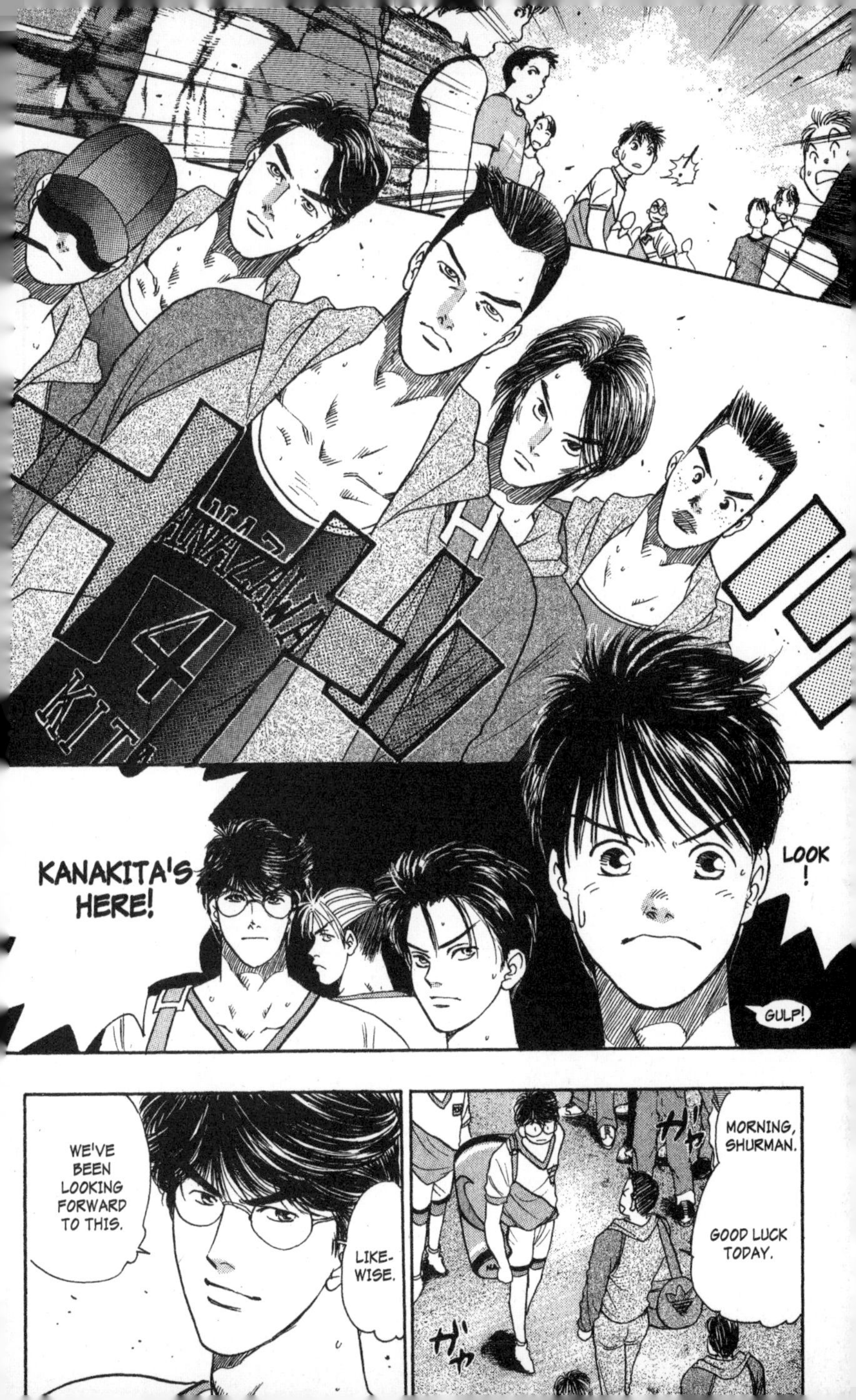
LOOK!
KANAKITA'S HERE!
GULP!
MORNING, SHURMAN.
GOOD LUCK TODAY.
WE'VE BEEN LOOKING FORWARD TO THIS.
LIKE-WISE.

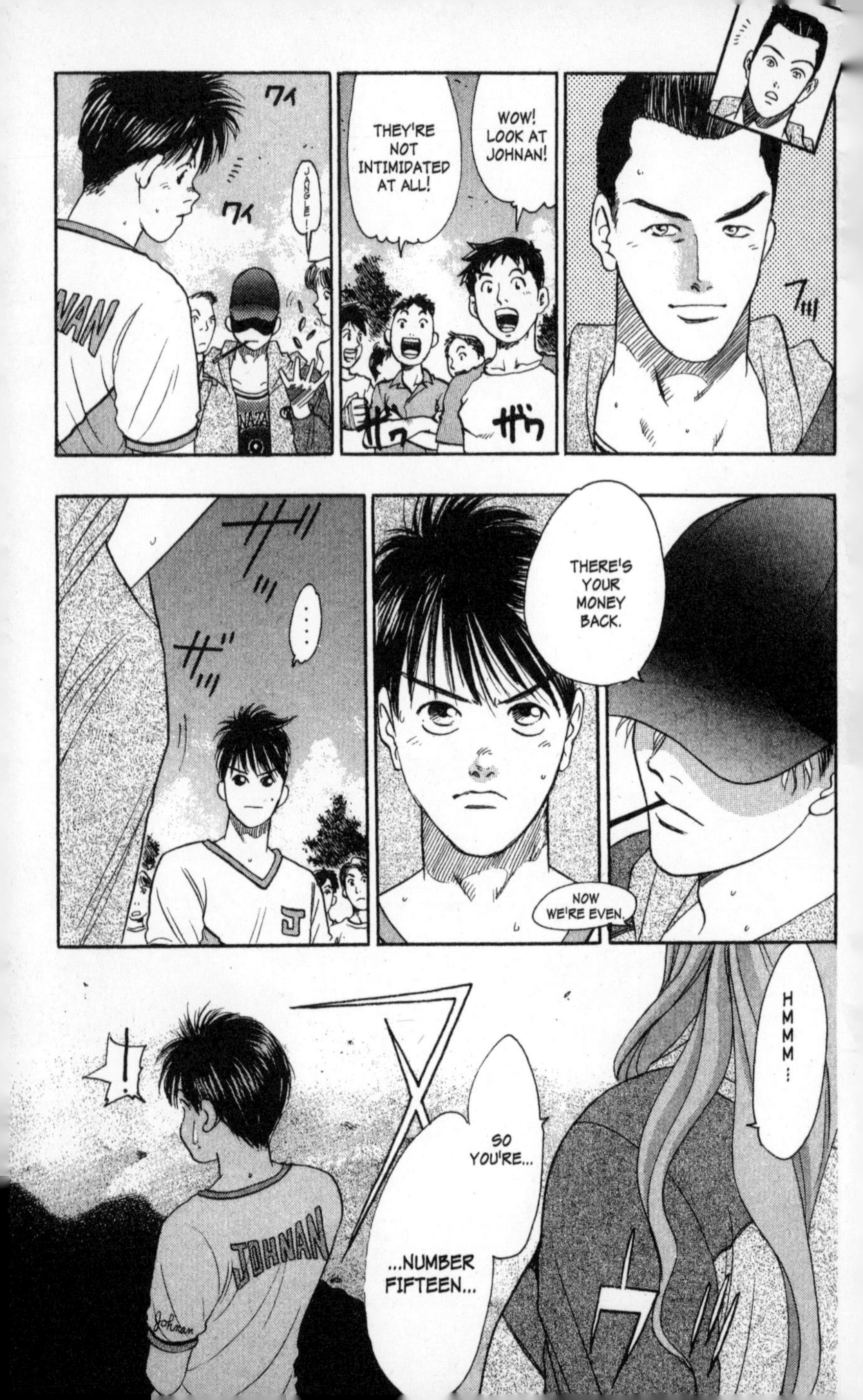
WOW! LOOK AT JOHNAN!
THEY'RE NOT INTIMIDATED AT ALL!
JANGLE!
THERE'S YOUR MONEY BACK.
NOW WE'RE EVEN.
HMMM..
SO YOU'RE...
...NUMBER FIFTEEN...
!

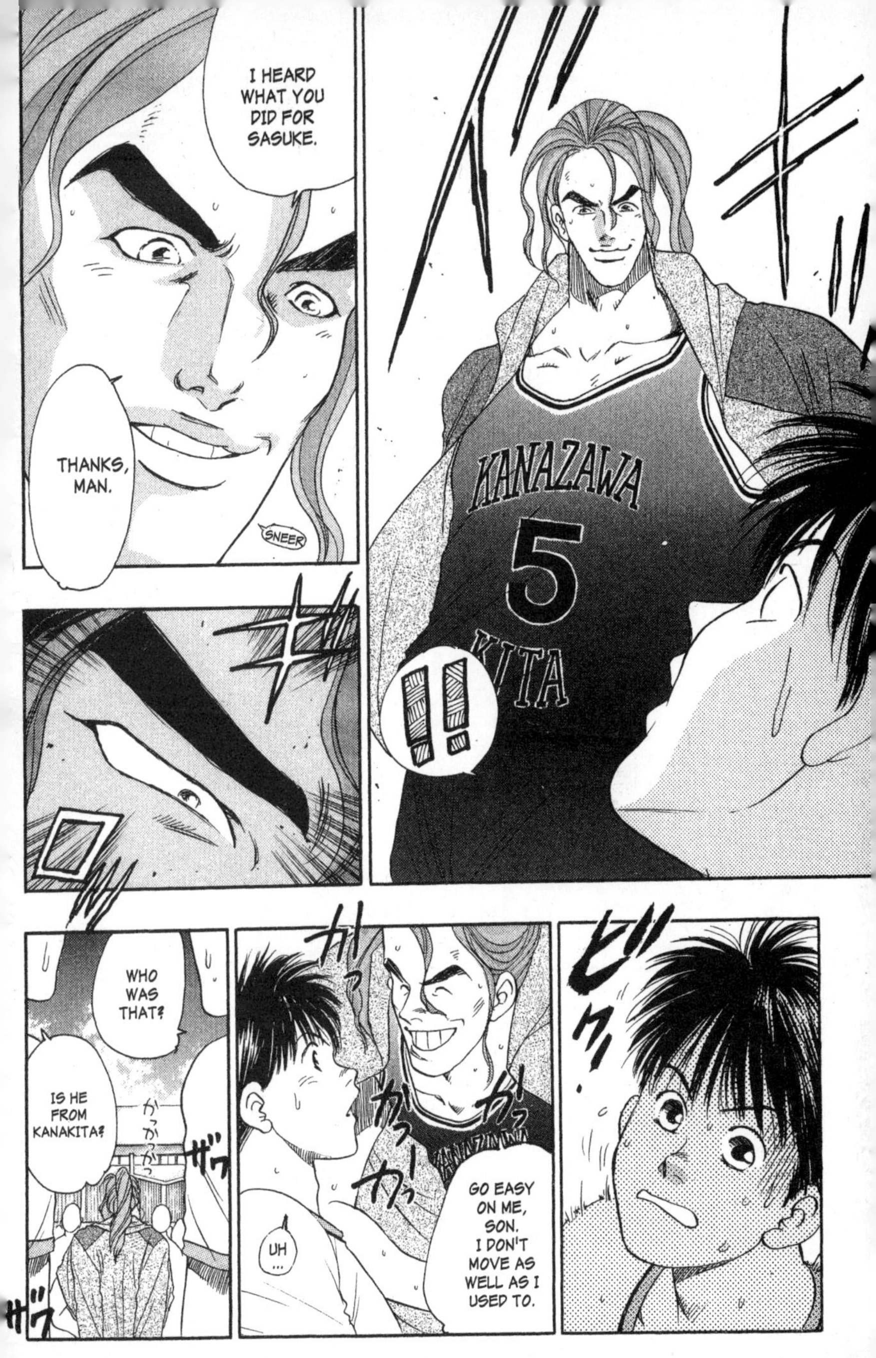
!!
I HEARD WHAT YOU DID FOR SASUKE.
THANKS, MAN.
SNEER
GO EASY ON ME, SON. I DON'T MOVE AS WELL AS I USED TO.
UH ...
WHO WAS THAT?
IS HE FROM KANAKITA?
かっかっかっ

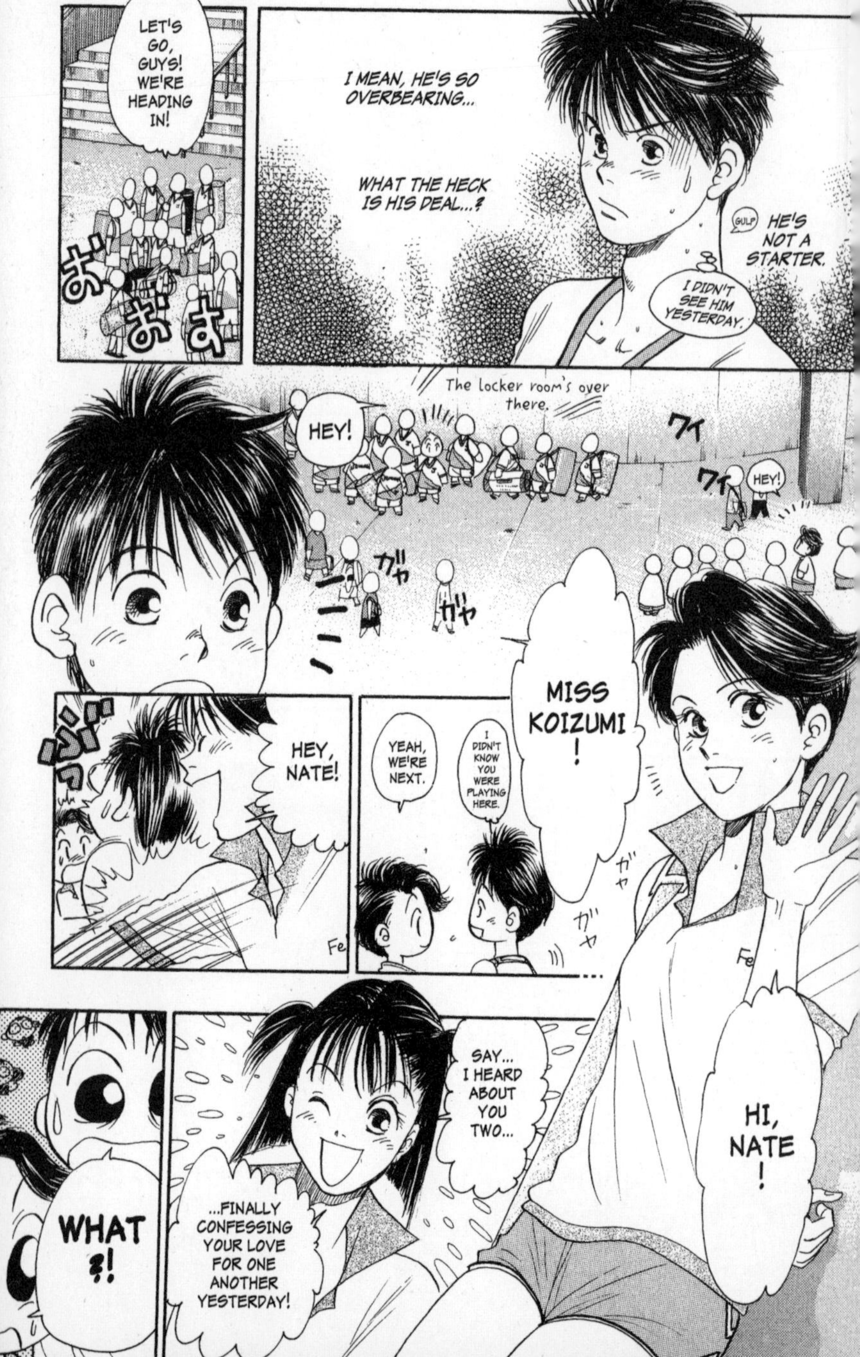
I MEAN, HE'S SO OVERBEARING...
WHAT THE HECK IS HIS DEAL...?
GULP
HE'S NOT A STARTER.
I DIDN'T SEE HIM YESTERDAY.
LET'S GO, GUYS! WE'RE HEADING IN!
The locker room's over there.
ワイ
ワイ
HEY!
HEY!
ガヤ
ガヤ
MISS KOIZUMI!
HI, NATE!
I DIDN'T KNOW YOU WERE PLAYING HERE.
YEAH, WE'RE NEXT.
ガヤ
ガヤ
HEY, NATE!
SAY... I HEARD ABOUT YOU TWO...
...FINALLY CONFESSING YOUR LOVE FOR ONE ANOTHER YESTERDAY!
WHAT?!

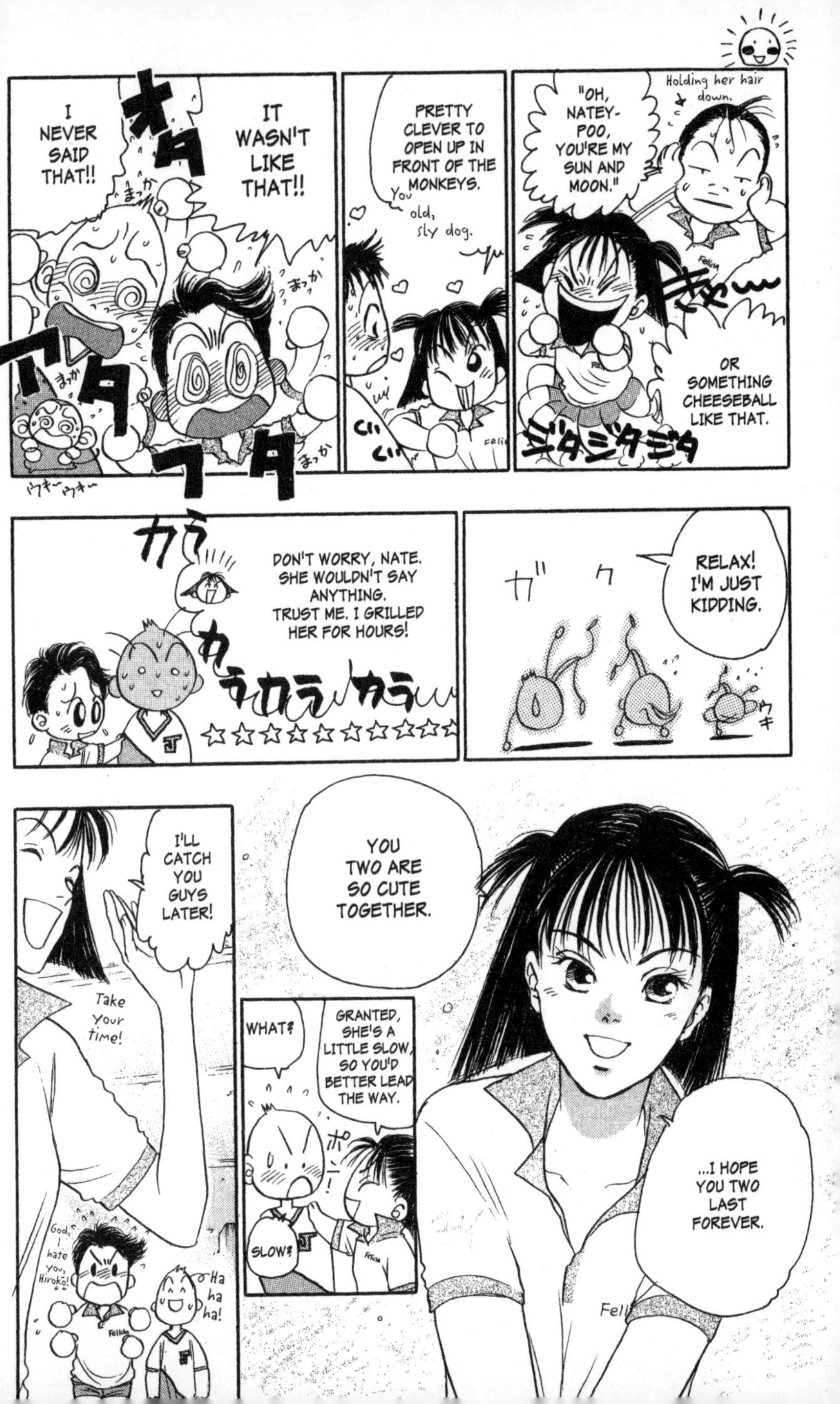
"OH, NATEY-POO, YOU'RE MY SUN AND MOON."
Holding her hair down.
OR SOMETHING CHEESEBALL LIKE THAT.
ジタジタジタ
PRETTY CLEVER TO OPEN UP IN FRONT OF THE MONKEYS.
You old, sly dog.
IT WASN'T LIKE THAT!!
I NEVER SAID THAT!!
RELAX! I'M JUST KIDDING.
DON'T WORRY, NATE. SHE WOULDN'T SAY ANYTHING. TRUST ME. I GRILLED HER FOR HOURS!
カラカラカラ
YOU TWO ARE SO CUTE TOGETHER.
GRANTED, SHE'S A LITTLE SLOW, SO YOU'D BETTER LEAD THE WAY.
WHAT?
SLOW?
...I HOPE YOU TWO LAST FOREVER.
I'LL CATCH YOU GUYS LATER!
Take your time!
God, I hate you, Hiroko!
Ha ha ha!

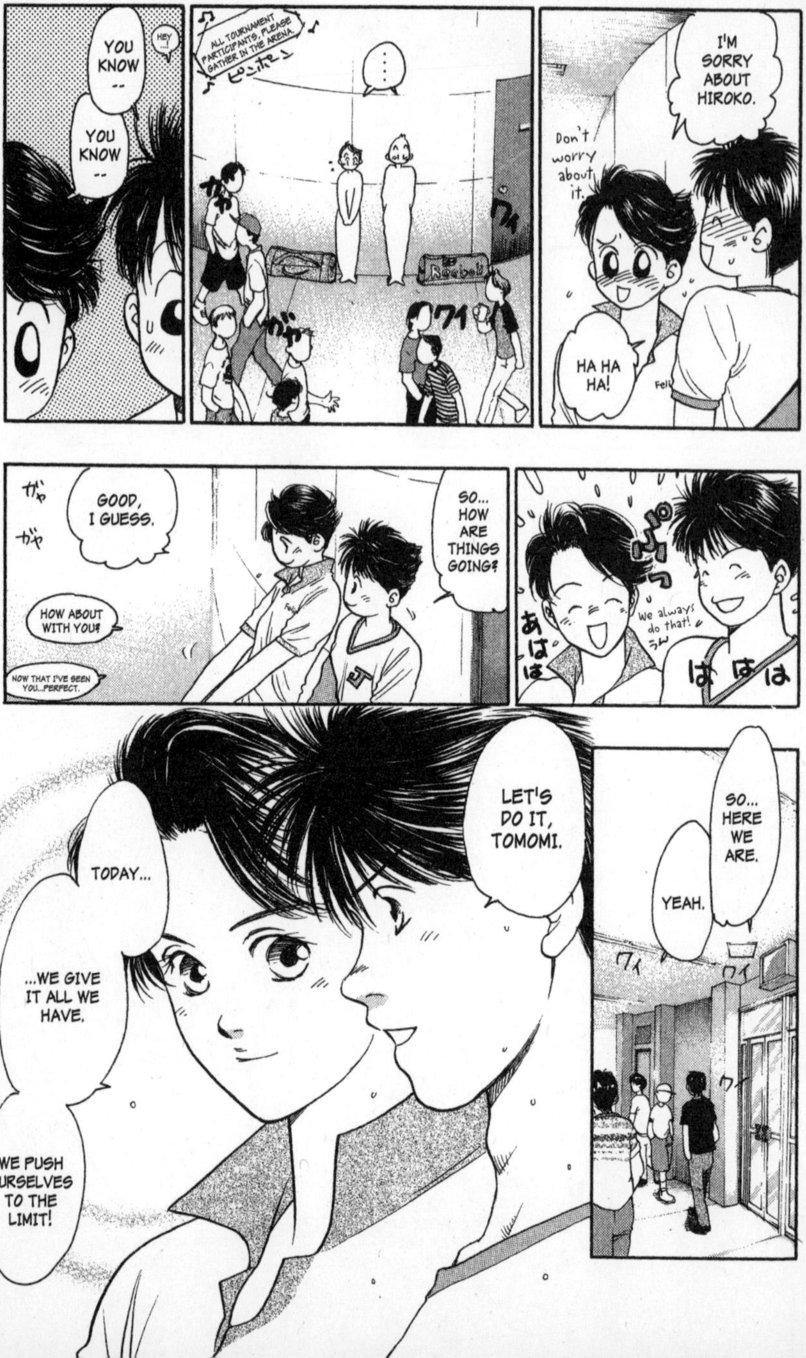
I'M SORRY ABOUT HIROKO.
Don't worry about it.
HA HA HA!
ALL TOURNAMENT PARTICIPANTS, PLEASE GATHER IN THE ARENA.
ピンポーン
...
ガヤ
ガヤ
ワイ
ワイ
HEY ...!
YOU KNOW --
YOU KNOW --
ぷっ
We always do that!
うん
あはは
ははは
SO... HOW ARE THINGS GOING?
GOOD, I GUESS.
HOW ABOUT WITH YOU?
NOW THAT I'VE SEEN YOU...PERFECT.
がや
がや
SO... HERE WE ARE.
YEAH.
LET'S DO IT, TOMOMI.
TODAY...
...WE GIVE IT ALL WE HAVE.
WE PUSH OURSELVES TO THE LIMIT!

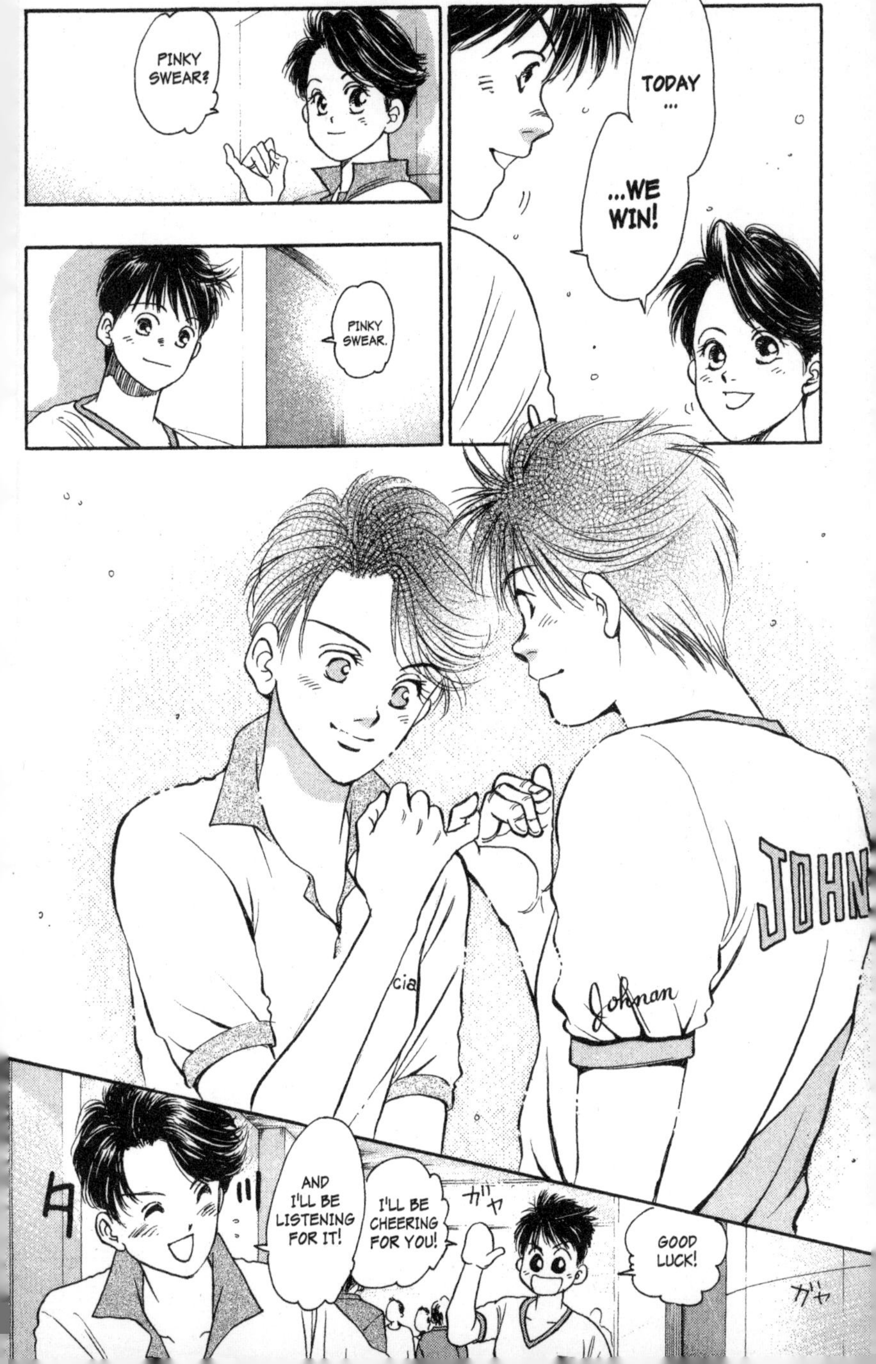
TODAY ...
...WE WIN!
PINKY SWEAR?
PINKY SWEAR.
JOHN
Johnan
GOOD LUCK!
ガヤ
ガヤ
I'LL BE CHEERING FOR YOU!
AND I'LL BE LISTENING FOR IT!

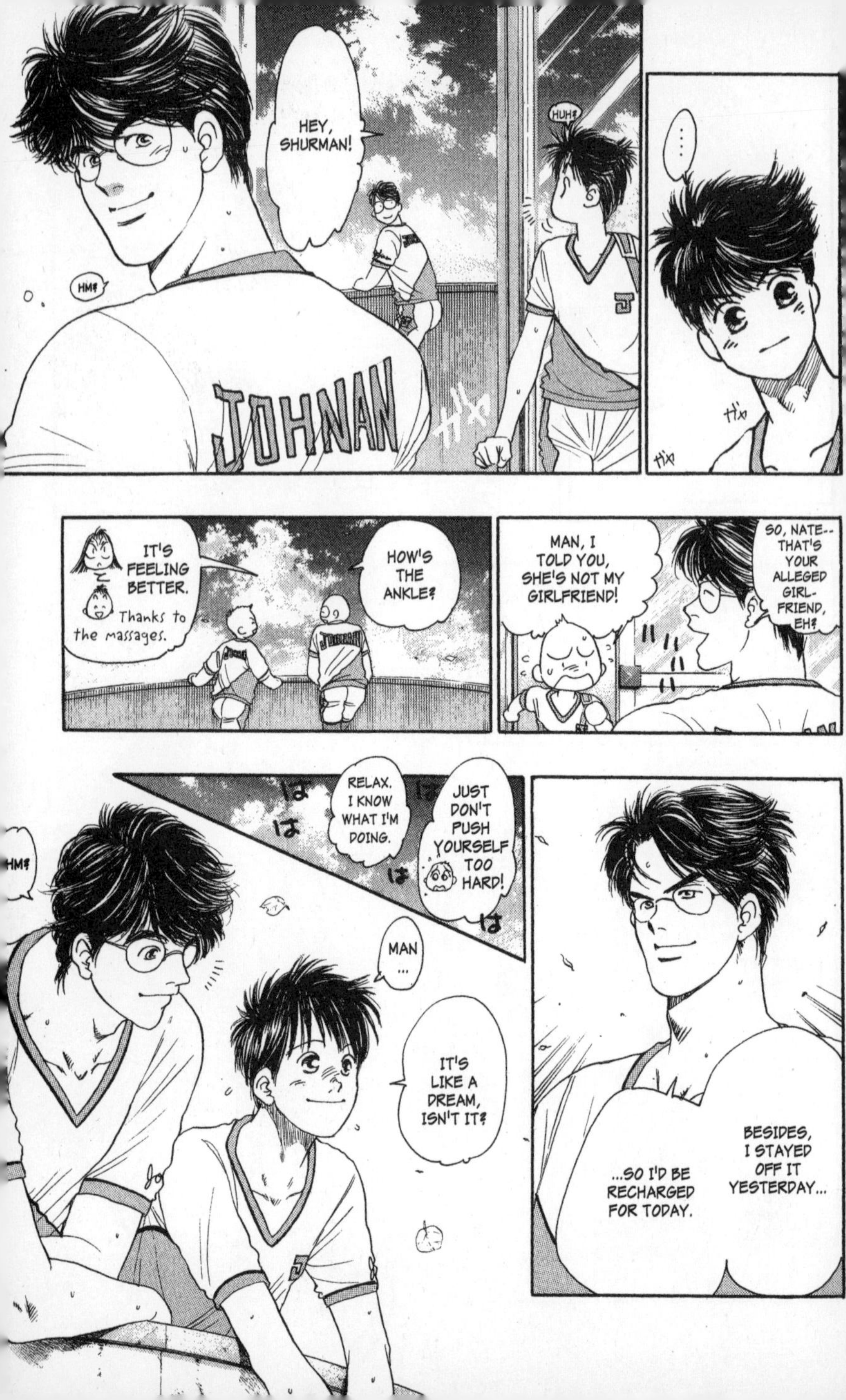
......
ガヤ
ガヤ
HUH?
HEY, SHURMAN!
HM?
JOHNAN
ガヤ
SO, NATE--THAT'S YOUR ALLEGED GIRLFRIEND, EH?
MAN, I TOLD YOU, SHE'S NOT MY GIRLFRIEND!
HOW'S THE ANKLE?
IT'S FEELING BETTER. Thanks to the massages.
BESIDES, I STAYED OFF IT YESTERDAY...
...SO I'D BE RECHARGED FOR TODAY.
は は は は は
JUST DON'T PUSH YOURSELF TOO HARD!
RELAX. I KNOW WHAT I'M DOING.
MAN ...
IT'S LIKE A DREAM, ISN'T IT?
HM?

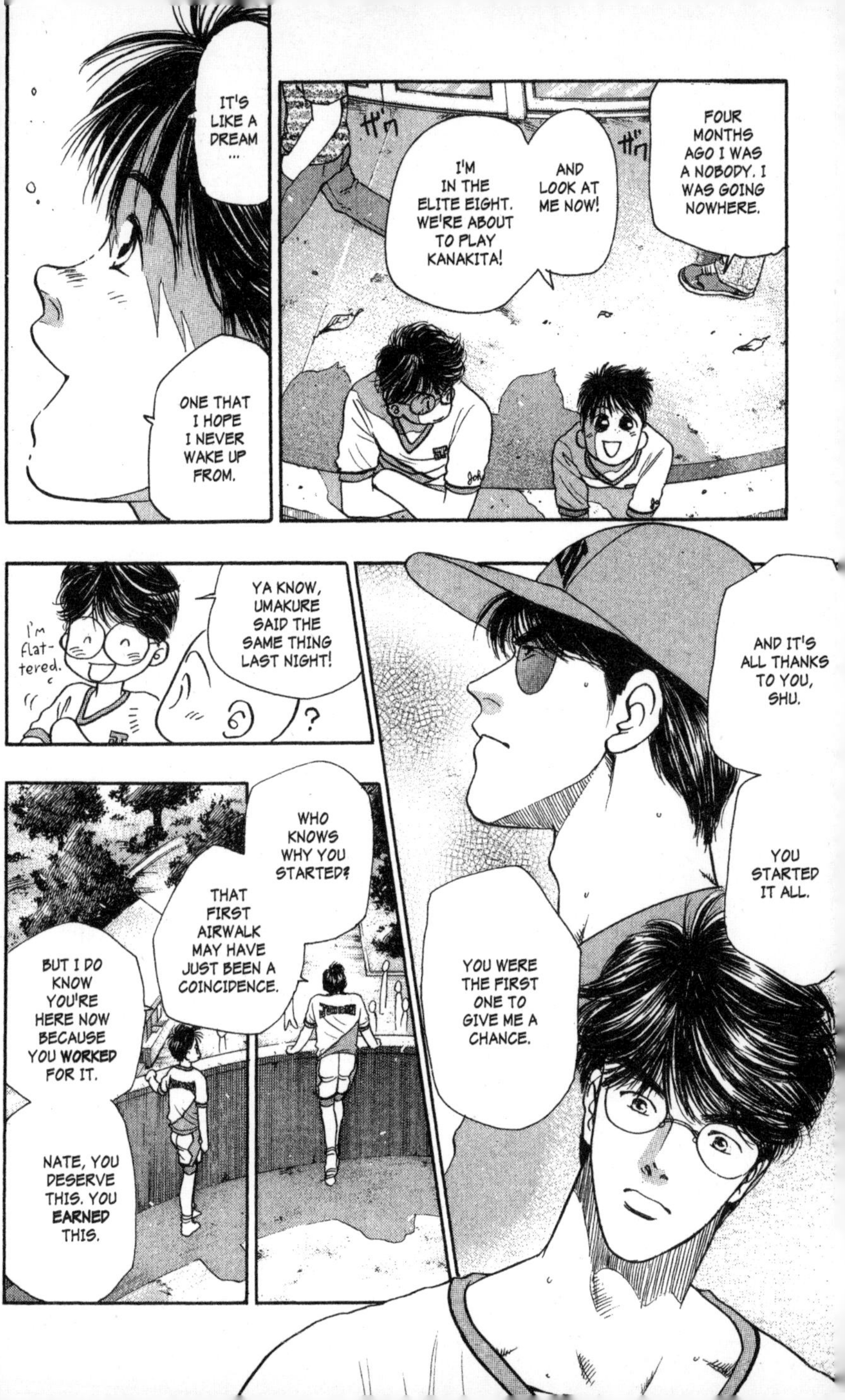

FOUR MONTHS AGO I WAS A NOBODY. I WAS GOING NOWHERE.
AND LOOK AT ME NOW!
I'M IN THE ELITE EIGHT. WE'RE ABOUT TO PLAY KANAKITA!
IT'S LIKE A DREAM ...
ONE THAT I HOPE I NEVER WAKE UP FROM.
AND IT'S ALL THANKS TO YOU, SHU.
YOU STARTED IT ALL.
YOU WERE THE FIRST ONE TO GIVE ME A CHANCE.
YA KNOW, UMAKURE SAID THE SAME THING LAST NIGHT!
I'm flattered.
?
WHO KNOWS WHY YOU STARTED?
THAT FIRST AIRWALK MAY HAVE JUST BEEN A COINCIDENCE.
BUT I DO KNOW YOU'RE HERE NOW BECAUSE YOU **WORKED** FOR IT.
NATE, YOU DESERVE THIS. YOU **EARNED** THIS.

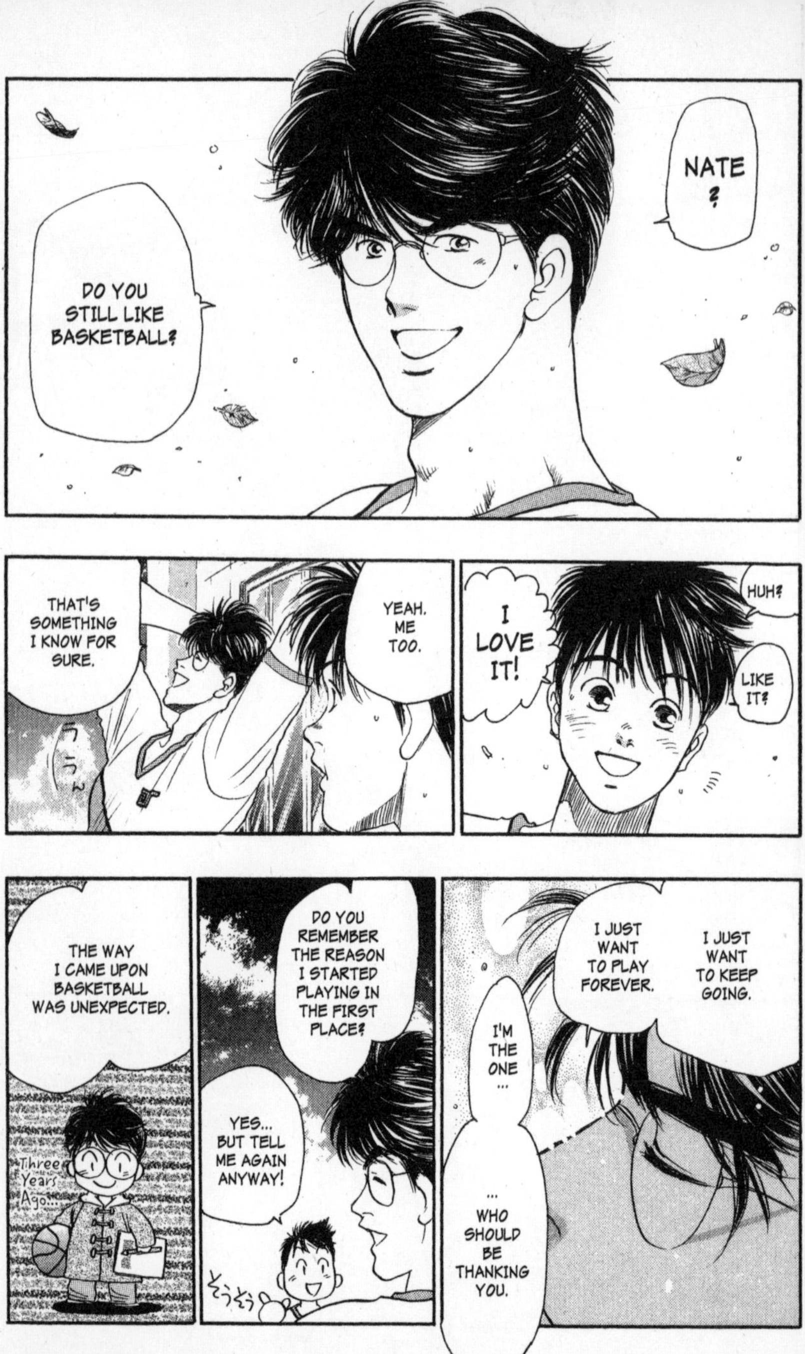

NATE?
DO YOU STILL LIKE BASKETBALL?
HUH?
LIKE IT?
I LOVE IT!
YEAH. ME TOO.
THAT'S SOMETHING I KNOW FOR SURE.
I JUST WANT TO KEEP GOING.
I JUST WANT TO PLAY FOREVER.
I'M THE ONE...
...WHO SHOULD BE THANKING YOU.
DO YOU REMEMBER THE REASON I STARTED PLAYING IN THE FIRST PLACE?
YES... BUT TELL ME AGAIN ANYWAY!
THE WAY I CAME UPON BASKETBALL WAS UNEXPECTED.
Three Years Ago...

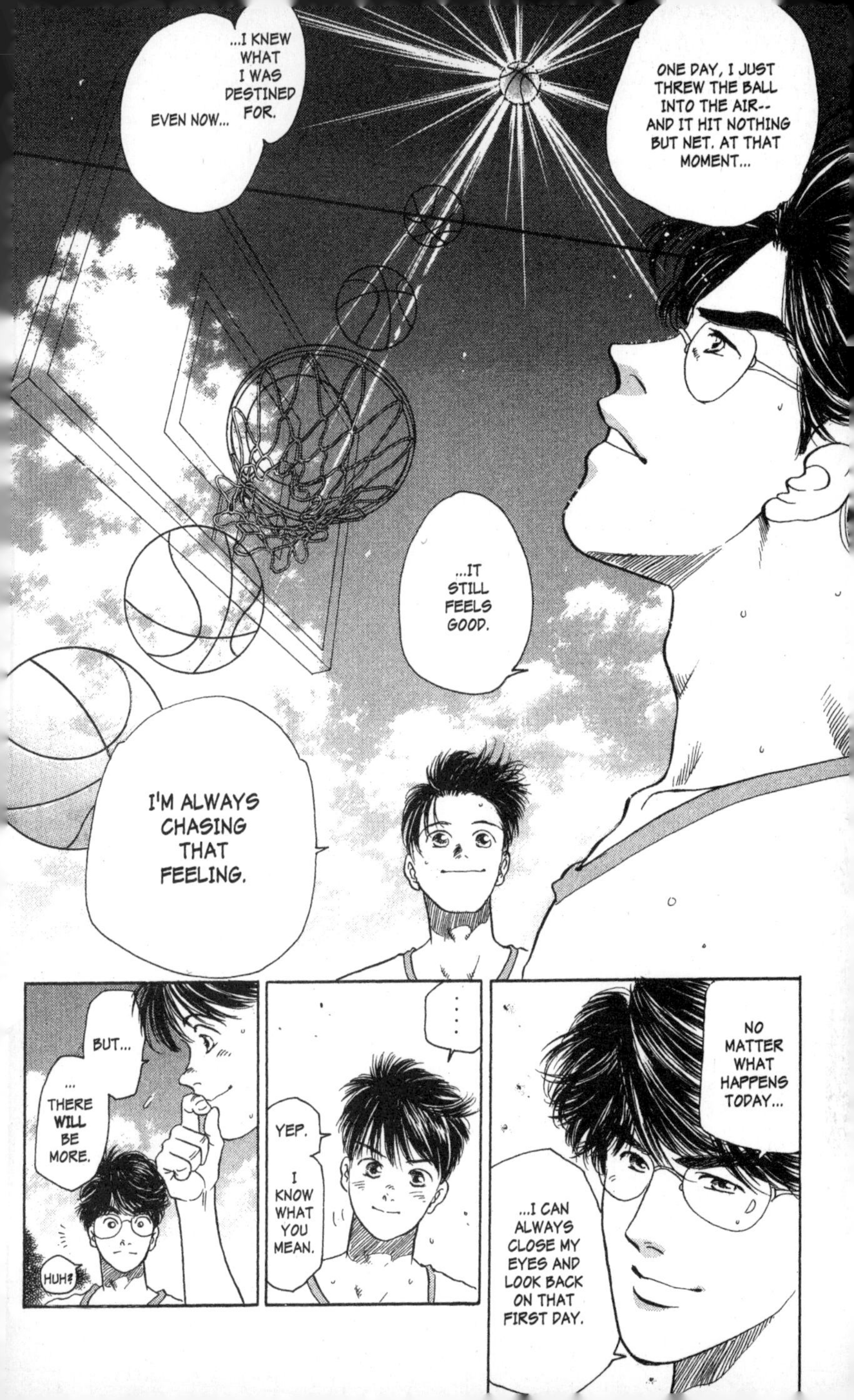
ONE DAY, I JUST THREW THE BALL INTO THE AIR-- AND IT HIT NOTHING BUT NET. AT THAT MOMENT...
...I KNEW WHAT I WAS DESTINED FOR.
EVEN NOW...
...IT STILL FEELS GOOD.
I'M ALWAYS CHASING THAT FEELING.
NO MATTER WHAT HAPPENS TODAY...
...I CAN ALWAYS CLOSE MY EYES AND LOOK BACK ON THAT FIRST DAY.
....
YEP.
I KNOW WHAT YOU MEAN.
BUT...
... THERE **WILL** BE MORE.
HUH?

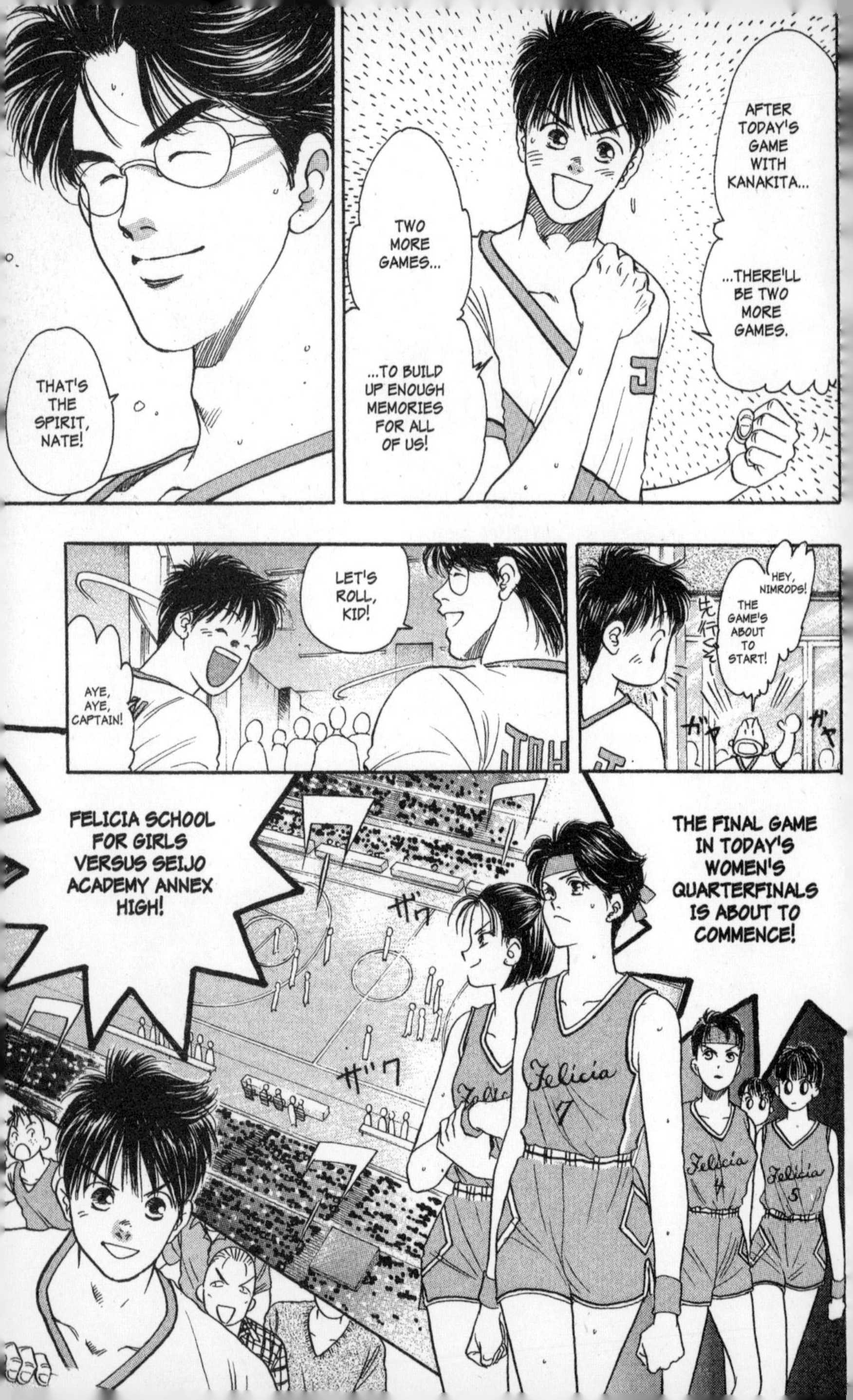
AFTER TODAY'S GAME WITH KANAKITA...
...THERE'LL BE TWO MORE GAMES.
TWO MORE GAMES...
...TO BUILD UP ENOUGH MEMORIES FOR ALL OF US!
THAT'S THE SPIRIT, NATE!
HEY, NIMRODS!
THE GAME'S ABOUT TO START!
ガヤ
ガヤ
LET'S ROLL, KID!
AYE, AYE, CAPTAIN!
THE FINAL GAME IN TODAY'S WOMEN'S QUARTERFINALS IS ABOUT TO COMMENCE!
FELICIA SCHOOL FOR GIRLS VERSUS SEIJO ACADEMY ANNEX HIGH!
ザワ
ザワ

You're Reading…

And now for a paid advertisement…

Are you a brooding teenager? Do you often find yourself unable to smile, unfurrow your brow, or even stop, much less smell the roses? Then you may qualify for Sasuke's new course, "Ten Weeks to Optimum Teenage Angst!" That's right! Buy our course and get your brood on!

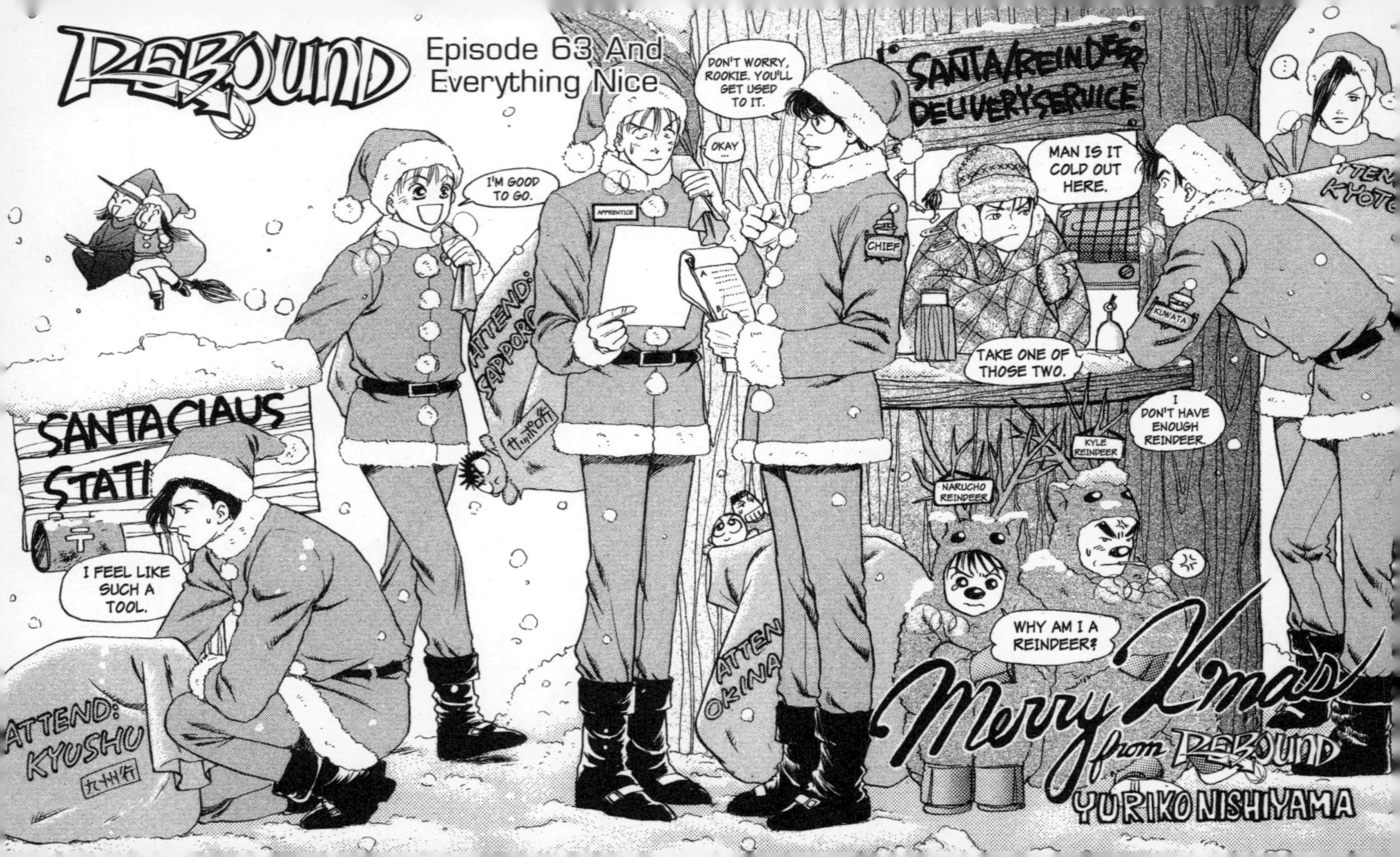

REBOUND
Episode 63 And Everything Nice
SANTA/REINDEER DELIVERY SERVICE
ATTEND: KYOTO
MAN IS IT COLD OUT HERE.
KUWATA
I DON'T HAVE ENOUGH REINDEER.
KYLE REINDEER
TAKE ONE OF THOSE TWO.
CHIEF
DON'T WORRY, ROOKIE. YOU'LL GET USED TO IT.
OKAY ...
APPRENTICE
NARUCHO REINDEER
WHY AM I A REINDEER?
ATTEN OKINA
ATTEND: SAPPORO
I'M GOOD TO GO.
SANTACLAUS STATI
I FEEL LIKE SUCH A TOOL.
ATTEND: KYUSHU
Merry Xmas from REBOUND
YURIKO NISHIYAMA

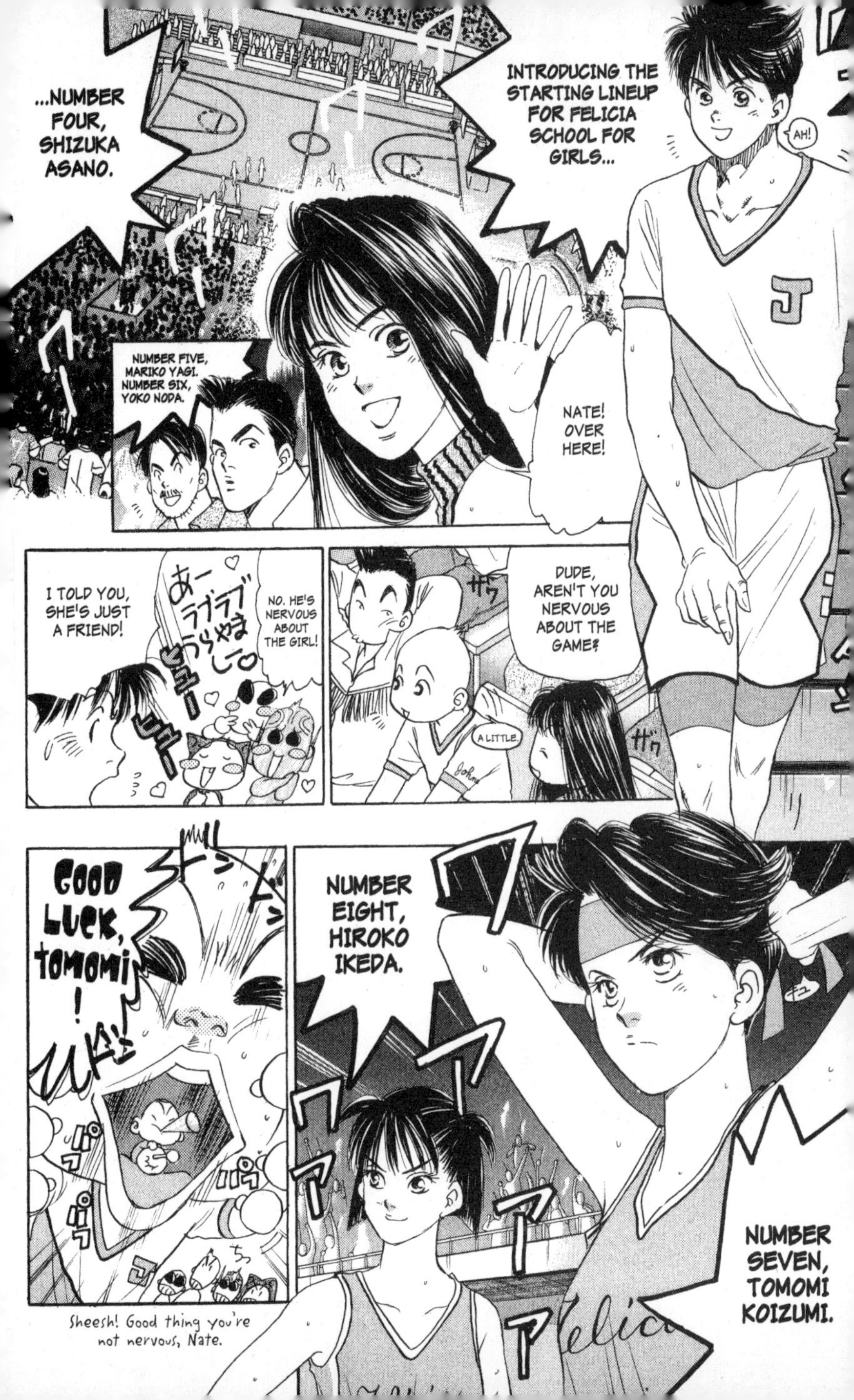

INTRODUCING THE STARTING LINEUP FOR FELICIA SCHOOL FOR GIRLS...
AH!
...NUMBER FOUR, SHIZUKA ASANO.
NATE! OVER HERE!
NUMBER FIVE, MARIKO YAGI. NUMBER SIX, YOKO NODA.
DUDE, AREN'T YOU NERVOUS ABOUT THE GAME?
A LITTLE.
NO. HE'S NERVOUS ABOUT THE GIRL!
あーラブラブうらやましー♡
I TOLD YOU, SHE'S JUST A FRIEND!
NUMBER SEVEN, TOMOMI KOIZUMI.
NUMBER EIGHT, HIROKO IKEDA.
GOOD LUCK, TOMOMI!
Sheesh! Good thing you're not nervous, Nate.

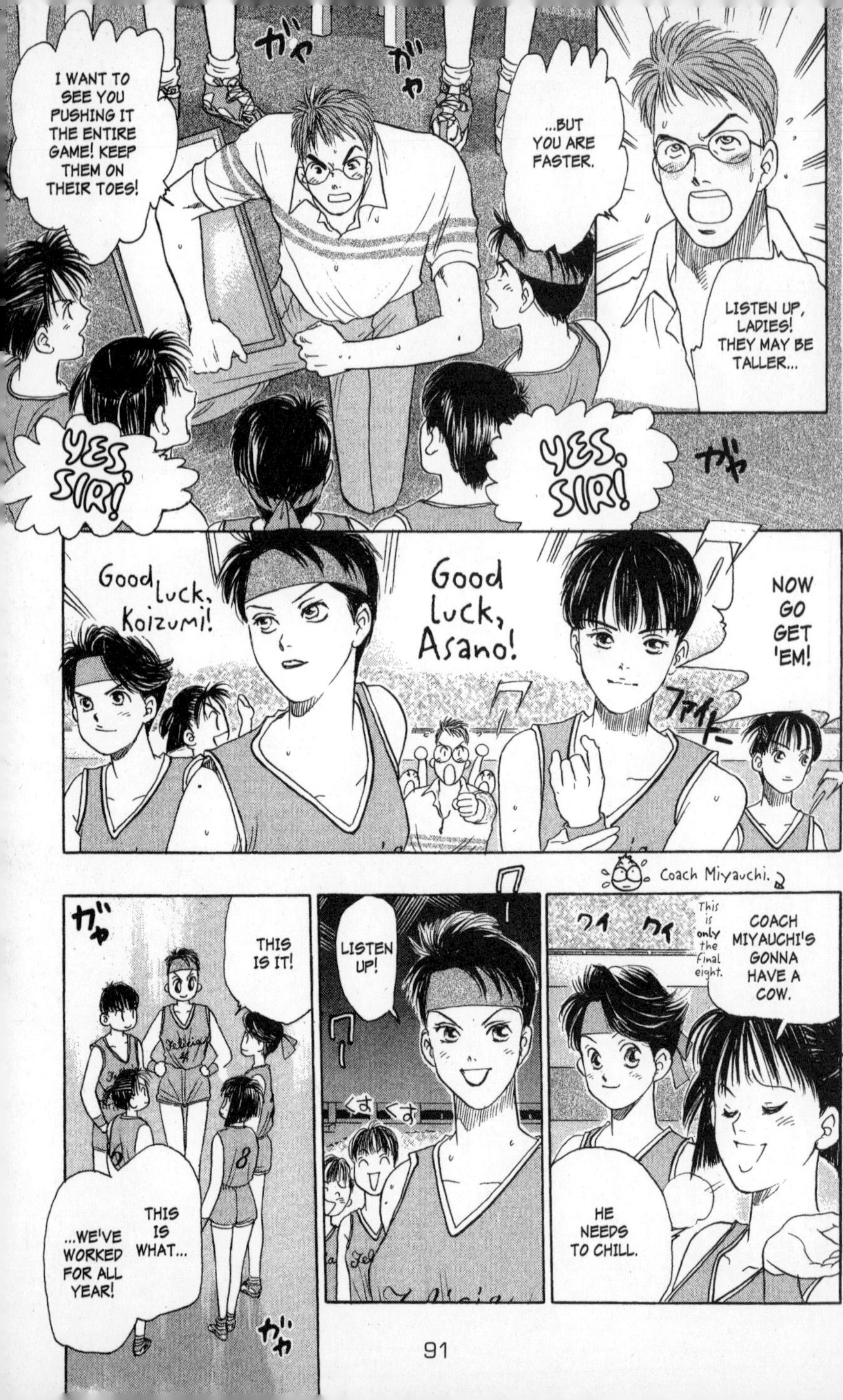
LISTEN UP, LADIES! THEY MAY BE TALLER...
...BUT YOU ARE FASTER.
がや
ガヤ
I WANT TO SEE YOU PUSHING IT THE ENTIRE GAME! KEEP THEM ON THEIR TOES!
がや
YES, SIR!
YES, SIR!
NOW GO GET 'EM!
ファイトー
Good luck, Asano!
Good luck, Koizumi!
Coach Miyauchi.
ワイ ワイ
This is only the final eight.
COACH MIYAUCHI'S GONNA HAVE A COW.
HE NEEDS TO CHILL.
LISTEN UP!
くすくす
ガヤ
THIS IS IT!
THIS IS WHAT...
...WE'VE WORKED FOR ALL YEAR!
がや

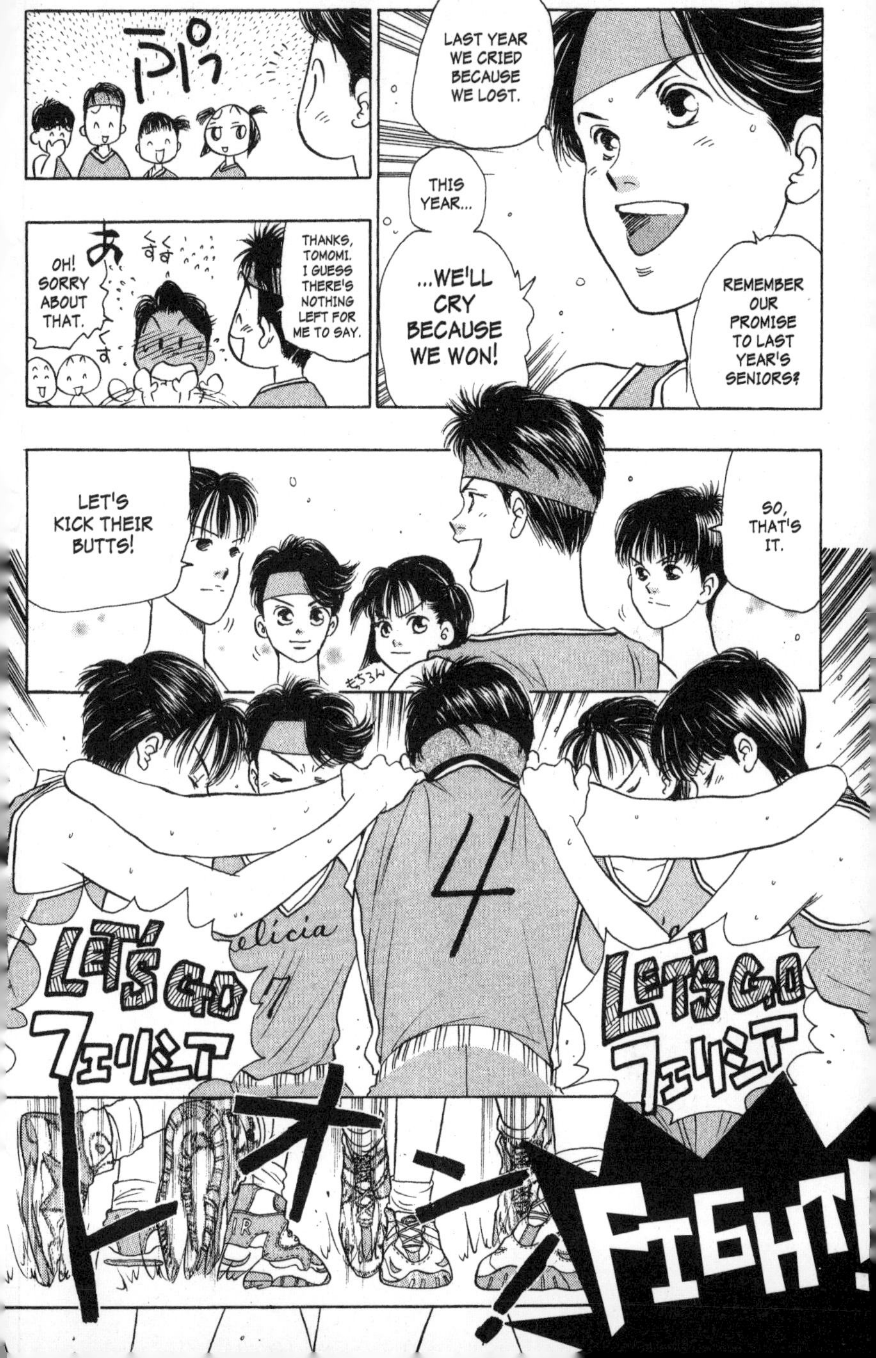
REMEMBER OUR PROMISE TO LAST YEAR'S SENIORS?
LAST YEAR WE CRIED BECAUSE WE LOST.
THIS YEAR...
...WE'LL CRY BECAUSE WE WON!
ぷぷっ
THANKS, TOMOMI. I GUESS THERE'S NOTHING LEFT FOR ME TO SAY.
あ
くすくす
OH! SORRY ABOUT THAT.
くすくす
SO, THAT'S IT.
もちろん
LET'S KICK THEIR BUTTS!
LET'S GO フェリシア
LET'S GO フェリシア
トオー!
FIGHT!

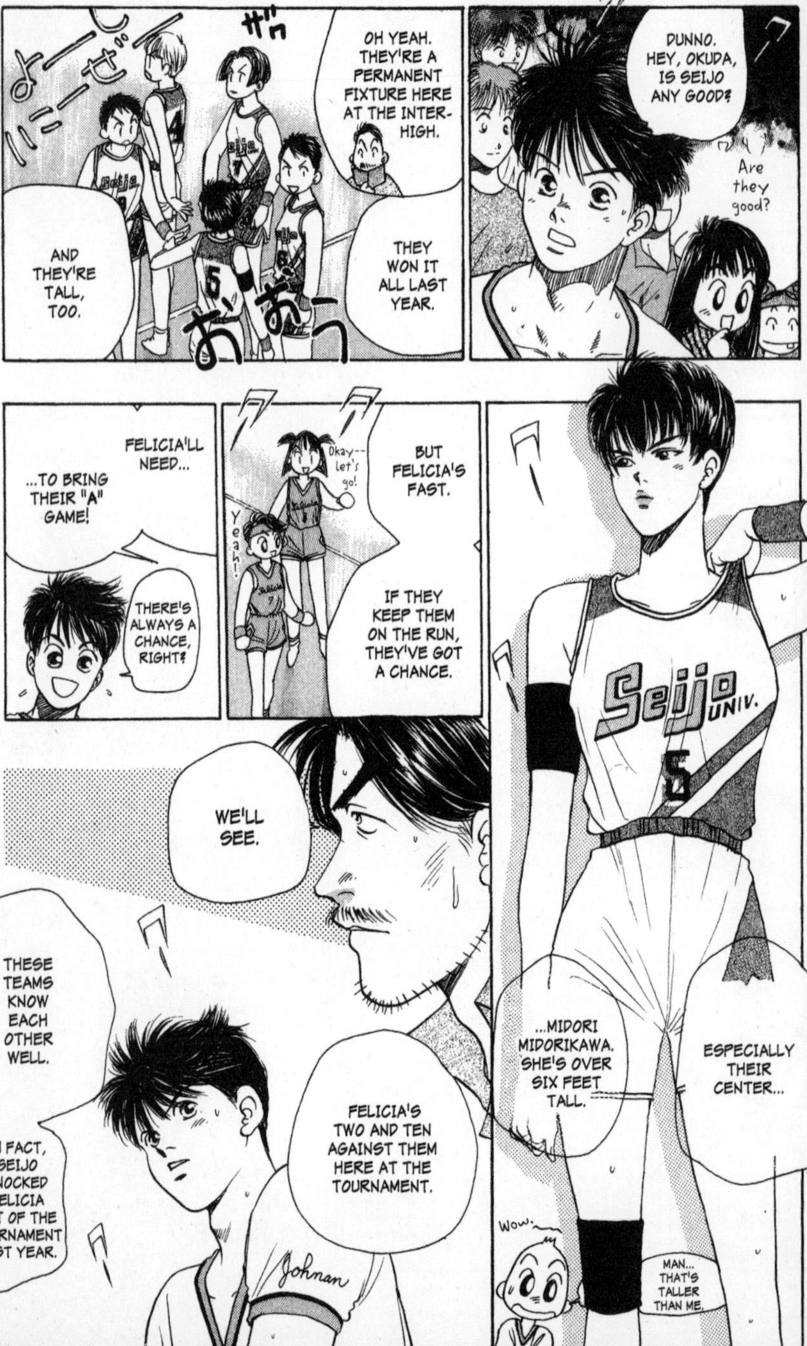
DUNNO. HEY, OKUDA, IS SEIJO ANY GOOD?
Are they good?
よーしいこーぜ
ザッ
OH YEAH. THEY'RE A PERMANENT FIXTURE HERE AT THE INTER-HIGH.
THEY WON IT ALL LAST YEAR.
AND THEY'RE TALL, TOO.
おおっ
ESPECIALLY THEIR CENTER...
...MIDORI MIDORIKAWA. SHE'S OVER SIX FEET TALL.
Seijo UNIV.
Wow.
MAN... THAT'S TALLER THAN ME.
BUT FELICIA'S FAST.
IF THEY KEEP THEM ON THE RUN, THEY'VE GOT A CHANCE.
Okay--let's go!
Yeah!
FELICIA'LL NEED...
...TO BRING THEIR "A" GAME!
THERE'S ALWAYS A CHANCE, RIGHT?
WE'LL SEE.
FELICIA'S TWO AND TEN AGAINST THEM HERE AT THE TOURNAMENT.
THESE TEAMS KNOW EACH OTHER WELL.
IN FACT, SEIJO KNOCKED FELICIA OUT OF THE TOURNAMENT LAST YEAR.
Johnan

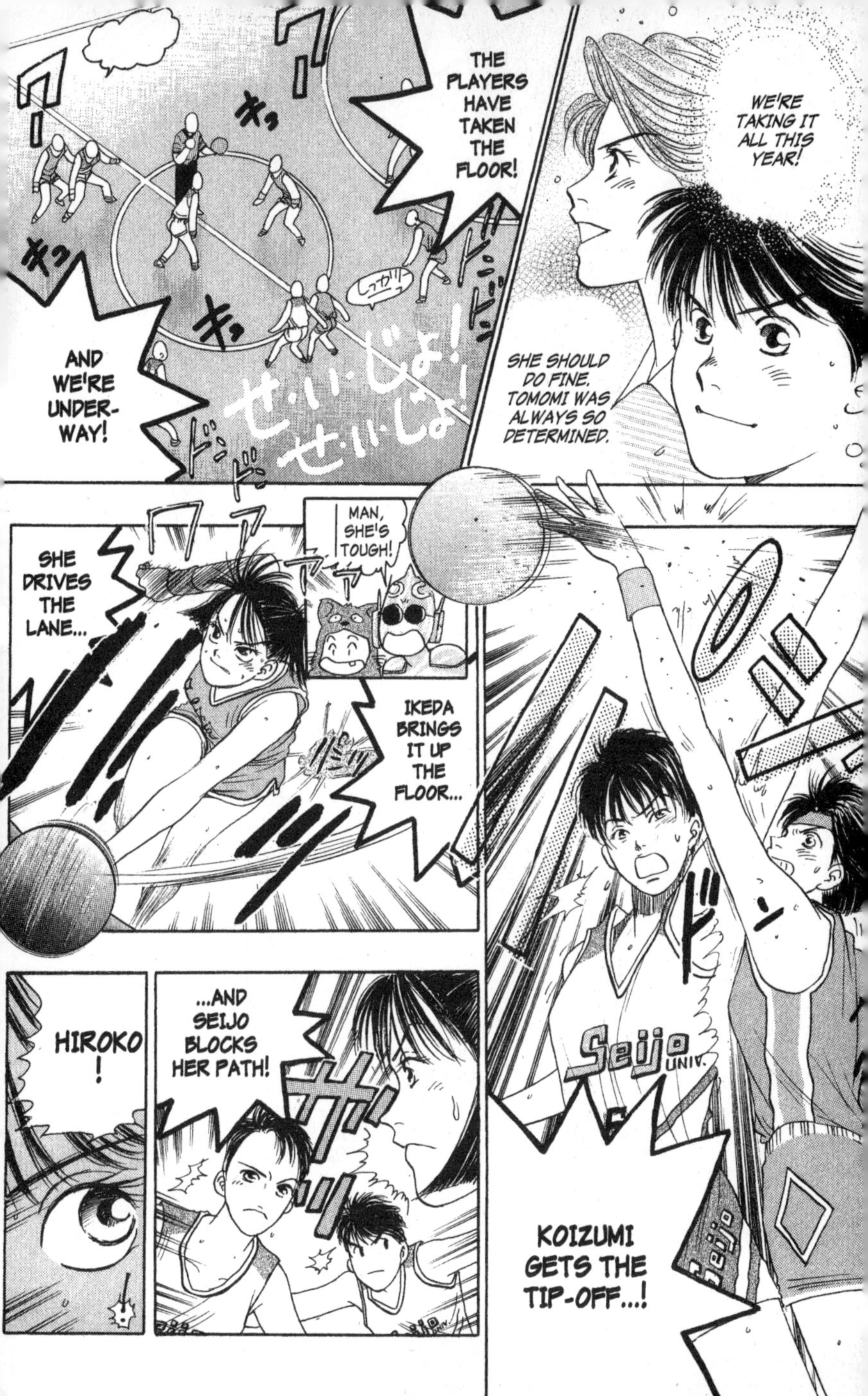

WE'RE TAKING IT ALL THIS YEAR!
SHE SHOULD DO FINE. TOMOMI WAS ALWAYS SO DETERMINED.
THE PLAYERS HAVE TAKEN THE FLOOR!
せ・い・じょ! せ・い・じょ!
AND WE'RE UNDER-WAY!
KOIZUMI GETS THE TIP-OFF...!
Seijo UNIV.
IKEDA BRINGS IT UP THE FLOOR...
MAN, SHE'S TOUGH!
SHE DRIVES THE LANE...
...AND SEIJO BLOCKS HER PATH!
HIROKO!

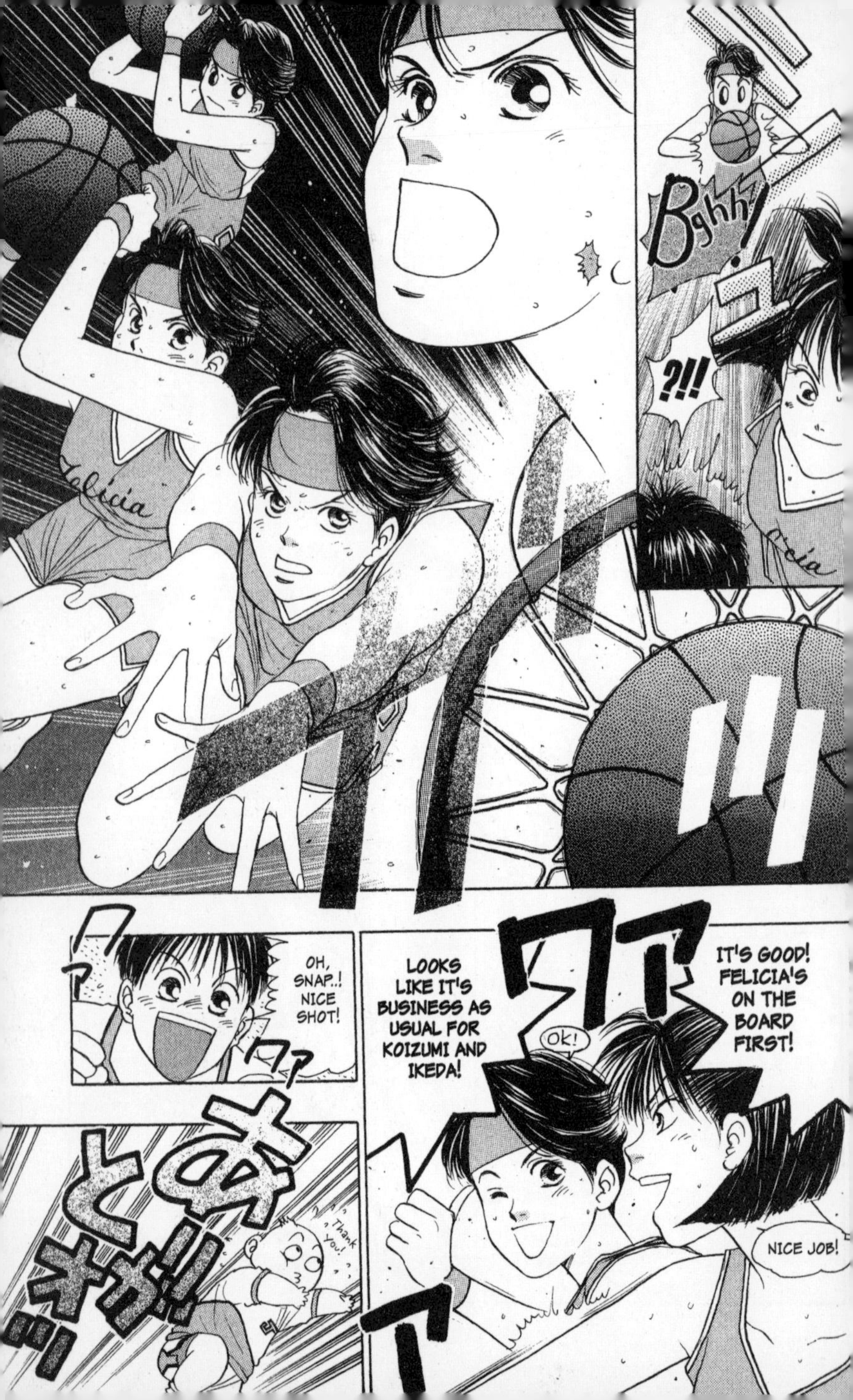
Bghh!
?!!
IT'S GOOD! FELICIA'S ON THE BOARD FIRST!
LOOKS LIKE IT'S BUSINESS AS USUAL FOR KOIZUMI AND IKEDA!
Ok!
NICE JOB!
OH, SNAP..! NICE SHOT!
Thank you!

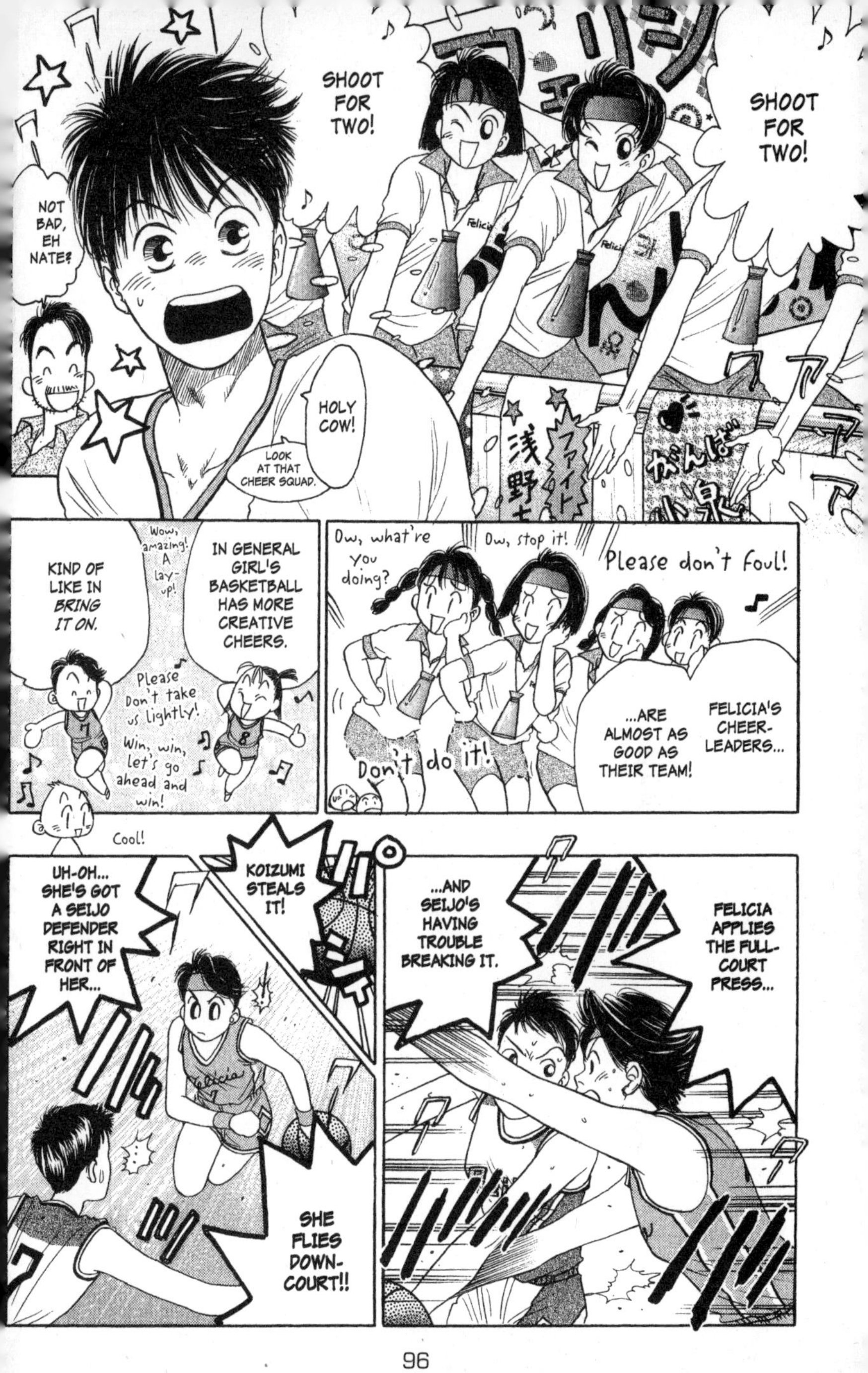
SHOOT FOR TWO!
SHOOT FOR TWO!
HOLY COW!
LOOK AT THAT CHEER SQUAD.
NOT BAD, EH NATE?
FELICIA'S CHEER-LEADERS...
...ARE ALMOST AS GOOD AS THEIR TEAM!
Please don't foul!
Ow, stop it!
Ow, what're you doing?
Don't do it!
IN GENERAL GIRL'S BASKETBALL HAS MORE CREATIVE CHEERS.
Wow, amazing! A lay-up!
KIND OF LIKE IN *BRING IT ON.*
Please Don't take us lightly!
Win, win, let's go ahead and win!
Cool!
FELICIA APPLIES THE FULL-COURT PRESS...
...AND SEIJO'S HAVING TROUBLE BREAKING IT.
KOIZUMI STEALS IT!
UH-OH... SHE'S GOT A SEIJO DEFENDER RIGHT IN FRONT OF HER...
SHE FLIES DOWN-COURT!!

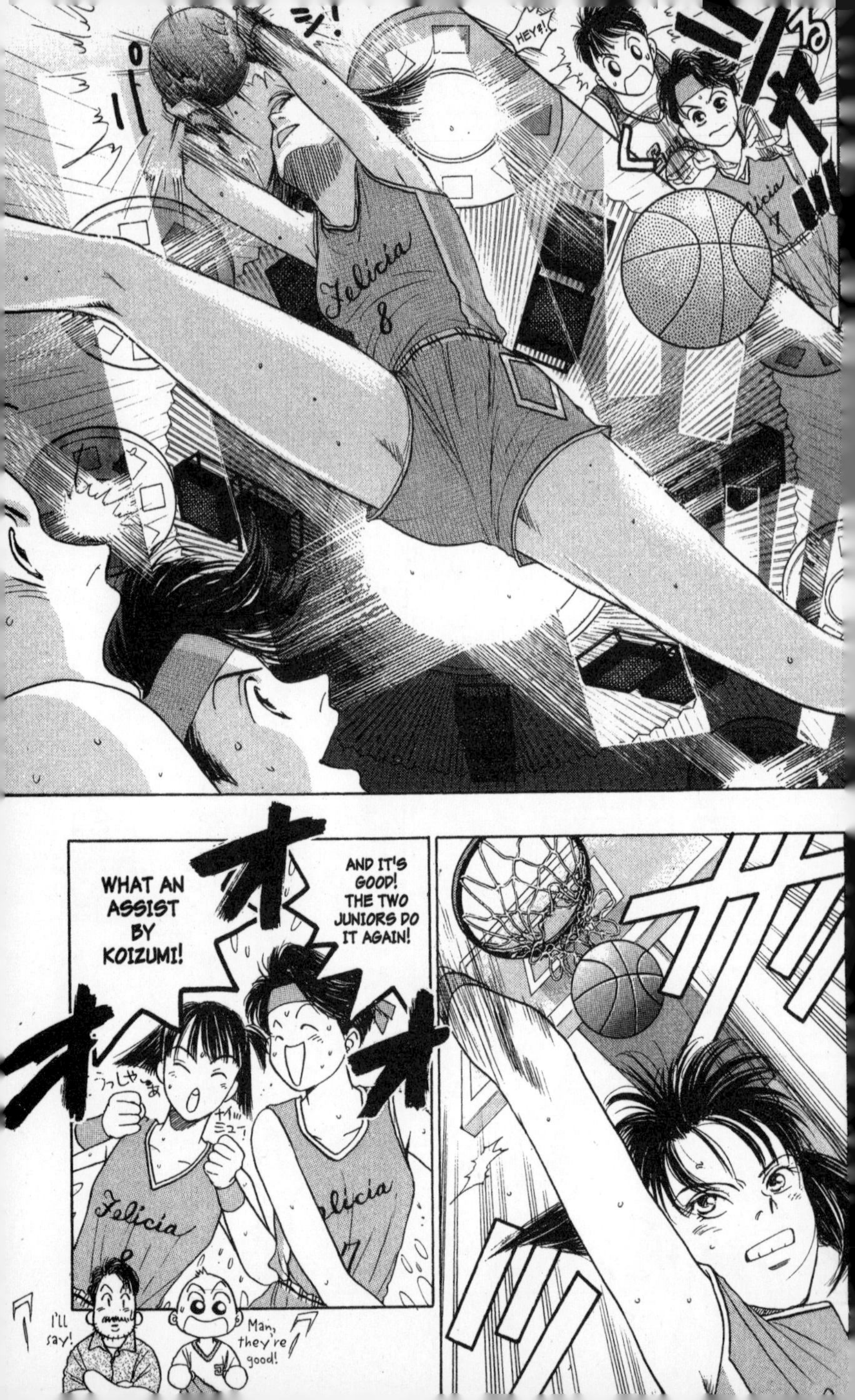
HEY?!
Felicia
8
AND IT'S GOOD! THE TWO JUNIORS DO IT AGAIN!
WHAT AN ASSIST BY KOIZUMI!
Felicia
Felicia
Man, they're good!
I'll say!

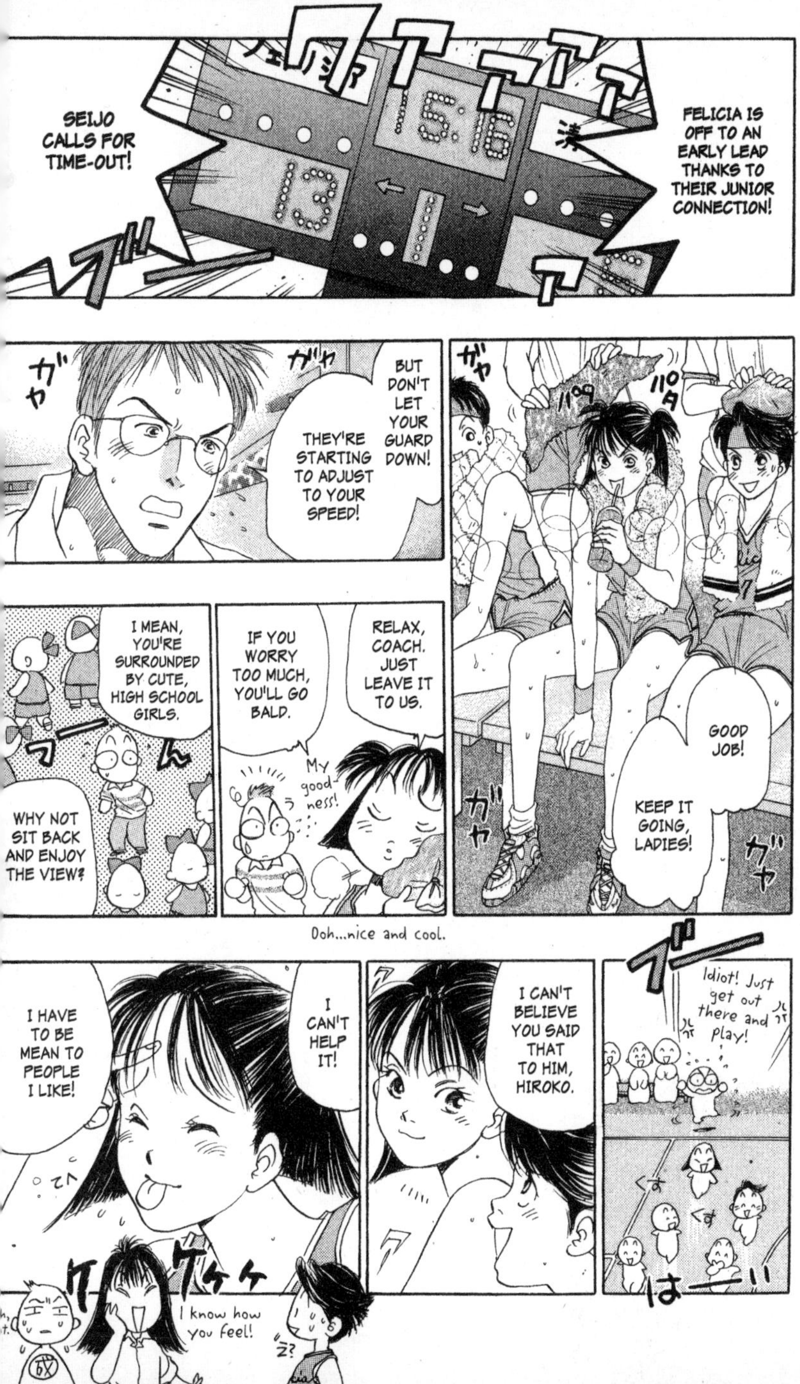
FELICIA IS OFF TO AN EARLY LEAD THANKS TO THEIR JUNIOR CONNECTION!
SEIJO CALLS FOR TIME-OUT!
GOOD JOB!
KEEP IT GOING, LADIES!
BUT DON'T LET YOUR GUARD DOWN!
THEY'RE STARTING TO ADJUST TO YOUR SPEED!
RELAX, COACH. JUST LEAVE IT TO US.
IF YOU WORRY TOO MUCH, YOU'LL GO BALD.
My goodness!
I MEAN, YOU'RE SURROUNDED BY CUTE, HIGH SCHOOL GIRLS.
WHY NOT SIT BACK AND ENJOY THE VIEW?
Ooh...nice and cool.
Idiot! Just get out there and play!
I CAN'T BELIEVE YOU SAID THAT TO HIM, HIROKO.
I CAN'T HELP IT!
I HAVE TO BE MEAN TO PEOPLE I LIKE!
I know how you feel!

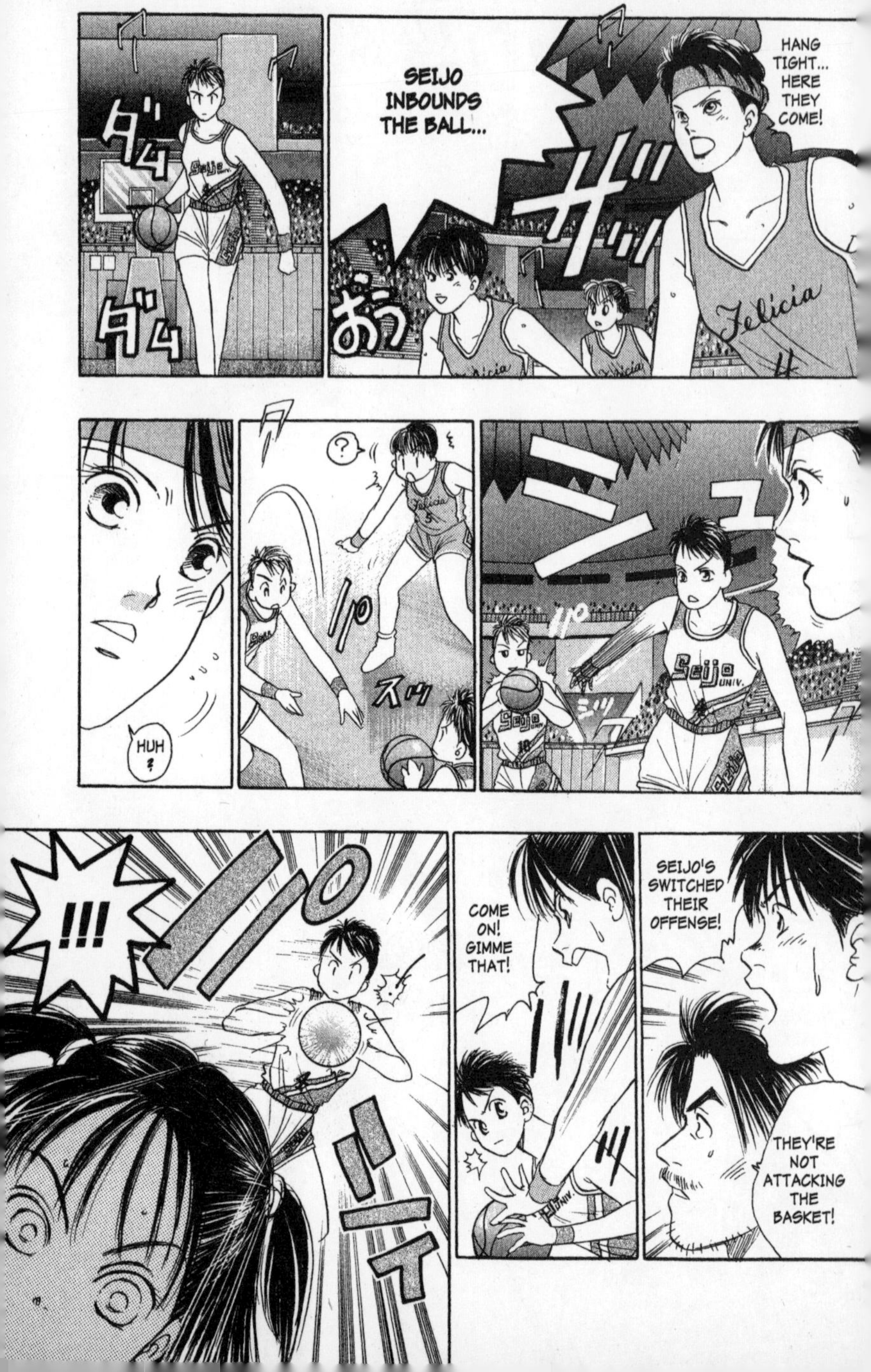

HANG TIGHT... HERE THEY COME!
ザッ
SEIJO INBOUNDS THE BALL...
おっ
ダム
ダム
パ
?
パ
スッ
HUH?
SEIJO'S SWITCHED THEIR OFFENSE!
THEY'RE NOT ATTACKING THE BASKET!
COME ON! GIMME THAT!
!!!

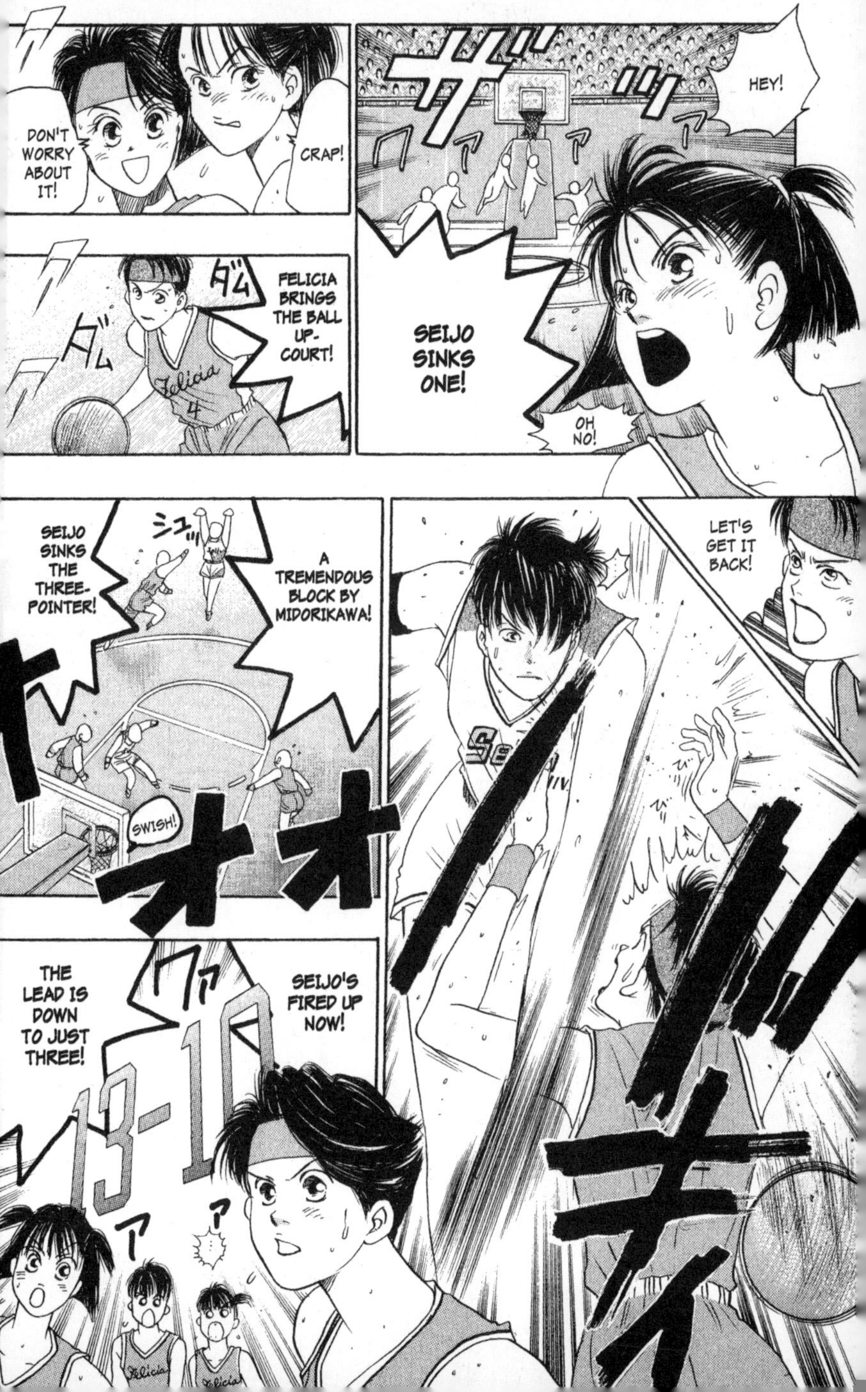
HEY!
SEIJO SINKS ONE!
OH NO!
CRAP!
DON'T WORRY ABOUT IT!
FELICIA BRINGS THE BALL UP-COURT!
LET'S GET IT BACK!
A TREMENDOUS BLOCK BY MIDORIKAWA!
SEIJO SINKS THE THREE-POINTER!
SWISH!
SEIJO'S FIRED UP NOW!
THE LEAD IS DOWN TO JUST THREE!
13-10

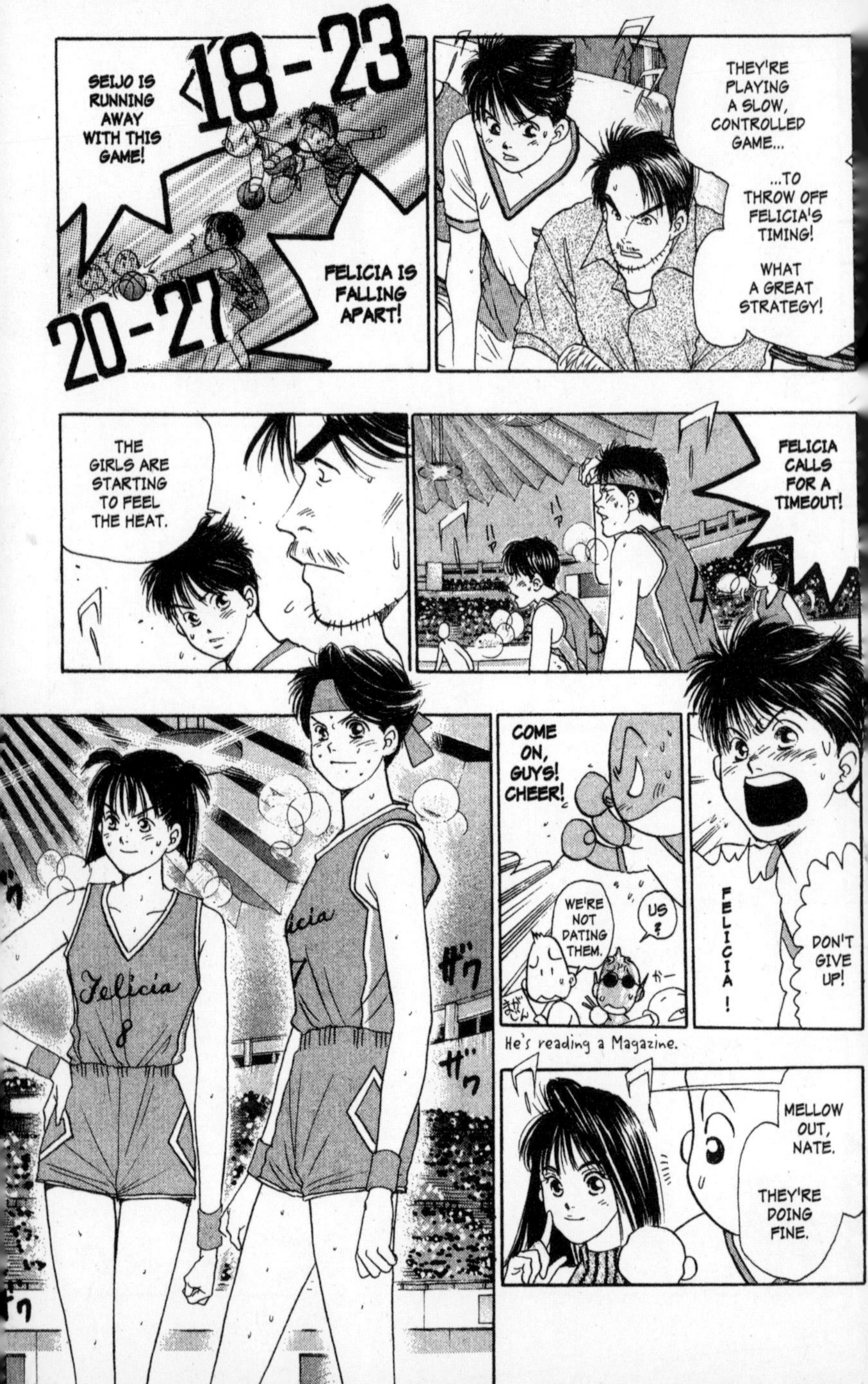
THEY'RE PLAYING A SLOW, CONTROLLED GAME...
...TO THROW OFF FELICIA'S TIMING!
WHAT A GREAT STRATEGY!
18-23
SEIJO IS RUNNING AWAY WITH THIS GAME!
FELICIA IS FALLING APART!
20-27
FELICIA CALLS FOR A TIMEOUT!
THE GIRLS ARE STARTING TO FEEL THE HEAT.
FELICIA!
DON'T GIVE UP!
COME ON, GUYS! CHEER!
US?
WE'RE NOT DATING THEM.
He's reading a Magazine.
MELLOW OUT, NATE.
THEY'RE DOING FINE.
ザワ
ザワ

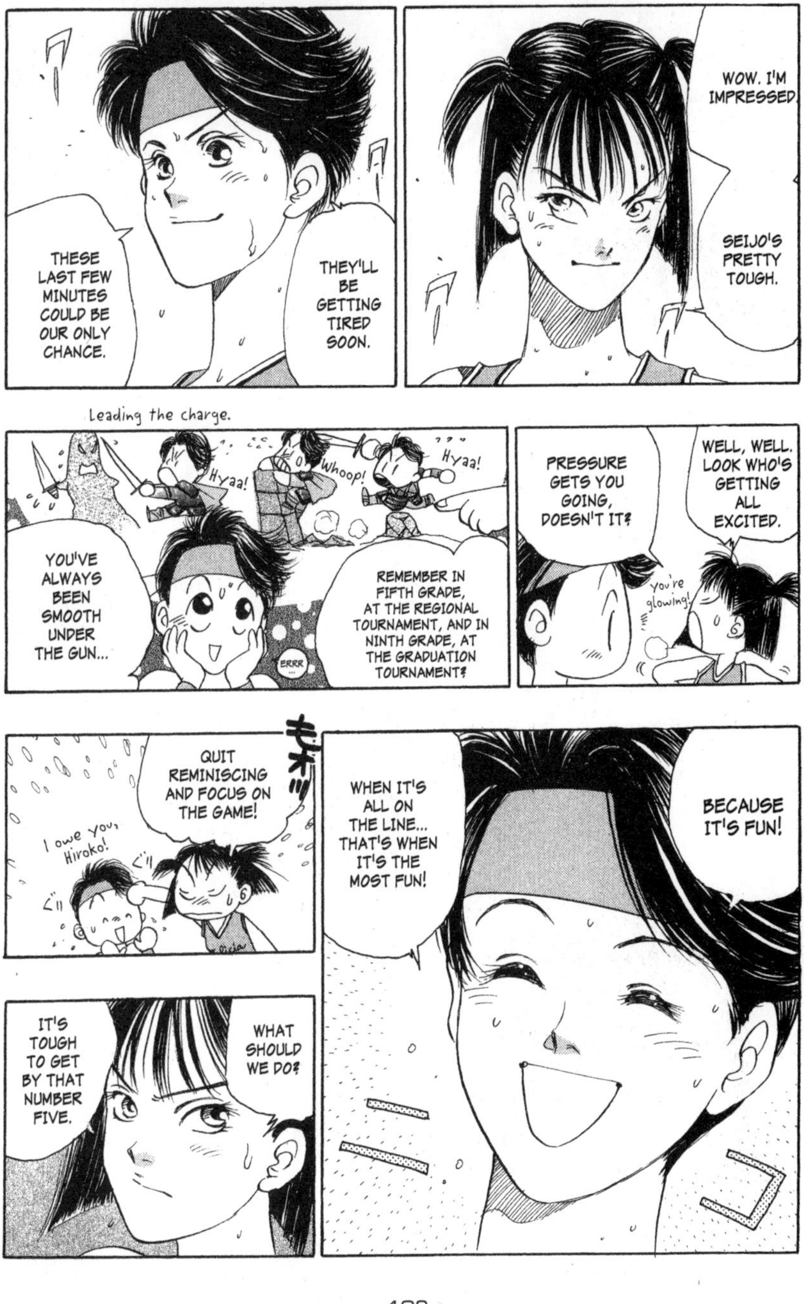
WOW. I'M IMPRESSED.
SEIJO'S PRETTY TOUGH.
THEY'LL BE GETTING TIRED SOON.
THESE LAST FEW MINUTES COULD BE OUR ONLY CHANCE.
WELL, WELL. LOOK WHO'S GETTING ALL EXCITED.
PRESSURE GETS YOU GOING, DOESN'T IT?
You're glowing!
Leading the charge.
Hyaa!
Whoop!
Hyaa!
REMEMBER IN FIFTH GRADE, AT THE REGIONAL TOURNAMENT, AND IN NINTH GRADE, AT THE GRADUATION TOURNAMENT?
YOU'VE ALWAYS BEEN SMOOTH UNDER THE GUN...
ERRR...
BECAUSE IT'S FUN!
WHEN IT'S ALL ON THE LINE... THAT'S WHEN IT'S THE MOST FUN!
QUIT REMINISCING AND FOCUS ON THE GAME!
I owe you, Hiroko!
WHAT SHOULD WE DO?
IT'S TOUGH TO GET BY THAT NUMBER FIVE.

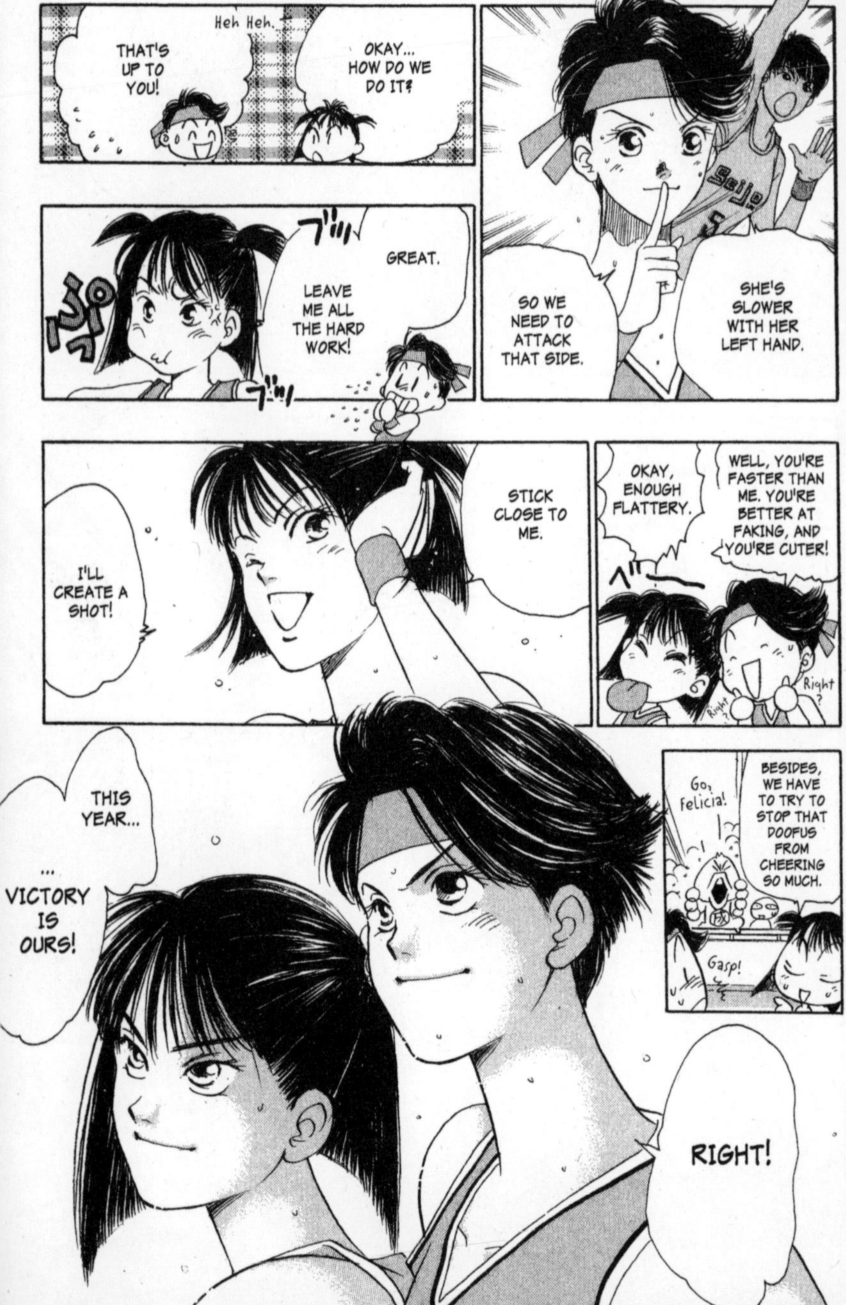
SHE'S SLOWER WITH HER LEFT HAND.
SO WE NEED TO ATTACK THAT SIDE.
OKAY... HOW DO WE DO IT?
Heh Heh.
THAT'S UP TO YOU!
GREAT.
LEAVE ME ALL THE HARD WORK!
WELL, YOU'RE FASTER THAN ME. YOU'RE BETTER AT FAKING, AND YOU'RE CUTER!
OKAY, ENOUGH FLATTERY.
Right?
Right?
STICK CLOSE TO ME.
I'LL CREATE A SHOT!
BESIDES, WE HAVE TO TRY TO STOP THAT DOOFUS FROM CHEERING SO MUCH.
Go, Felicia!
Gasp!
THIS YEAR...
... VICTORY IS OURS!
RIGHT!

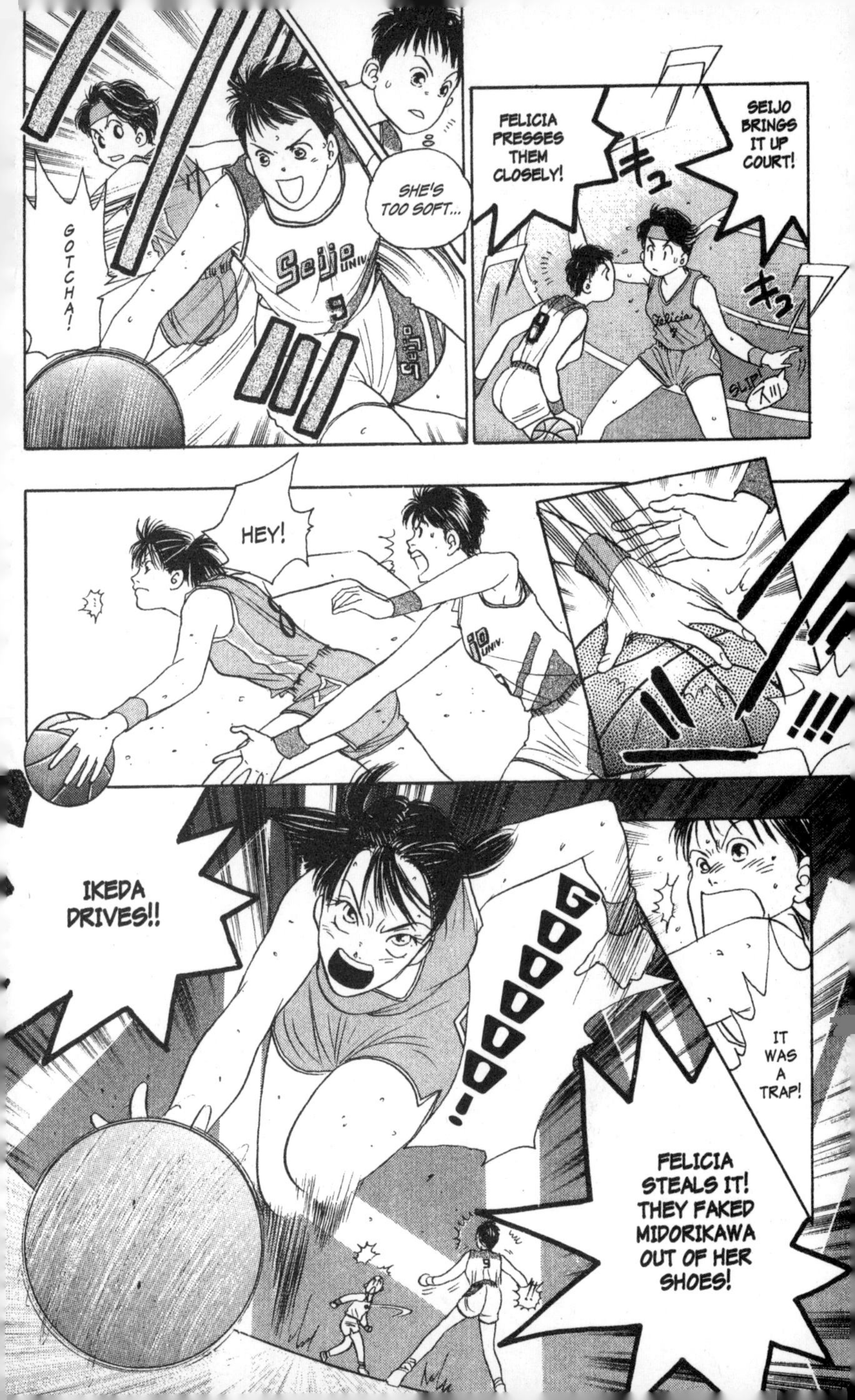
SEIJO BRINGS IT UP COURT!
FELICIA PRESSES THEM CLOSELY!
キュ
キュ
SLIP!
SHE'S TOO SOFT...
GOTCHA!
!!!
HEY!
IT WAS A TRAP!
GOOOOOO!
IKEDA DRIVES!!
FELICIA STEALS IT! THEY FAKED MIDORIKAWA OUT OF HER SHOES!

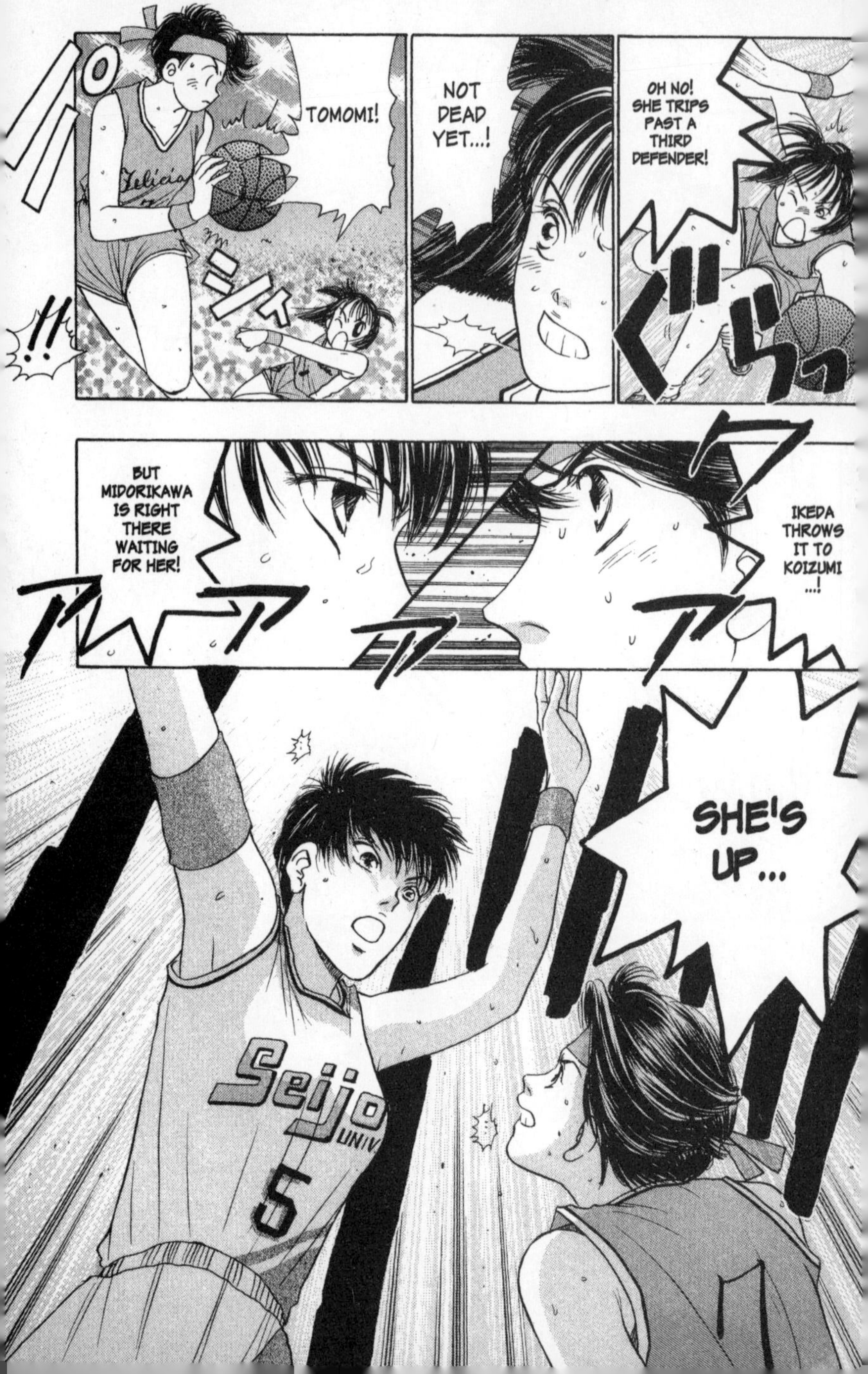
OH NO! SHE TRIPS PAST A THIRD DEFENDER!
NOT DEAD YET...!
TOMOMI!
!!
IKEDA THROWS IT TO KOIZUMI ...!
BUT MIDORIKAWA IS RIGHT THERE WAITING FOR HER!
SHE'S UP...
Seijo UNIV
5

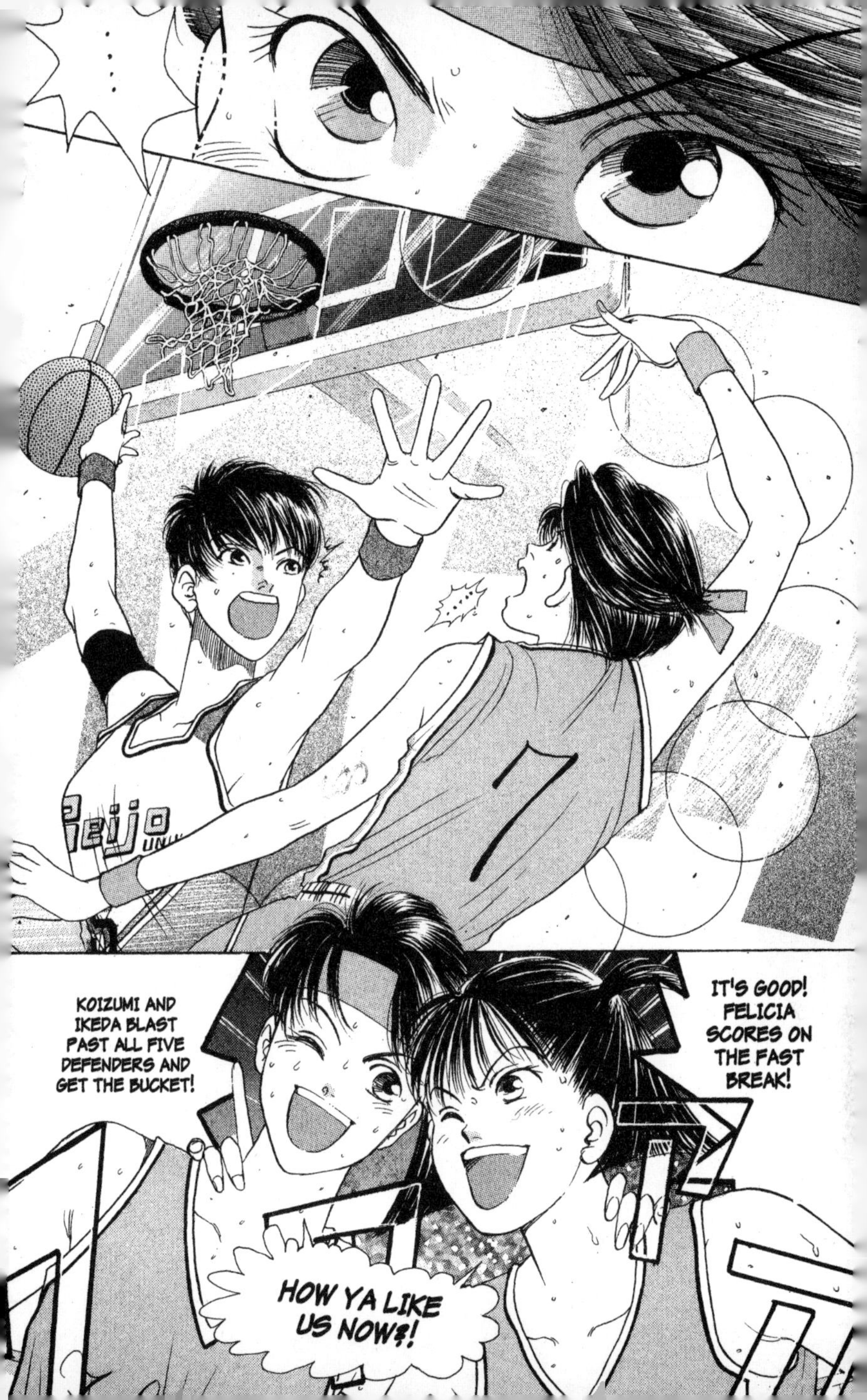
IT'S GOOD! FELICIA SCORES ON THE FAST BREAK!
KOIZUMI AND IKEDA BLAST PAST ALL FIVE DEFENDERS AND GET THE BUCKET!
HOW YA LIKE US NOW?!

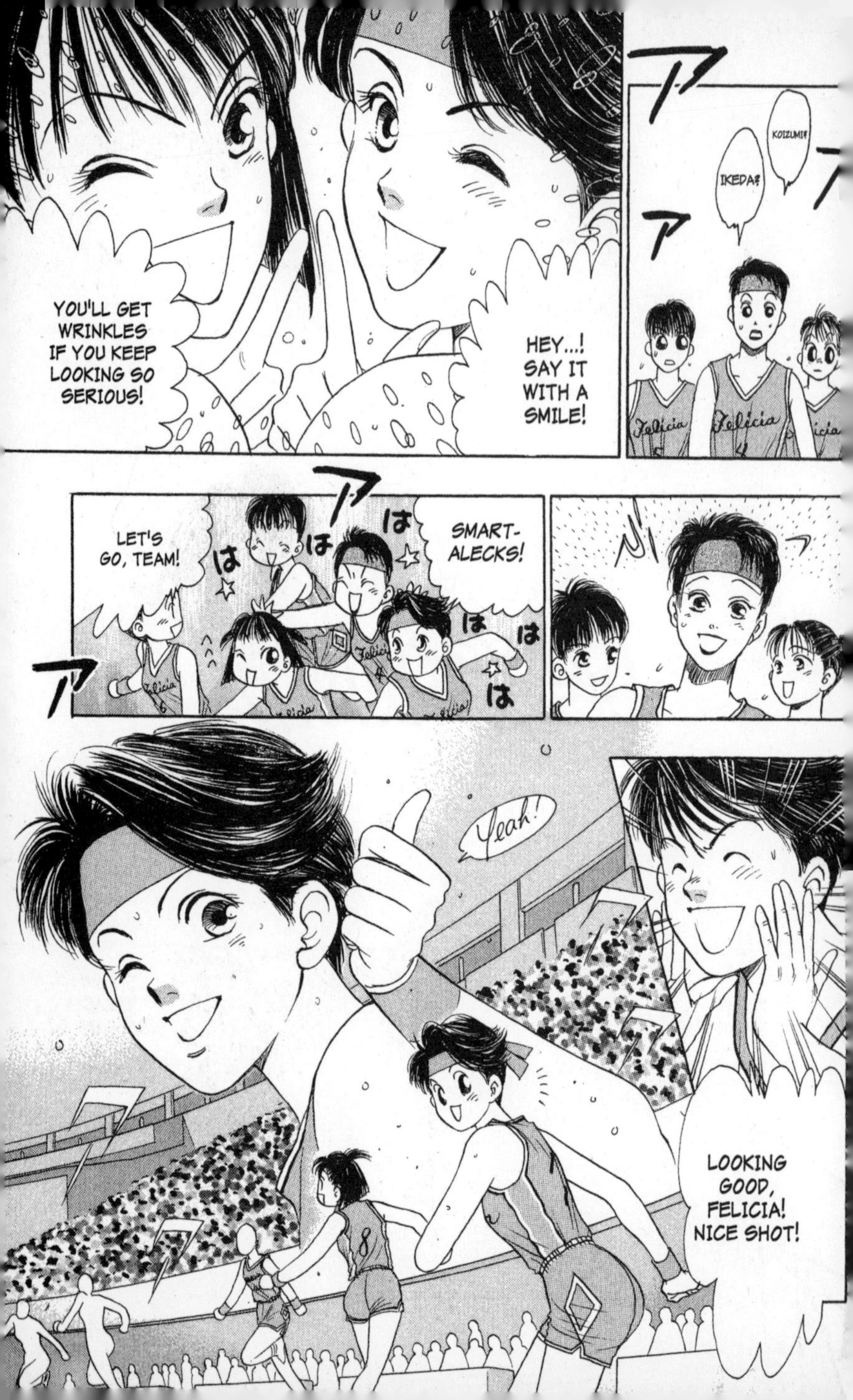

KOIZUMI?
IKEDA?
HEY...! SAY IT WITH A SMILE!
YOU'LL GET WRINKLES IF YOU KEEP LOOKING SO SERIOUS!
SMART-ALECKS!
LET'S GO, TEAM!
LOOKING GOOD, FELICIA! NICE SHOT!
Yeah!

You're Reading...

REBOUND

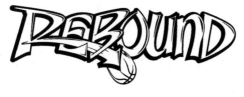

REBOUND

# Episode 64
# Girls Gone Wild!

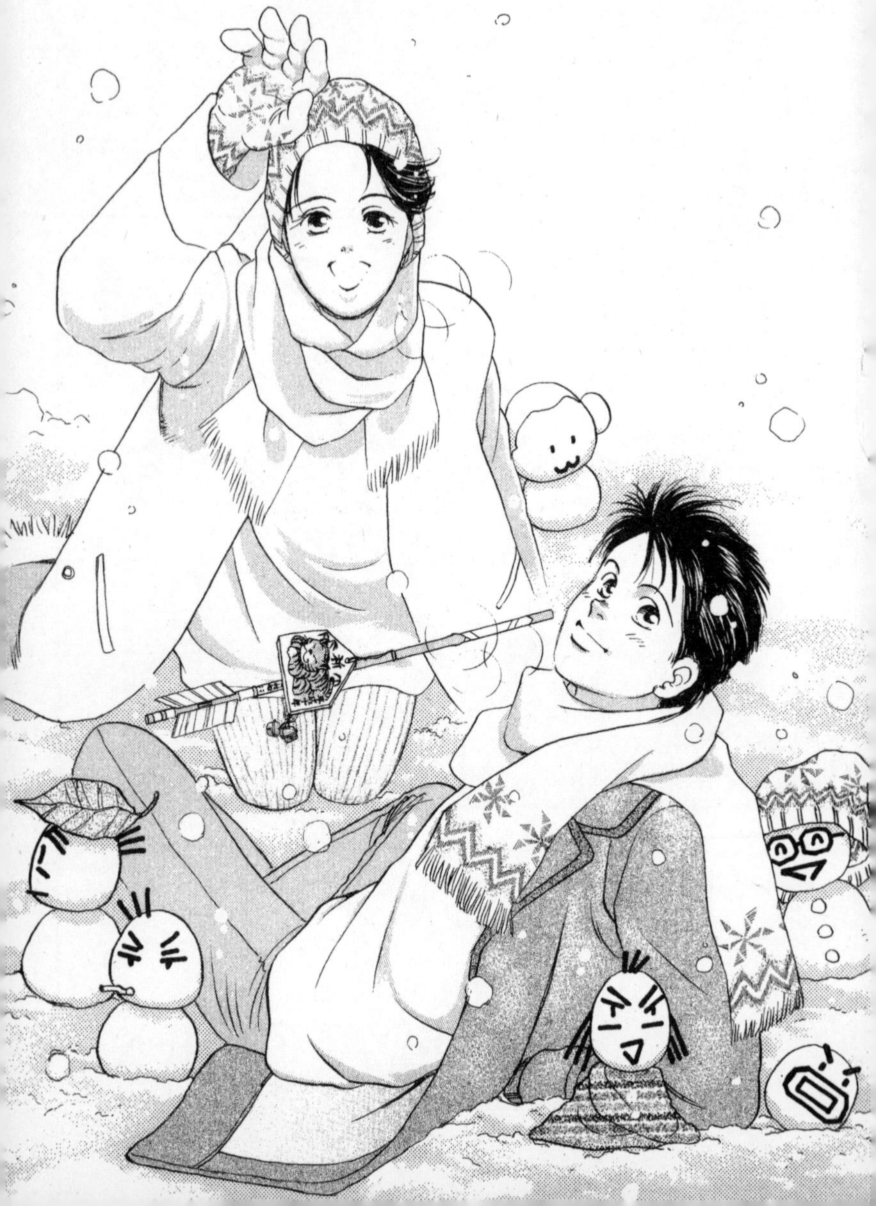

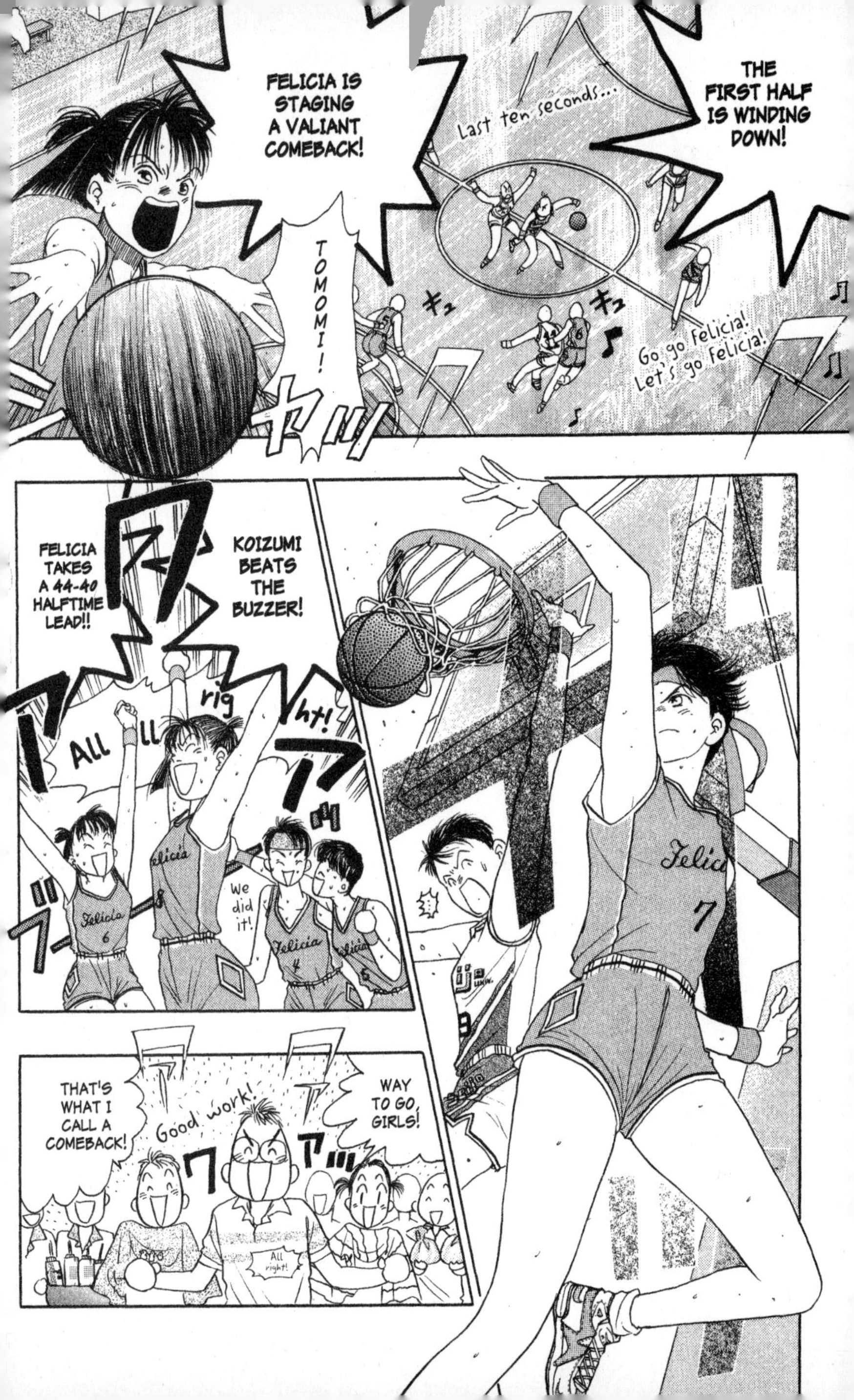
THE FIRST HALF IS WINDING DOWN!
Last ten seconds...
FELICIA IS STAGING A VALIANT COMEBACK!
Go go Felicia! Let's go Felicia!
TOMOMI!
KOIZUMI BEATS THE BUZZER!
FELICIA TAKES A 44-40 HALFTIME LEAD!!
All right!
We did it!
WAY TO GO, GIRLS!
Good work!
THAT'S WHAT I CALL A COMEBACK!
All right!

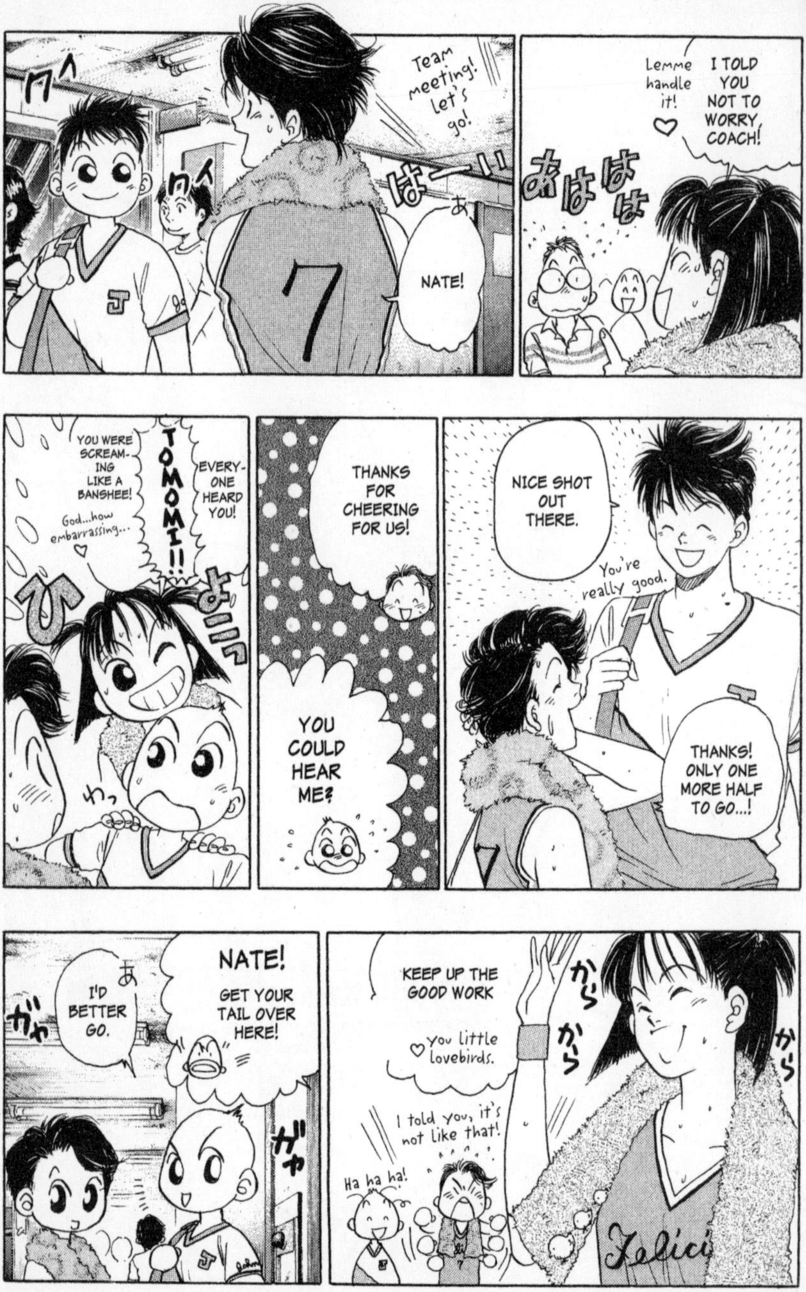
I TOLD YOU NOT TO WORRY, COACH!
Lemme handle it!
あははは
Team meeting! let's go!
はーい
あ
NATE!
ワイ
NICE SHOT OUT THERE.
You're really good.
THANKS! ONLY ONE MORE HALF TO GO...!
THANKS FOR CHEERING FOR US!
YOU COULD HEAR ME?
EVERY-ONE HEARD YOU!
TOMOMI!!
YOU WERE SCREAM-ING LIKE A BANSHEE!
God...how embarrassing...
ひょこっ
わっ
から
から
から
KEEP UP THE GOOD WORK
You little lovebirds.
I told you, it's not like that!
Ha ha ha!
NATE!
GET YOUR TAIL OVER HERE!
あ
I'D BETTER GO.
がや
がや

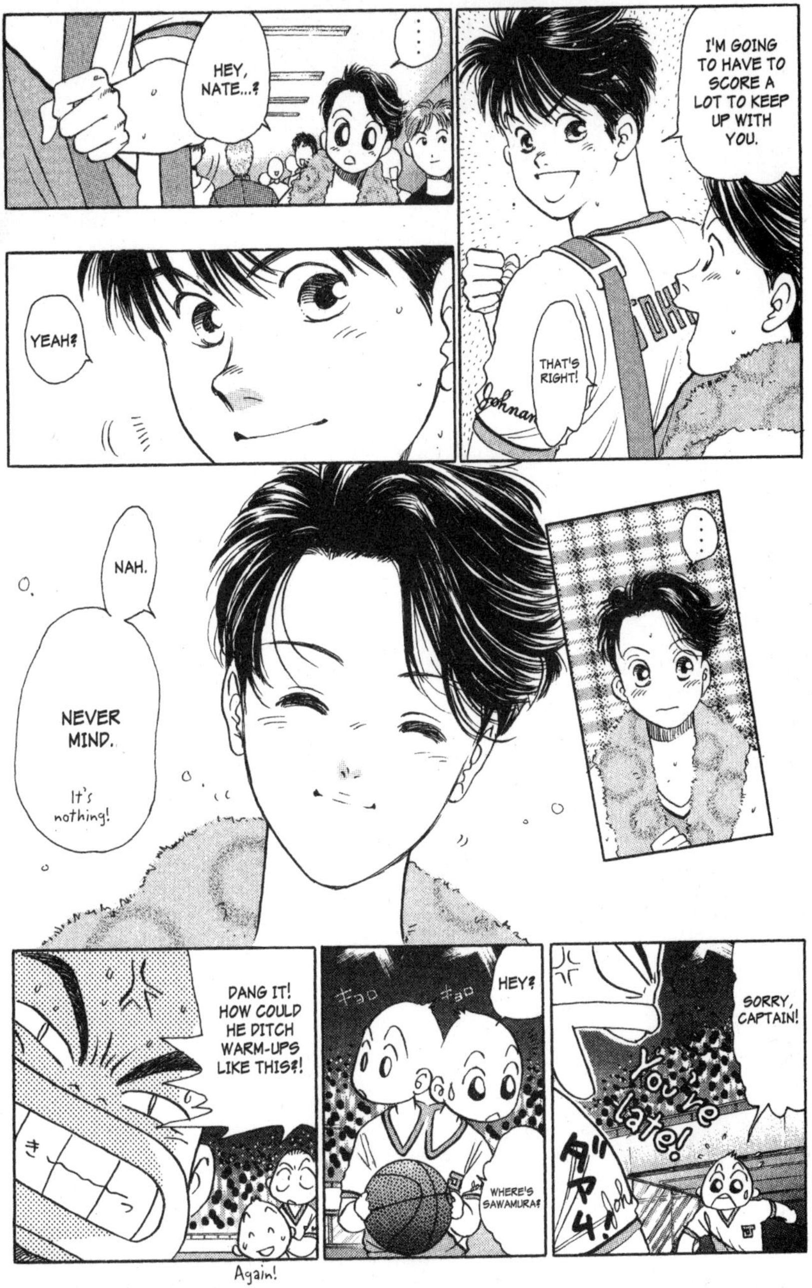
I'M GOING TO HAVE TO SCORE A LOT TO KEEP UP WITH YOU.
THAT'S RIGHT!
HEY, NATE...?
...
YEAH?
...
NAH.
NEVER MIND.
It's nothing!
SORRY, CAPTAIN!
You're late!
HEY?
キョロ
キョロ
WHERE'S SAWAMURA?
DANG IT! HOW COULD HE DITCH WARM-UPS LIKE THIS?!
Again!

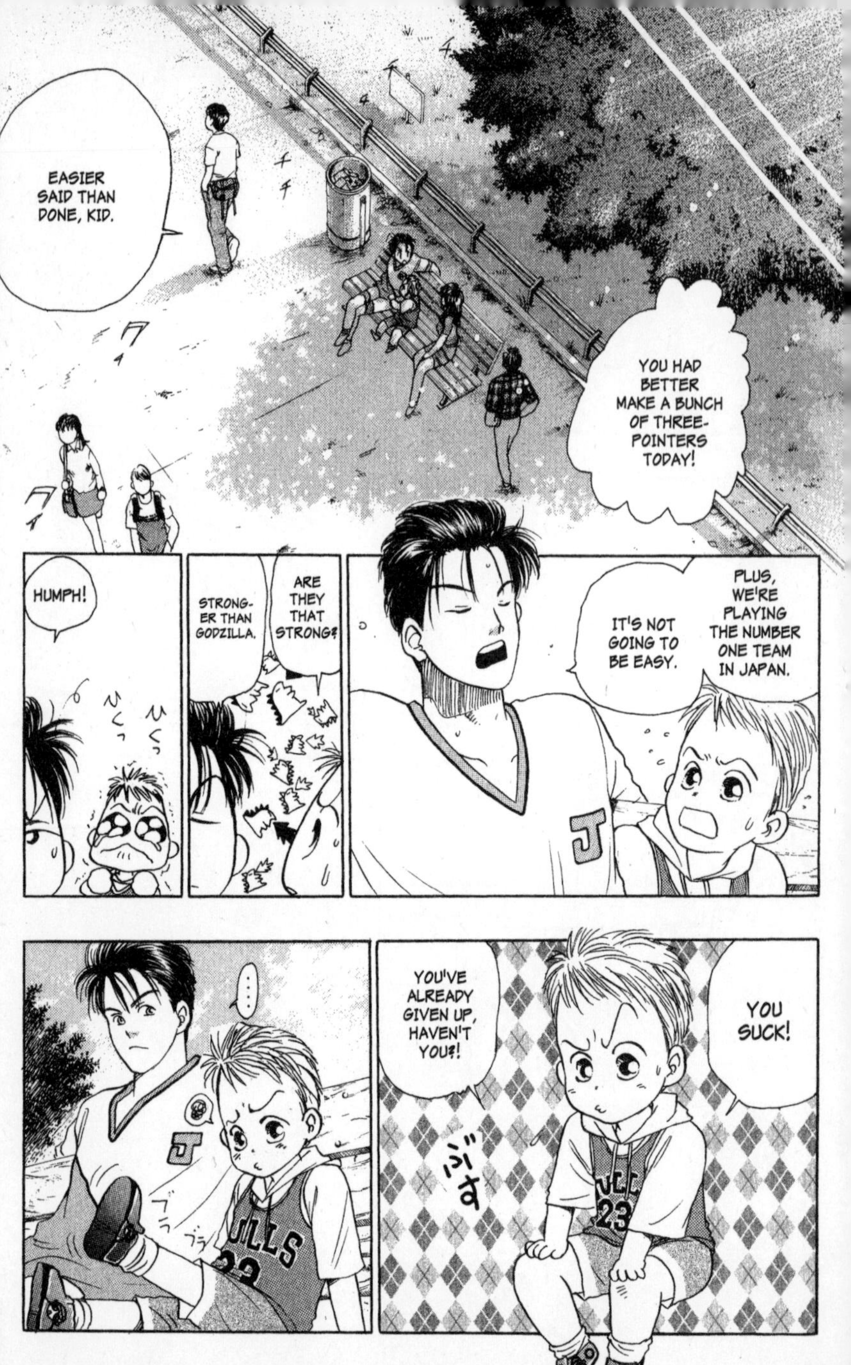
YOU HAD BETTER MAKE A BUNCH OF THREE-POINTERS TODAY!
EASIER SAID THAN DONE, KID.
PLUS, WE'RE PLAYING THE NUMBER ONE TEAM IN JAPAN.
IT'S NOT GOING TO BE EASY.
ARE THEY THAT STRONG?
STRONGER THAN GODZILLA.
HUMPH!
ひくっ
ひくっ
YOU SUCK!
YOU'VE ALREADY GIVEN UP, HAVEN'T YOU?!
ぶす
.....

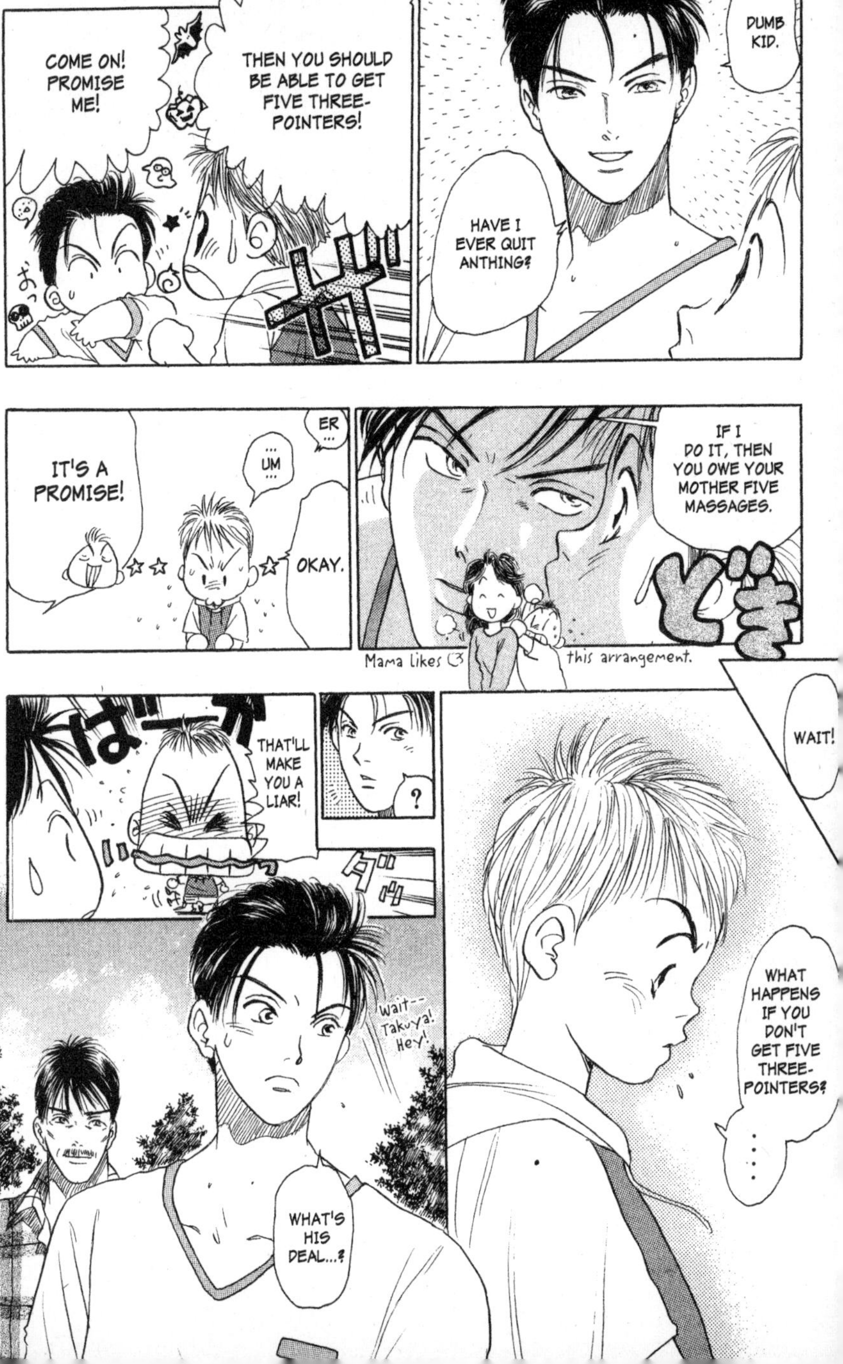
DUMB KID.
HAVE I EVER QUIT ANTHING?
THEN YOU SHOULD BE ABLE TO GET FIVE THREE-POINTERS!
COME ON! PROMISE ME!
おっ
IF I DO IT, THEN YOU OWE YOUR MOTHER FIVE MASSAGES.
Mama likes ♡ this arrangement.
ER...
...UM...
OKAY.
IT'S A PROMISE!
WAIT!
WHAT HAPPENS IF YOU DON'T GET FIVE THREE-POINTERS?
....
?
THAT'LL MAKE YOU A LIAR!
Wait-- Takuya! Hey!
WHAT'S HIS DEAL...?

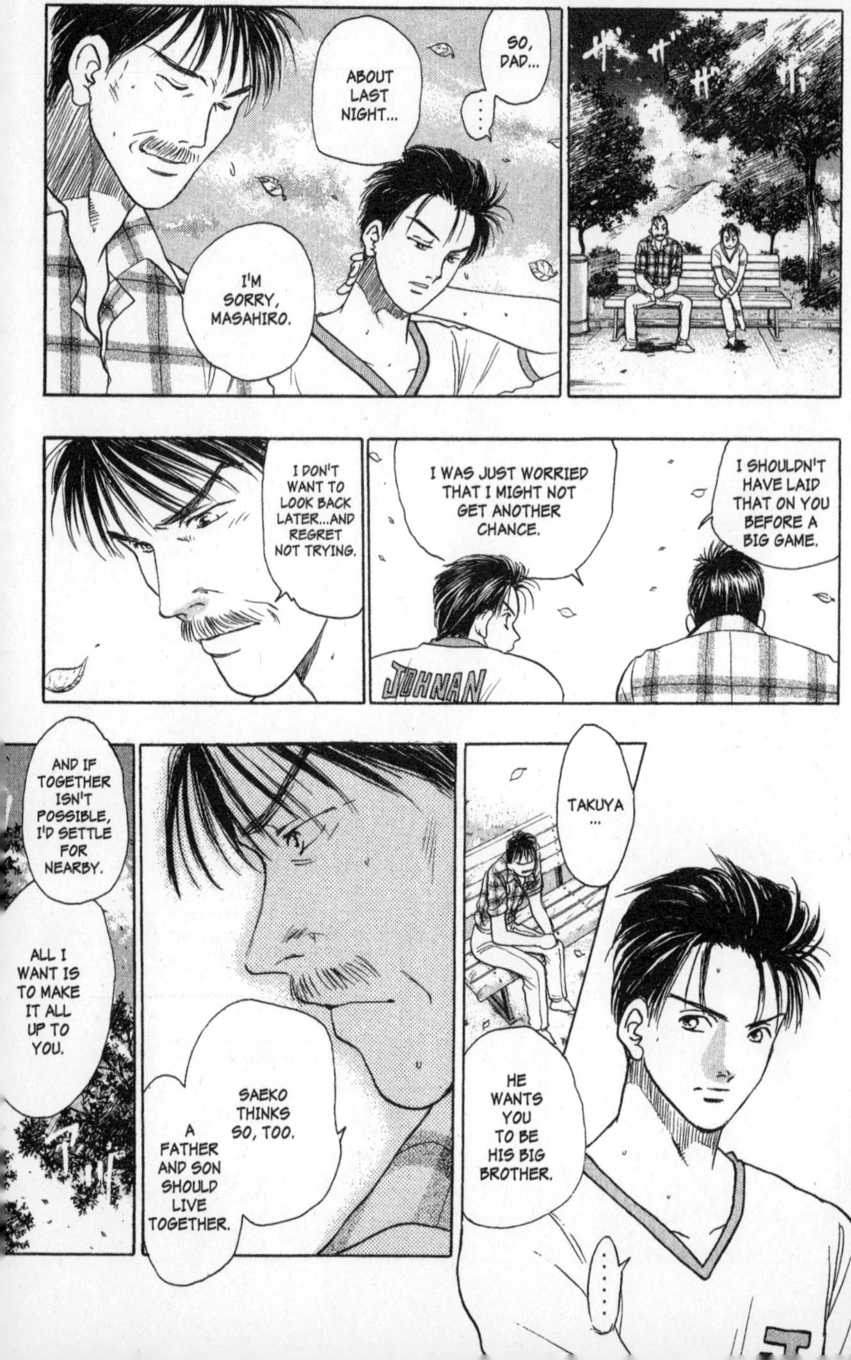
SO, DAD...
......
ABOUT LAST NIGHT...
I'M SORRY, MASAHIRO.
I SHOULDN'T HAVE LAID THAT ON YOU BEFORE A BIG GAME.
I WAS JUST WORRIED THAT I MIGHT NOT GET ANOTHER CHANCE.
JOHNAN
I DON'T WANT TO LOOK BACK LATER...AND REGRET NOT TRYING.
TAKUYA ...
HE WANTS YOU TO BE HIS BIG BROTHER.
......
SAEKO THINKS SO, TOO.
A FATHER AND SON SHOULD LIVE TOGETHER.
AND IF TOGETHER ISN'T POSSIBLE, I'D SETTLE FOR NEARBY.
ALL I WANT IS TO MAKE IT ALL UP TO YOU.

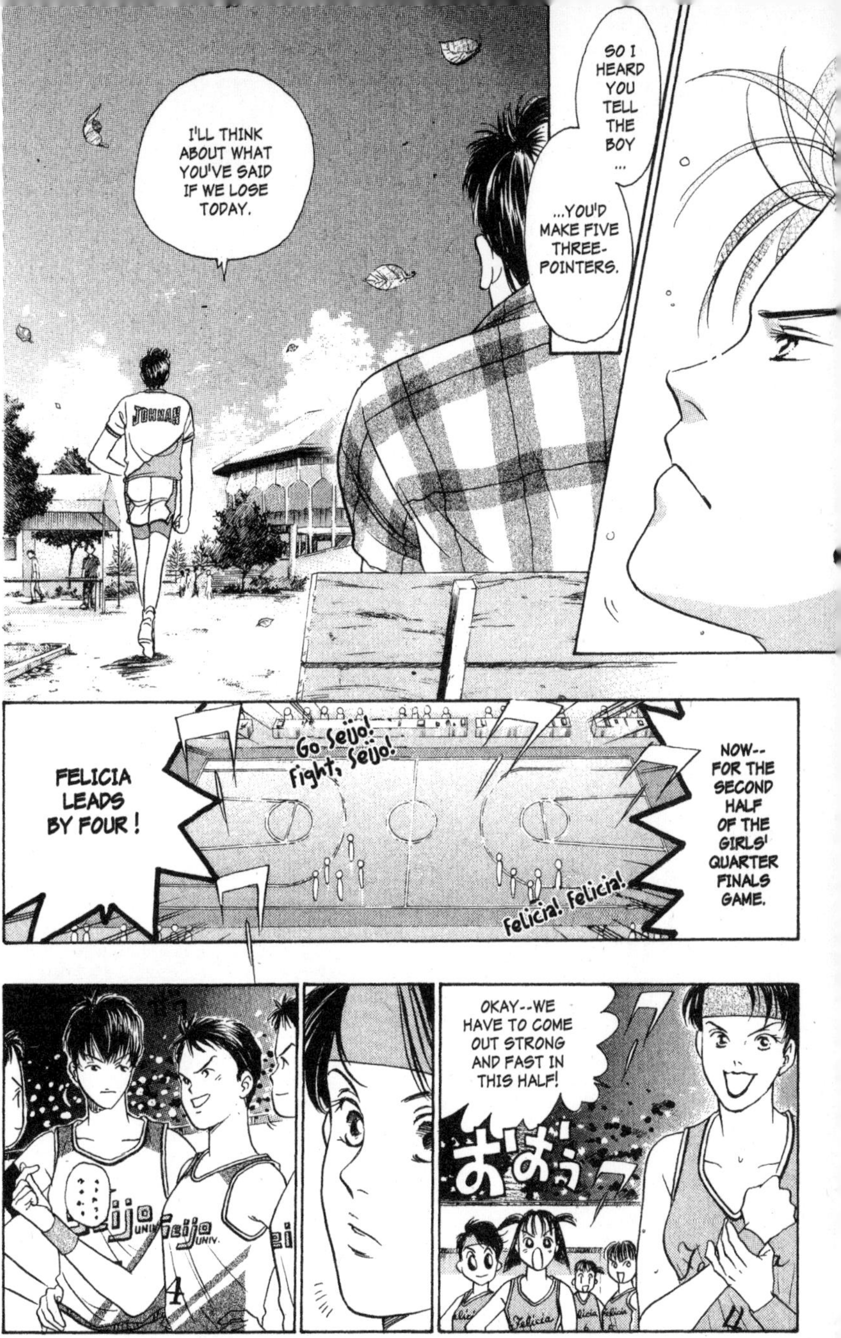
SO I HEARD YOU TELL THE BOY ...
...YOU'D MAKE FIVE THREE-POINTERS.
I'LL THINK ABOUT WHAT YOU'VE SAID IF WE LOSE TODAY.
NOW-- FOR THE SECOND HALF OF THE GIRLS' QUARTER FINALS GAME.
Go Seijo! Fight, Seijo!
Felicia! Felicia!
FELICIA LEADS BY FOUR!
OKAY--WE HAVE TO COME OUT STRONG AND FAST IN THIS HALF!
おおぅ

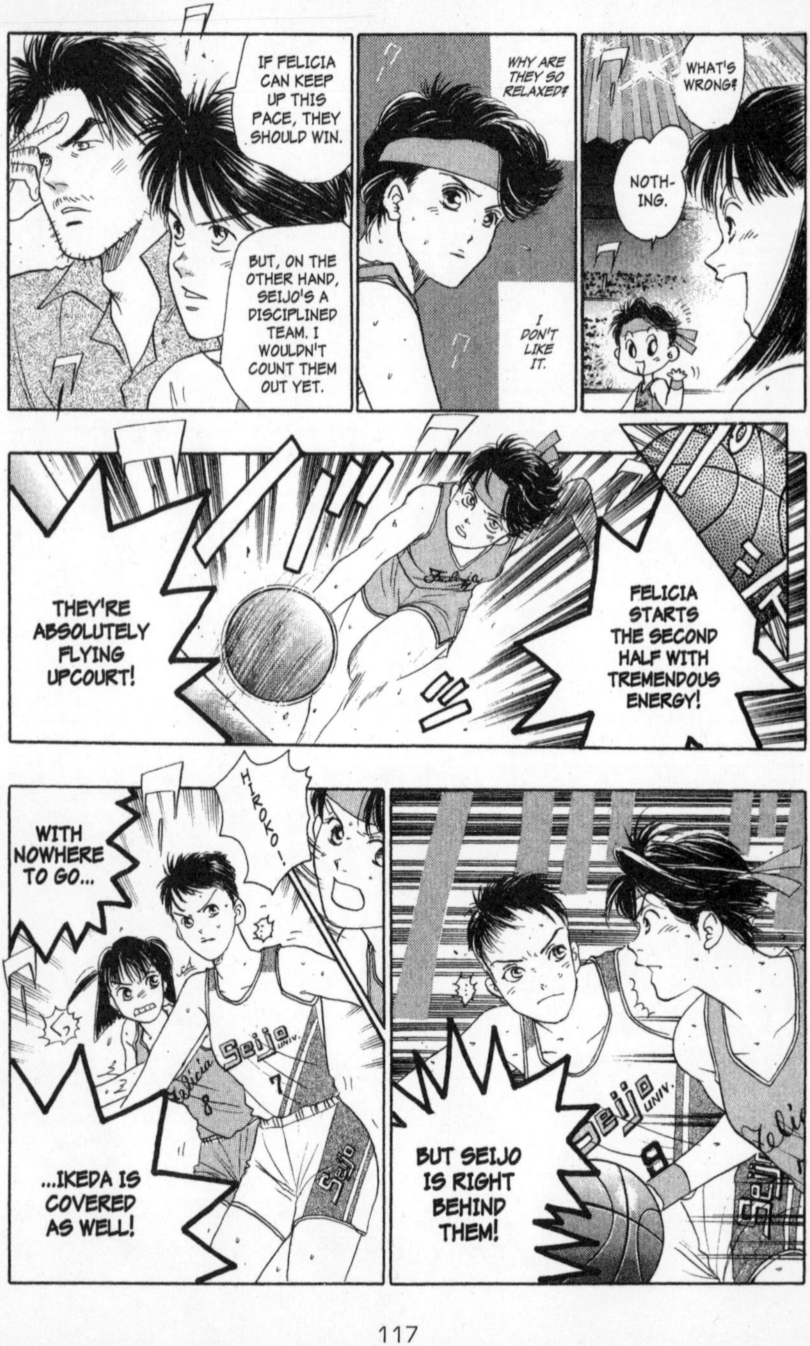
WHAT'S WRONG?
NOTH-ING.
WHY ARE THEY SO RELAXED?
I DON'T LIKE IT.
IF FELICIA CAN KEEP UP THIS PACE, THEY SHOULD WIN.
BUT, ON THE OTHER HAND, SEIJO'S A DISCIPLINED TEAM. I WOULDN'T COUNT THEM OUT YET.
FELICIA STARTS THE SECOND HALF WITH TREMENDOUS ENERGY!
THEY'RE ABSOLUTELY FLYING UPCOURT!
BUT SEIJO IS RIGHT BEHIND THEM!
HIROKO!
WITH NOWHERE TO GO...
...IKEDA IS COVERED AS WELL!

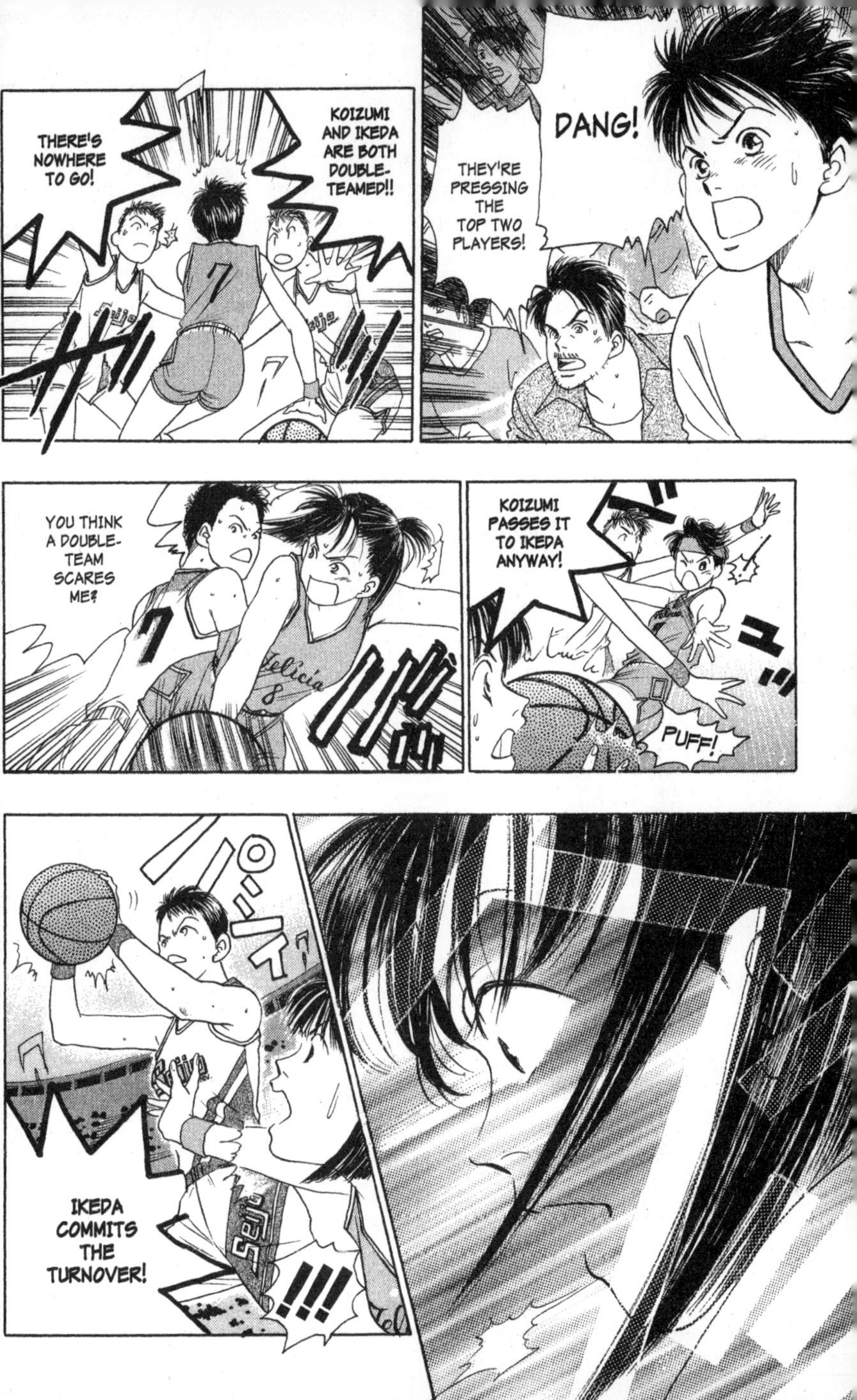
DANG!
THEY'RE PRESSING THE TOP TWO PLAYERS!
KOIZUMI AND IKEDA ARE BOTH DOUBLE-TEAMED!!
THERE'S NOWHERE TO GO!
KOIZUMI PASSES IT TO IKEDA ANYWAY!
PUFF!
YOU THINK A DOUBLE-TEAM SCARES ME?
IKEDA COMMITS THE TURNOVER!
!!!

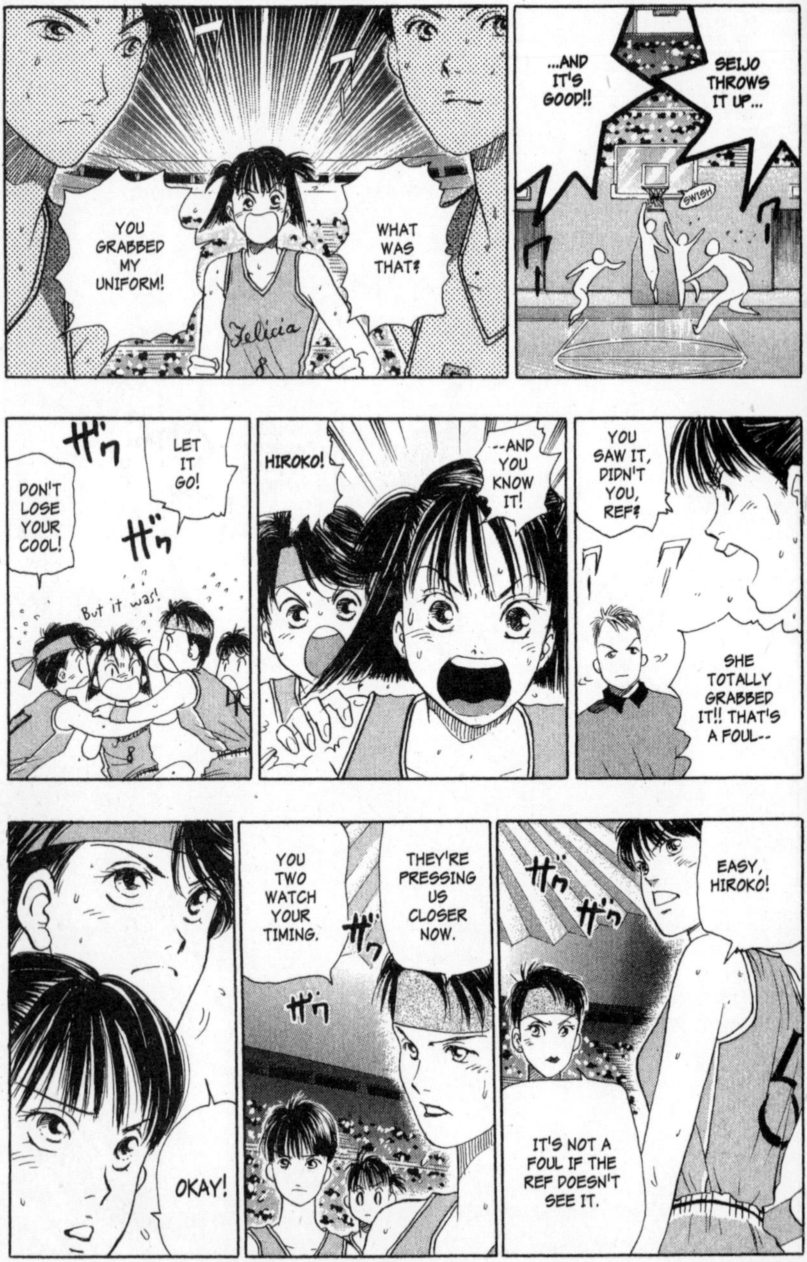
SEIJO THROWS IT UP...
...AND IT'S GOOD!!
SWISH
WHAT WAS THAT?
YOU GRABBED MY UNIFORM!
YOU SAW IT, DIDN'T YOU, REF?
SHE TOTALLY GRABBED IT!! THAT'S A FOUL--
--AND YOU KNOW IT!
HIROKO!
ザワ
LET IT GO!
ザワ
DON'T LOSE YOUR COOL!
But it was!
EASY, HIROKO!
ザワ ザワ
IT'S NOT A FOUL IF THE REF DOESN'T SEE IT.
THEY'RE PRESSING US CLOSER NOW.
YOU TWO WATCH YOUR TIMING.
ザワ
ザワ
OKAY!

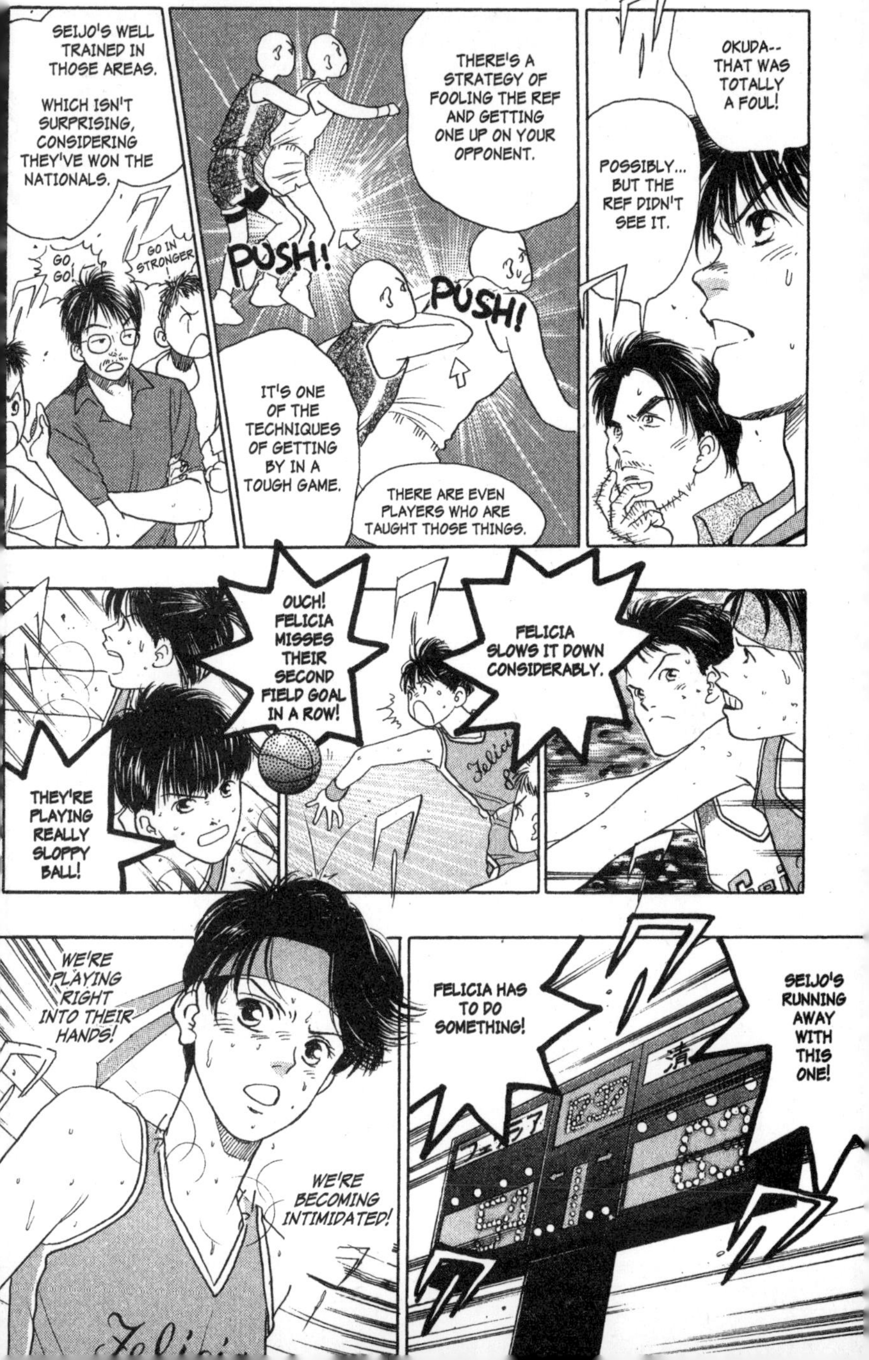
OKUDA-- THAT WAS TOTALLY A FOUL!
POSSIBLY... BUT THE REF DIDN'T SEE IT.
THERE'S A STRATEGY OF FOOLING THE REF AND GETTING ONE UP ON YOUR OPPONENT.
PUSH!
PUSH!
IT'S ONE OF THE TECHNIQUES OF GETTING BY IN A TOUGH GAME.
THERE ARE EVEN PLAYERS WHO ARE TAUGHT THOSE THINGS.
SEIJO'S WELL TRAINED IN THOSE AREAS.
WHICH ISN'T SURPRISING, CONSIDERING THEY'VE WON THE NATIONALS.
GO IN STRONGER!
GO, GO!
FELICIA SLOWS IT DOWN CONSIDERABLY.
OUCH! FELICIA MISSES THEIR SECOND FIELD GOAL IN A ROW!
THEY'RE PLAYING REALLY SLOPPY BALL!
SEIJO'S RUNNING AWAY WITH THIS ONE!
FELICIA HAS TO DO SOMETHING!
WE'RE PLAYING RIGHT INTO THEIR HANDS!
WE'RE BECOMING INTIMIDATED!

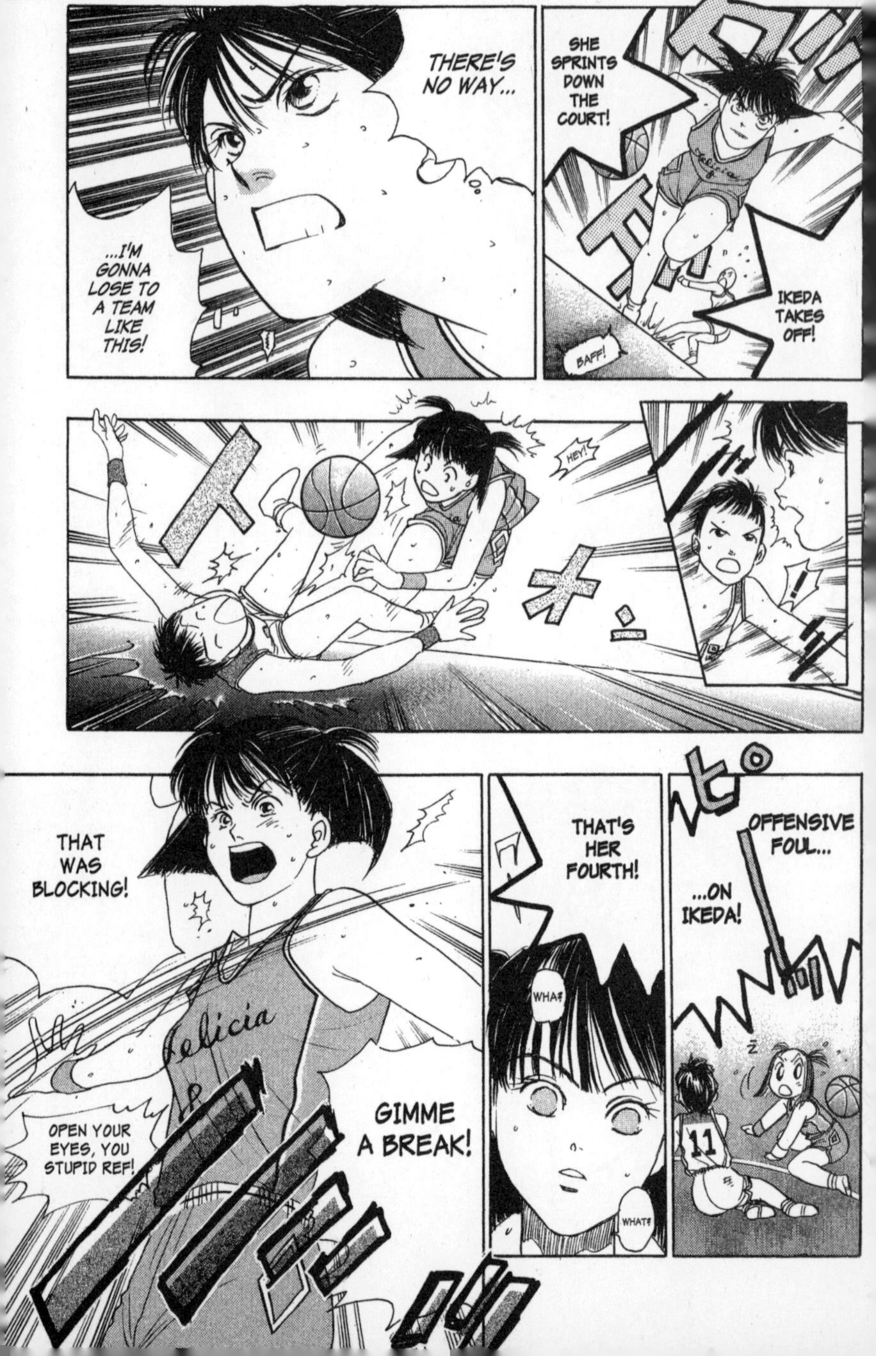
SHE SPRINTS DOWN THE COURT!
IKEDA TAKES OFF!
BAFF!
THERE'S NO WAY...
...I'M GONNA LOSE TO A TEAM LIKE THIS!
HEY!
OFFENSIVE FOUL...
...ON IKEDA!
THAT'S HER FOURTH!
WHA?
WHAT?
THAT WAS BLOCKING!
GIMME A BREAK!
OPEN YOUR EYES, YOU STUPID REF!

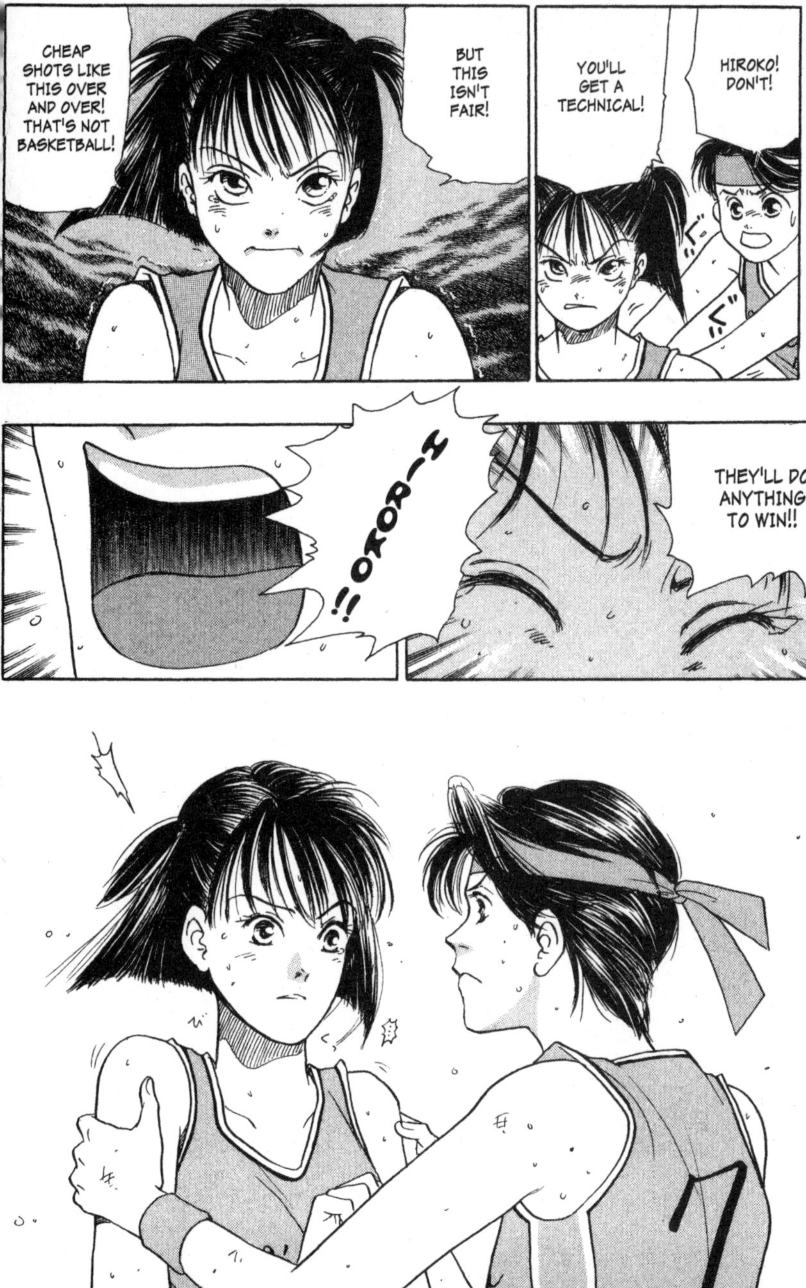
HIROKO! DON'T!
YOU'LL GET A TECHNICAL!
BUT THIS ISN'T FAIR!
CHEAP SHOTS LIKE THIS OVER AND OVER! THAT'S NOT BASKETBALL!
THEY'LL DO ANYTHING TO WIN!!
HIROTO!!

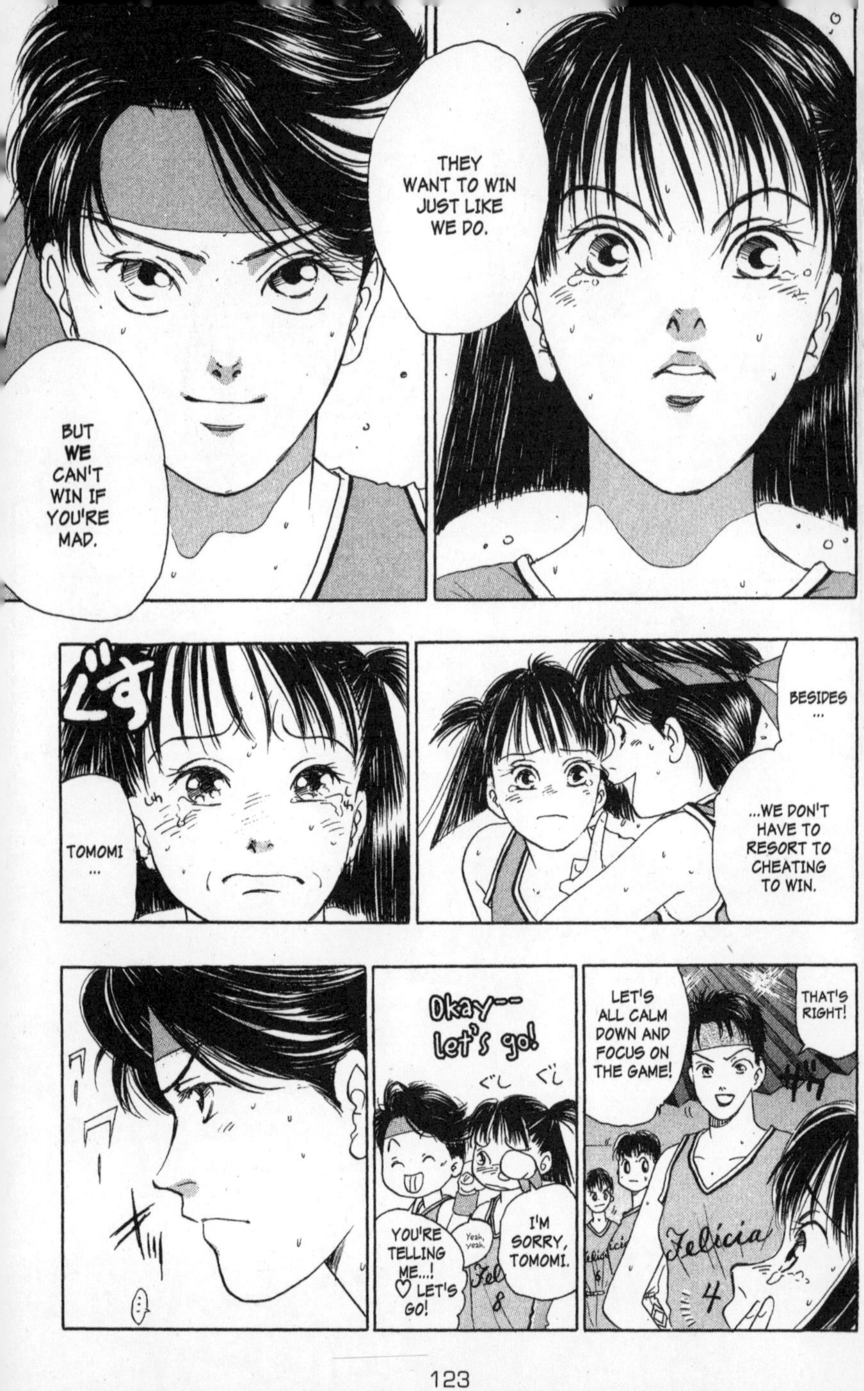
THEY WANT TO WIN JUST LIKE WE DO.
BUT WE CAN'T WIN IF YOU'RE MAD.
BESIDES...
...WE DON'T HAVE TO RESORT TO CHEATING TO WIN.
ぐす
TOMOMI...
THAT'S RIGHT!
LET'S ALL CALM DOWN AND FOCUS ON THE GAME!
Okay-- let's go!
ぐし ぐし
I'M SORRY, TOMOMI.
Yeah, yeah.
YOU'RE TELLING ME...! ♡ LET'S GO!
...

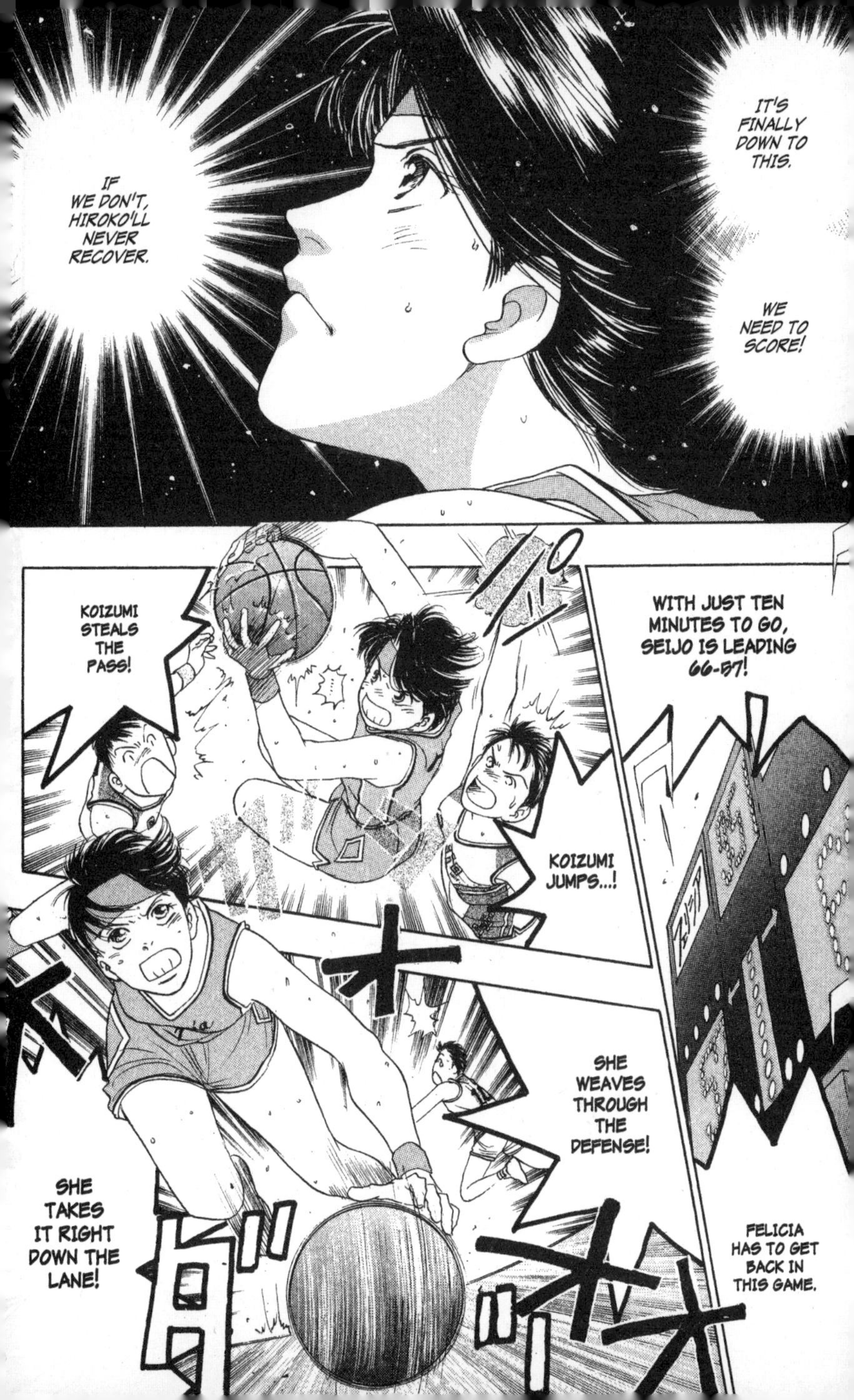
IT'S FINALLY DOWN TO THIS.
WE NEED TO SCORE!
IF WE DON'T, HIROKO'LL NEVER RECOVER.
WITH JUST TEN MINUTES TO GO, SEIJO IS LEADING 66-57!
FELICIA HAS TO GET BACK IN THIS GAME.
KOIZUMI STEALS THE PASS!
KOIZUMI JUMPS...!
SHE WEAVES THROUGH THE DEFENSE!
SHE TAKES IT RIGHT DOWN THE LANE!

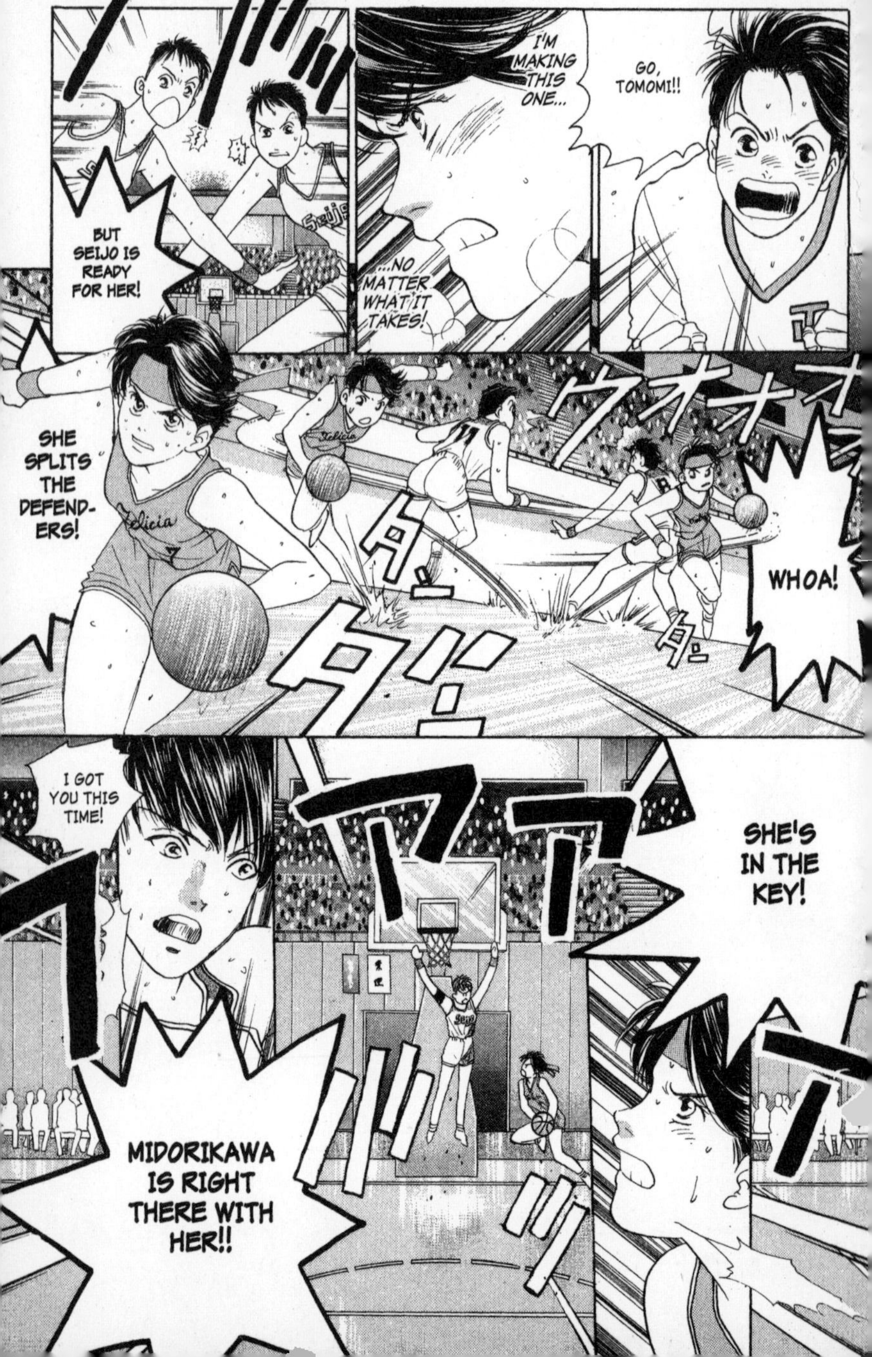
GO, TOMOMI!!
I'M MAKING THIS ONE...
...NO MATTER WHAT IT TAKES!
BUT SEIJO IS READY FOR HER!
ウオオオ
WHOA!
SHE SPLITS THE DEFENDERS!
SHE'S IN THE KEY!
I GOT YOU THIS TIME!
MIDORIKAWA IS RIGHT THERE WITH HER!!

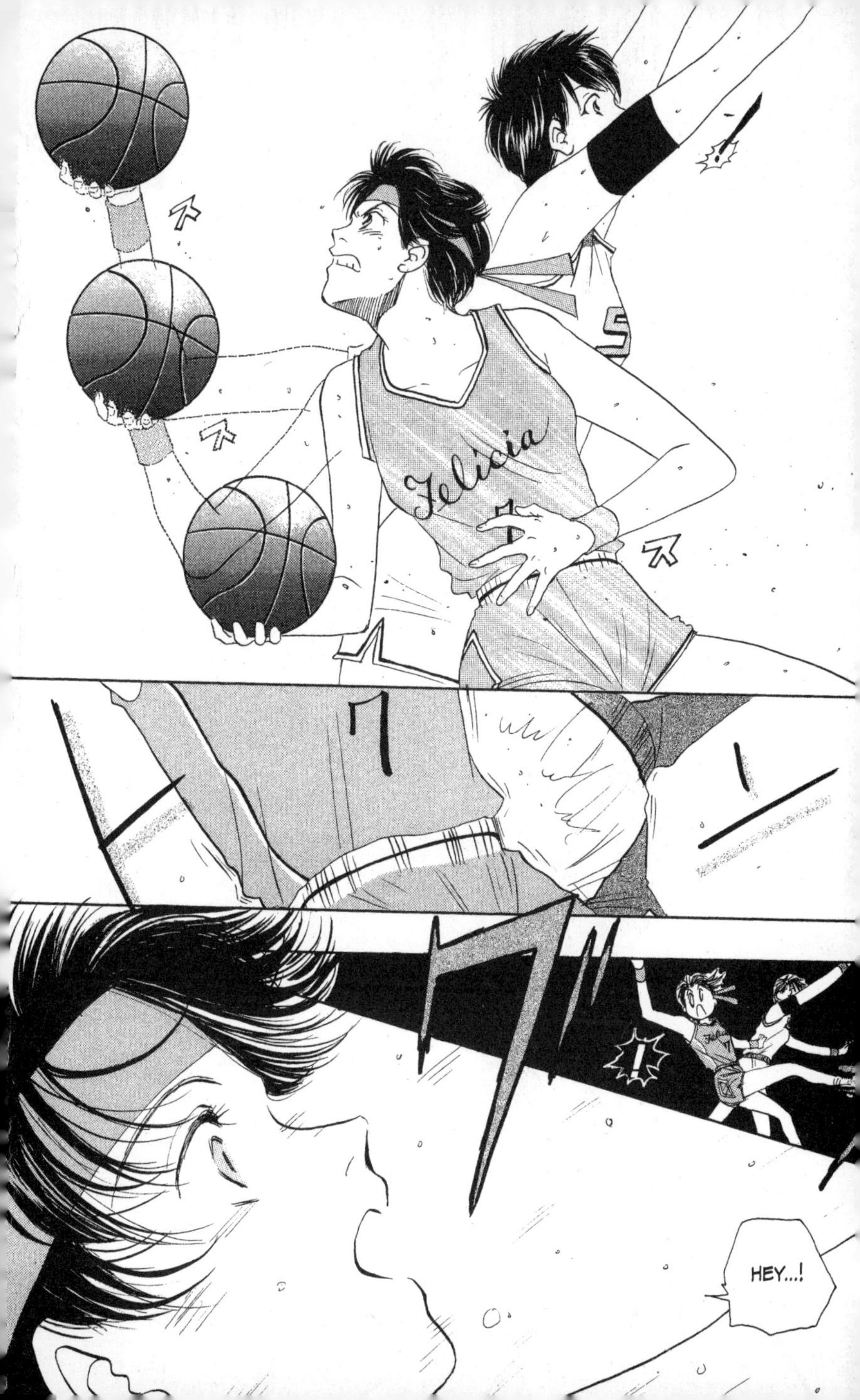
Felicia
7
HEY...!

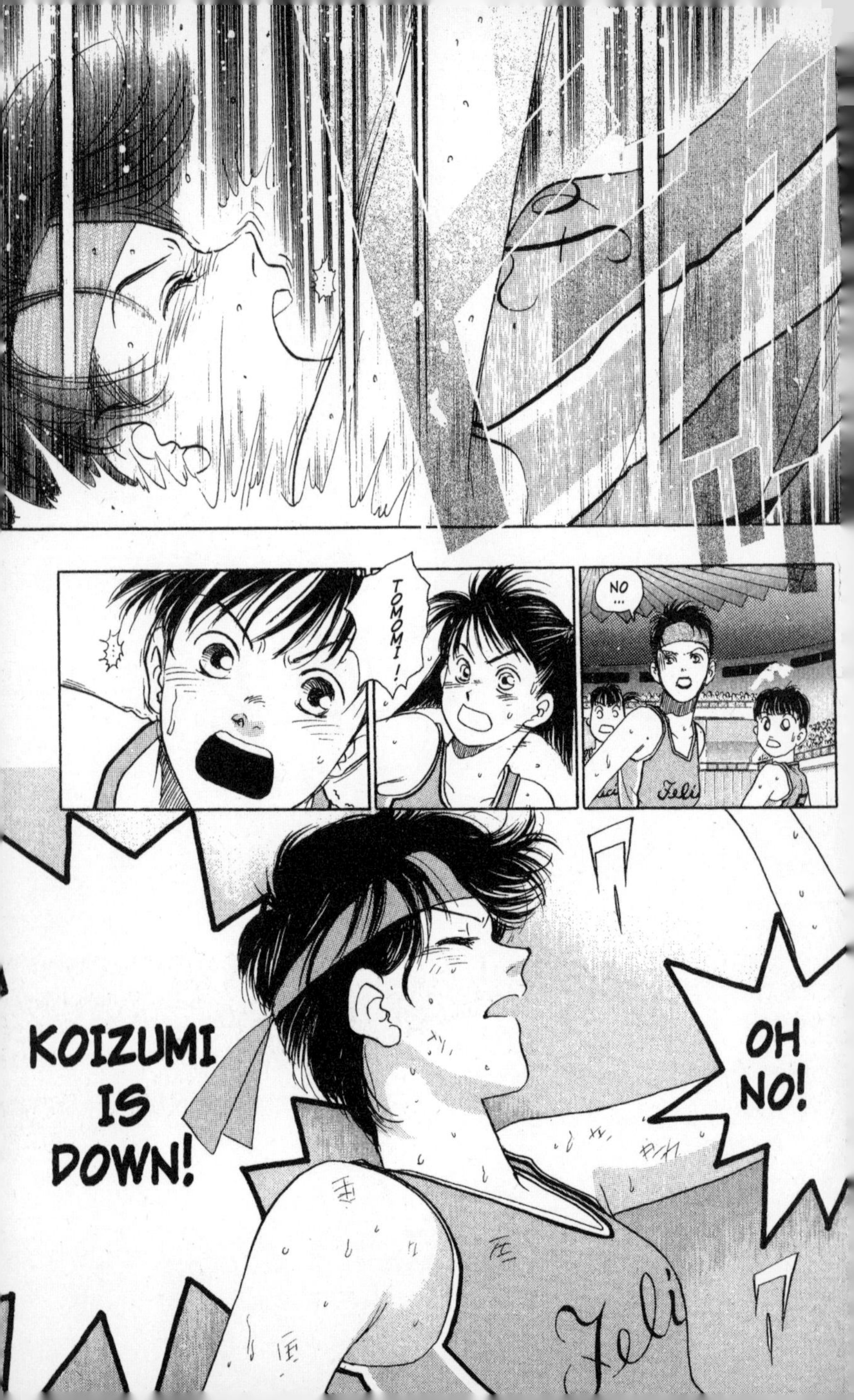
NO ...
TOMOMI!
OH NO!
KOIZUMI IS DOWN!

You're Reading...

# REBOUND

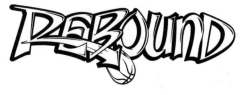

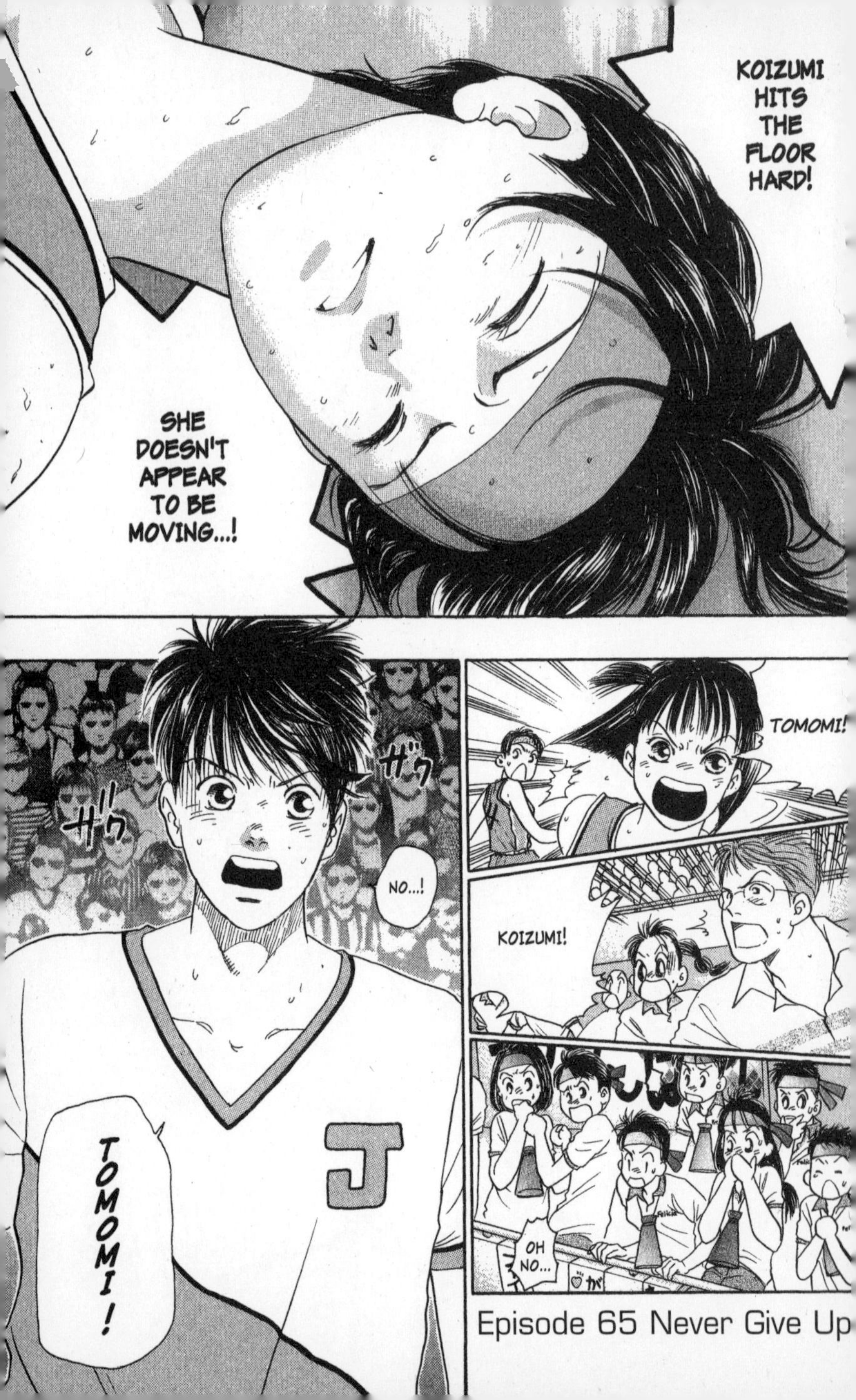
KOIZUMI HITS THE FLOOR HARD!
SHE DOESN'T APPEAR TO BE MOVING...!
TOMOMI!
KOIZUMI!
OH NO...
NO...!
TOMOMI!

Episode 65 Never Give Up

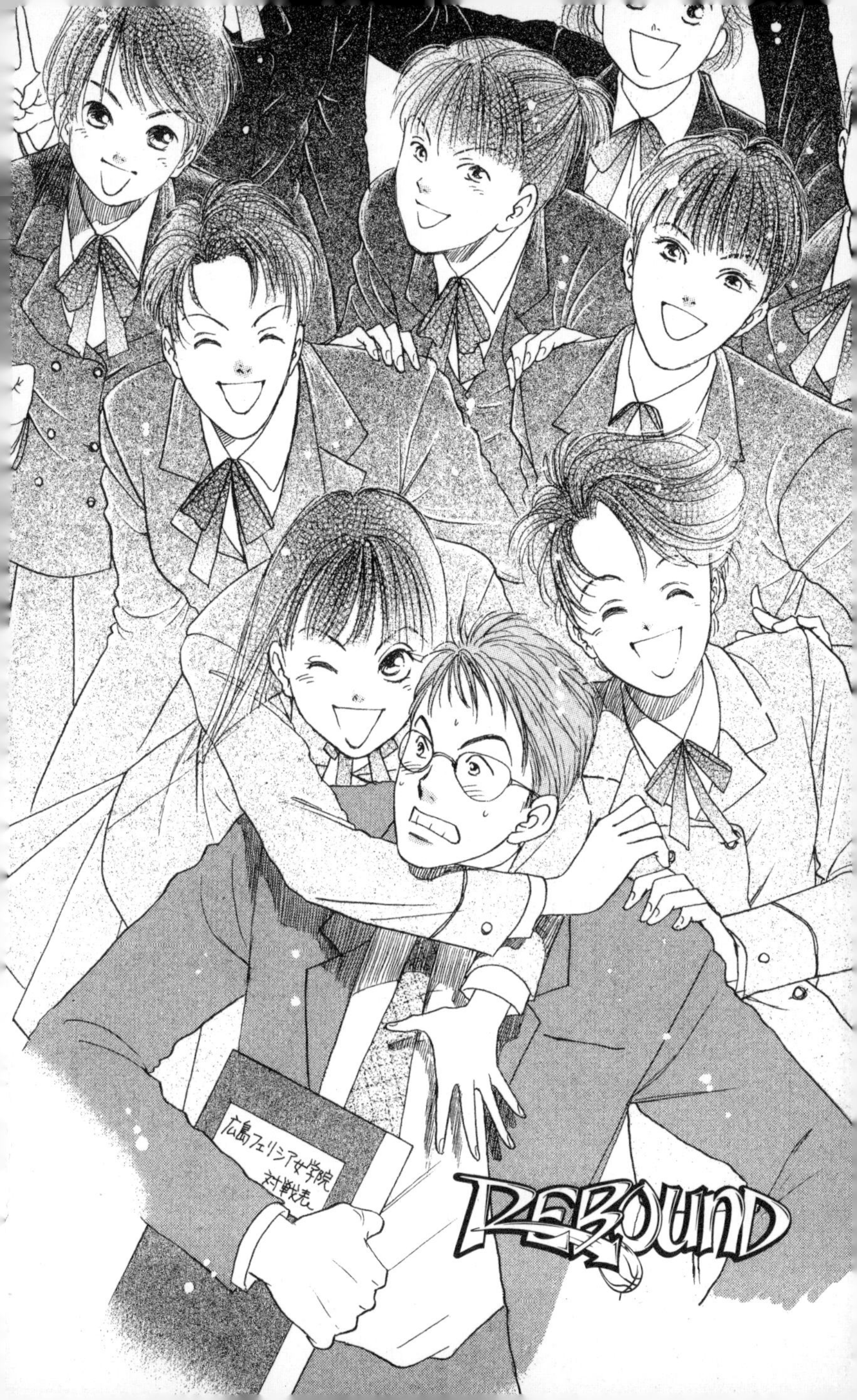
広島フェリシア女学院
対戦表
REBOUND

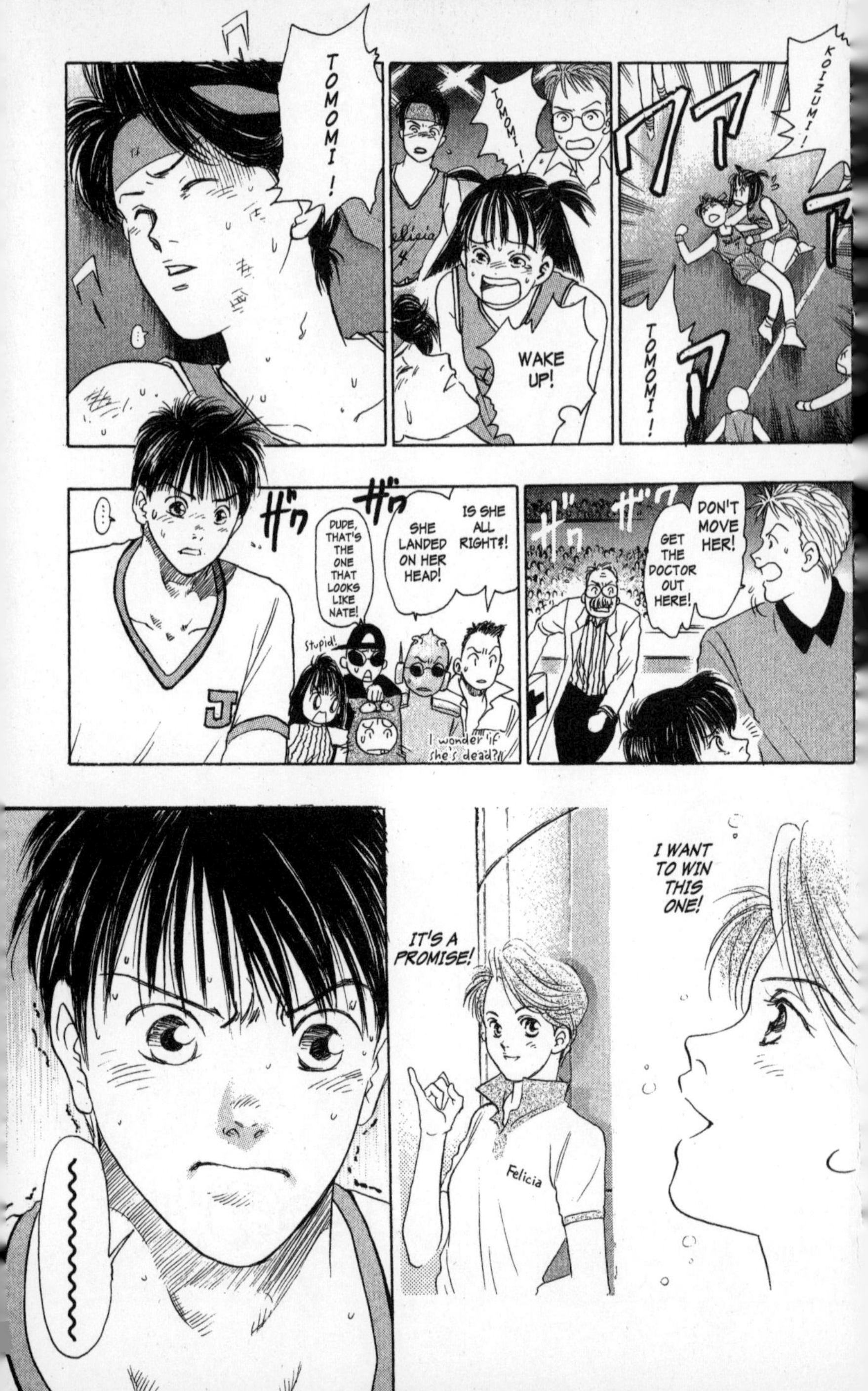
KOIZUMI!
TOMOMI!
TOMOMI!
WAKE UP!
TOMOMI!
...
DON'T MOVE HER!
GET THE DOCTOR OUT HERE!
IS SHE ALL RIGHT?!
SHE LANDED ON HER HEAD!
DUDE, THAT'S THE ONE THAT LOOKS LIKE NATE!
Stupid!
I wonder if she's dead?!
...
I WANT TO WIN THIS ONE!
IT'S A PROMISE!

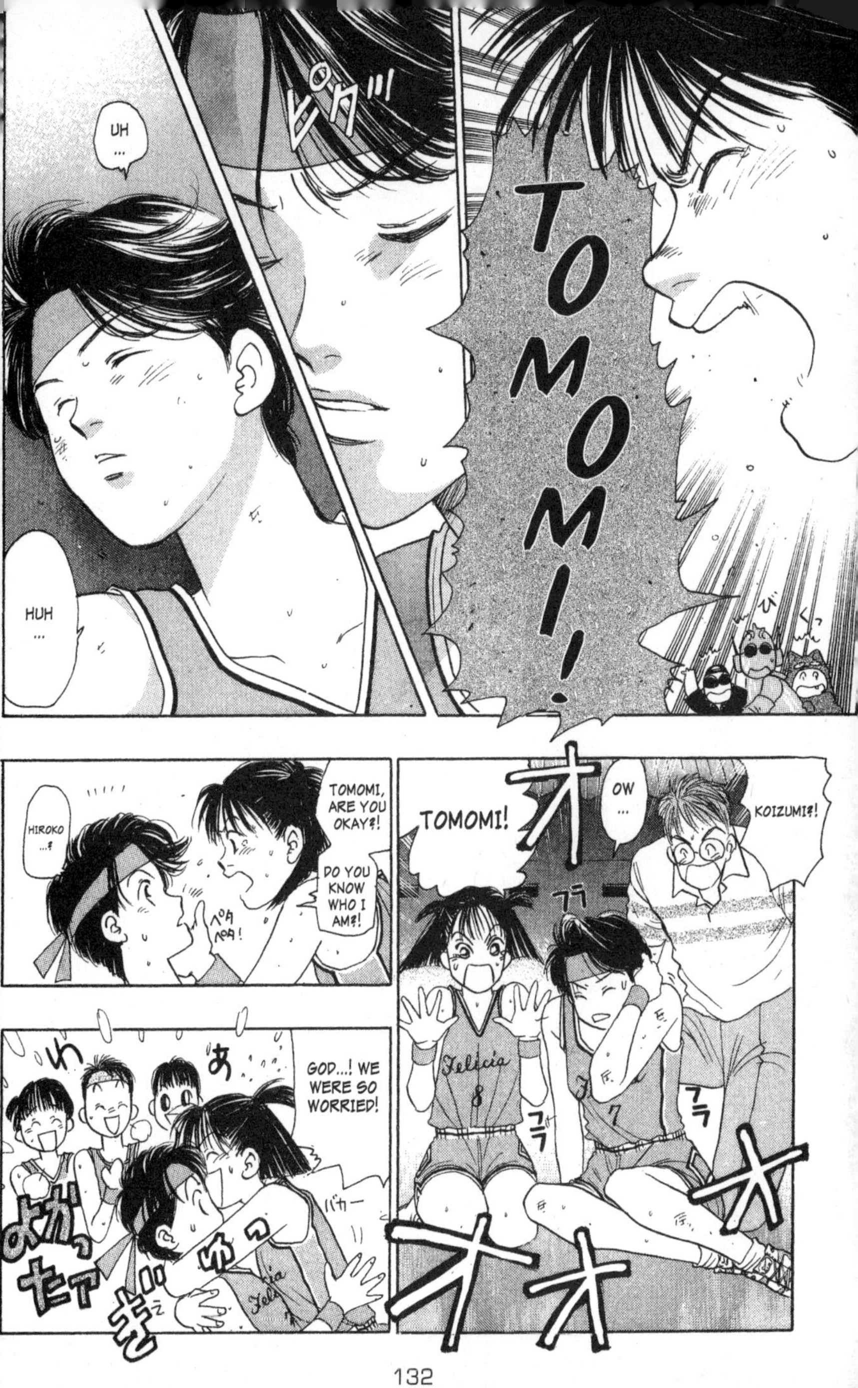
TOMOMI!!
UH ...
HUH ...
KOIZUMI?!
OW ...
TOMOMI!
TOMOMI, ARE YOU OKAY?!
DO YOU KNOW WHO I AM?!
HIROKO ...?
GOD...! WE WERE SO WORRIED!

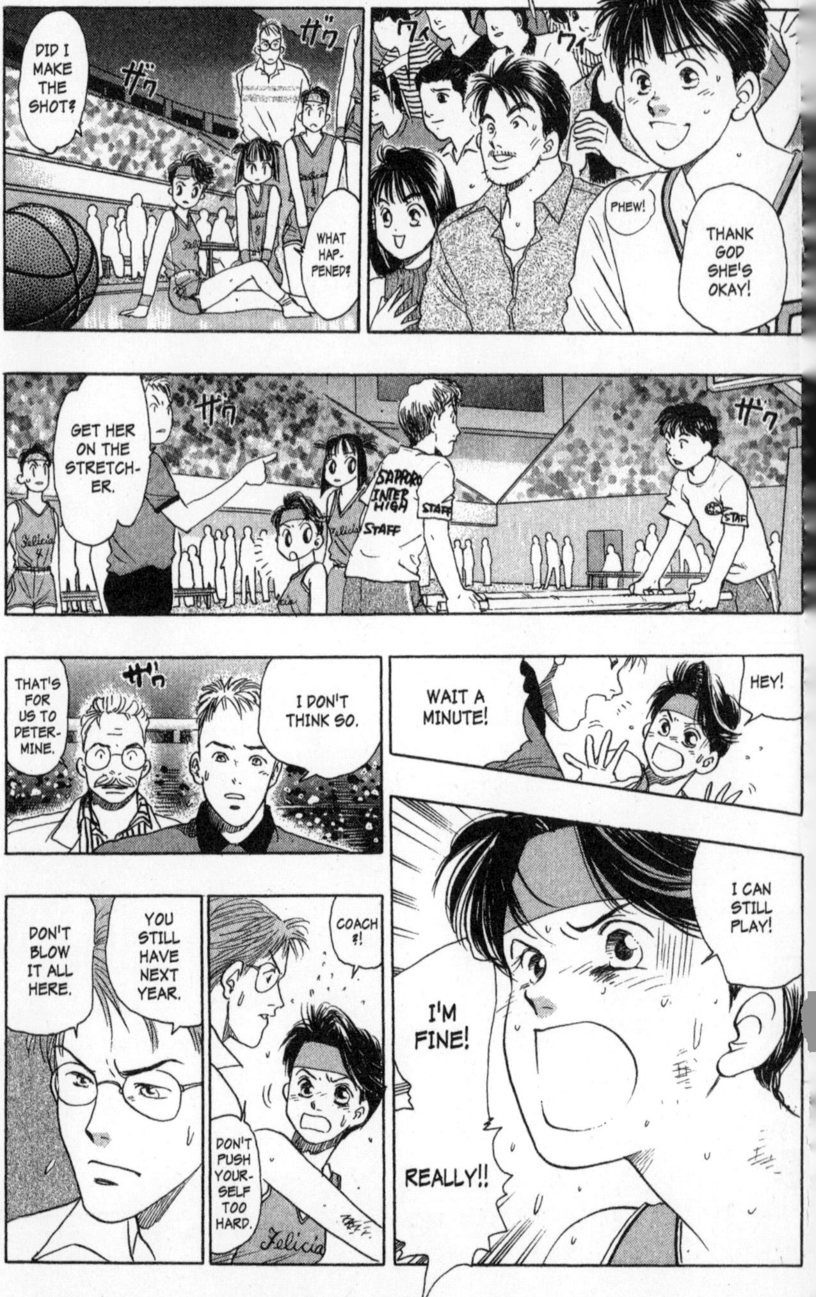
ワイ
ワイ
PHEW!
THANK GOD SHE'S OKAY!
ザワ
ザワ
WHAT HAP-PENED?
DID I MAKE THE SHOT?
ザワ
ザワ
GET HER ON THE STRETCH-ER.
SAPPORO INTER HIGH STAFF
STAFF
STAFF
HEY!
WAIT A MINUTE!
I CAN STILL PLAY!
I'M FINE!
REALLY!!
ザワ
I DON'T THINK SO.
THAT'S FOR US TO DETER-MINE.
COACH?!
DON'T PUSH YOUR-SELF TOO HARD.
YOU STILL HAVE NEXT YEAR.
DON'T BLOW IT ALL HERE.

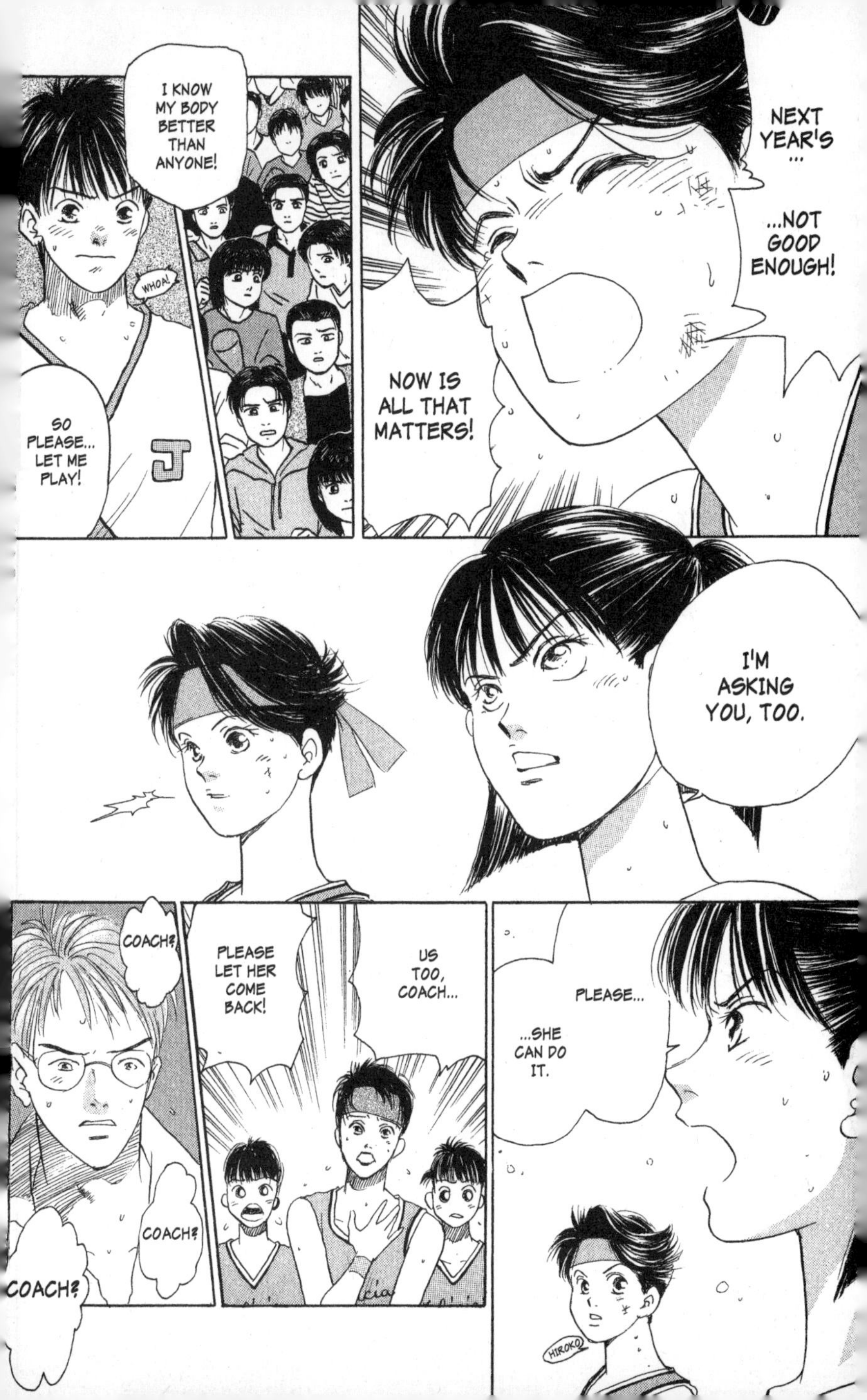
NEXT YEAR'S...
...NOT GOOD ENOUGH!
NOW IS ALL THAT MATTERS!
I KNOW MY BODY BETTER THAN ANYONE!
WHOA!
SO PLEASE... LET ME PLAY!
I'M ASKING YOU, TOO.
PLEASE...
...SHE CAN DO IT.
HIROKO
US TOO, COACH...
PLEASE LET HER COME BACK!
COACH?
COACH?
COACH?

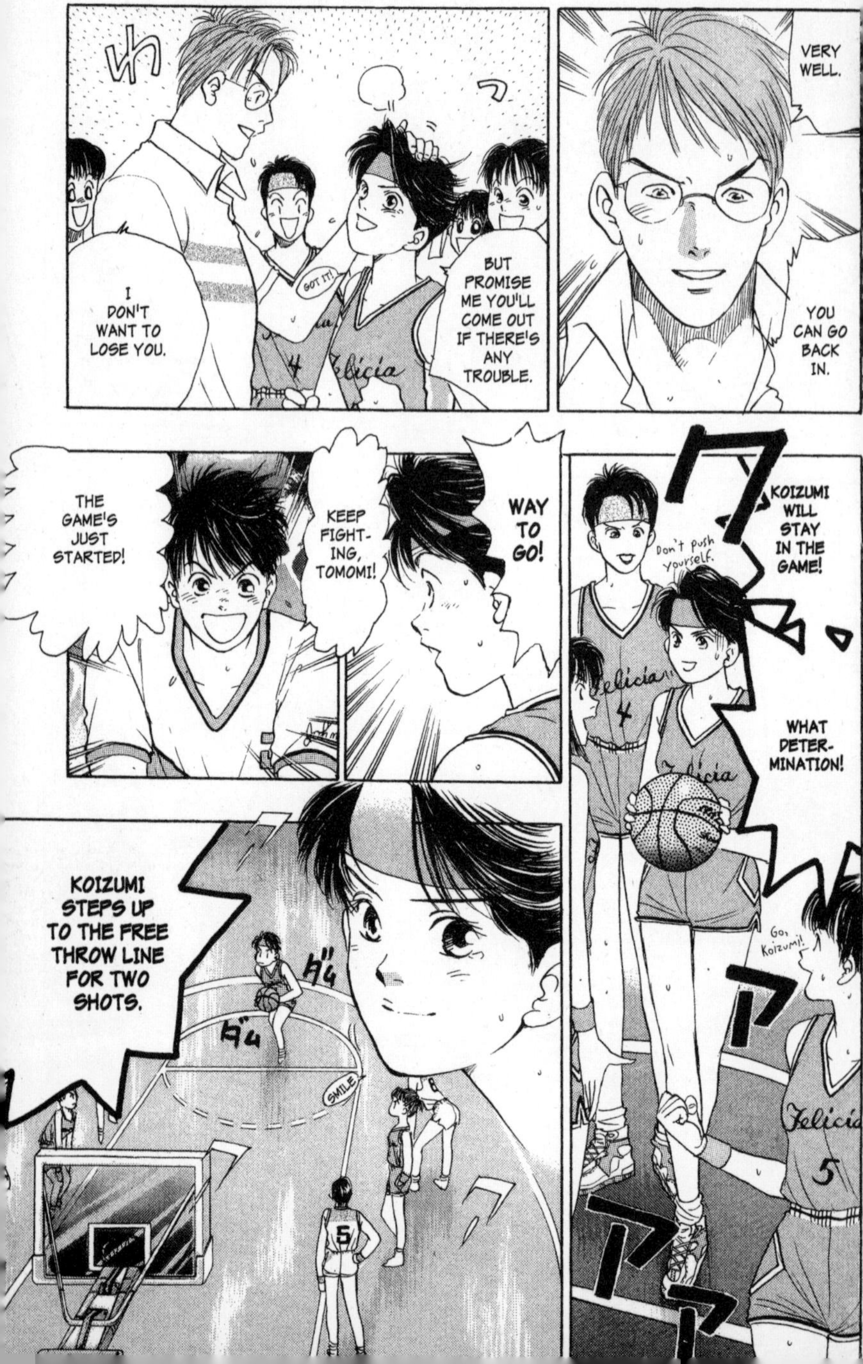
VERY WELL.
YOU CAN GO BACK IN.
BUT PROMISE ME YOU'LL COME OUT IF THERE'S ANY TROUBLE.
GOT IT!
I DON'T WANT TO LOSE YOU.
KOIZUMI WILL STAY IN THE GAME!
Don't push yourself.
WHAT DETERMINATION!
Go, Koizumi!
WAY TO GO!
KEEP FIGHT-ING, TOMOMI!
THE GAME'S JUST STARTED!
SMILE
KOIZUMI STEPS UP TO THE FREE THROW LINE FOR TWO SHOTS.

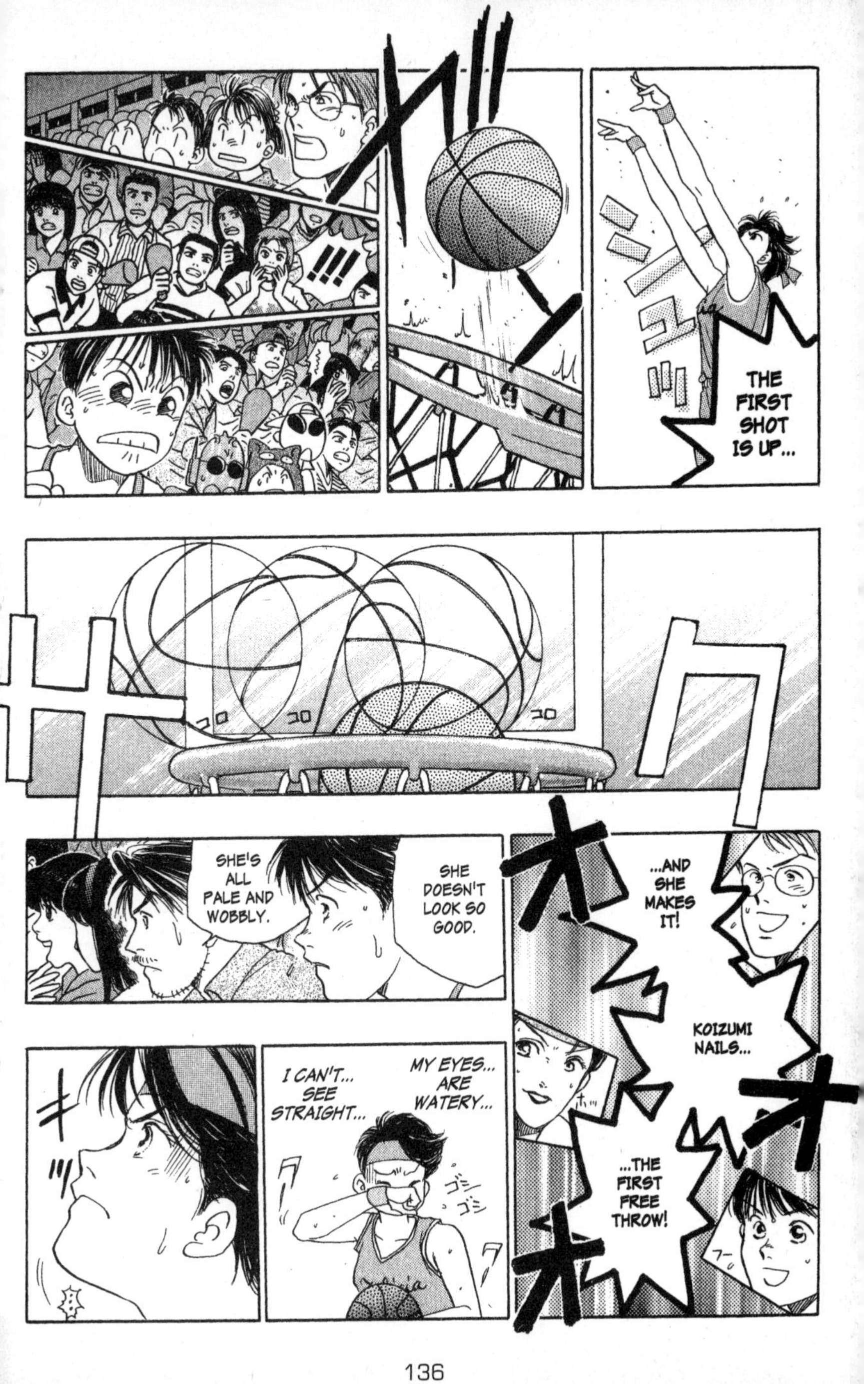

THE FIRST SHOT IS UP...
...AND SHE MAKES IT!
KOIZUMI NAILS...
...THE FIRST FREE THROW!
SHE DOESN'T LOOK SO GOOD.
SHE'S ALL PALE AND WOBBLY.
MY EYES... ARE WATERY...
I CAN'T... SEE STRAIGHT...

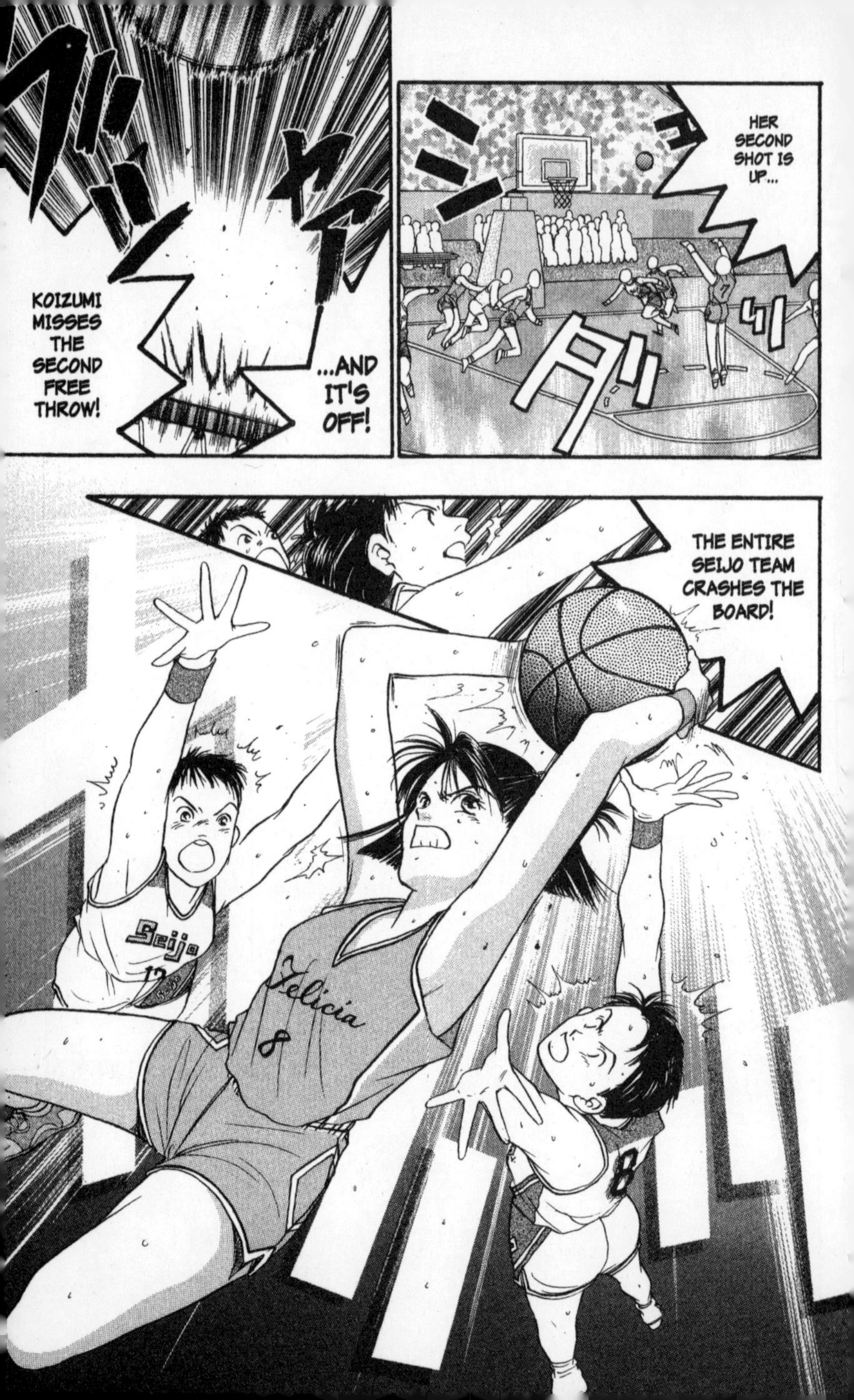
HER SECOND SHOT IS UP...
...AND IT'S OFF!
KOIZUMI MISSES THE SECOND FREE THROW!
THE ENTIRE SEIJO TEAM CRASHES THE BOARD!

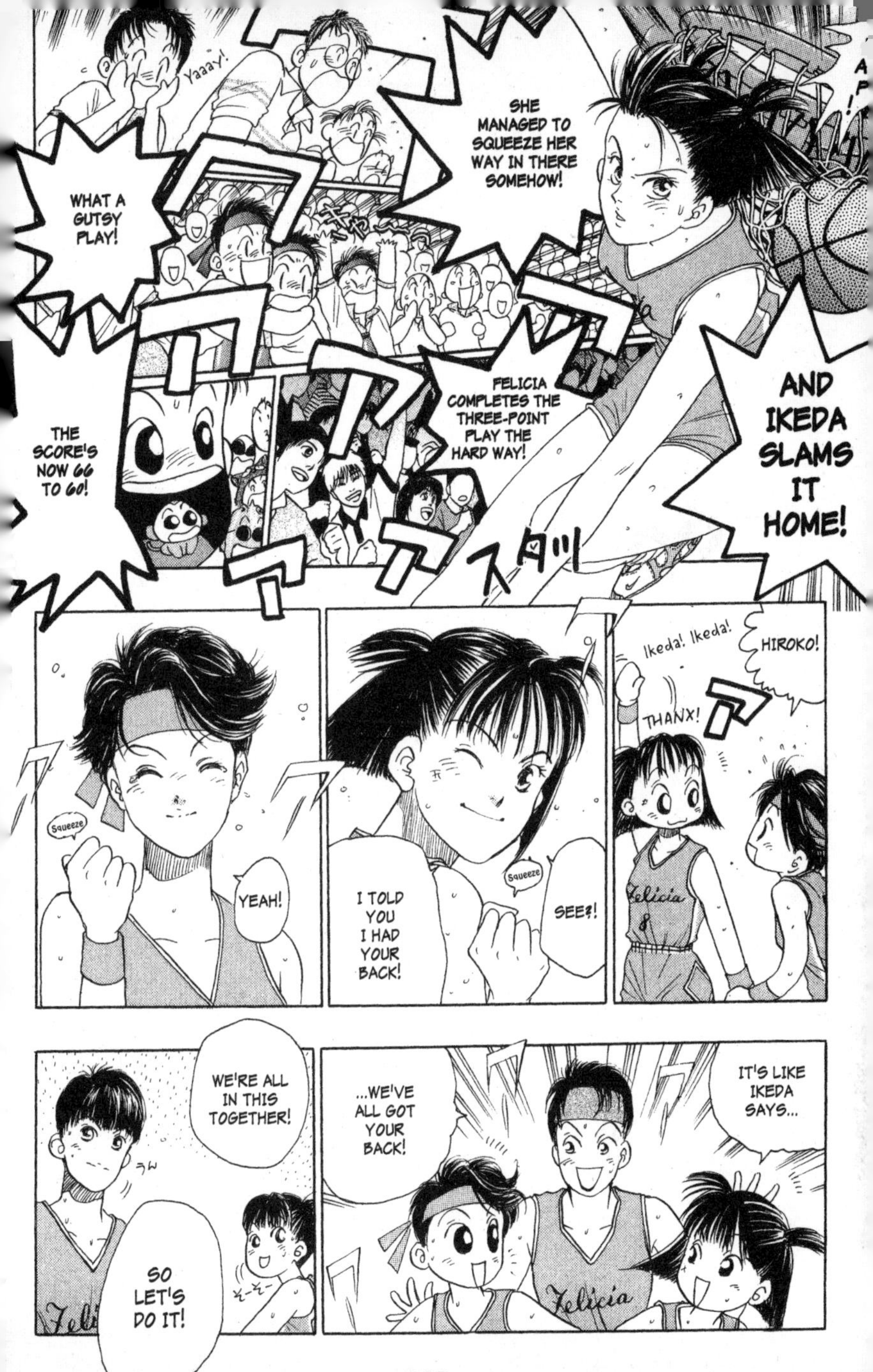
SHE MANAGED TO SQUEEZE HER WAY IN THERE SOMEHOW!
Yaaay!
WHAT A GUTSY PLAY!
AND IKEDA SLAMS IT HOME!
FELICIA COMPLETES THE THREE-POINT PLAY THE HARD WAY!
THE SCORE'S NOW 66 TO 60!
HIROKO!
Ikeda! Ikeda!
THANX!
SEE?!
Squeeze
I TOLD YOU I HAD YOUR BACK!
YEAH!
Squeeze
IT'S LIKE IKEDA SAYS...
...WE'VE ALL GOT YOUR BACK!
WE'RE ALL IN THIS TOGETHER!
SO LET'S DO IT!

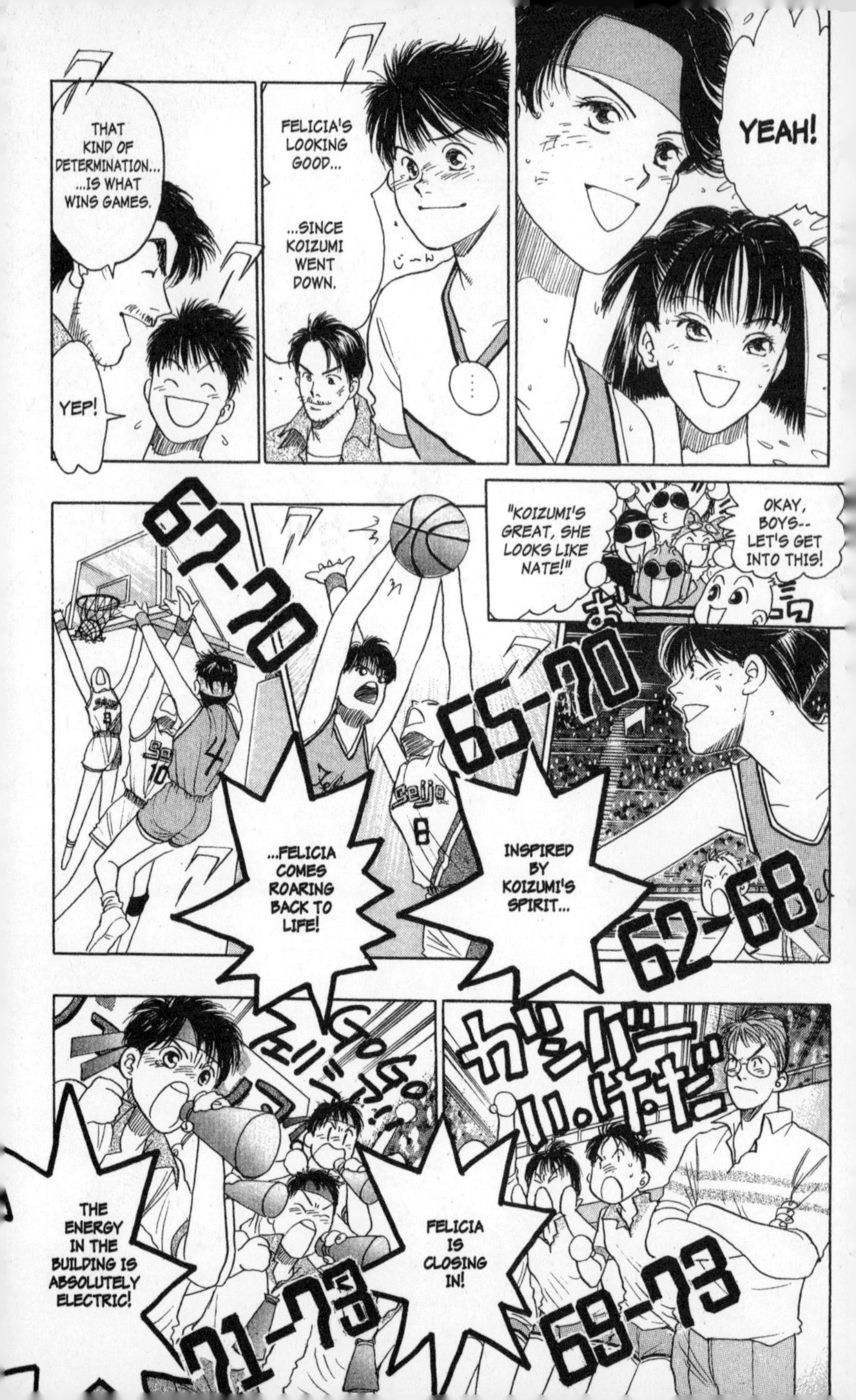
YEAH!
FELICIA'S LOOKING GOOD...
...SINCE KOIZUMI WENT DOWN.
...
THAT KIND OF DETERMINATION... ...IS WHAT WINS GAMES.
YEP!
OKAY, BOYS-- LET'S GET INTO THIS!
"KOIZUMI'S GREAT, SHE LOOKS LIKE NATE!"
62-68
INSPIRED BY KOIZUMI'S SPIRIT...
65-70
67-70
...FELICIA COMES ROARING BACK TO LIFE!
69-73
FELICIA IS CLOSING IN!
GO GO
71-73
THE ENERGY IN THE BUILDING IS ABSOLUTELY ELECTRIC!

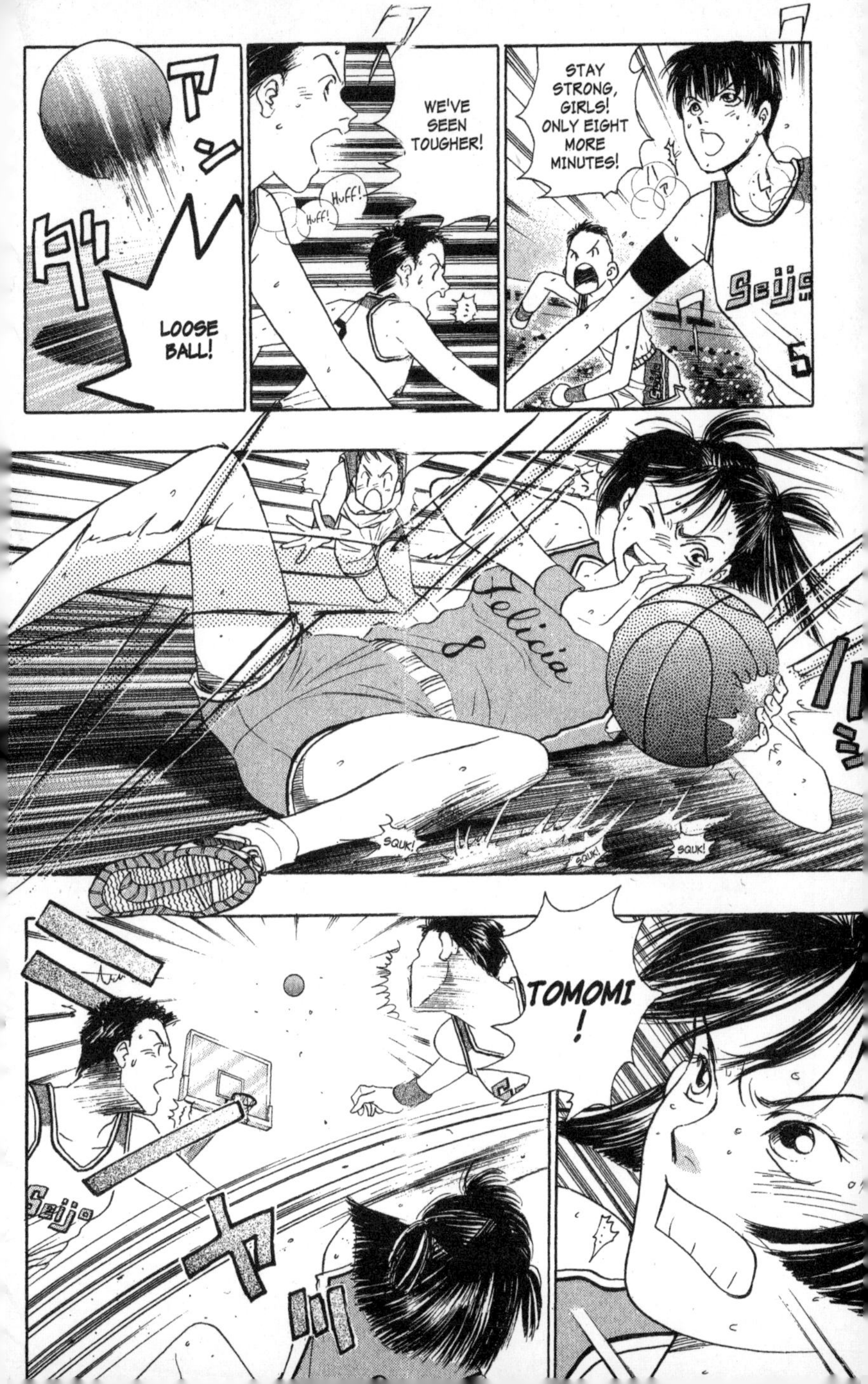
STAY STRONG, GIRLS! ONLY EIGHT MORE MINUTES!
WE'VE SEEN TOUGHER!
Huff!
Huff!
LOOSE BALL!
SQUK!
SQUK!
SQUK!
TOMOMI!

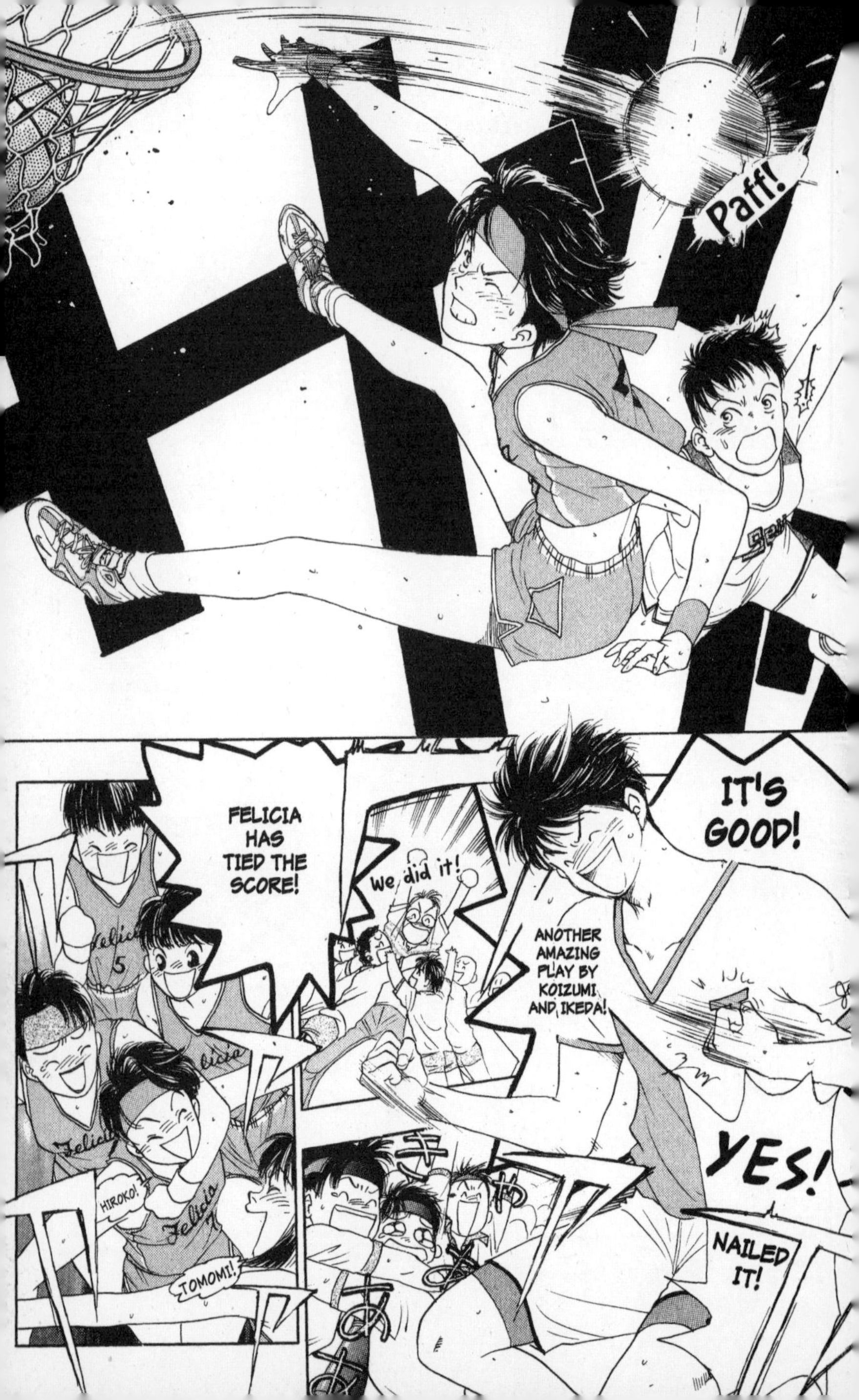
Paff!
IT'S GOOD!
ANOTHER AMAZING PLAY BY KOIZUMI AND IKEDA!
YES!
NAILED IT!
We did it!
FELICIA HAS TIED THE SCORE!
HIROKO!
TOMOMI!

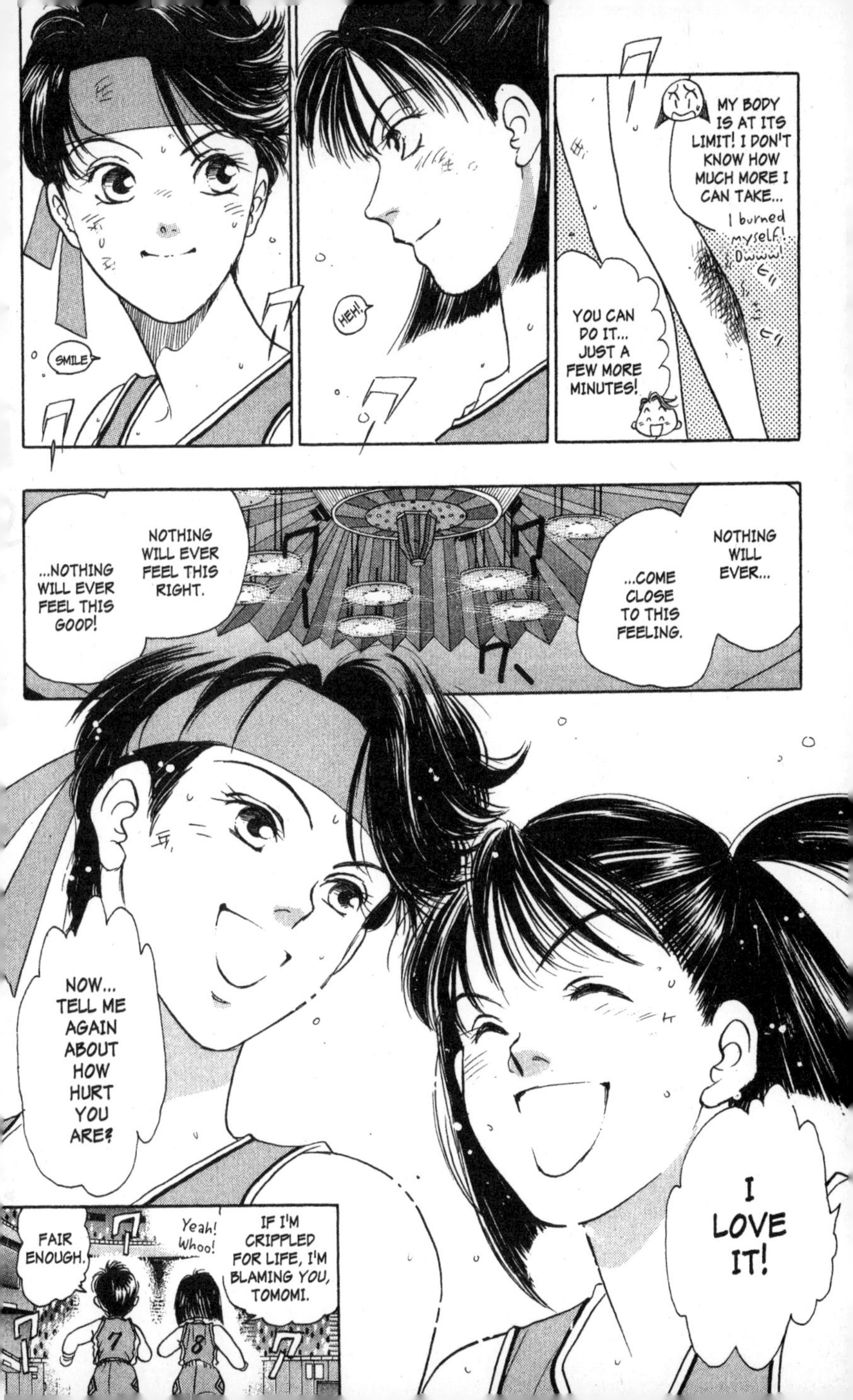
MY BODY IS AT ITS LIMIT! I DON'T KNOW HOW MUCH MORE I CAN TAKE...
I burned myself! Owww!
YOU CAN DO IT... JUST A FEW MORE MINUTES!
HEH!
SMILE
NOTHING WILL EVER...
...COME CLOSE TO THIS FEELING.
NOTHING WILL EVER FEEL THIS RIGHT.
...NOTHING WILL EVER FEEL THIS GOOD!
I LOVE IT!
NOW... TELL ME AGAIN ABOUT HOW HURT YOU ARE?
IF I'M CRIPPLED FOR LIFE, I'M BLAMING YOU, TOMOMI.
Yeah! Whoo!
FAIR ENOUGH.

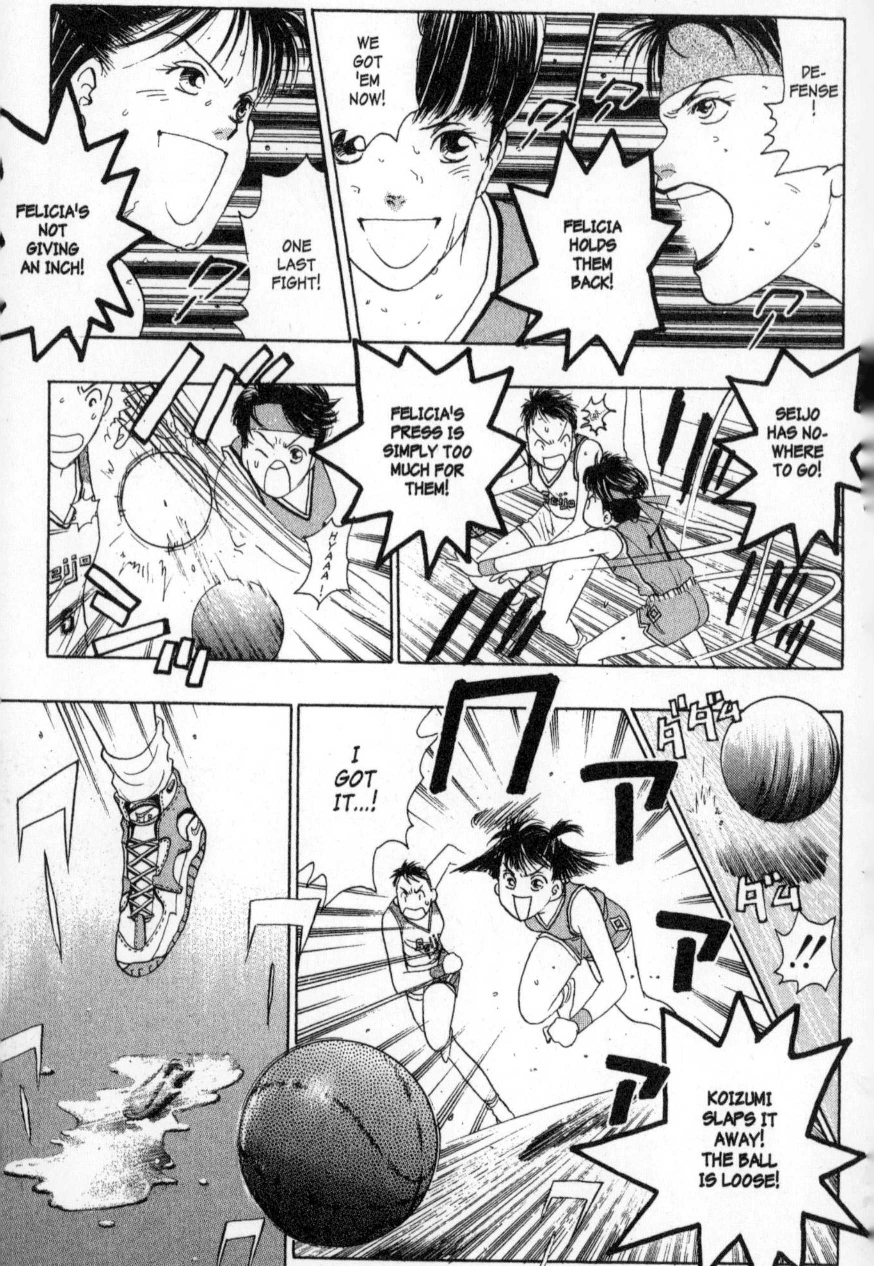
DE-FENSE!
FELICIA HOLDS THEM BACK!
WE GOT 'EM NOW!
ONE LAST FIGHT!
FELICIA'S NOT GIVING AN INCH!
SEIJO HAS NO-WHERE TO GO!
FELICIA'S PRESS IS SIMPLY TOO MUCH FOR THEM!
HYAAA!
!!
KOIZUMI SLAPS IT AWAY! THE BALL IS LOOSE!
I GOT IT...!

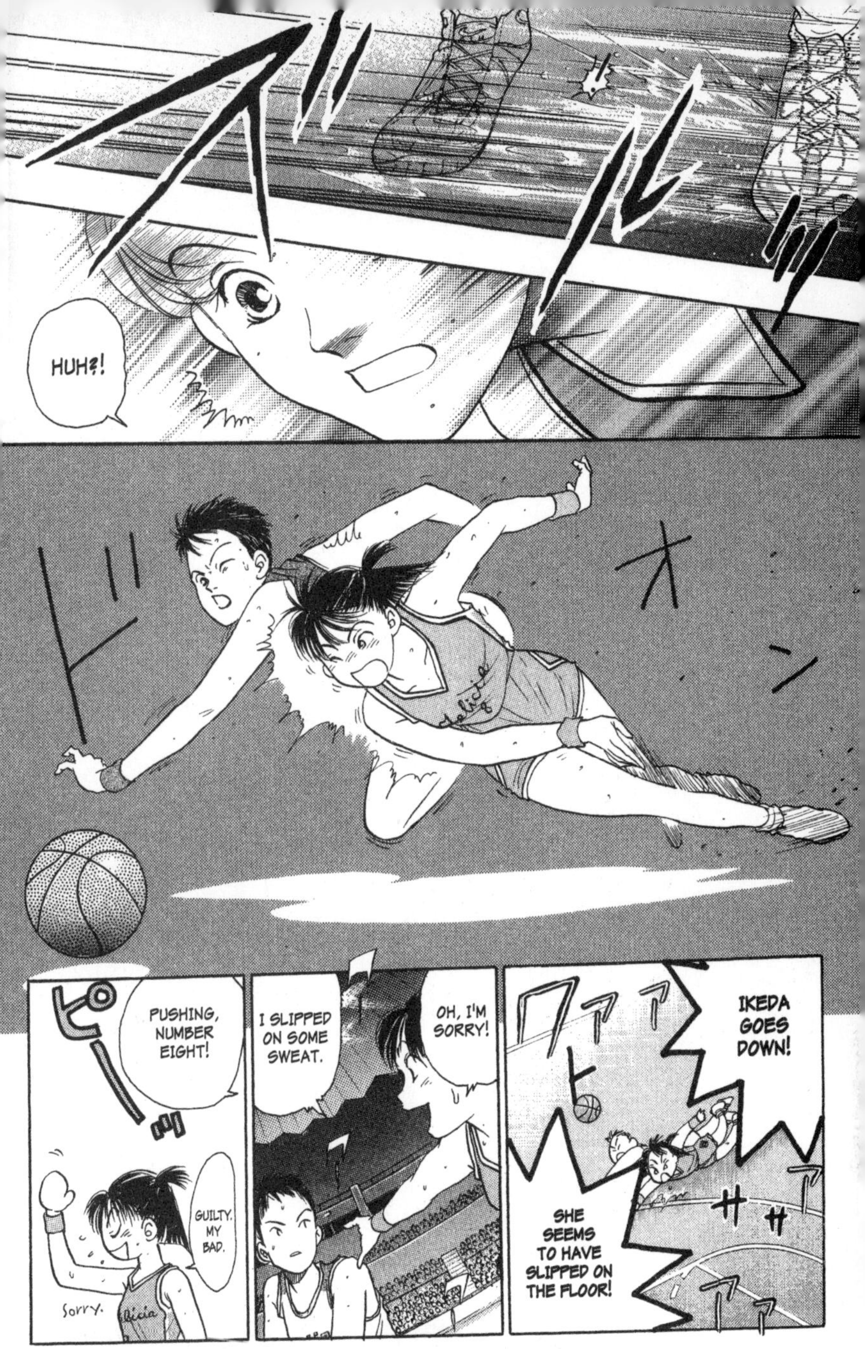
HUH?!
IKEDA GOES DOWN!
SHE SEEMS TO HAVE SLIPPED ON THE FLOOR!
OH, I'M SORRY!
I SLIPPED ON SOME SWEAT.
PUSHING, NUMBER EIGHT!
GUILTY. MY BAD.
Sorry.

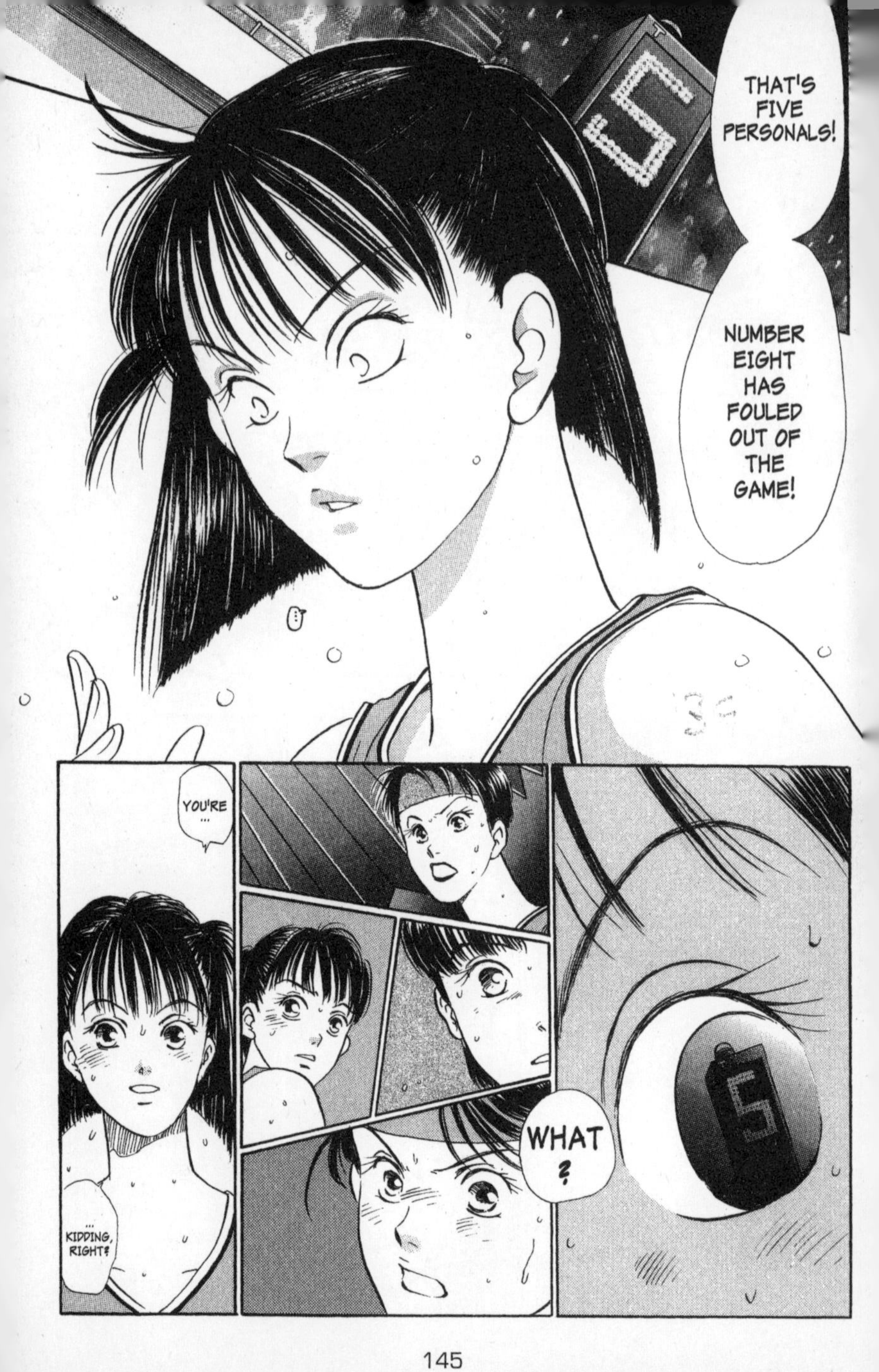
THAT'S FIVE PERSONALS!
NUMBER EIGHT HAS FOULED OUT OF THE GAME!
WHAT?
YOU'RE...
...KIDDING, RIGHT?

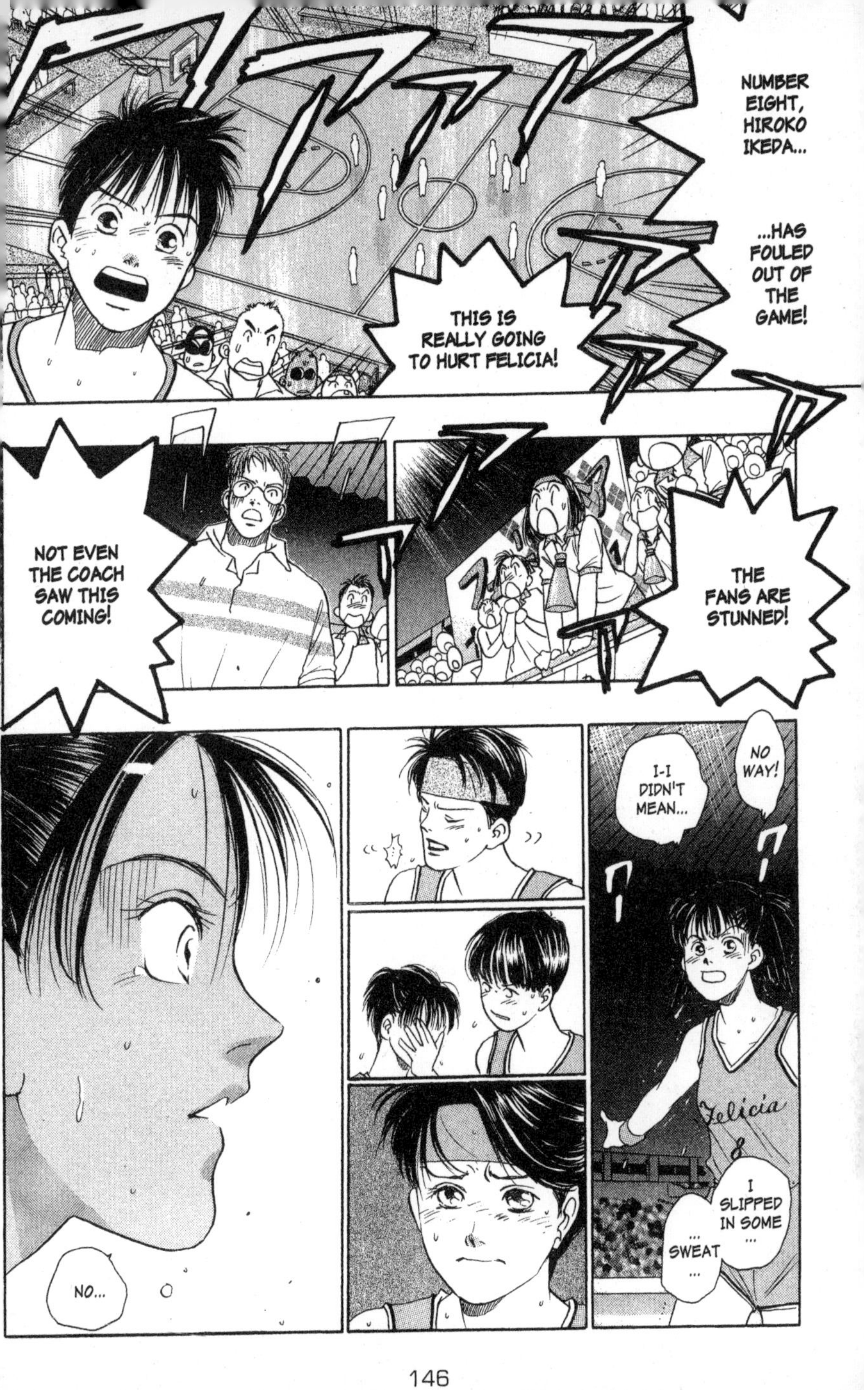
NUMBER EIGHT, HIROKO IKEDA...
...HAS FOULED OUT OF THE GAME!
THIS IS REALLY GOING TO HURT FELICIA!
THE FANS ARE STUNNED!
NOT EVEN THE COACH SAW THIS COMING!
NO WAY!
I-I DIDN'T MEAN...
I SLIPPED IN SOME...
...SWEAT...
NO...

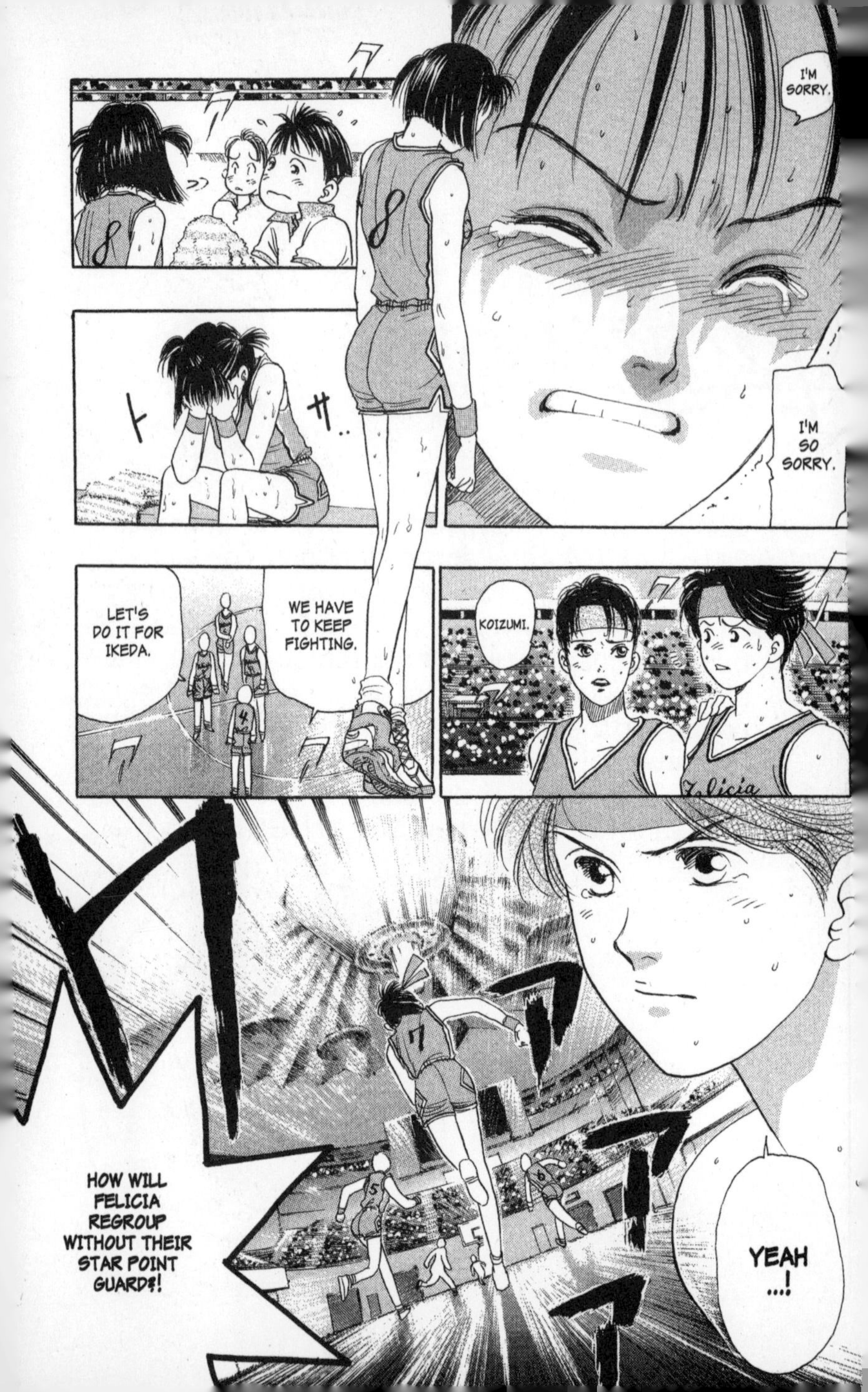
I'M SORRY.
I'M SO SORRY.
ト
サ..
KOIZUMI.
WE HAVE TO KEEP FIGHTING.
LET'S DO IT FOR IKEDA.
YEAH ...!
HOW WILL FELICIA REGROUP WITHOUT THEIR STAR POINT GUARD?!

You're Reading...

Coming Soon!! From TOKYOPOP, in association with Ain't I A Stinker productions—the action packed sequel to last volume's runaway blockbuster Monkey Boy Wonder! You've seen our champion chimp fling feces in the face of death—but never has he faced the sheer power of the League of Scarily Insane Flight Attendants!! Coffee, tea, or red, flaming DEATH!! Which will our hero chose? Find out this summer when you see—MB2: Enter the Simian!!

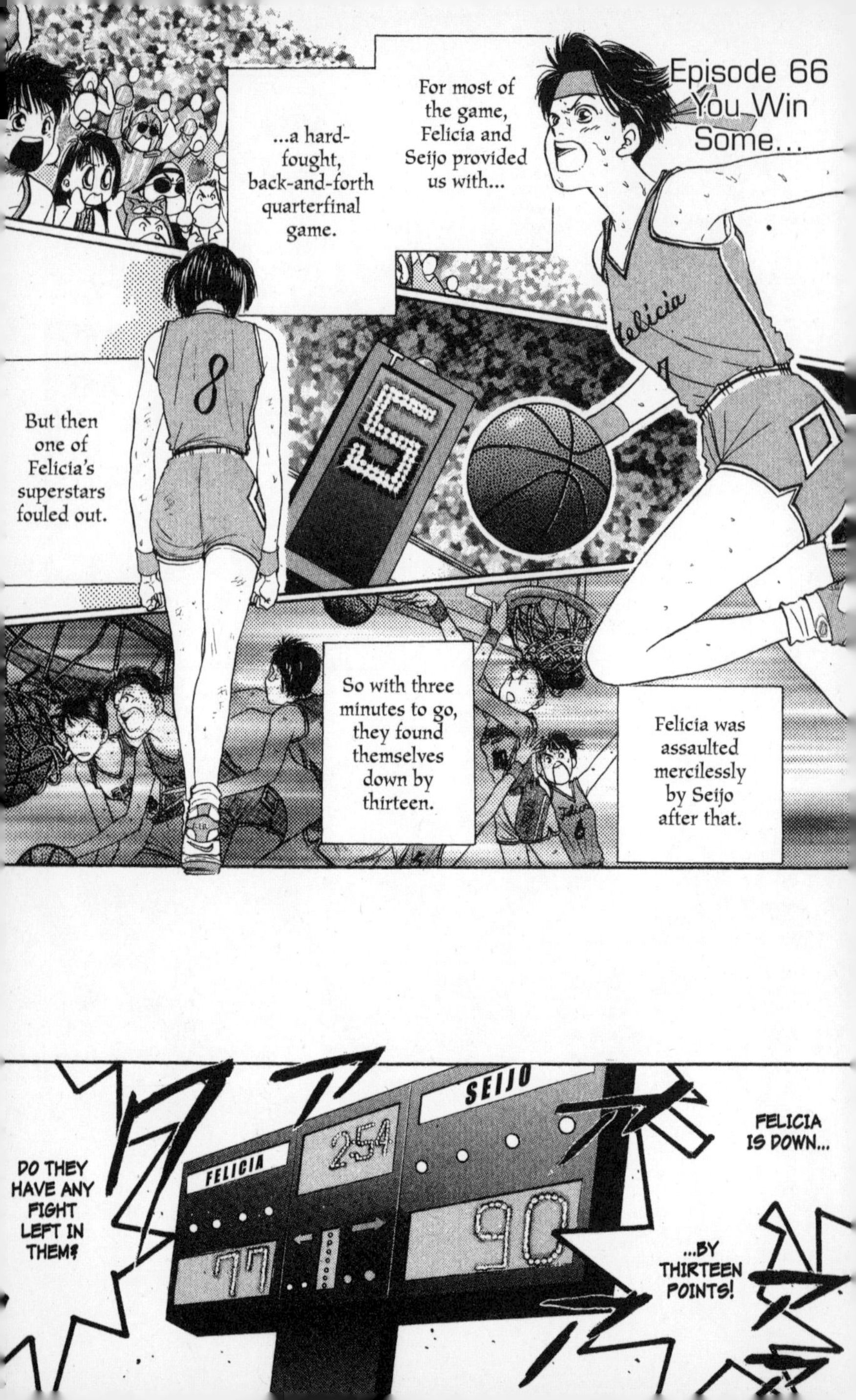
Episode 66
You Win
Some...
For most of the game, Felicia and Seijo provided us with...
...a hard-fought, back-and-forth quarterfinal game.
But then one of Felicia's superstars fouled out.
Felicia was assaulted mercilessly by Seijo after that.
So with three minutes to go, they found themselves down by thirteen.
SEIJO
2:54
FELICIA
77
90
FELICIA IS DOWN...
...BY THIRTEEN POINTS!
DO THEY HAVE ANY FIGHT LEFT IN THEM?

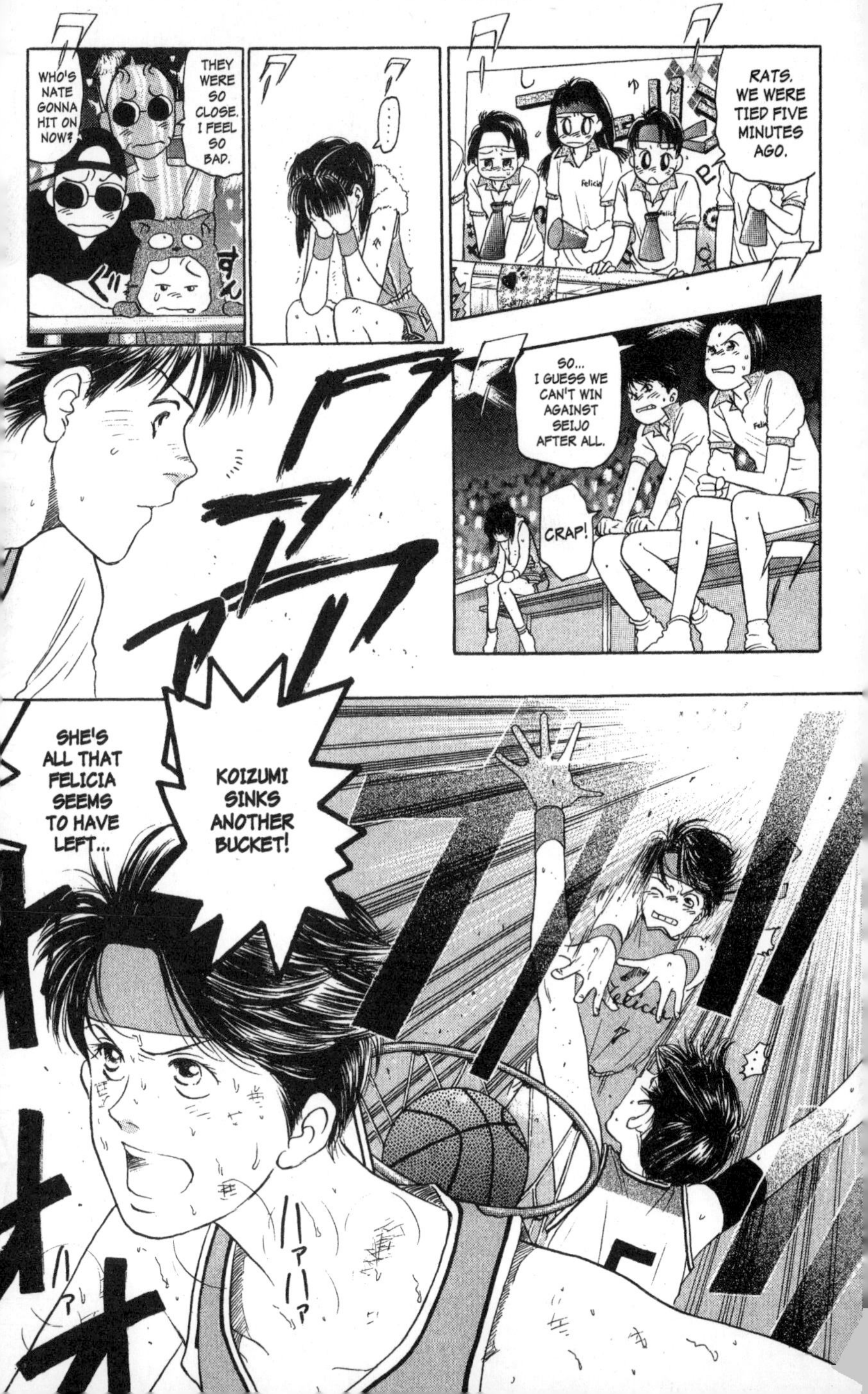
RATS. WE WERE TIED FIVE MINUTES AGO.
...
THEY WERE SO CLOSE. I FEEL SO BAD.
WHO'S NATE GONNA HIT ON NOW?
SO... I GUESS WE CAN'T WIN AGAINST SEIJO AFTER ALL.
CRAP!
KOIZUMI SINKS ANOTHER BUCKET!
SHE'S ALL THAT FELICIA SEEMS TO HAVE LEFT...

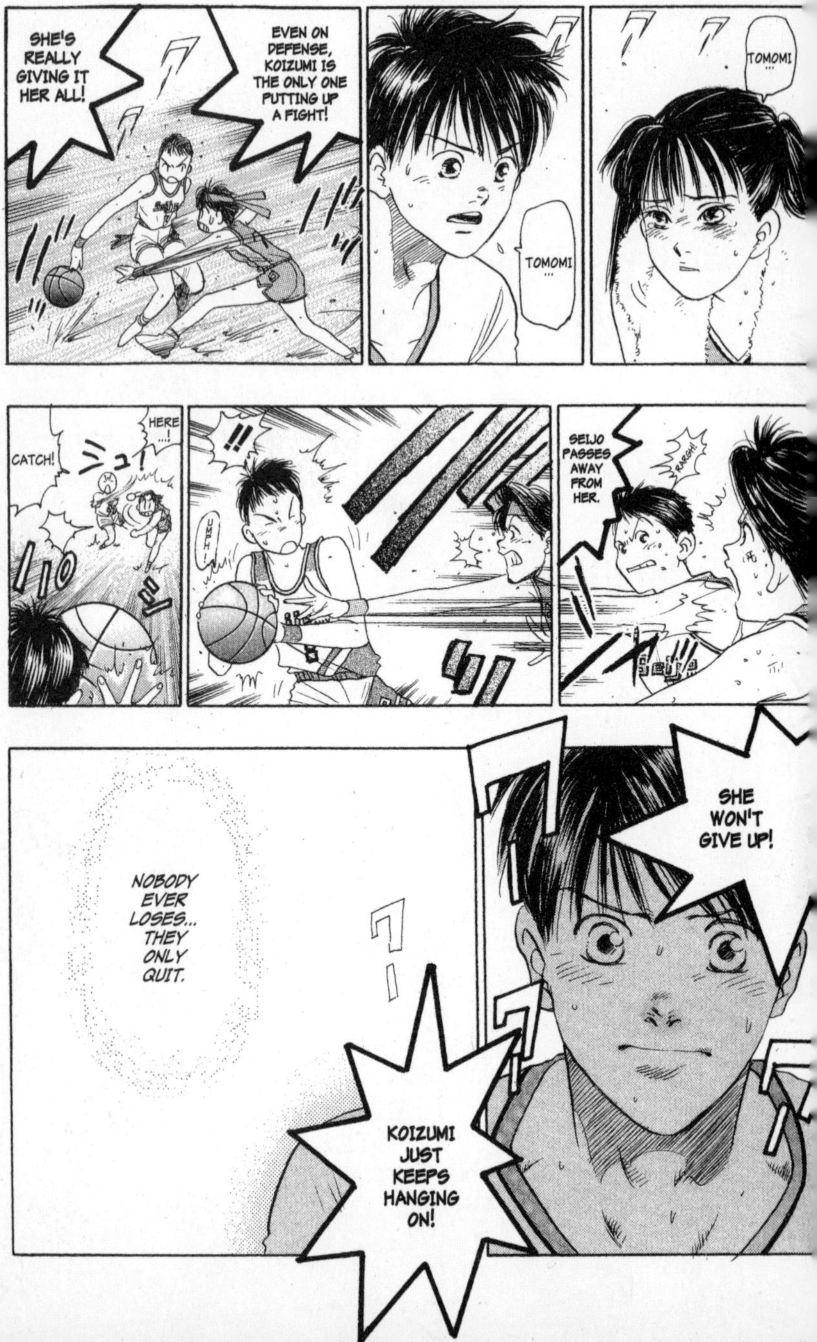
TOMOMI...
TOMOMI...
EVEN ON DEFENSE, KOIZUMI IS THE ONLY ONE PUTTING UP A FIGHT!
SHE'S REALLY GIVING IT HER ALL!
RARGH!
SEIJO PASSES AWAY FROM HER.
!!
UMPH!
HERE...!
CATCH!
SHE WON'T GIVE UP!
KOIZUMI JUST KEEPS HANGING ON!
NOBODY EVER LOSES... THEY ONLY QUIT.

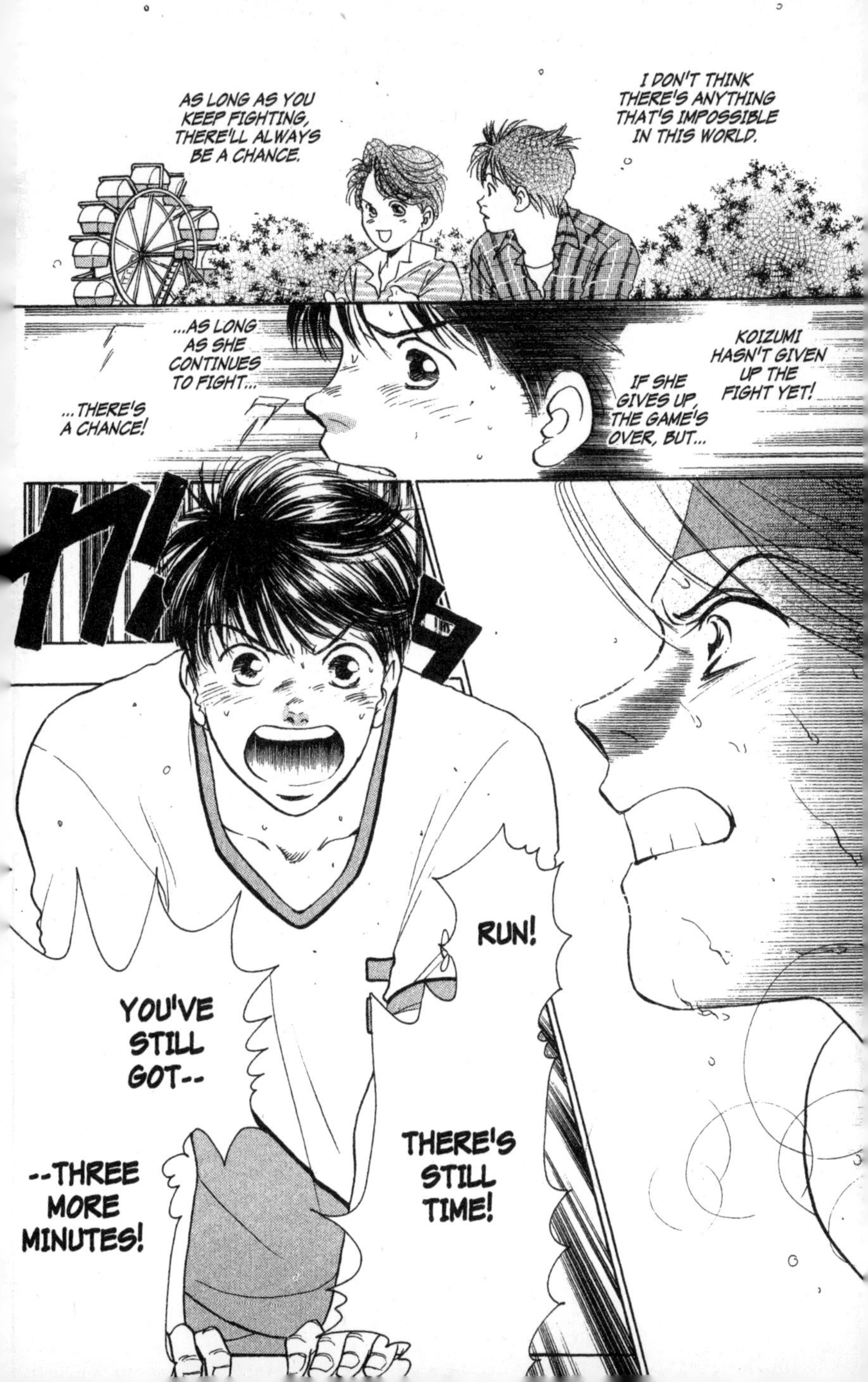
I DON'T THINK THERE'S ANYTHING THAT'S IMPOSSIBLE IN THIS WORLD.
AS LONG AS YOU KEEP FIGHTING, THERE'LL ALWAYS BE A CHANCE.
KOIZUMI HASN'T GIVEN UP THE FIGHT YET!
IF SHE GIVES UP, THE GAME'S OVER, BUT...
...AS LONG AS SHE CONTINUES TO FIGHT...
...THERE'S A CHANCE!
RUN!
YOU'VE STILL GOT--
THERE'S STILL TIME!
--THREE MORE MINUTES!

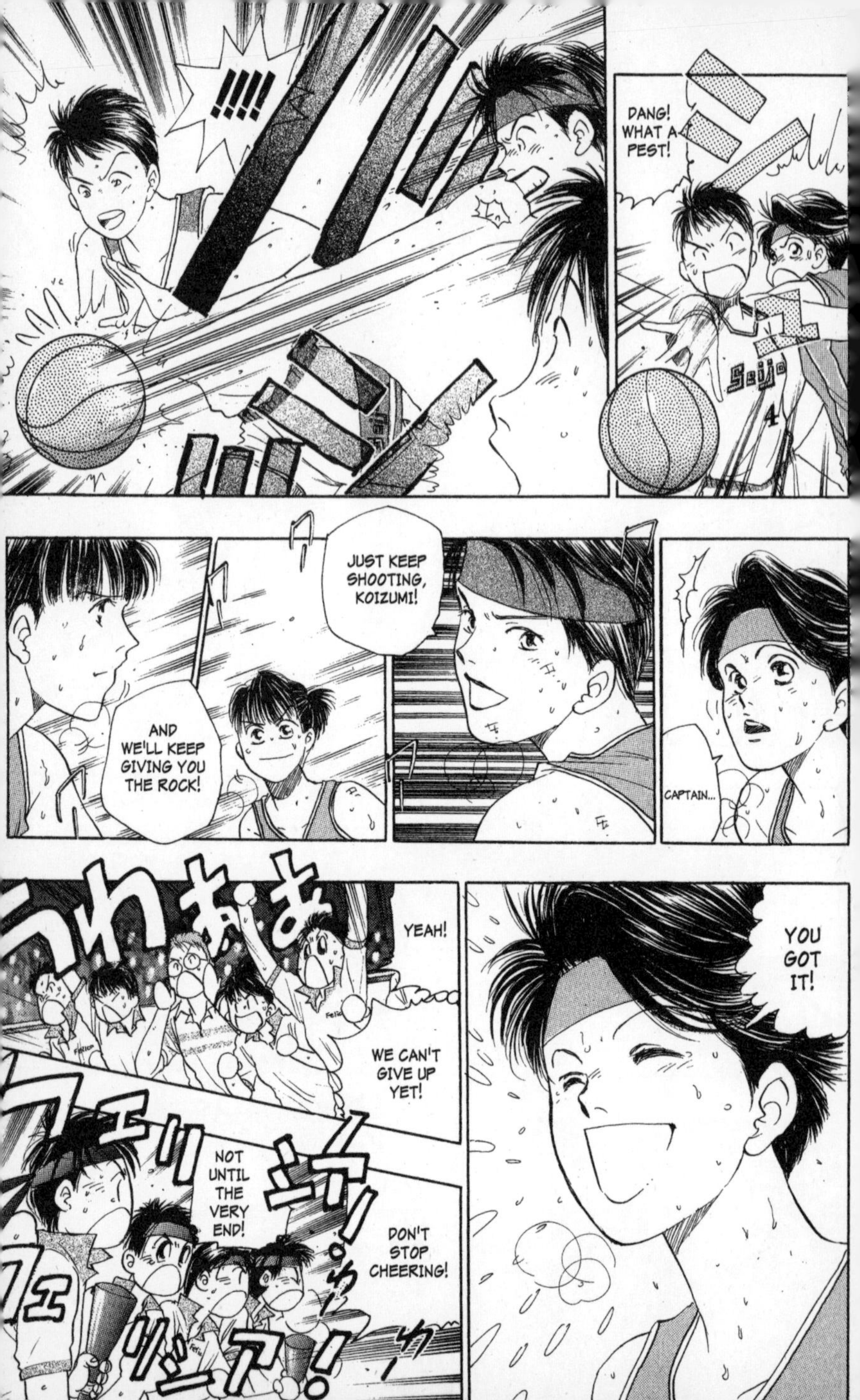
DANG! WHAT A PEST!
!!!!!
CAPTAIN...
JUST KEEP SHOOTING, KOIZUMI!
AND WE'LL KEEP GIVING YOU THE ROCK!
YOU GOT IT!
YEAH!
WE CAN'T GIVE UP YET!
NOT UNTIL THE VERY END!
DON'T STOP CHEERING!

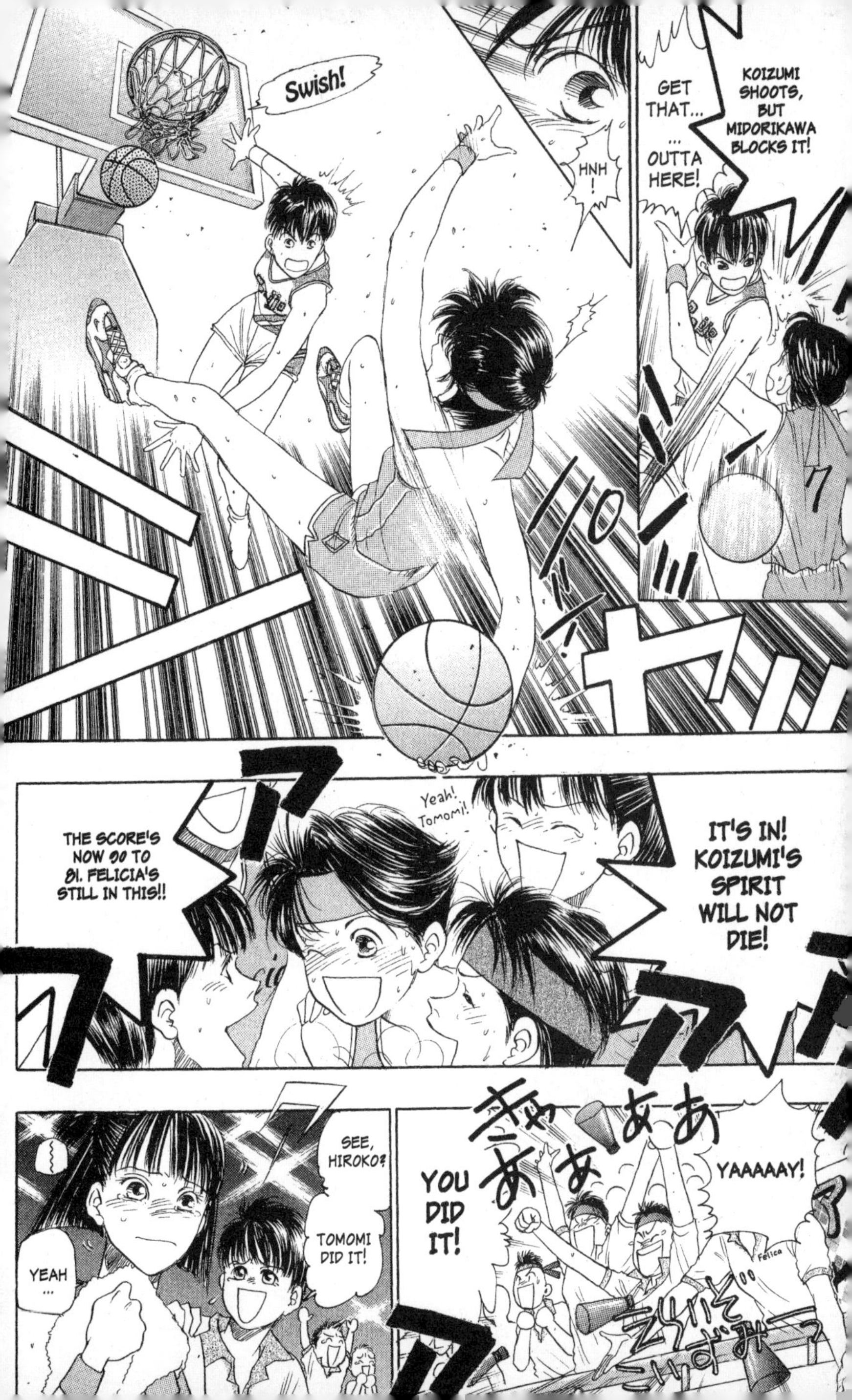
KOIZUMI SHOOTS, BUT MIDORIKAWA BLOCKS IT!
GET THAT... ... OUTTA HERE!
HNH !
Swish!
IT'S IN! KOIZUMI'S SPIRIT WILL NOT DIE!
Yeah! Tomomi!
THE SCORE'S NOW 90 TO 81. FELICIA'S STILL IN THIS!!
YAAAAAY!
YOU DID IT!
Felica
SEE, HIROKO?
TOMOMI DID IT!
YEAH ...

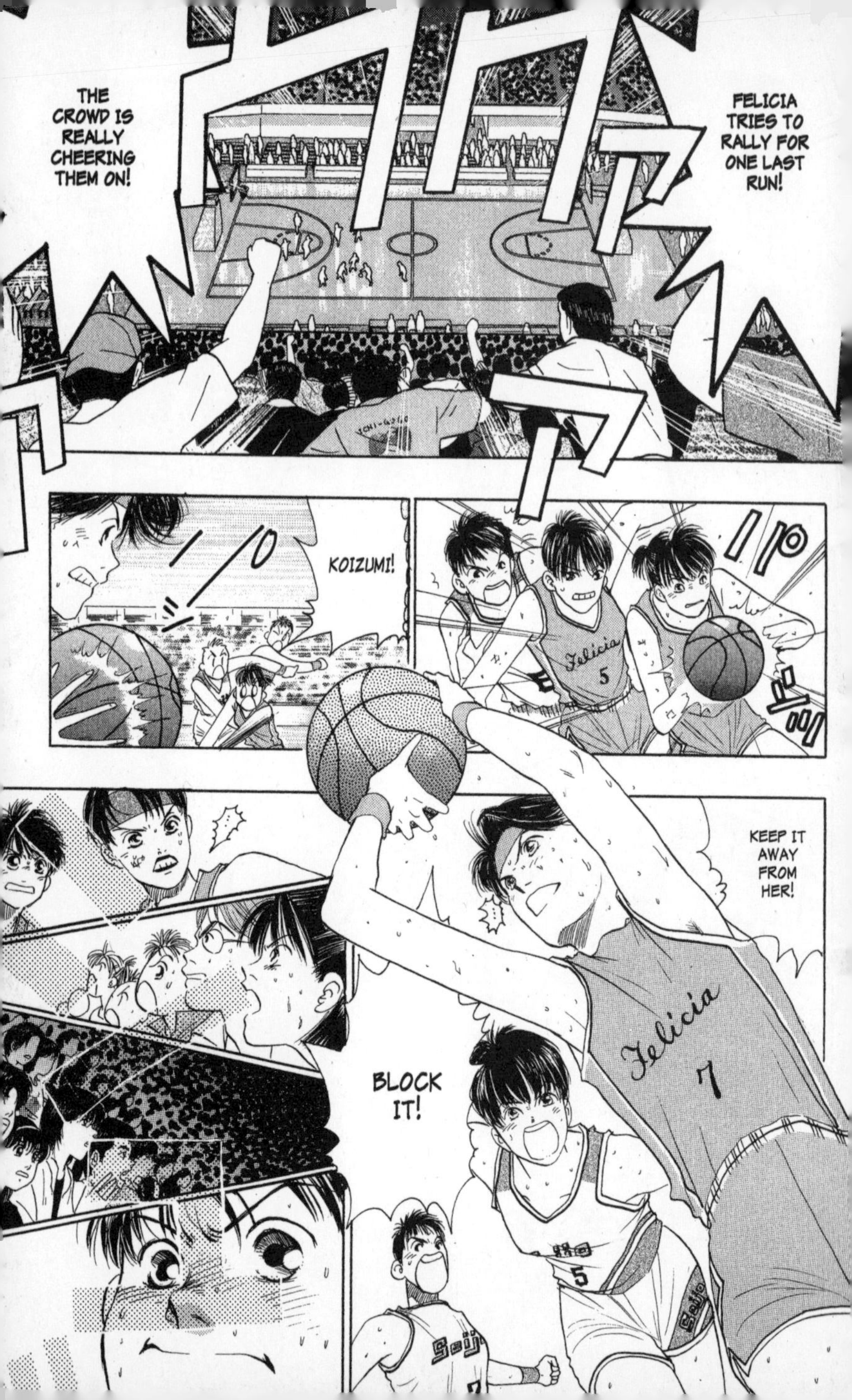
FELICIA TRIES TO RALLY FOR ONE LAST RUN!
THE CROWD IS REALLY CHEERING THEM ON!
KOIZUMI!
KEEP IT AWAY FROM HER!
BLOCK IT!

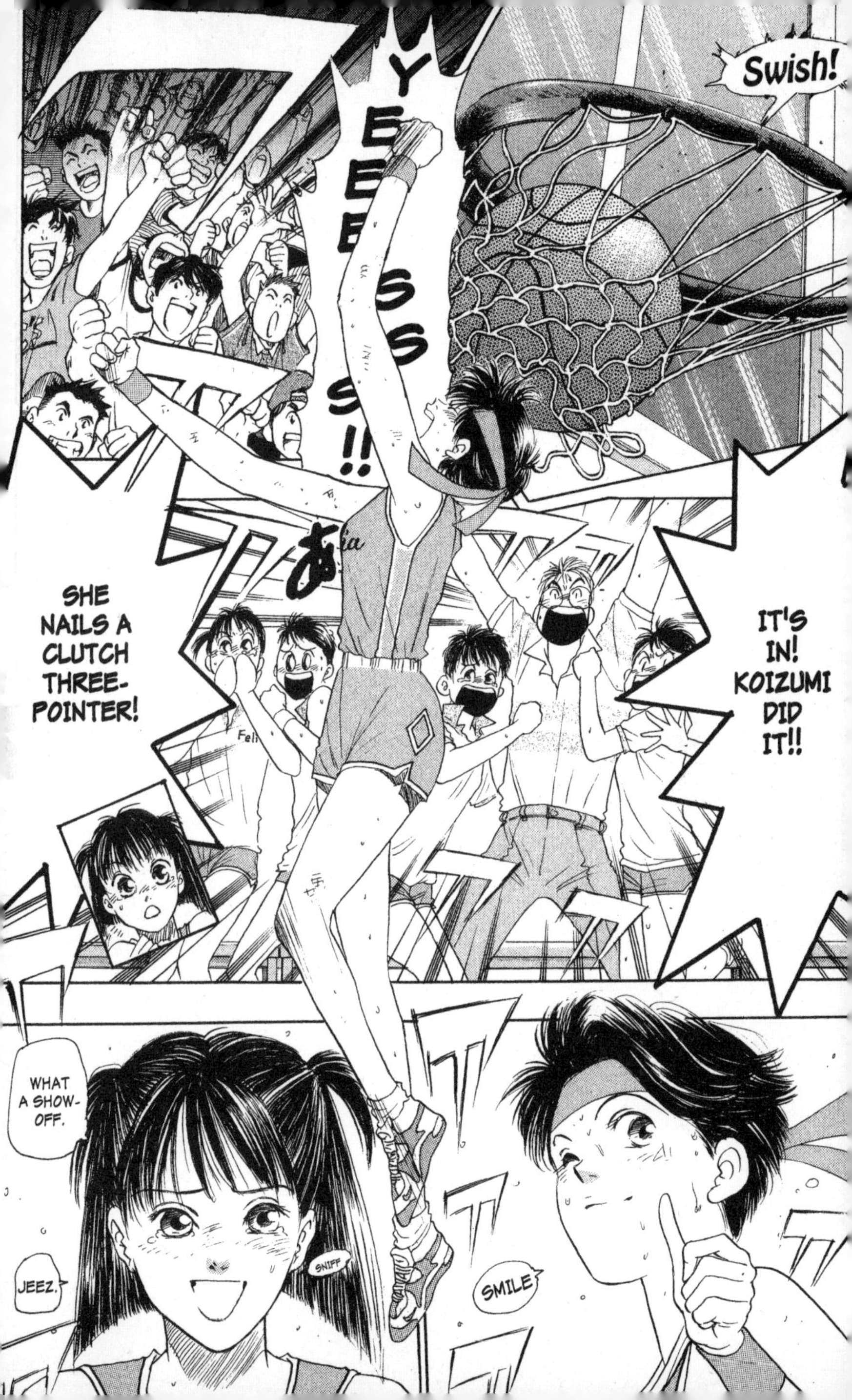
Swish!
YEEESSS!!
IT'S IN! KOIZUMI DID IT!!
SHE NAILS A CLUTCH THREE-POINTER!
SMILE
WHAT A SHOW-OFF.
SNIFF
JEEZ.

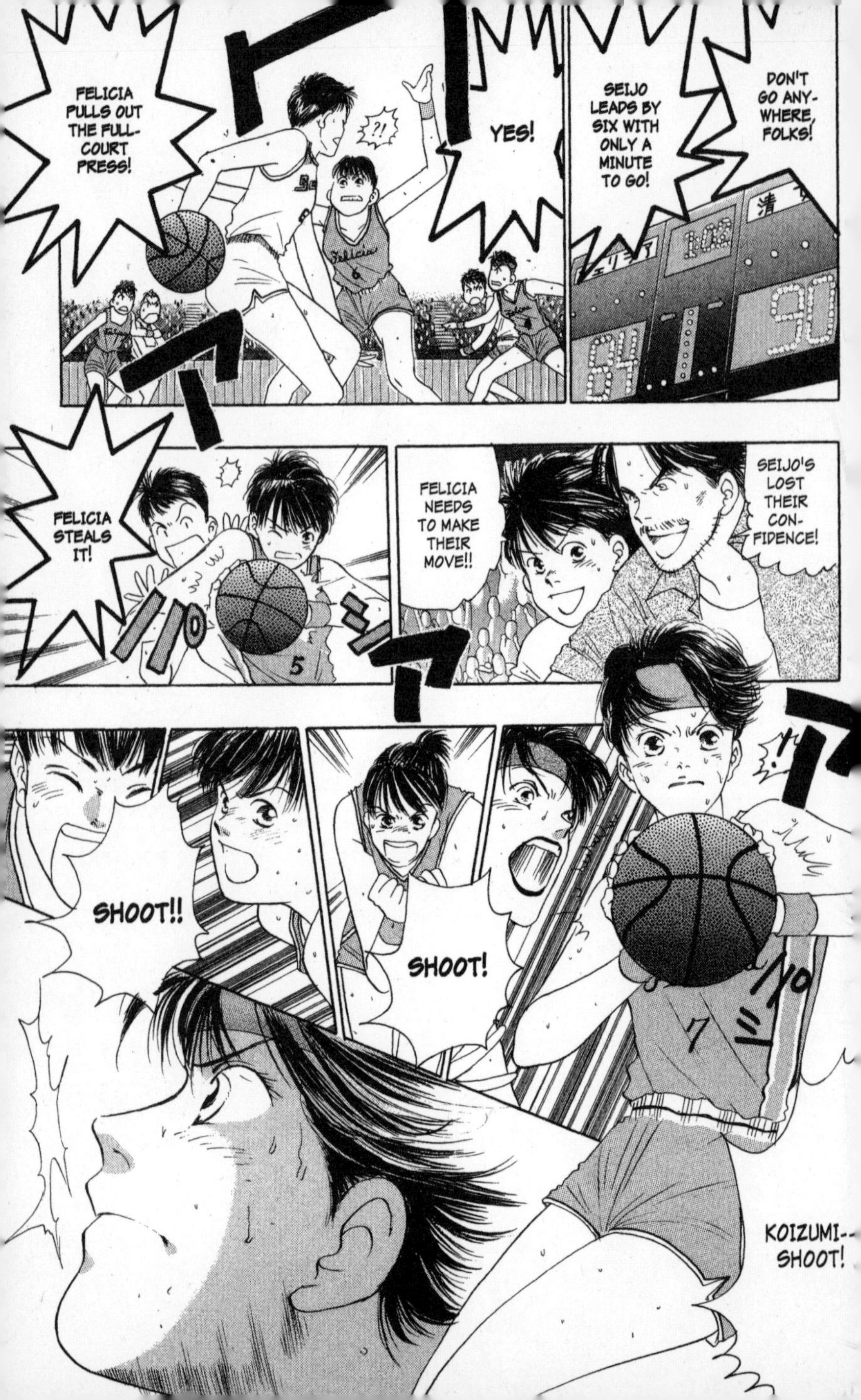
DON'T GO ANYWHERE, FOLKS!
SEIJO LEADS BY SIX WITH ONLY A MINUTE TO GO!
YES!
FELICIA PULLS OUT THE FULL-COURT PRESS!
?!
SEIJO'S LOST THEIR CONFIDENCE!
FELICIA NEEDS TO MAKE THEIR MOVE!!
FELICIA STEALS IT!
KOIZUMI-- SHOOT!
!
SHOOT!
SHOOT!!

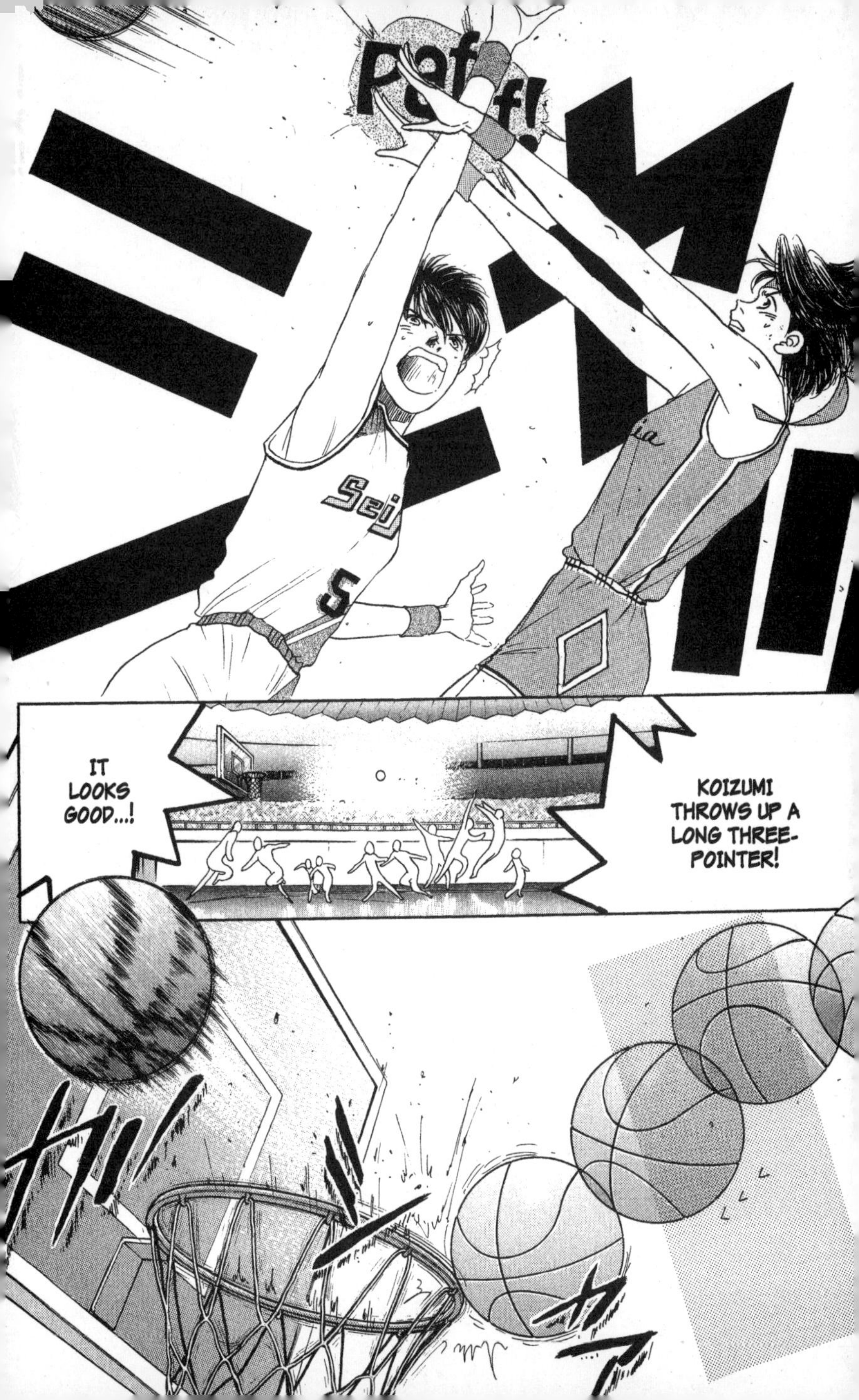
Paff!
KOIZUMI THROWS UP A LONG THREE-POINTER!
IT LOOKS GOOD...!

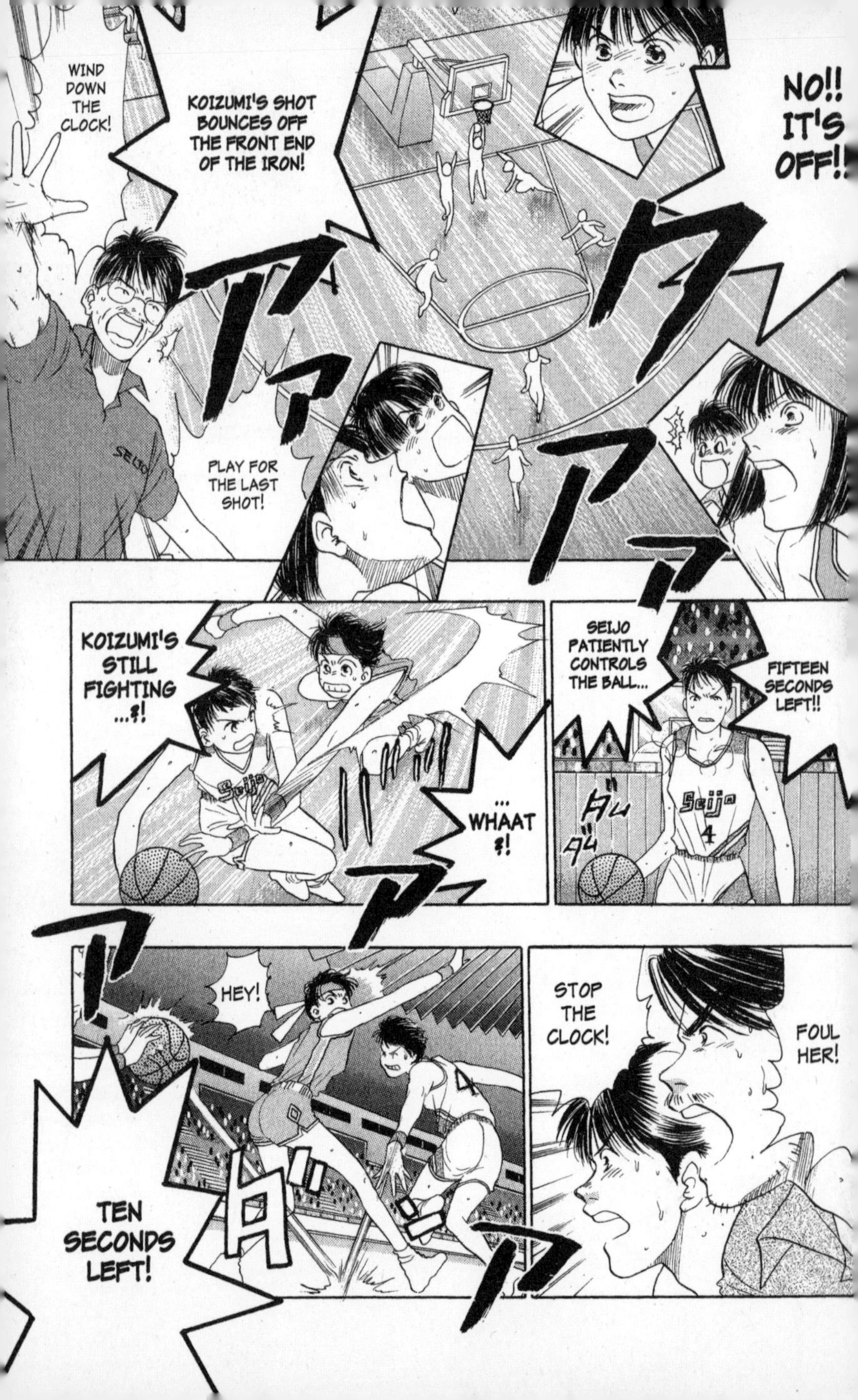
NO!! IT'S OFF!!
KOIZUMI'S SHOT BOUNCES OFF THE FRONT END OF THE IRON!
WIND DOWN THE CLOCK!
PLAY FOR THE LAST SHOT!
FIFTEEN SECONDS LEFT!!
SEIJO PATIENTLY CONTROLS THE BALL...
ダム ダム
... WHAAT ?!
KOIZUMI'S STILL FIGHTING ...?!
FOUL HER!
STOP THE CLOCK!
HEY!
TEN SECONDS LEFT!

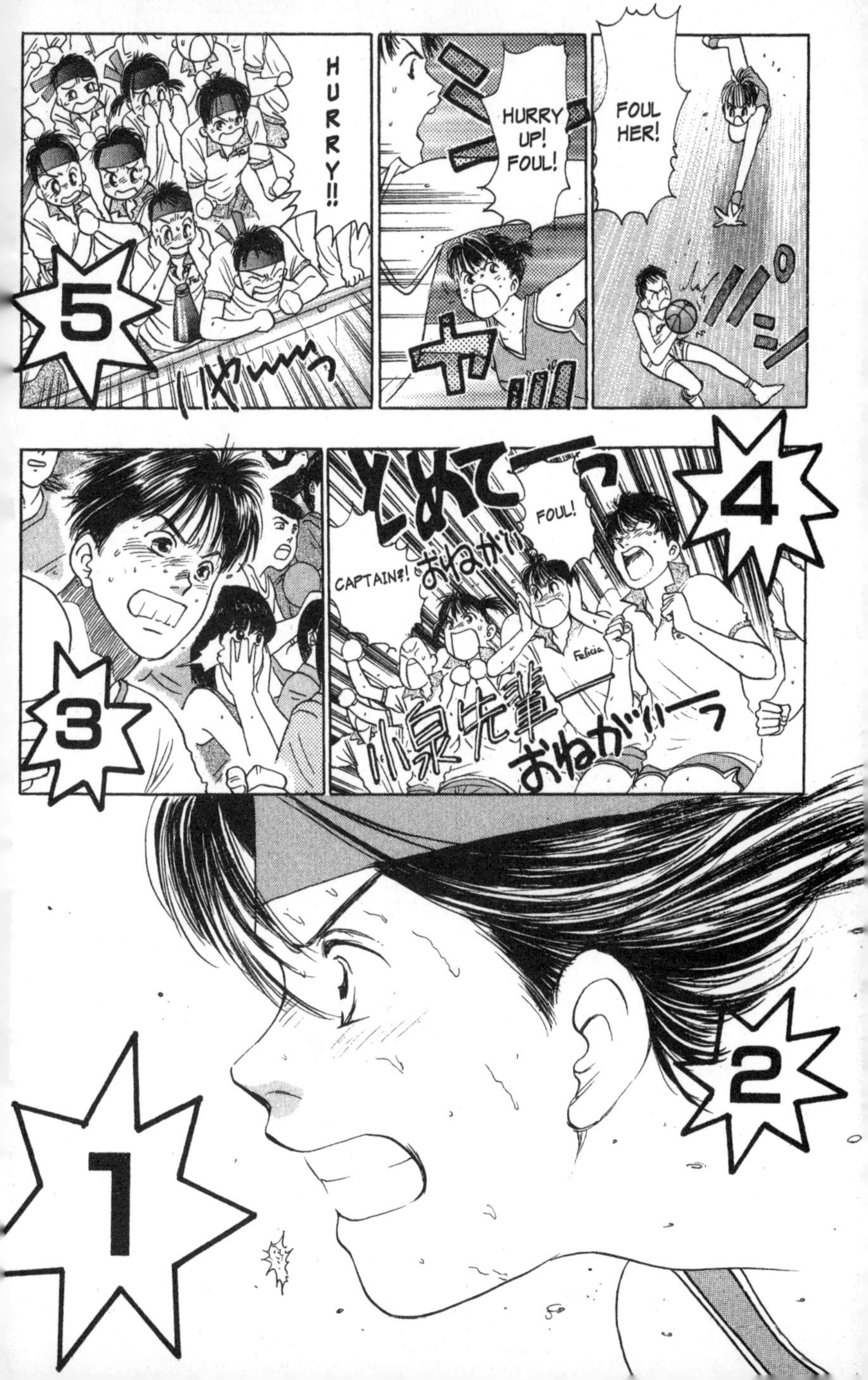

FOUL HER!
HURRY UP! FOUL!
HURRY!!
5
とめてーっ
FOUL!
CAPTAIN?!
おねがい
小泉先輩おねがいーっ
4
3
2
1

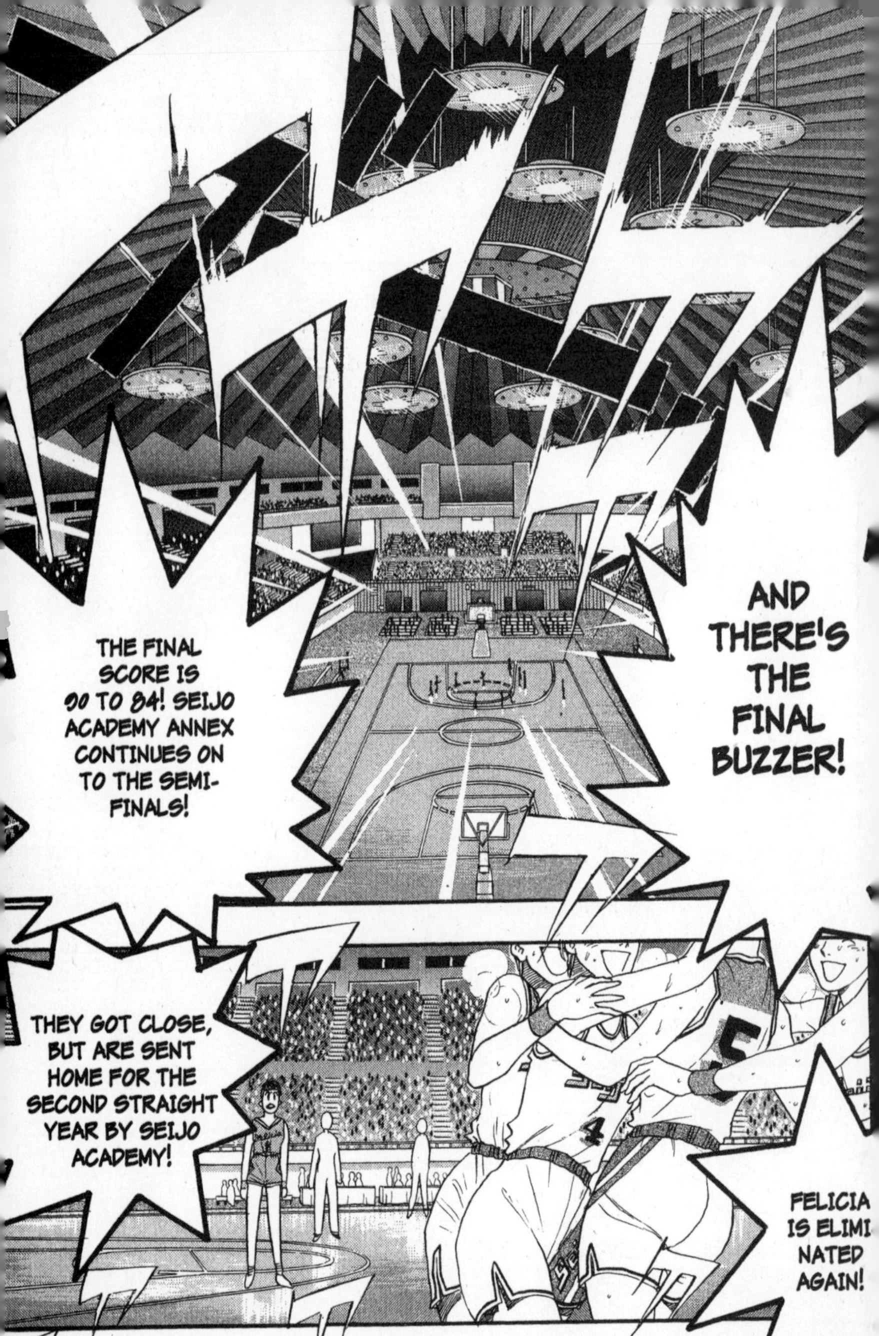
AND THERE'S THE FINAL BUZZER!
THE FINAL SCORE IS 90 TO 84! SEIJO ACADEMY ANNEX CONTINUES ON TO THE SEMI-FINALS!
THEY GOT CLOSE, BUT ARE SENT HOME FOR THE SECOND STRAIGHT YEAR BY SEIJO ACADEMY!
FELICIA IS ELIMI NATED AGAIN!

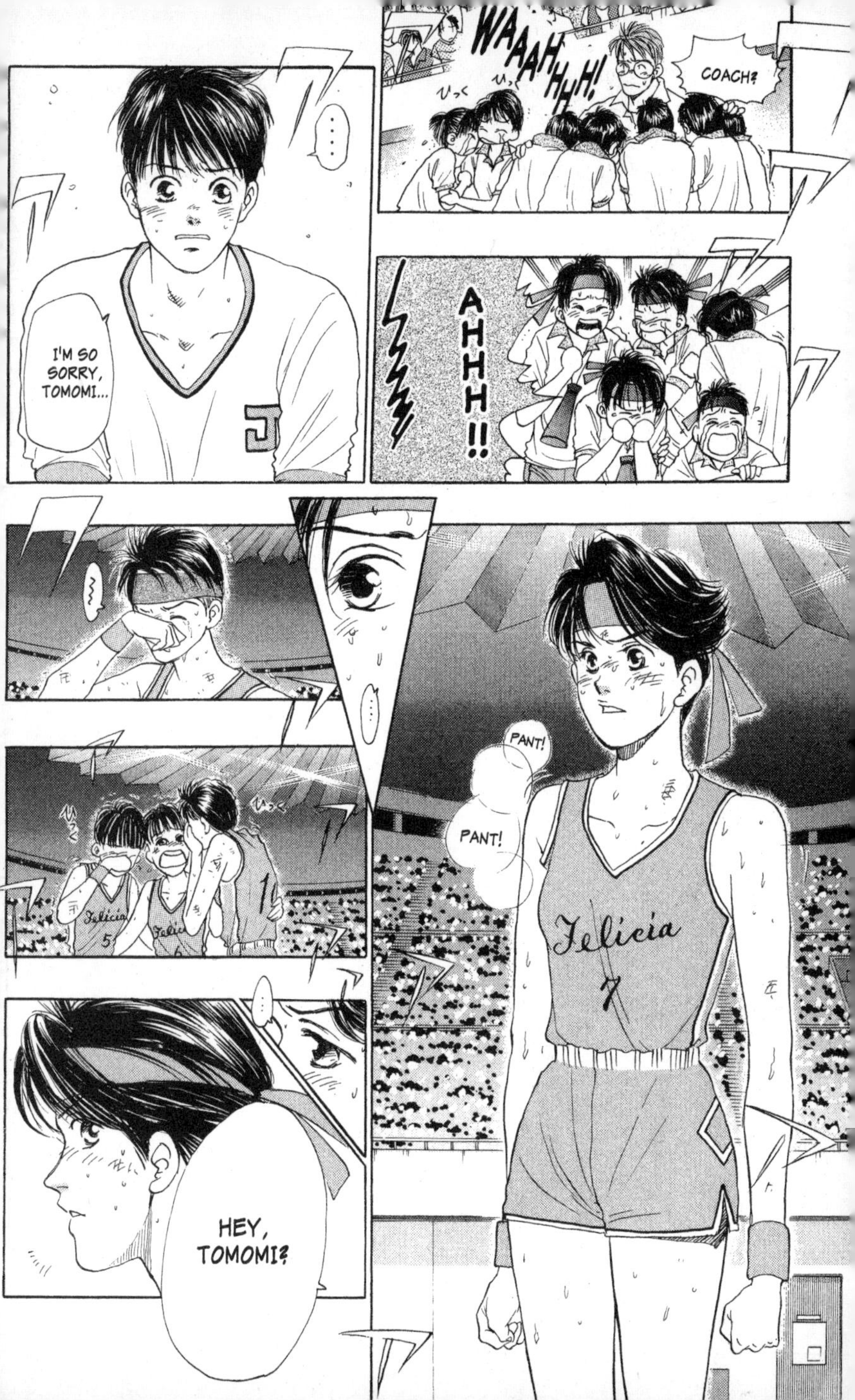
WAAAHHHH!
びっく
ひっく
COACH?
AHHHH!!
...
I'M SO SORRY, TOMOMI...
PANT!
PANT!
...
ひっく
ひっく
...
HEY, TOMOMI?

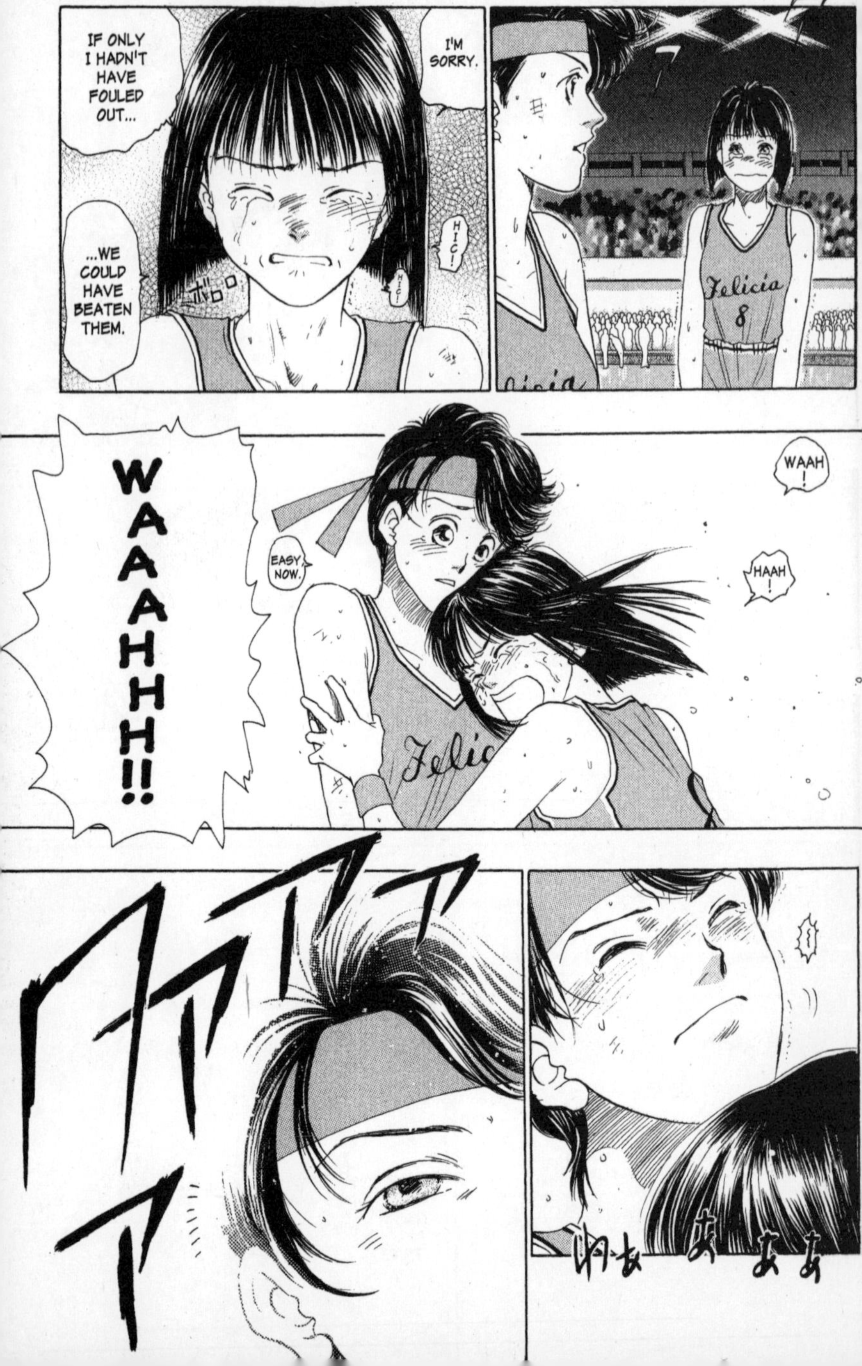
I'M SORRY.
IF ONLY I HADN'T HAVE FOULED OUT...
HIC!
HIC!
...WE COULD HAVE BEATEN THEM.
WAAH!
HAAH!
EASY NOW.
WAAAHHHH!!

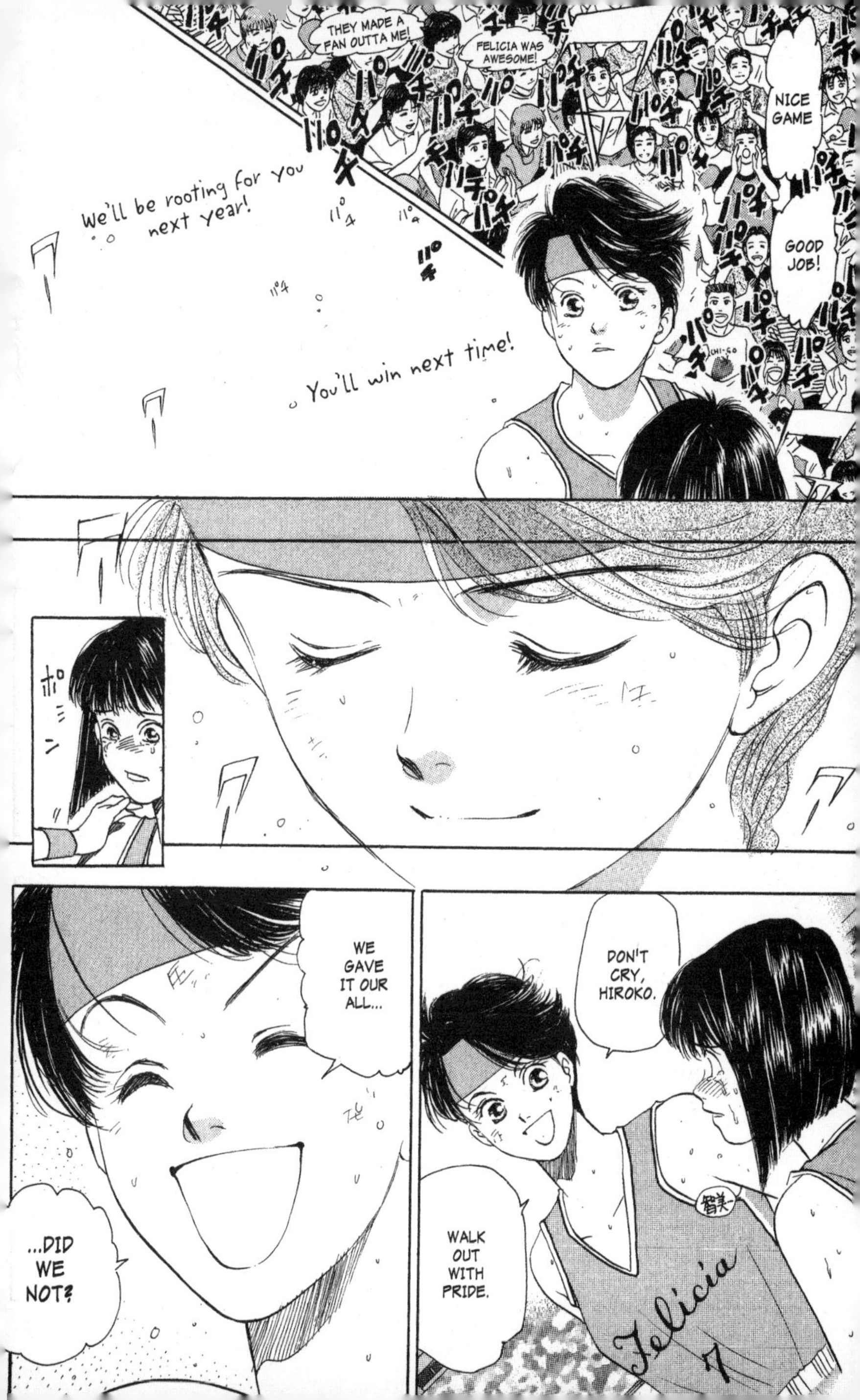
NICE GAME
GOOD JOB!
FELICIA WAS AWESOME!
THEY MADE A FAN OUTTA ME!
We'll be rooting for you next year!
You'll win next time!
DON'T CRY, HIROKO.
WALK OUT WITH PRIDE.
Felicia 7
WE GAVE IT OUR ALL...
...DID WE NOT?

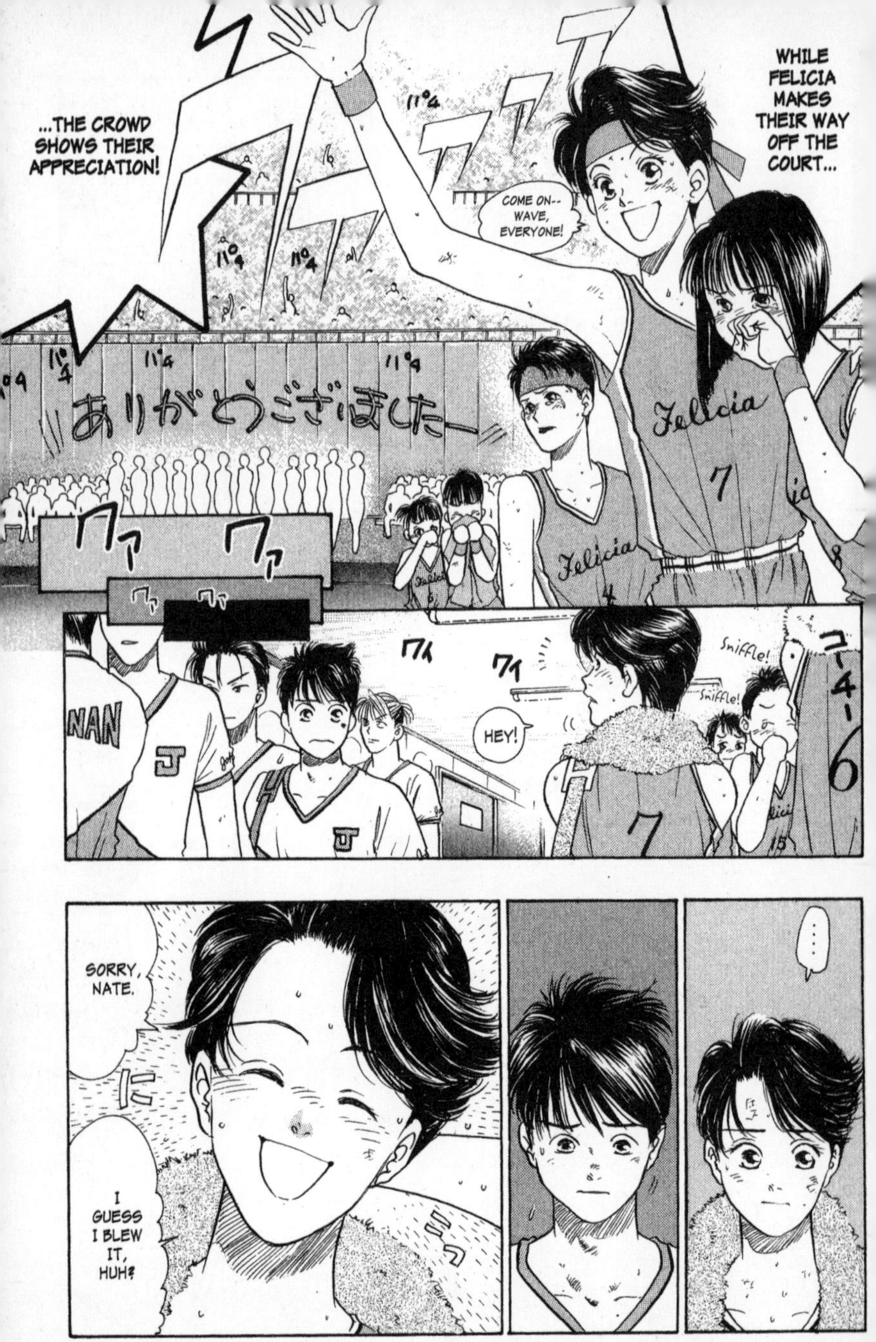
WHILE FELICIA MAKES THEIR WAY OFF THE COURT...
COME ON-- WAVE, EVERYONE!
...THE CROWD SHOWS THEIR APPRECIATION!
ありがとうございましたー
ワァ ワァ
HEY!
Sniffle!
Sniffle!
...
SORRY, NATE.
I GUESS I BLEW IT, HUH?

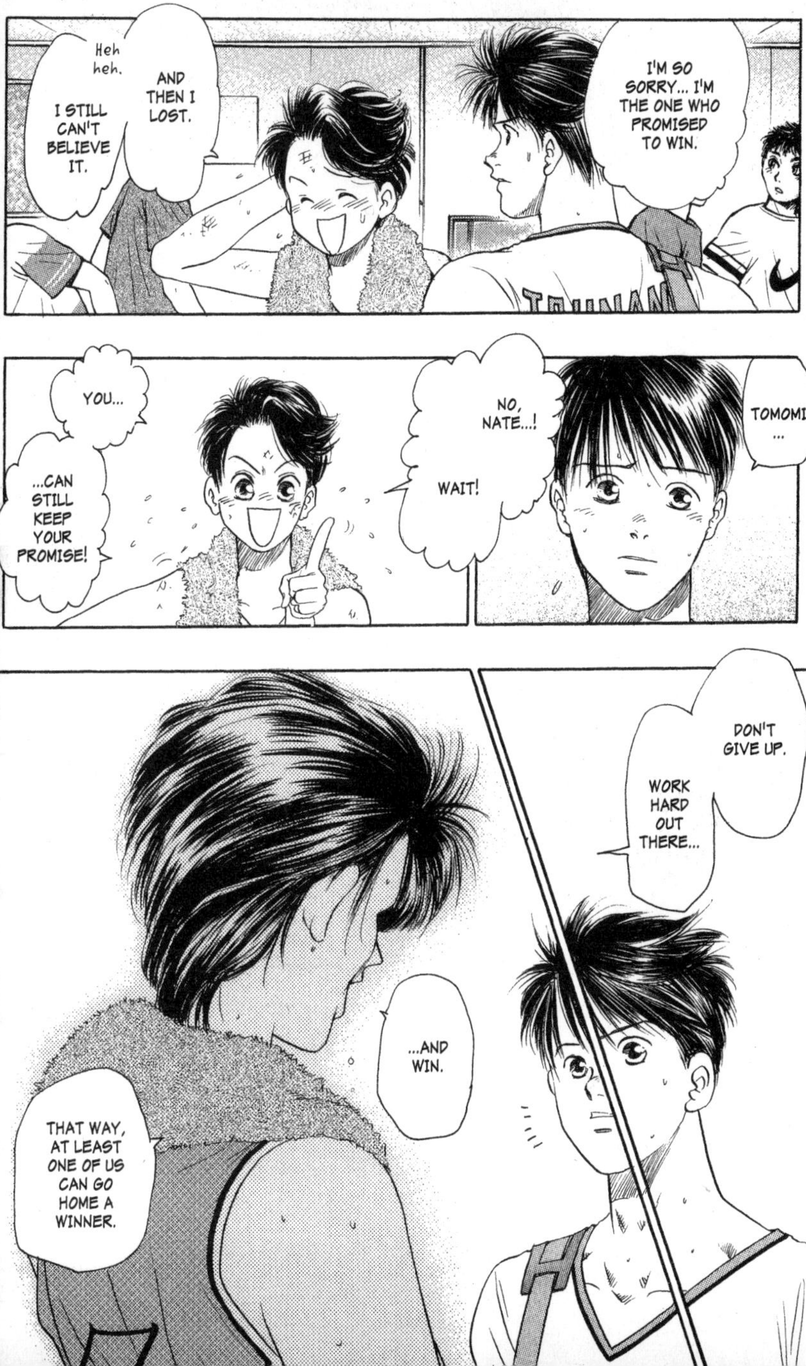

I'M SO SORRY... I'M THE ONE WHO PROMISED TO WIN.
AND THEN I LOST.
Heh heh.
I STILL CAN'T BELIEVE IT.
TOMOMI ...
NO, NATE...!
WAIT!
YOU...
...CAN STILL KEEP YOUR PROMISE!
DON'T GIVE UP.
WORK HARD OUT THERE...
...AND WIN.
THAT WAY, AT LEAST ONE OF US CAN GO HOME A WINNER.

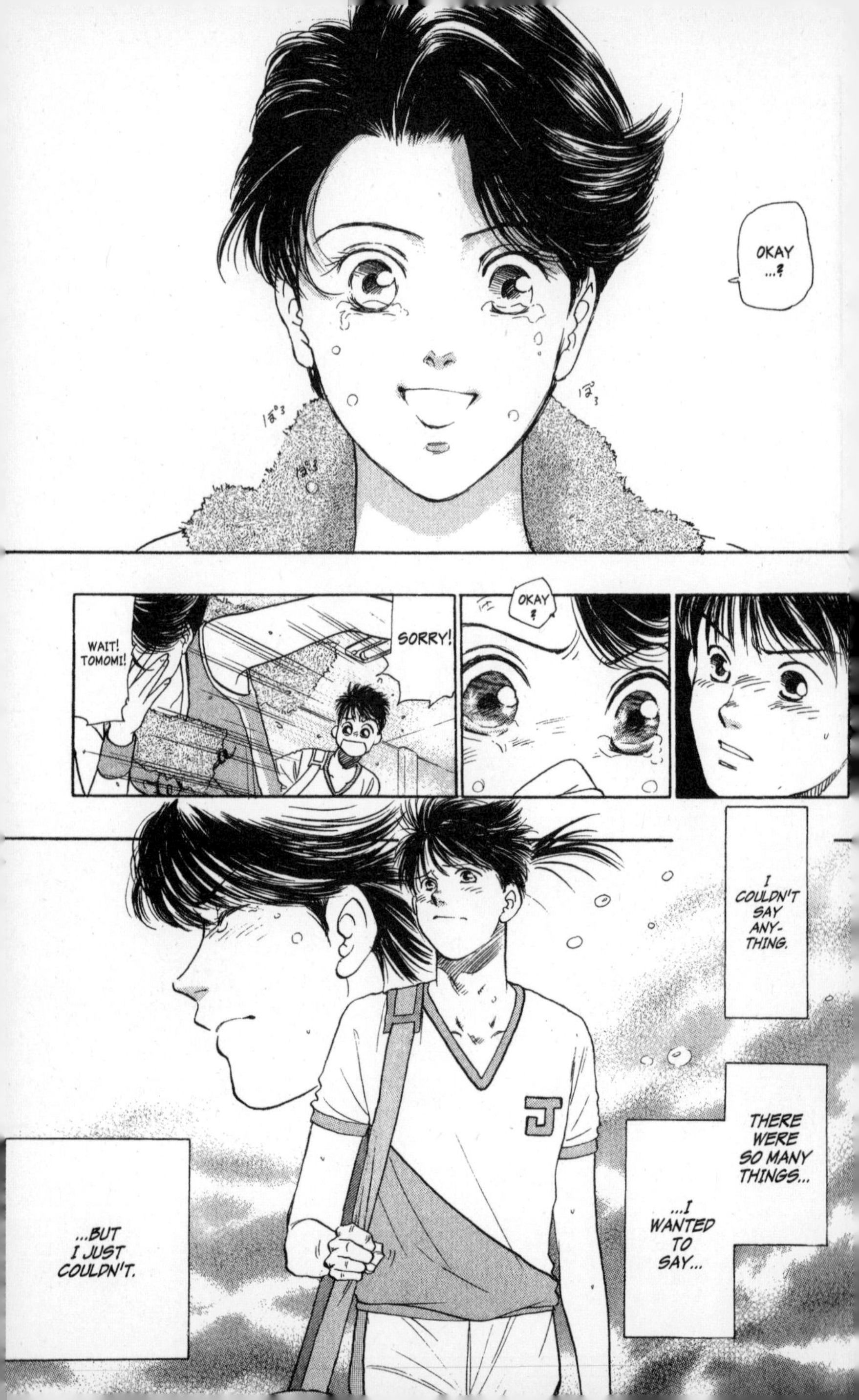
OKAY ...?
OKAY ?
SORRY!
WAIT! TOMOMI!
I COULDN'T SAY ANYTHING.
THERE WERE SO MANY THINGS...
...I WANTED TO SAY...
...BUT I JUST COULDN'T.

You're Reading...

REBOUND

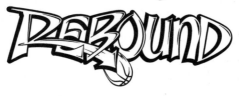

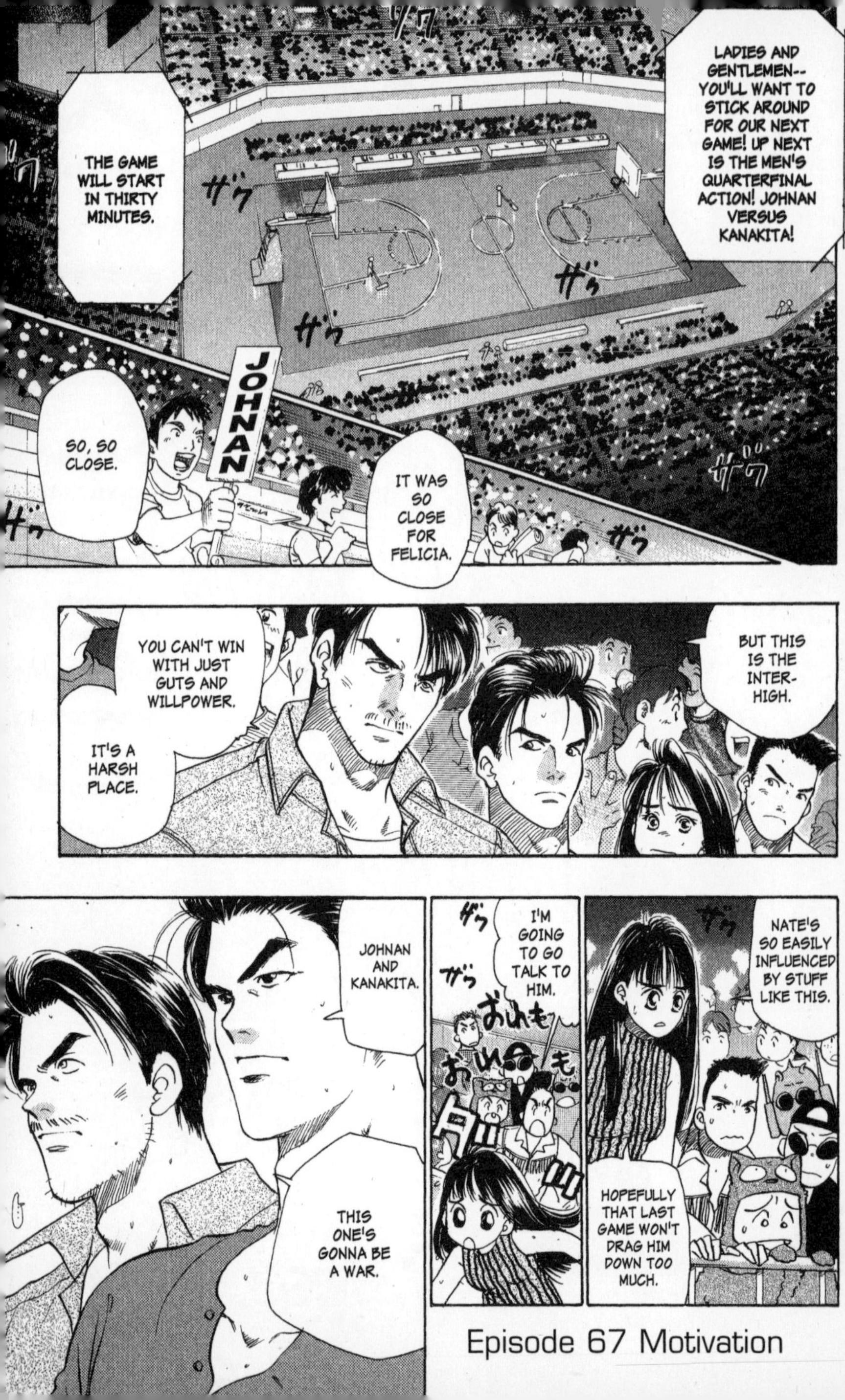
LADIES AND GENTLEMEN-- YOU'LL WANT TO STICK AROUND FOR OUR NEXT GAME! UP NEXT IS THE MEN'S QUARTERFINAL ACTION! JOHNAN VERSUS KANAKITA!
THE GAME WILL START IN THIRTY MINUTES.
JOHNAN
IT WAS SO CLOSE FOR FELICIA.
SO, SO CLOSE.
BUT THIS IS THE INTER-HIGH.
YOU CAN'T WIN WITH JUST GUTS AND WILLPOWER.
IT'S A HARSH PLACE.
NATE'S SO EASILY INFLUENCED BY STUFF LIKE THIS.
HOPEFULLY THAT LAST GAME WON'T DRAG HIM DOWN TOO MUCH.
I'M GOING TO GO TALK TO HIM.
JOHNAN AND KANAKITA.
THIS ONE'S GONNA BE A WAR.

# Episode 67 Motivation

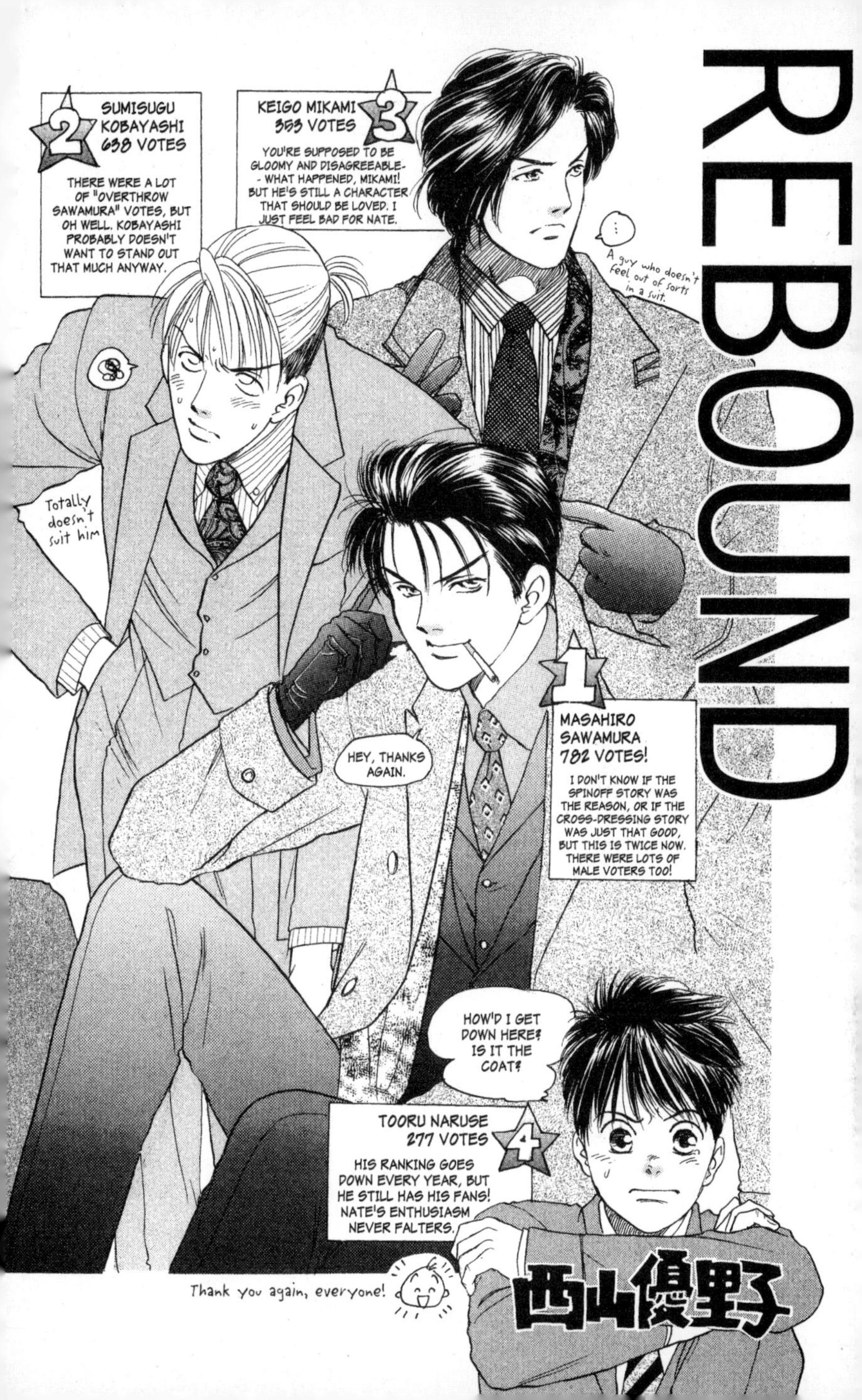

REBOUND
KEIGO MIKAMI 353 VOTES
3
YOU'RE SUPPOSED TO BE GLOOMY AND DISAGREEABLE- - WHAT HAPPENED, MIKAMI! BUT HE'S STILL A CHARACTER THAT SHOULD BE LOVED. I JUST FEEL BAD FOR NATE.
2
SUMISUGU KOBAYASHI 638 VOTES
THERE WERE A LOT OF "OVERTHROW SAWAMURA" VOTES, BUT OH WELL. KOBAYASHI PROBABLY DOESN'T WANT TO STAND OUT THAT MUCH ANYWAY.
...
A guy who doesn't feel out of sorts in a suit.
Totally doesn't suit him
1
MASAHIRO SAWAMURA 782 VOTES!
I DON'T KNOW IF THE SPINOFF STORY WAS THE REASON, OR IF THE CROSS-DRESSING STORY WAS JUST THAT GOOD, BUT THIS IS TWICE NOW. THERE WERE LOTS OF MALE VOTERS TOO!
HEY, THANKS AGAIN.
HOW'D I GET DOWN HERE? IS IT THE COAT?
4
TOORU NARUSE 277 VOTES
HIS RANKING GOES DOWN EVERY YEAR, BUT HE STILL HAS HIS FANS! NATE'S ENTHUSIASM NEVER FALTERS.
西山優里子
Thank you again, everyone!

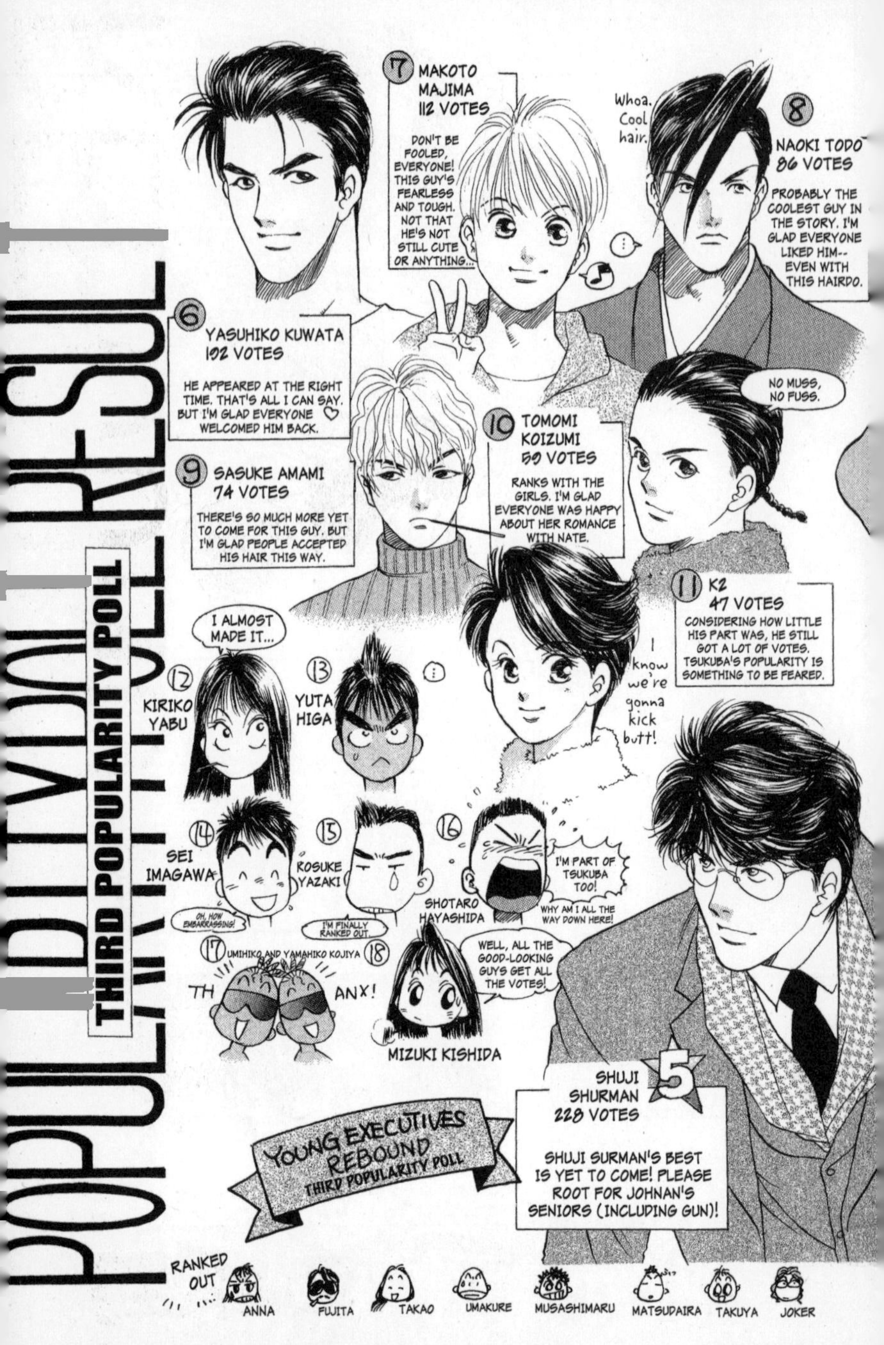

POPULARITY POLL RESUL
THIRD POPULARITY POLL
8
NAOKI TODO
86 VOTES
PROBABLY THE COOLEST GUY IN THE STORY. I'M GLAD EVERYONE LIKED HIM-- EVEN WITH THIS HAIRDO.
Whoa. Cool hair.
7
MAKOTO MAJIMA
112 VOTES
DON'T BE FOOLED, EVERYONE! THIS GUY'S FEARLESS AND TOUGH. NOT THAT HE'S NOT STILL CUTE OR ANYTHING...
6
YASUHIKO KUWATA
192 VOTES
HE APPEARED AT THE RIGHT TIME. THAT'S ALL I CAN SAY. BUT I'M GLAD EVERYONE ♡ WELCOMED HIM BACK.
NO MUSS, NO FUSS.
10
TOMOMI KOIZUMI
59 VOTES
RANKS WITH THE GIRLS. I'M GLAD EVERYONE WAS HAPPY ABOUT HER ROMANCE WITH NATE.
9
SASUKE AMAMI
74 VOTES
THERE'S SO MUCH MORE YET TO COME FOR THIS GUY. BUT I'M GLAD PEOPLE ACCEPTED HIS HAIR THIS WAY.
11
K2
47 VOTES
CONSIDERING HOW LITTLE HIS PART WAS, HE STILL GOT A LOT OF VOTES. TSUKUBA'S POPULARITY IS SOMETHING TO BE FEARED.
I know we're gonna kick butt!
13
YUTA HIGA
12
KIRIKO YABU
I ALMOST MADE IT...
16
SHOTARO HAYASHIDA
I'M PART OF TSUKUBA TOO!
WHY AM I ALL THE WAY DOWN HERE!
15
ROSUKE YAZAKI
I'M FINALLY RANKED OUT.
14
SEI IMAGAWA
OH, HOW EMBARRASSING!
18
MIZUKI KISHIDA
WELL, ALL THE GOOD-LOOKING GUYS GET ALL THE VOTES!
17
UMIHIKO AND YAMAHIKO KOJIYA
TH ANX!
5
SHUJI SHURMAN
228 VOTES
SHUJI SURMAN'S BEST IS YET TO COME! PLEASE ROOT FOR JOHNAN'S SENIORS (INCLUDING GUN)!
YOUNG EXECUTIVES REBOUND
THIRD POPULARITY POLL
RANKED OUT
ANNA
FUJITA
TAKAO
UMAKURE
MUSASHIMARU
MATSUDAIRA
TAKUYA
JOKER

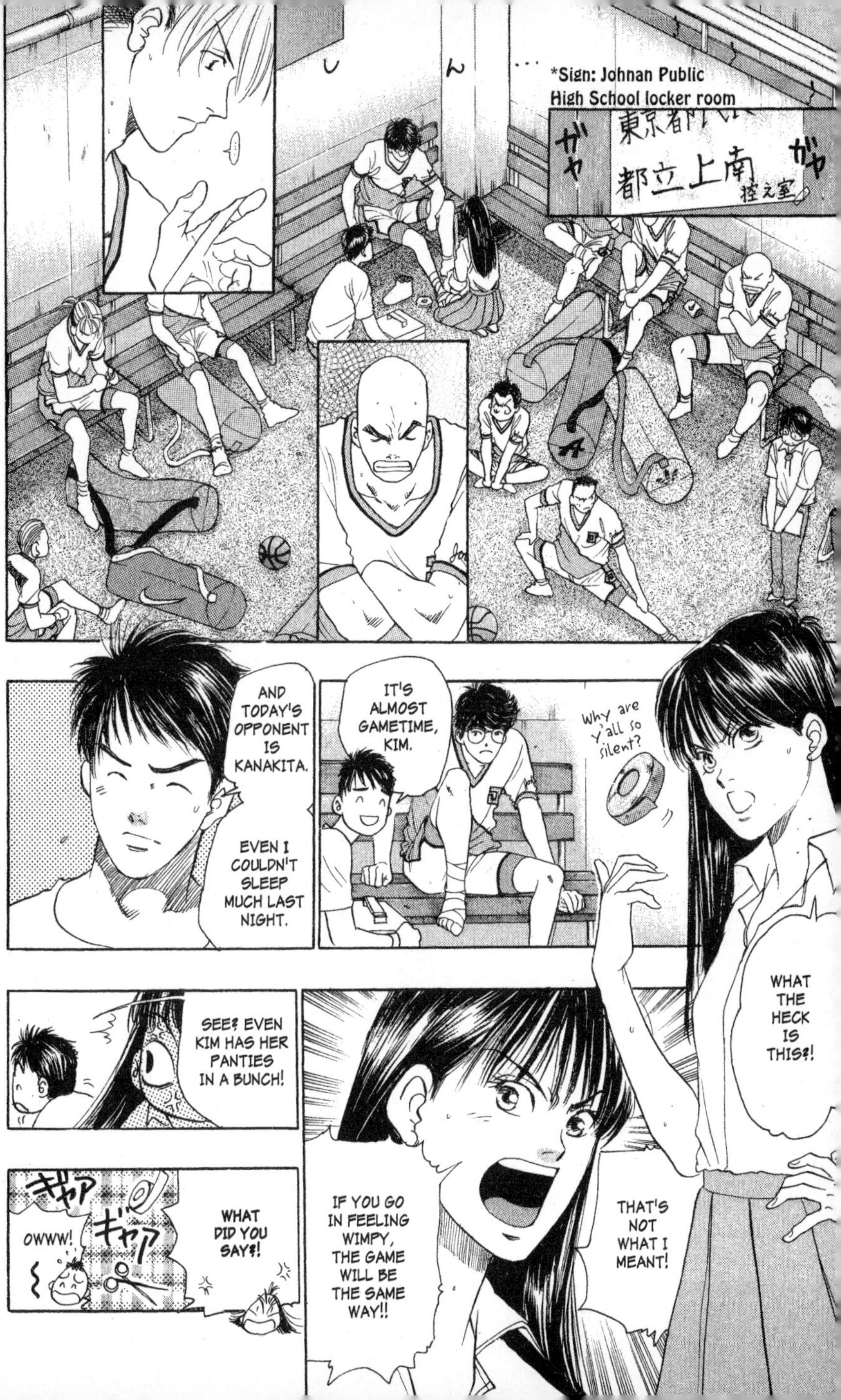
しん…
*Sign: Johnan Public High School locker room
ガヤ
都立上南
控え室
ガヤ
…
Why are y'all so silent?
IT'S ALMOST GAMETIME, KIM.
AND TODAY'S OPPONENT IS KANAKITA.
EVEN I COULDN'T SLEEP MUCH LAST NIGHT.
WHAT THE HECK IS THIS?!
THAT'S NOT WHAT I MEANT!
IF YOU GO IN FEELING WIMPY, THE GAME WILL BE THE SAME WAY!!
SEE? EVEN KIM HAS HER PANTIES IN A BUNCH!
WHAT DID YOU SAY?!
ギャア
ギャア
OWWW!

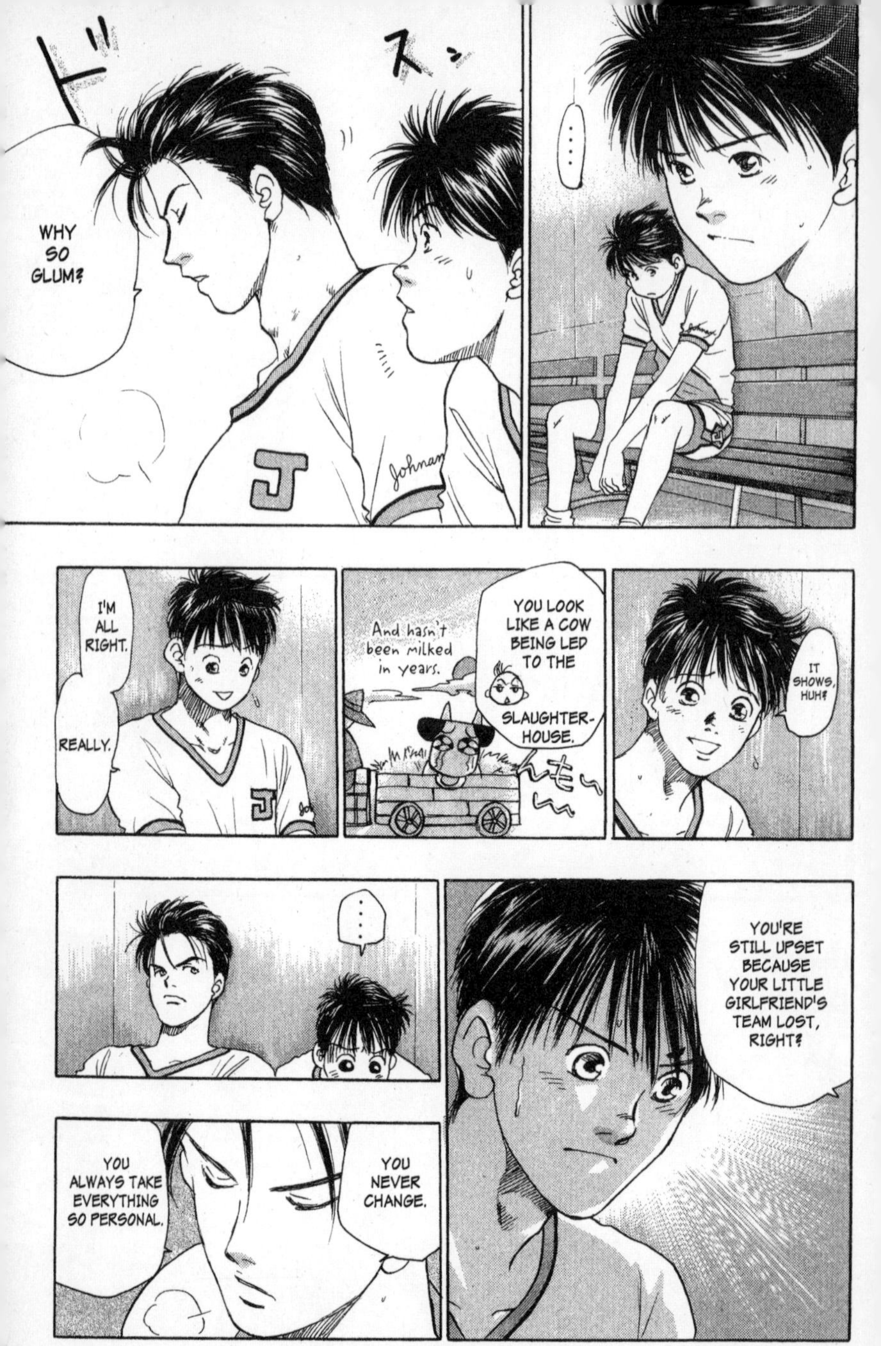
. . . . .
ドスッ
WHY SO GLUM?
IT SHOWS, HUH?
YOU LOOK LIKE A COW BEING LED TO THE SLAUGHTER-HOUSE.
And hasn't been milked in years.
I'M ALL RIGHT.
REALLY.
YOU'RE STILL UPSET BECAUSE YOUR LITTLE GIRLFRIEND'S TEAM LOST, RIGHT?
. . . . .
YOU NEVER CHANGE.
YOU ALWAYS TAKE EVERYTHING SO PERSONAL.

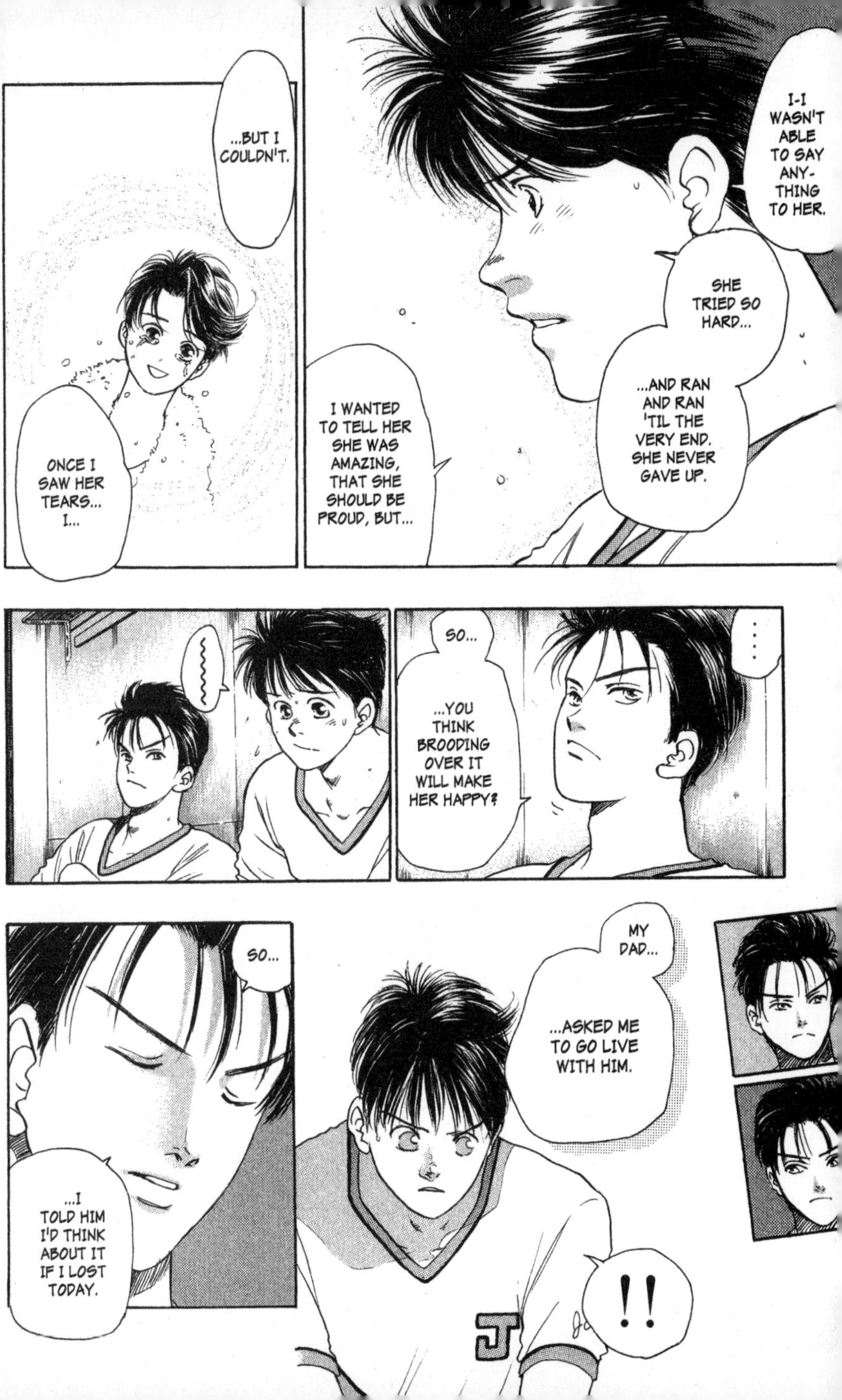
I-I WASN'T ABLE TO SAY ANY-THING TO HER.
SHE TRIED SO HARD...
...AND RAN AND RAN 'TIL THE VERY END. SHE NEVER GAVE UP.
I WANTED TO TELL HER SHE WAS AMAZING, THAT SHE SHOULD BE PROUD, BUT...
...BUT I COULDN'T.
ONCE I SAW HER TEARS... I...
SO...
...YOU THINK BROODING OVER IT WILL MAKE HER HAPPY?
....
MY DAD...
...ASKED ME TO GO LIVE WITH HIM.
!!
SO...
...I TOLD HIM I'D THINK ABOUT IT IF I LOST TODAY.

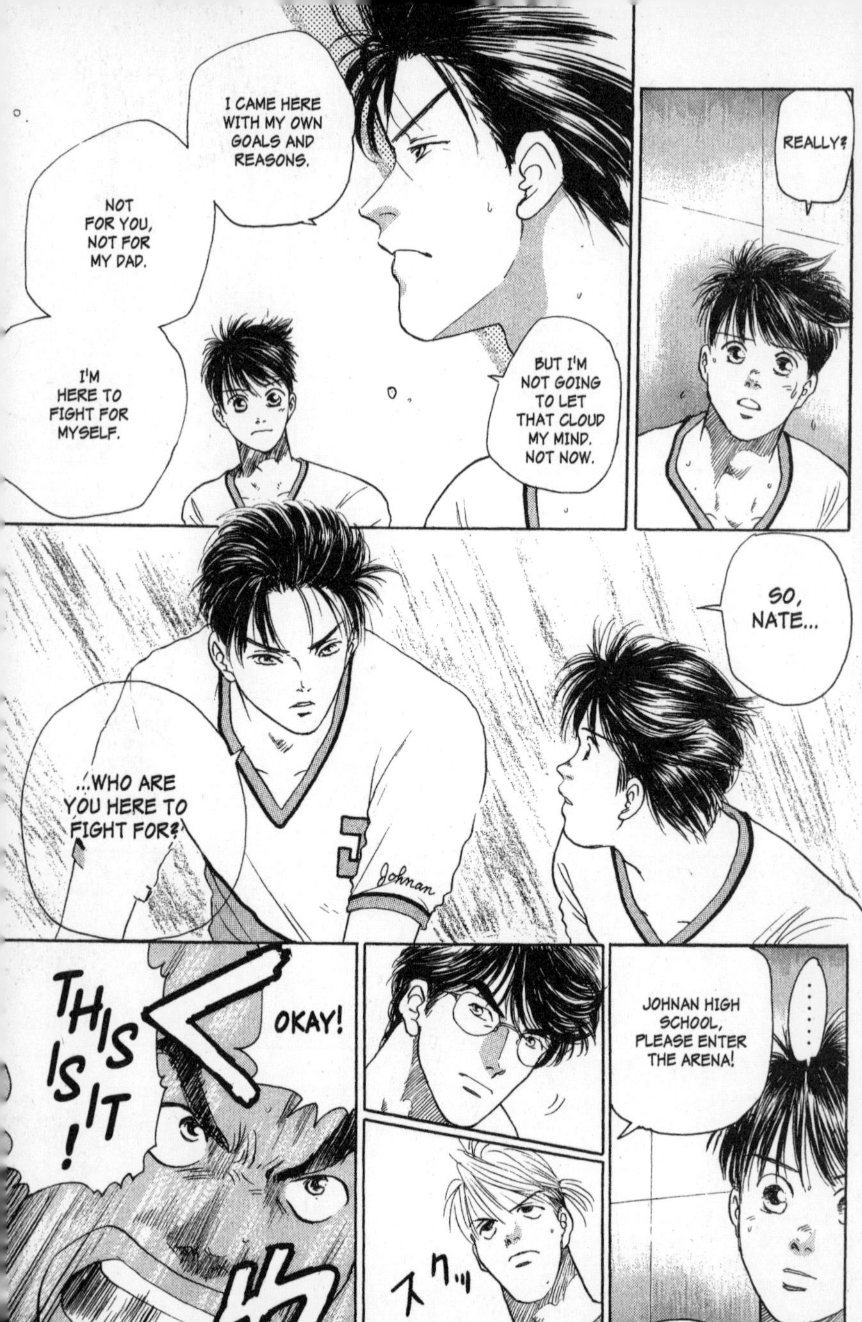
REALLY?
I CAME HERE WITH MY OWN GOALS AND REASONS.
NOT FOR YOU, NOT FOR MY DAD.
I'M HERE TO FIGHT FOR MYSELF.
BUT I'M NOT GOING TO LET THAT CLOUD MY MIND. NOT NOW.
SO, NATE...
...WHO ARE YOU HERE TO FIGHT FOR?
......
JOHNAN HIGH SCHOOL, PLEASE ENTER THE ARENA!
OKAY!
THIS IS IT!

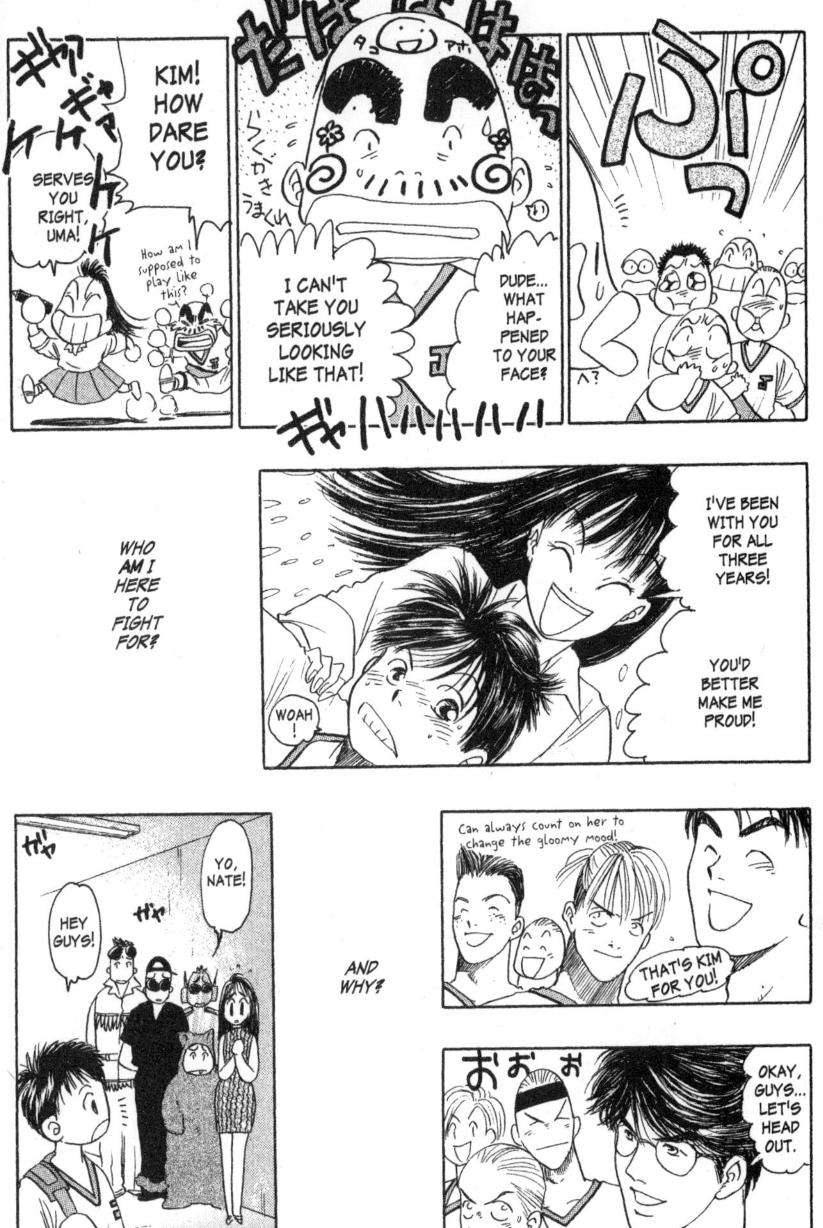
ぷっ
へ?
だはははは
DUDE... WHAT HAP-PENED TO YOUR FACE?
I CAN'T TAKE YOU SERIOUSLY LOOKING LIKE THAT!
ギャハハハハハ
KIM! HOW DARE YOU?
SERVES YOU RIGHT, UMA!
How am I supposed to play like this?
I'VE BEEN WITH YOU FOR ALL THREE YEARS!
YOU'D BETTER MAKE ME PROUD!
WOAH!
WHO AM I HERE TO FIGHT FOR?
Can always count on her to change the gloomy mood!
THAT'S KIM FOR YOU!
おおお
OKAY, GUYS... LET'S HEAD OUT.
AND WHY?
YO, NATE!
HEY GUYS!

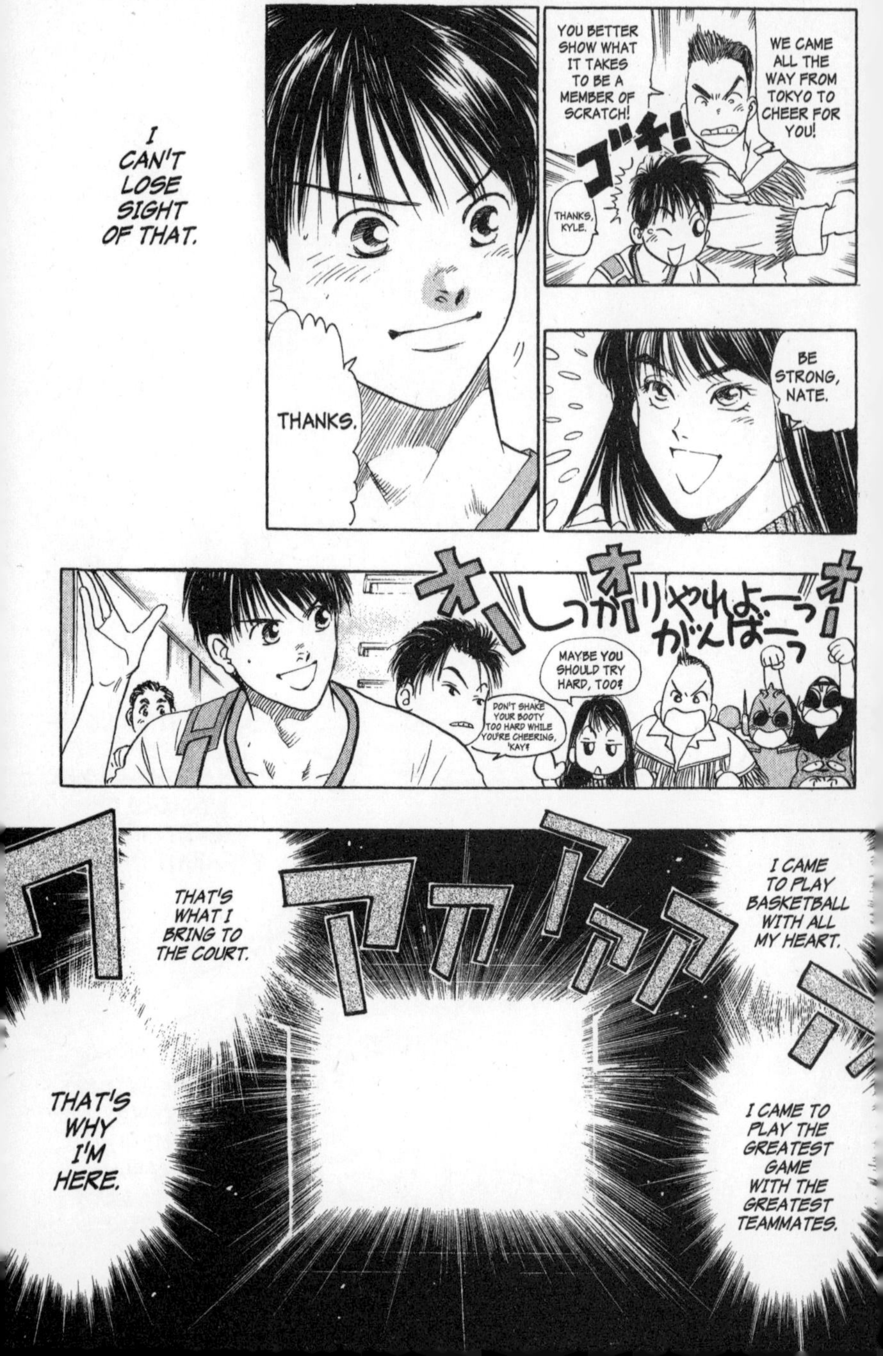

WE CAME ALL THE WAY FROM TOKYO TO CHEER FOR YOU!
YOU BETTER SHOW WHAT IT TAKES TO BE A MEMBER OF SCRATCH!
ゴチ!
THANKS, KYLE.
BE STRONG, NATE.
THANKS.
I CAN'T LOSE SIGHT OF THAT.
しっかりやれよーっ
がんばーっ
MAYBE YOU SHOULD TRY HARD, TOO?
DON'T SHAKE YOUR BOOTY TOO HARD WHILE YOU'RE CHEERING, 'KAY?
I CAME TO PLAY BASKETBALL WITH ALL MY HEART.
THAT'S WHAT I BRING TO THE COURT.
I CAME TO PLAY THE GREATEST GAME WITH THE GREATEST TEAMMATES.
THAT'S WHY I'M HERE.

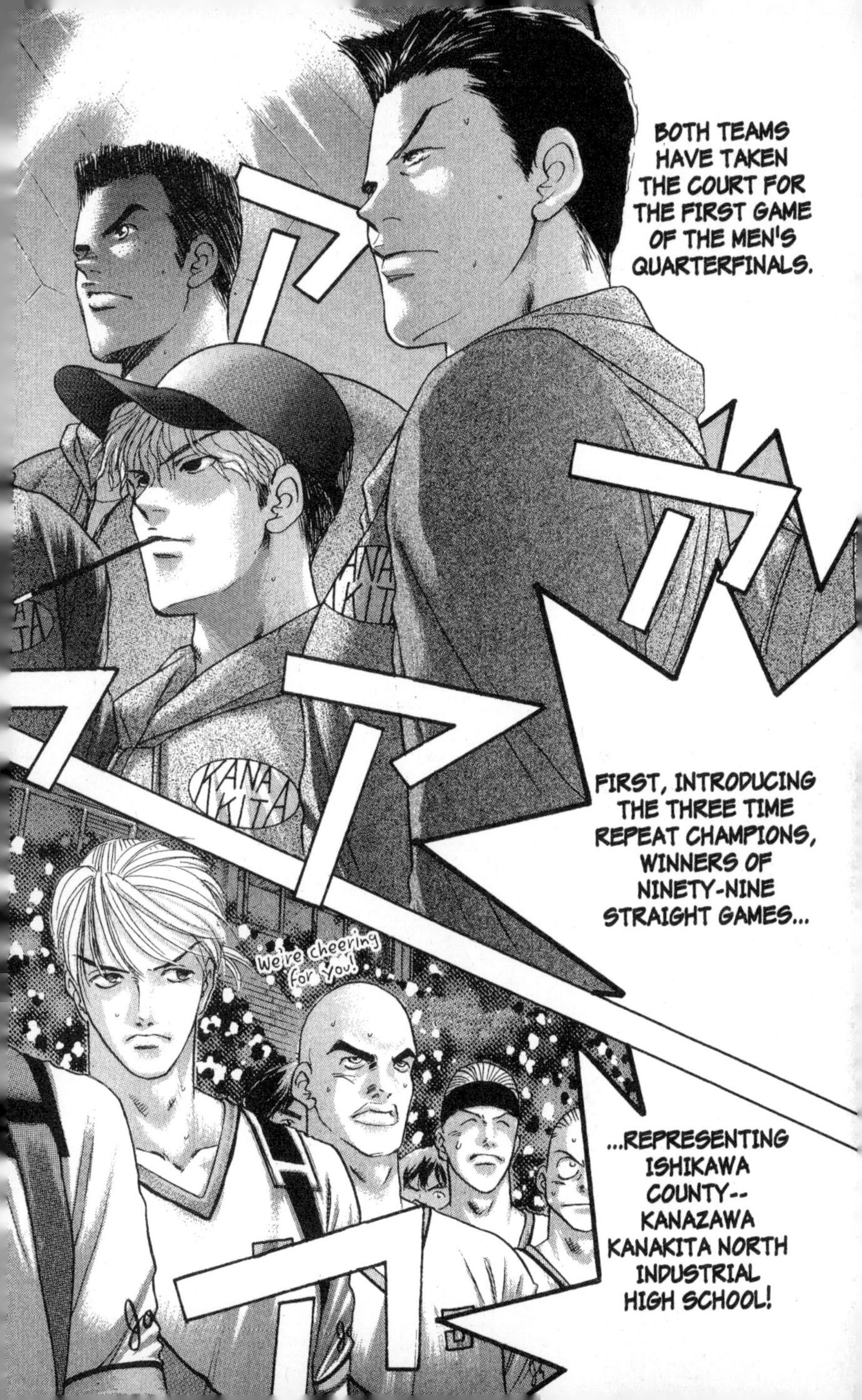
BOTH TEAMS HAVE TAKEN THE COURT FOR THE FIRST GAME OF THE MEN'S QUARTERFINALS.
KANA KITA
FIRST, INTRODUCING THE THREE TIME REPEAT CHAMPIONS, WINNERS OF NINETY-NINE STRAIGHT GAMES...
We're cheering for you!
...REPRESENTING ISHIKAWA COUNTY-- KANAZAWA KANAKITA NORTH INDUSTRIAL HIGH SCHOOL!

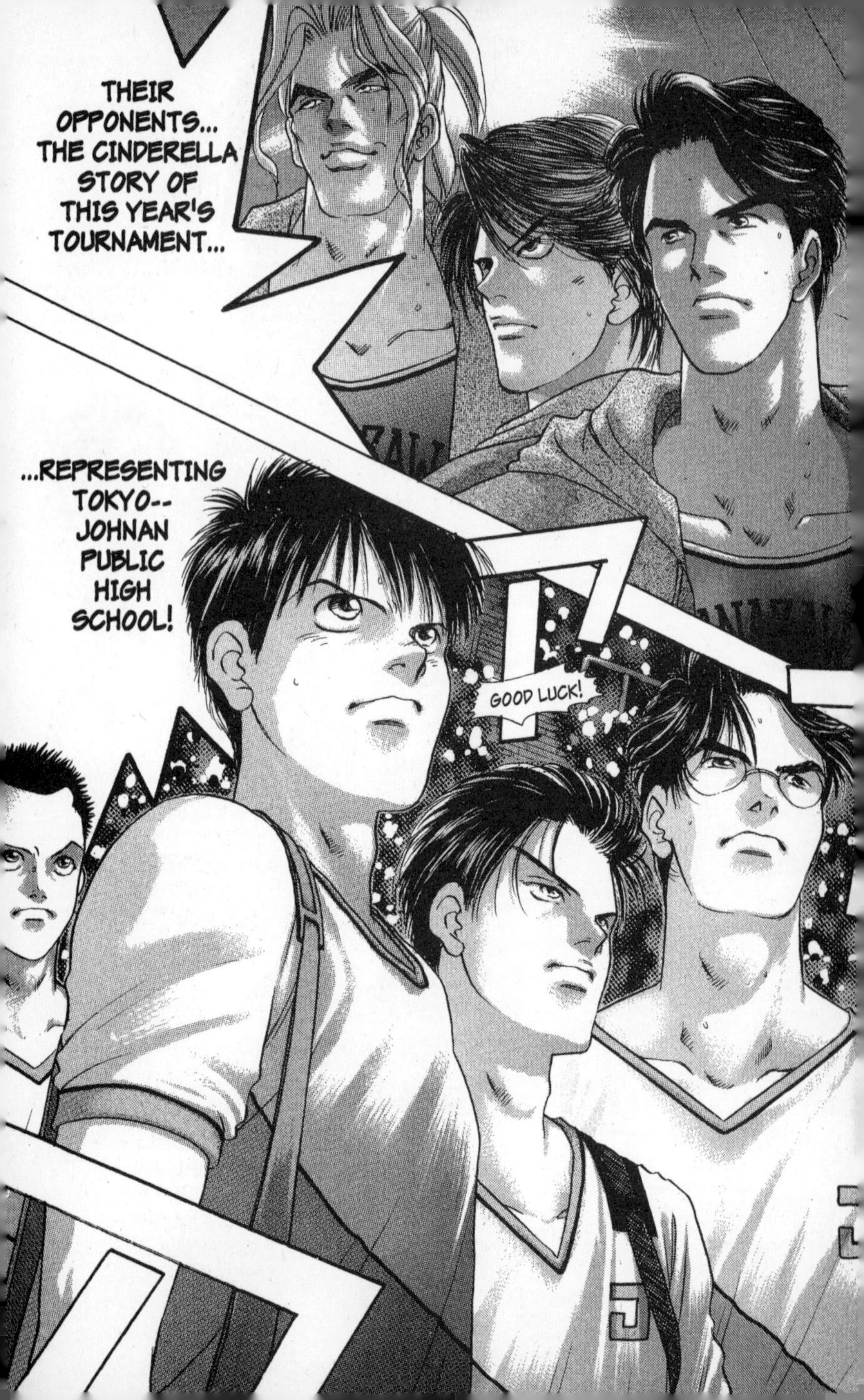
THEIR OPPONENTS... THE CINDERELLA STORY OF THIS YEAR'S TOURNAMENT...
...REPRESENTING TOKYO-- JOHNAN PUBLIC HIGH SCHOOL!
GOOD LUCK!

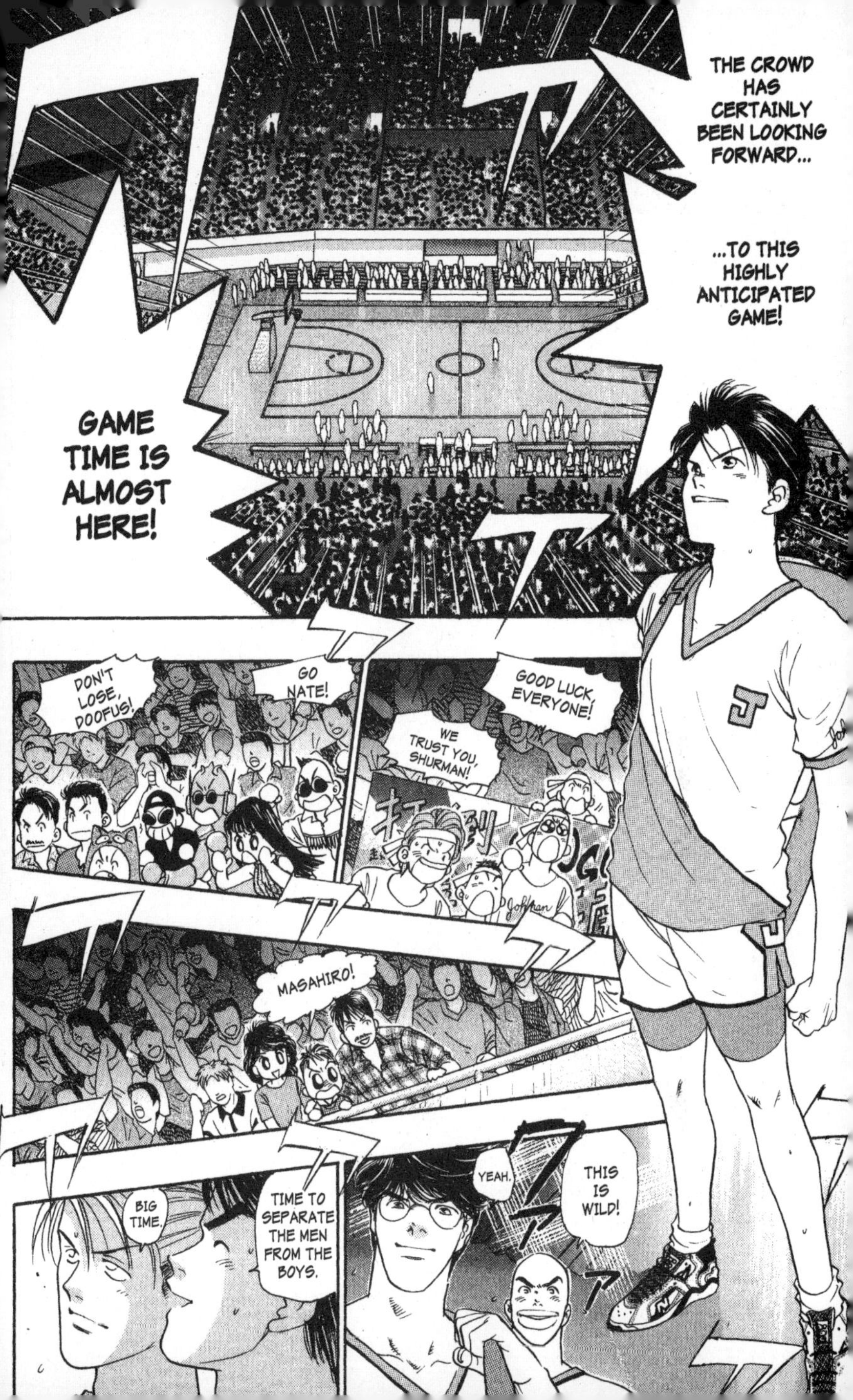
THE CROWD HAS CERTAINLY BEEN LOOKING FORWARD...
...TO THIS HIGHLY ANTICIPATED GAME!
GAME TIME IS ALMOST HERE!
GOOD LUCK, EVERYONE!
WE TRUST YOU, SHURMAN!
GO NATE!
DON'T LOSE, DOOFUS!
MASAHIRO!
THIS IS WILD!
YEAH.
TIME TO SEPARATE THE MEN FROM THE BOYS.
BIG TIME.

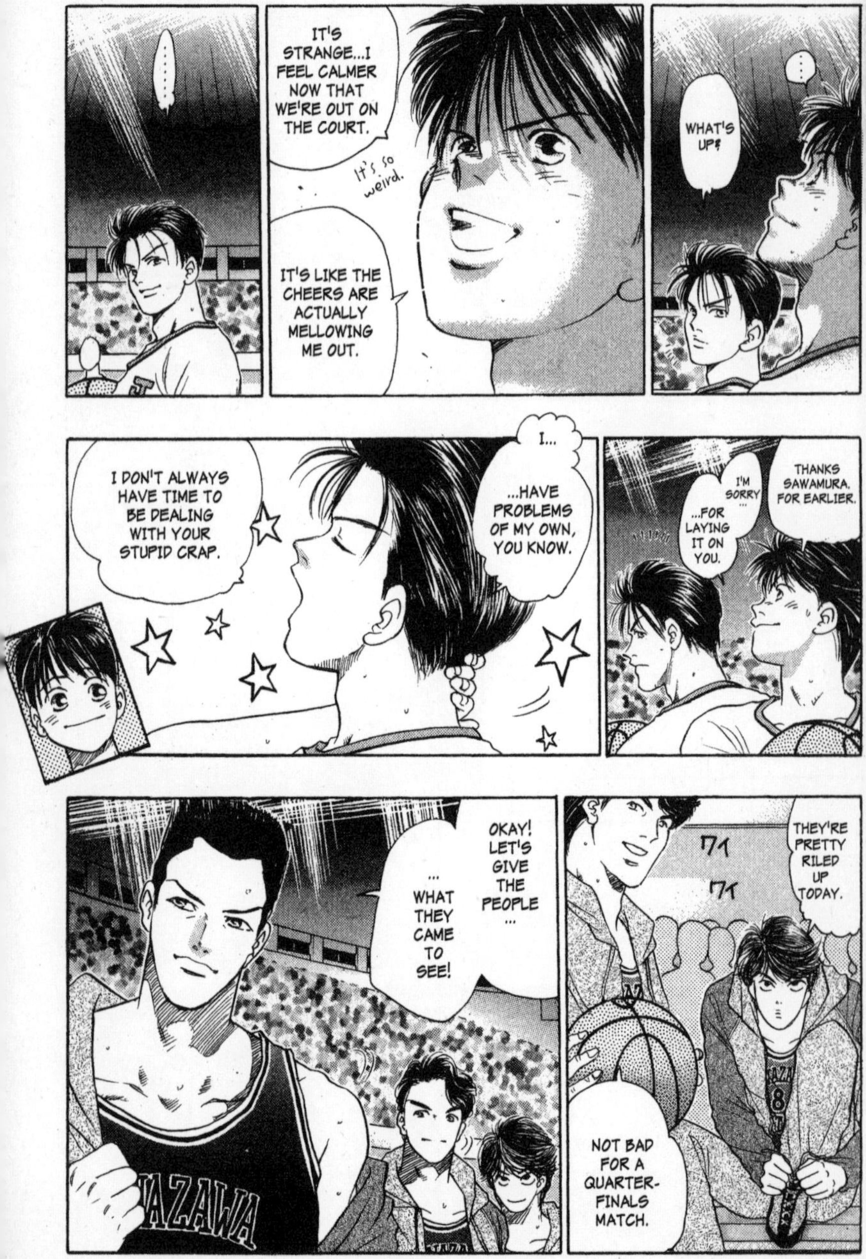
...!
WHAT'S UP?
IT'S STRANGE...I FEEL CALMER NOW THAT WE'RE OUT ON THE COURT.
It's so weird.
IT'S LIKE THE CHEERS ARE ACTUALLY MELLOWING ME OUT.
......
THANKS SAWAMURA. FOR EARLIER.
I'M SORRY ...
...FOR LAYING IT ON YOU.
I...
...HAVE PROBLEMS OF MY OWN, YOU KNOW.
I DON'T ALWAYS HAVE TIME TO BE DEALING WITH YOUR STUPID CRAP.
THEY'RE PRETTY RILED UP TODAY.
ワイ
ワイ
NOT BAD FOR A QUARTER-FINALS MATCH.
OKAY! LET'S GIVE THE PEOPLE ...
... WHAT THEY CAME TO SEE!

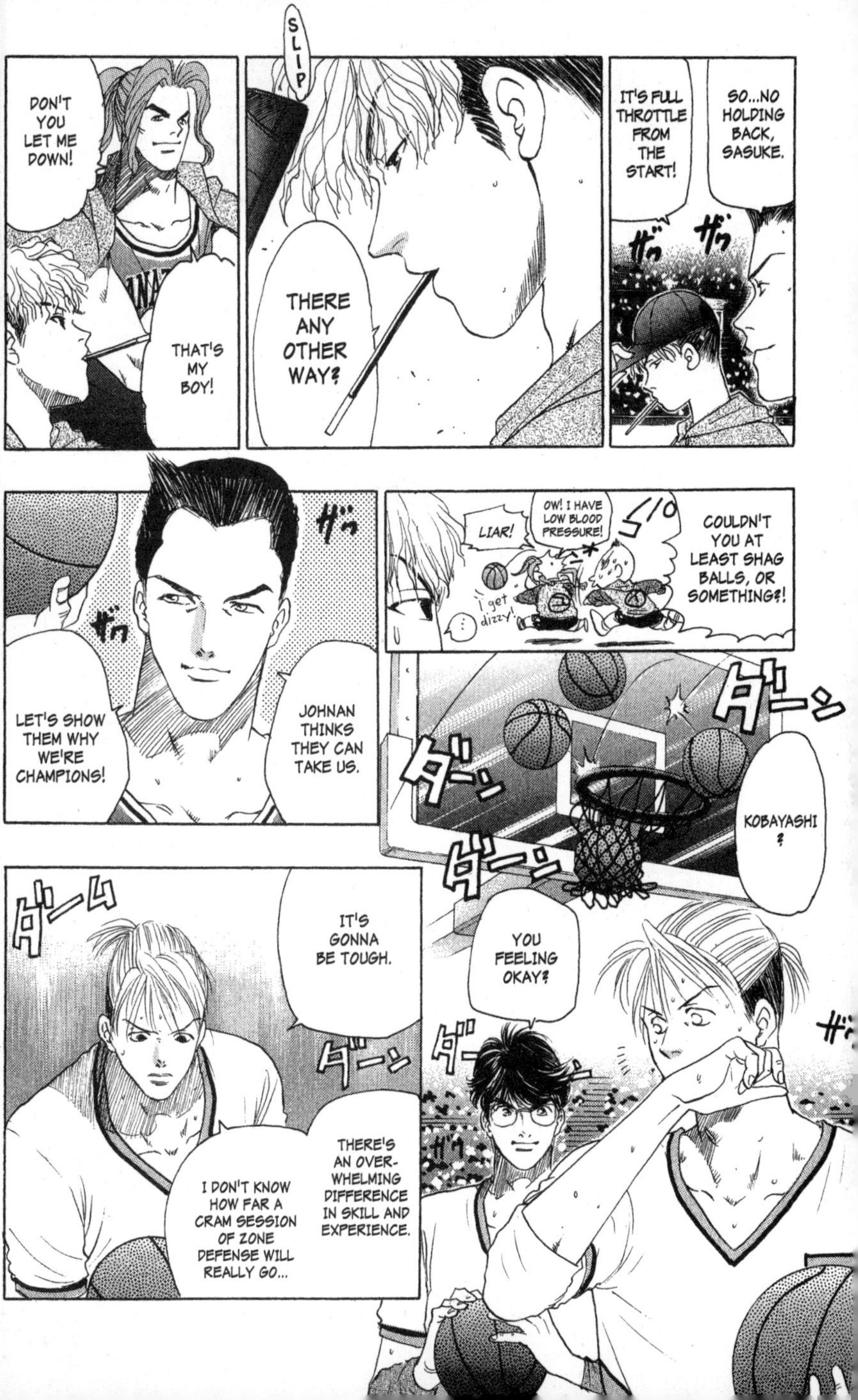
SO...NO HOLDING BACK, SASUKE.
IT'S FULL THROTTLE FROM THE START!
SLIP
THERE ANY OTHER WAY?
DON'T YOU LET ME DOWN!
THAT'S MY BOY!
COULDN'T YOU AT LEAST SHAG BALLS, OR SOMETHING?!
OW! I HAVE LOW BLOOD PRESSURE!
LIAR!
I get dizzy!
...
JOHNAN THINKS THEY CAN TAKE US.
LET'S SHOW THEM WHY WE'RE CHAMPIONS!
KOBAYASHI?
YOU FEELING OKAY?
IT'S GONNA BE TOUGH.
THERE'S AN OVER-WHELMING DIFFERENCE IN SKILL AND EXPERIENCE.
I DON'T KNOW HOW FAR A CRAM SESSION OF ZONE DEFENSE WILL REALLY GO...

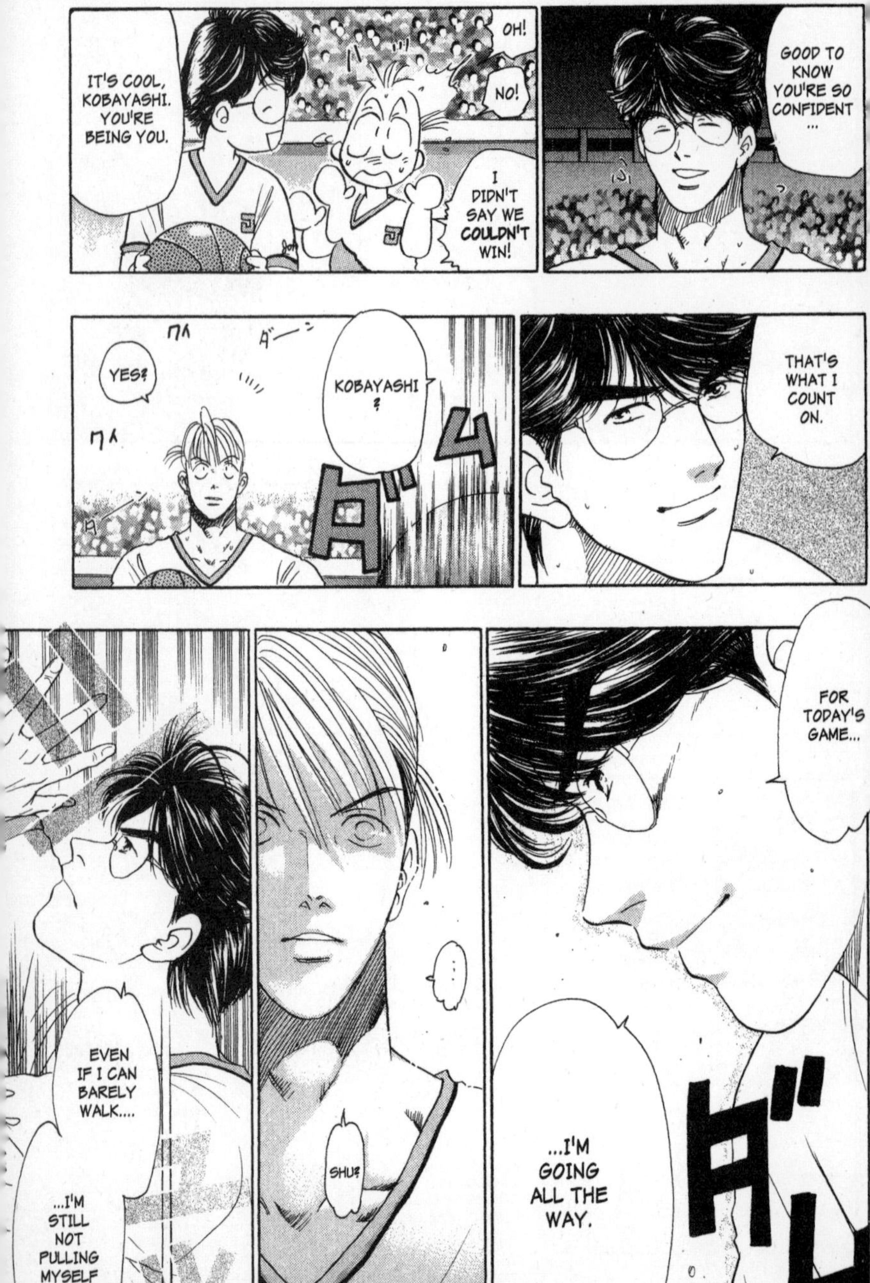
GOOD TO KNOW YOU'RE SO CONFIDENT ...
OH!
NO!
I DIDN'T SAY WE COULDN'T WIN!
IT'S COOL, KOBAYASHI. YOU'RE BEING YOU.
THAT'S WHAT I COUNT ON.
KOBAYASHI?
YES?
FOR TODAY'S GAME...
...I'M GOING ALL THE WAY.
...
SHU?
EVEN IF I CAN BARELY WALK....
...I'M STILL NOT PULLING MYSELF OUT.

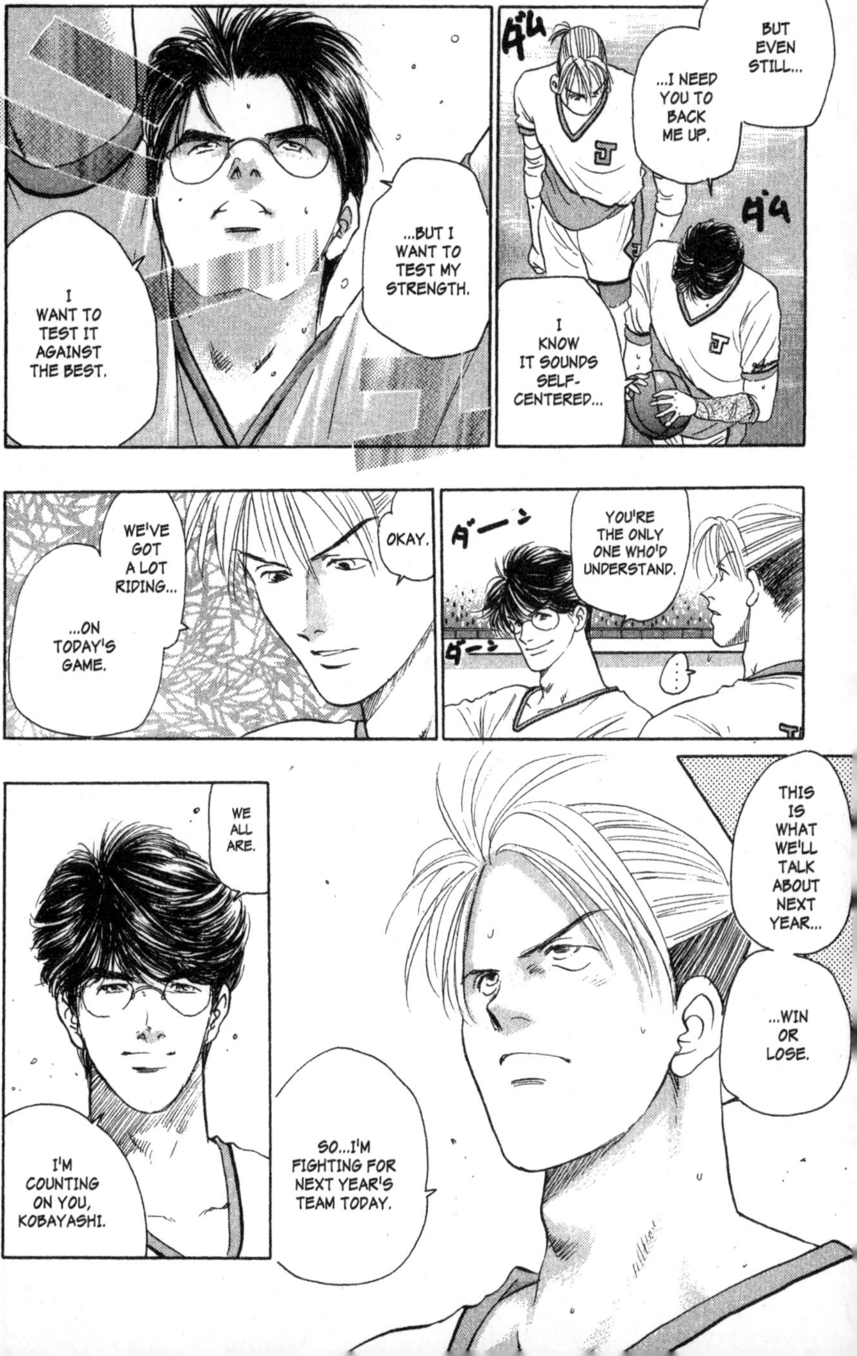
ダム
BUT EVEN STILL...
...I NEED YOU TO BACK ME UP.
ダム
I KNOW IT SOUNDS SELF-CENTERED...
...BUT I WANT TO TEST MY STRENGTH.
I WANT TO TEST IT AGAINST THE BEST.
YOU'RE THE ONLY ONE WHO'D UNDERSTAND.
...
OKAY.
WE'VE GOT A LOT RIDING...
...ON TODAY'S GAME.
THIS IS WHAT WE'LL TALK ABOUT NEXT YEAR...
...WIN OR LOSE.
SO...I'M FIGHTING FOR NEXT YEAR'S TEAM TODAY.
WE ALL ARE.
I'M COUNTING ON YOU, KOBAYASHI.

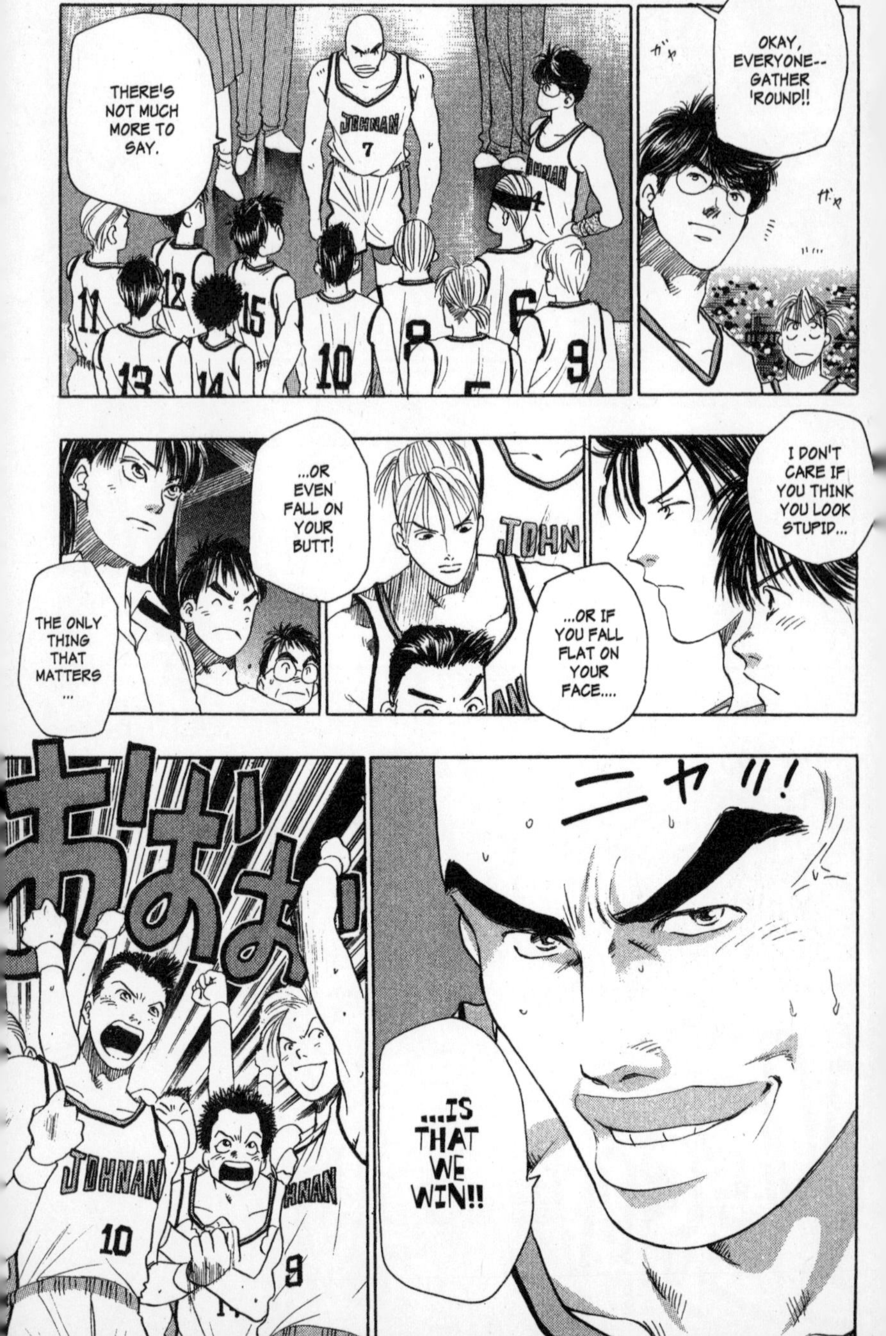
OKAY, EVERYONE-- GATHER 'ROUND!!
THERE'S NOT MUCH MORE TO SAY.
I DON'T CARE IF YOU THINK YOU LOOK STUPID...
...OR IF YOU FALL FLAT ON YOUR FACE....
...OR EVEN FALL ON YOUR BUTT!
THE ONLY THING THAT MATTERS ...
ニヤリ!
...IS THAT WE WIN!!

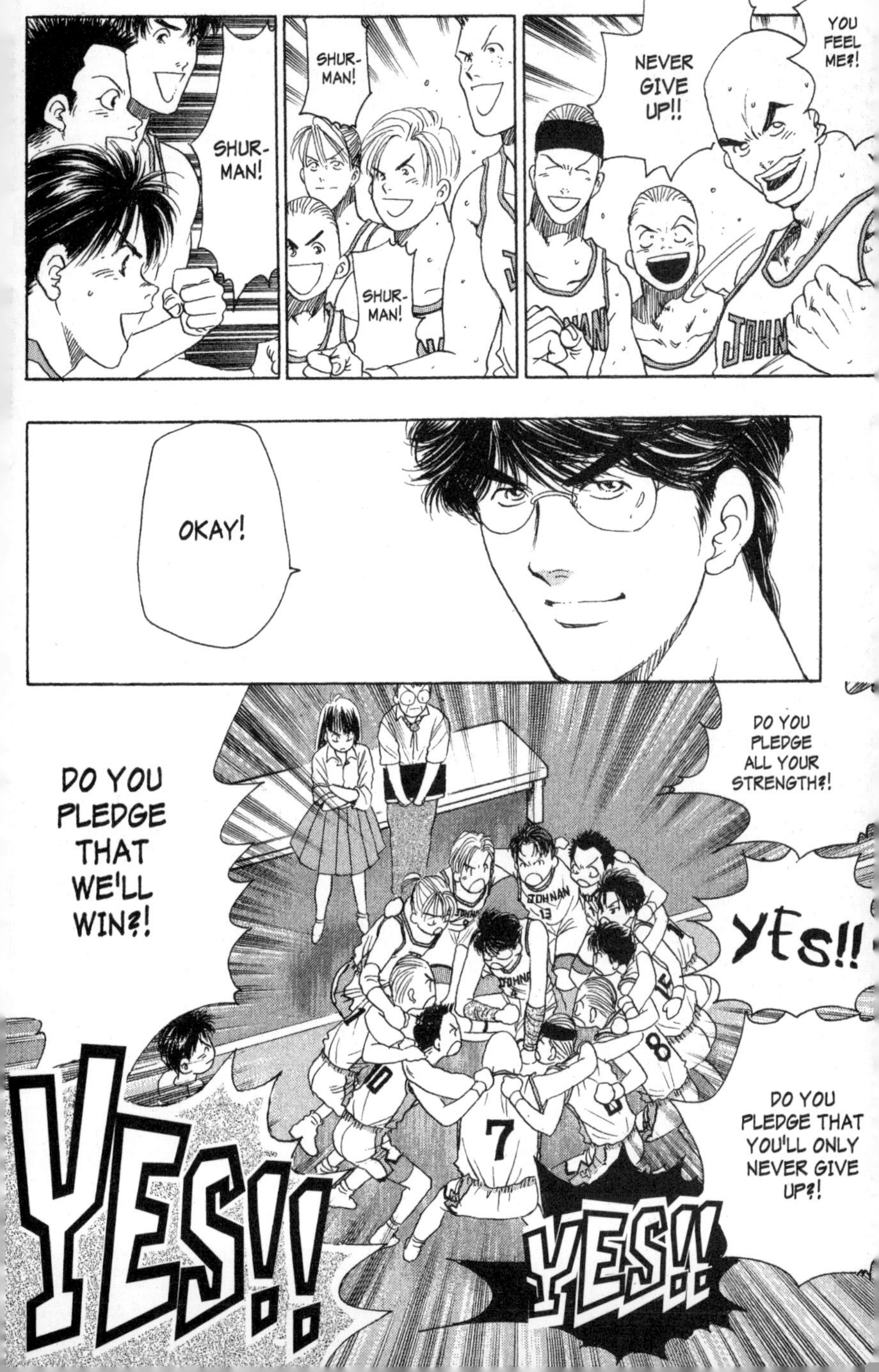
YOU FEEL ME?!
NEVER GIVE UP!!
SHUR-MAN!
SHUR-MAN!
SHUR-MAN!
OKAY!
DO YOU PLEDGE ALL YOUR STRENGTH?!
DO YOU PLEDGE THAT WE'LL WIN?!
YES!!
DO YOU PLEDGE THAT YOU'LL ONLY NEVER GIVE UP?!
YES!!
YES!!

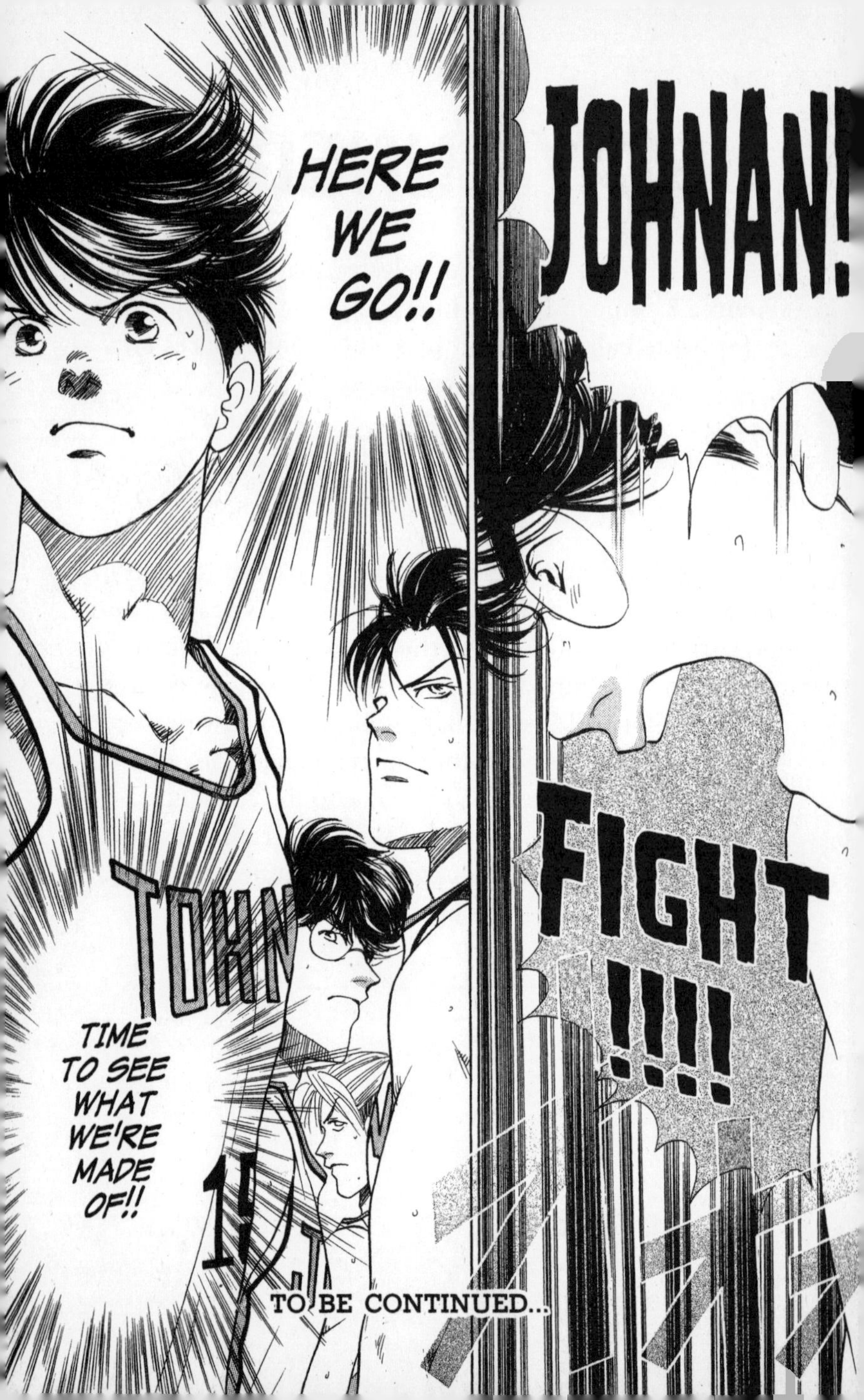
JOHNAN!
FIGHT!!!!
HERE WE GO!!
TIME TO SEE WHAT WE'RE MADE OF!!
TO BE CONTINUED...

# STAY TUNED!!!

We hope you enjoyed your selected manga, Rebound Volume 8. Tune in two months from now when the quest for basketball glory continues when Johnan faces off with Kanakita…

Preview for  Volume 9

This is it! Johnan and Kanakita finally go head to head in intense basketball action! Will all of Johnan's practice and preparation pay off? Or will they choke in the clutches of Kanakita's Unlimited Triangle? Can Nate's air walk turn the tide? Or will Sasuke make good on his vow to stop him at every turn? And as for Shurman--he finally gets his chance to play the best. Will he rise to the challenge, or choke under pressure? Only one thing is certain--it's going to be a battle of not only basketball fundamentals, but of wills as well…

And now, a commercial break…

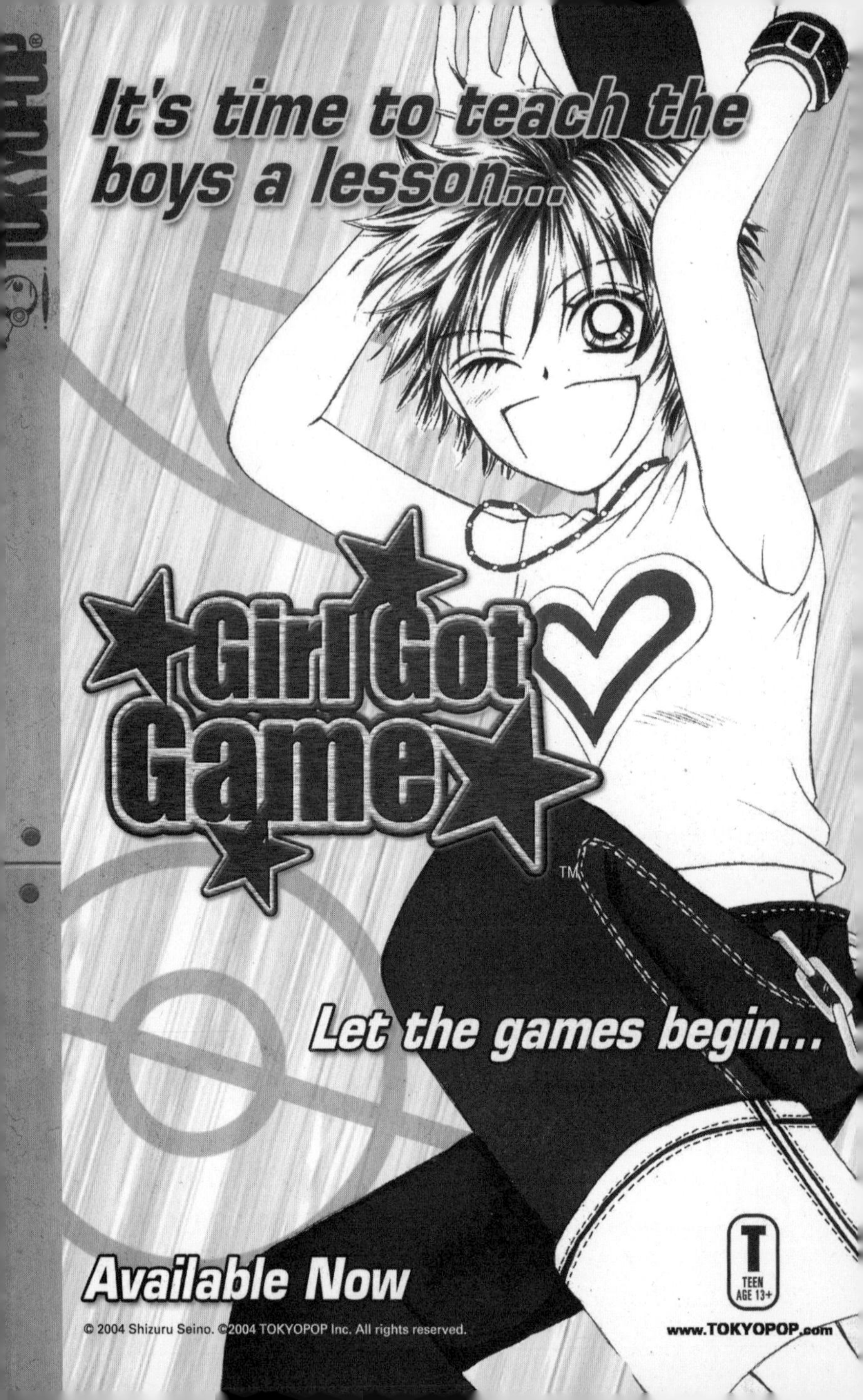

TOKYOPOP®
It's time to teach the boys a lesson...
Girl Got Game™
Let the games begin...
Available Now
T TEEN AGE 13+
© 2004 Shizuru Seino. ©2004 TOKYOPOP Inc. All rights reserved.
www.TOKYOPOP.com

# ALSO AVAILABLE FROM TOKYOPOP

**For more
information visit
www.TOKYOPOP.com**

03.30.04Y

# ALSO AVAILABLE FROM 🐾TOKYOPOP®

## MANGA

.HACK//LEGEND OF THE TWILIGHT
ANGELIC LAYER
BABY BIRTH
BRAIN POWERED
BRIGADOON
B'TX
CANDIDATE FOR GODDESS, THE
CARDCAPTOR SAKURA
CARDCAPTOR SAKURA - MASTER OF THE CLOW
CHRONICLES OF THE CURSED SWORD
CLAMP SCHOOL DETECTIVES
CLOVER
COMIC PARTY
CORRECTOR YUI
COWBOY BEBOP
COWBOY BEBOP: SHOOTING STAR
CRAZY LOVE STORY
CRESCENT MOON
CROSS
CULDCEPT
CYBORG 009
D•N•ANGEL
DEMON DIARY
DEMON ORORON, THE
DIABOLO
DIGIMON
DIGIMON TAMERS
DIGIMON ZERO TWO
DRAGON HUNTER
DRAGON KNIGHTS
DRAGON VOICE
DREAM SAGA
DUKLYON: CLAMP SCHOOL DEFENDERS
ET CETERA
ETERNITY
FAERIES' LANDING
FLCL
FLOWER OF THE DEEP SLEEP
FORBIDDEN DANCE
FRUITS BASKET
G GUNDAM
GATEKEEPERS
GIRL GOT GAME
GIRLS' EDUCATIONAL CHARTER
GUNDAM BLUE DESTINY
GUNDAM SEED ASTRAY
GUNDAM WING
GUNDAM WING: BATTLEFIELD OF PACIFISTS
GUNDAM WING: ENDLESS WALTZ

GUNDAM WING: THE LAST OUTPOST (G-UNIT)
HANDS OFF!
HARLEM BEAT
HONEY MUSTARD
IMMORTAL RAIN
I.N.V.U.
INITIAL D
INSTANT TEEN: JUST ADD NUTS
JING: KING OF BANDITS
JING: KING OF BANDITS - TWILIGHT TALES
JULINE
KARE KANO
KILL ME, KISS ME
KINDAICHI CASE FILES, THE
KING OF HELL
KODOCHA: SANA'S STAGE
LEGEND OF CHUN HYANG, THE
MAGIC KNIGHT RAYEARTH I
MAGIC KNIGHT RAYEARTH II
MAN OF MANY FACES
MARMALADE BOY
MARS
MARS: HORSE WITH NO NAME
MINK
MIRACLE GIRLS
MODEL
MY LOVE
NECK AND NECK
ONE
ONE I LOVE, THE
PEACH GIRL
PEACH GIRL: CHANGE OF HEART
PITA-TEN
PLANET LADDER
PLANETES
PRINCESS AI
PSYCHIC ACADEMY
QUEEN'S KNIGHT, THE
RAGNAROK
RAVE MASTER
REALITY CHECK
REBIRTH
REBOUND
RISING STARS OF MANGA
SAILOR MOON
SAINT TAIL
SAMURAI GIRL REAL BOUT HIGH SCHOOL
SEIKAI TRILOGY, THE
SGT. FROG
SHAOLIN SISTERS

03.30.04Y

# STOP!

## This is the back of the book.
## You wouldn't want to spoil a great ending!

This book is printed "manga-style," in the authentic Japanese right-to-left format. Since none of the artwork has been flipped or altered, readers get to experience the story just as the creator intended. You've been asking for it, so TOKYOPOP® delivered: authentic, hot-off-the-press, and far more fun!

## DIRECTIONS

If this is your first time reading manga-style, here's a quick guide to help you understand how it works.

It's easy... just start in the top right panel and follow the numbers. Have fun, and look for more 100% authentic manga from TOKYOPOP®!